The PHOTOSHOP 5/5.5 WOW! BOOK

Linnea Dayton & Jack Davis

Peachpit Press

The Photoshop 5/5.5 Wow! Book, Windows/Mac Edition

Linnea Dayton and Jack Davis

Peachpit Press
1249 Eighth Street
Berkeley, CA 94710
(510) 524-2178
(510) 524-2221 (fax)

Find us on the World Wide Web at:
http://www.peachpit.com/wow

Peachpit Press is a division of Addison Wesley Longman.

ISBN 0-201-35371-7

0 9 8 7 6 5 4 3 2

Printed and bound in the United States of America.

To Nancy Ruenzel, for years of editorial inspiration

— Linnea Dayton

To Geno Andrews, for moral, spiritual, and comic support

— Jack Davis

ACKNOWLEDGMENTS

This book would not have been possible without a great deal of support. First, we would like to thank the Photoshop artists who have allowed us to include their work and describe their techniques in this book; their names are listed in the Appendix. We are also grateful to many Photoshop artists whose work does not appear in this edition of the book but who have passed along some of their Photoshop knowledge and experience; among them are Cher Threinen-Pendarvis, Sharon Steuer, Russell Brown, Jeff Girard, Laurie Grace, and Ellie Dickson. We appreciate the support of the folks at Adobe Systems, Inc., who kept us up to date on the development of Photoshop and other Adobe programs, supplied us with software, and answered our technical questions.

We are grateful to Jill Davis, whose book design made the writing and illustrating much easier; to Janet Ashford, who wrote many of the new "Gallery" pages for this edition; to Elizabeth Ryder and Karla Huebner, who helped us acquire and manage materials; to Melissa Ryder for copyediting and proofreading; and to Jackie Estrada for again preparing the index. And words can't express our thanks to Jonathan Parker, who once again made room in his design studio's schedule to produce this edition, and even prepared the font that let us set the ⌘ symbols, both standard weight and boldface.

We'd like to thank the friends, family, colleagues, and co-workers, including those at Peachpit Press, who have so far supported us through seven editions of this endeavor. In particular, we thank Victor Gavenda for his technical support and Cary Norsworthy, our editor, for being such a supportive and effective member of our team.

And finally, we'd like to thank those readers of previous editions who have let us know that *The Photoshop Wow! Book* has been useful and important to them, as well as those who have just quietly used and appreciated it. Thanks also for pointing out where we could improve the book so all of us can get the most "Wow!" from our favorite tool — Photoshop.

CONTENTS

WELCOME TO *THE PHOTOSHOP 5/5.5 WOW! BOOK*

ADOBE PHOTOSHOP IS ONE OF THE MOST POWERFUL visual communication tools ever to appear on the desktop. The program has expanded the visual vocabulary of designers and illustrators to include color photo imagery, making photos the "raw material" for creative expression. It also lets photographers do their magic in the light, without chemicals! It allows the new generation of information architects to forge ahead in creating on-screen imagery for the Web and other interactive digital delivery systems. And it makes it much easier to do the resizing, cropping, and basic color correction of production work, both for print and for the Web. Beyond that, it provides a laboratory for synthesizing textures, patterns, and special effects that can be applied to photos, graphics, video, or film. It can even automate many of these tasks, everything from routine production operations to graphics special effects.

Versions 5 and 5.5 have only increased the Photoshop "Wow!" factor, with the addition of new features like **Layer Effects** for a quick, interactive way to add dimensional effects like shadows, glows, and embossing and to keep them "live" so it's easy to make changes; **improved type** tools that let you assign font and style character-by-character, and type layers that let you edit the text, even after you apply layer effects; the **History palette** for delivering the "multiple Undos" that Photoshop aficionados have longed for; improvements to the way **Actions** are recorded and played back; and new **"magnetic" versions** of the lasso and pen tools that can automatically follow the edges of the element you want to select. Changes to Photoshop's color handling seem to be a mixed blessing, with the welcome addition of **spot color** channels and the somewhat confusing changes to the RGB color space.

Brand-new in version 5.5 are a whole suite of **tools for preparing images for the Web;** the **Extract** command and the **background eraser**, for automating and fine-tuning the trickiest of silhouetting tasks, like selecting hair; the **Auto Contrast** command, a refinement of Auto Levels; and the **Art History brush,** which "intelligently" applies textured strokes to turn your image into a painting.

HOW TO USE THIS BOOK

For those who have enjoyed the earlier editions of this book, this one — though it's completely revised and expanded — works basically the same way, with a few exceptions. For instance, since

"Photoshop Fundamentals" are covered primarily in Chapters 1 and 2 and in the introductory pages of the other chapters.

1

WINDOWS OR MAC?

Photoshop 5 and 5.5 work almost identically under Windows and MacOS, with just a few differences in the keyboard shortcuts. In almost all cases, these key correspondences apply:

• The **Ctrl** key on a Windows machine is equivalent to the ⌘ key on the Mac.

• The Windows **Alt** key is the same as the **Option** key on the Mac.

• Where you'd press the **right mouse button** in Windows, you'll use the Mac's **Control** key instead.

2b **CHANGING TONE BUT NOT HUE**

The Auto Contrast command — new in Photoshop 5.5's Image, Adjust submenu — makes an overall adjustment to the dynamic range of tones in an image like the Auto Levels command does. But it guards against the color shifts that sometimes occur with Auto Levels.

(To achieve the same result in Photoshop 5, you can apply an Auto Levels change by means of a Levels Adjustment layer with its blending mode set to Luminosity, as illustrated on page 104.)

Photoshop 5 and 5.5 work virtually identically on Macintosh and Windows machines, and since many artists now work on both platforms, with this edition of the book we've combined the two versions into one. In doing so we've included the keyboard shortcuts, platform-specific directions, and tips for both kinds of machines.

The **key shortcuts** are given with the Windows modifier key first, followed by a slash and then the Mac modifier key, and then a hyphen and the character key. So, for instance, "Ctrl/⌘-R" means "hold down the Windows Ctrl key (called the 'Control' key) or the Mac ⌘ key (called the 'Command' key) as you press the 'R' key."

You'll find **seven kinds of information** in this book: (1) basic information about how Photoshop's tools and functions work, (2) short tips for making your work quicker and easier, (3) step-by-step techniques for particular kinds of projects, (4) galleries of work done by experienced Photoshop artists, (5) "illustrated lists" of resources, and (6) the Wow! CD-ROM.

1 You'll find the **Basics** sections at the beginning of each of the nine chapters of this book. But *The Photoshop 5/5.5 Wow! Book* wasn't designed to be a substitute for the *Adobe Photoshop User Guide*, which has always been an excellent reference manual. Instead, our goal is to provide the kind of inspirational examples and practical "nuts-and-bolts" info that will help you maximize the program's performance and your own creativity and productivity with it.

Most of the chapter introductions are short, with most of the meat of the chapter in the techniques sections that follow. The exceptions are Chapters 1 and 2. Since these two chapters cover the fundamentals of using Photoshop 5 and 5.5, it's a good idea to read these two sections, as well as the introduction for the chapter you're working in, before you start in on that chapter's techniques.

Whether or not you start by reading Chapters 1 and 2, at some point you're going to come up against the need for some "Photoshop fundamentals." When you do, here's where to look:

• To **maximize your efficiency**, from stocking your system with RAM and disk storage space, to constructing your files to give yourself as many options for change as possible, to recovering from mistakes, read the **"Working Smart"** section of Chapter 1, starting on page 14. It's well worth the time it takes to read these pages!

• To learn how to **scan a photo or artwork so you get enough information** to make a good print, read **"Resolution, Color Depth, and File Size"** on page 50 and then follow the procedure in **"Setting Up a Scan"** on page 53.

• To **get the color you expect** when you print, read **"Getting Consistent Color"** on page 40.

3a

If an example shown in the book was done with an earlier versions of Photoshop, we've completely updated the step-by-step directions so the techniques are current for version 5 and 5.5.

3b

An "Action indicator" at the beginning of a technique section tells you that you can find a similar effect, automated as a Photoshop Wow! Action, on the CD-ROM that comes with the book. An "Image indicator" tells you that the CD-ROM includes the file used as the starting point for creating the result shown at the top of the page, as well as the final layered file.

- To learn how to choose component images that can work together in a seamless **montage,** read **"Choosing and Preparing Components"** on page 152 at the beginning of Chapter 4.

- To find out how to **make a clean selection** of part of an image without spending all day at it, read **"Making Selections," "Selecting by Color," "Selecting by Shape,"** and **"Selecting by Shape *and* Color,"** at the beginning of Chapter 2. And while you're in Chapter 2, check out **"Modifying Selections"** and **"Storing Selections: Alpha Channels."**

- To **clean up a selection**, getting rid of ragged edges or a fringe effect when smooth selecting simply isn't possible, read **"Cleaning Up a Selection"** and the **"Cleaning Up Masks"** tip on page 78.

- For a quick and fun **tutorial on using layers,** layer masks, Adjustment layers, Effects layers, clipping groups, and the Layers palette, work through **"Exercising Layers"** in Chapter 2, using Tommy Yune's **Elaine** and **Liz** files provided on the Wow! CD-ROM that comes with this book.

- To learn the basics of using **layer masks** to combine several selected elements into an effective **collage,** see **"Making Seamless Transitions"** on page 154 in Chapter 4.

- To **set up assembly-line production and reliable repeatability,** read **"Automating with Actions,"** starting on page 27 in Chapter 1.

2 To collect the kind of hands-on information that can make you instantly more efficient, flip through the book and scan the **Tips.** You can easily identify them by the gray title bar on top. The tips are a kind of hypertext — linked bits of information that we've positioned alongside the basics and techniques wherever we thought they'd be most helpful. But each one also stands on its own, and you can pick up a lot of useful information quickly by flipping through the book and reading them. You can identify the hottest new **tips for version 5.5** by the yellow background behind them.

3 Each **Technique**, presented in 1 to 6 pages, is designed to give you enough step-by-step information so you can carry it out in Photoshop. Our goal was to provide enough written and pictorial instructions so you wouldn't have to hunt through the *Adobe Photoshop User Guide* or continuously consult Photoshop's excellent online Help to follow the steps. But to spare you a lot of repetition, we've assumed you know the basic Windows or Mac interface — how to open and save files, for instance — and we've focused on specific techniques in some cases, rather than explaining every detail of every method used in a particular project. Some of the

4

Without taking you through a project step-by-step, the Gallery sections provide insight into artists' techniques that you can apply to your own work.

5

The "Filter Demos" section of Chapter 5 is one of the book's "Resources" sections.

techniques are simple and introductory; others are more advanced and challenging. If something isn't clear to you, go back to review Chapters 1 and 2, as well as the introductory pages for that chapter.

Some techniques are presented with artwork created specifically for the demonstration. Other techniques are descriptions of the methods artists used to create particular illustrations or parts of illustrations. Where possible, we've provided the **starting images,** as well as any other files you might need to complete the projects, on the **Wow CD-ROM** in the pocket at the back of the book, so you can follow the steps to get the result shown, before trying the technique on other images.

The step-by-step techniques start with an introductory paragraph that explains the objective of the technique. If the technique works best on a particular kind of photo — one with bright white specular highlights, or with a foreground subject that extends to the bottom of the image, for instance — the introduction tells you this, too, so you can figure out whether the technique will work with the photo you're thinking of applying it to.

The rest of each technique consists of numbered, illustrated instructions. The first step tells, briefly, how to get to the starting point for the project. If you need to know more about some process described in step 1, check the index at the back of the book for references to other sections.

The techniques sections are more like recipes than like TV dinners — you follow the directions to combine the ingredients. When you want the equivalent of a microwavable meal, turn to the **Wow Actions** on the Wow CD-ROM. After you've enjoyed a no-fuss-no-muss Action effect, you can dissect the resulting file and the Action itself to learn about that particular technique and about making Actions in general.

As you work with Photoshop 5/5.5, you'll notice that there seem to be at least a dozen ways to do everything — you can choose from a menu, use a keyboard shortcut, or click in the customizable Actions palette; you can cut and paste, or drag and drop; you can combine images with layer masks or load selections from alpha channels and then cut and paste; you can make color adjustments or apply special effects directly, or add Adjustment layers or Layer Effects to do it. Because of the variety of possibilities, you'll find varied approaches used in the techniques sections, so you'll get a broad exposure to the different ways Photoshop can work. But, in general, the methods presented are the ones that we have found to be the most efficient and effective — approaches that will save you time, produce high-quality results, and leave you with the most flexibility to make the inevitable last-minute changes.

4 The images in the **Galleries** are for inspiration, but their captions also include a lot of useful information about how the artwork was produced. Many of the methods mentioned in the

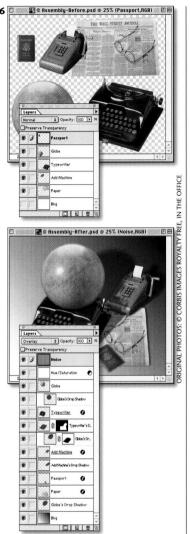

6

"Before" and "After" versions of many of the techniques in the book are provided in the Wow Layered Images folder on the CD-ROM that comes with this book.

ORIGINAL PHOTOS: © CORBIS IMAGES ROYALTY FREE, IN THE OFFICE

Galleries are described more fully elsewhere in the book. Check the index if you need help finding a particular technique.

On the Wow CD-ROM we've provided both the starting materials and the finished layered files for many of the techniques. These are organized by chapter in the **Wow Layered Images** folder. Also, in the **Wow Actions** folder you'll find Actions that produce results similar to those in some of the Techniques sections.

5 Throughout the book, and especially in Chapter 5, "Using Filters," and in the Appendixes at the back, is information you can use to locate the kinds of **Resources** Photoshop users need to know about, such as stock photo images and plug-in filters.

6 Don't miss the **Wow CD-ROM** — in addition to the tutorial image files and Actions, it's filled with other images and plug-ins from leading photo stock and filter resources, as well as demo programs.

In response to requests from readers of earlier editions, the **"Study Guide"** pages in Acrobat PDF form on the Wow CD-ROM include suggestions for using *The Photoshop 5/5.5 Wow! Book* and CD-ROM either for teaching classes in computerized imagery and design with Photoshop 5 or 5.5, or for self-paced exploration and mastery of the program.

Experiment! The aim of this book is to get you started using the tools if you're new at it, and to give you some new insight and ideas if you're an old hand. As you read the book and try out the tips, techniques, and Actions, we hope you'll use them as a jumping off place for your own fearless experimentation. *Wow*

A LOOK AT PHOTOSHOP 5 AND 5.5

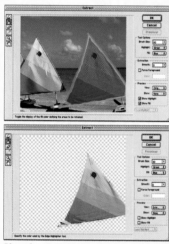

*Photoshop 5.5's **Extract** command, found in the Image menu, lets you "paint" a band that roughly defines the selection you want and designate the area inside (you fill it with color) and outside (you leave it unfilled). Within the band itself, Photoshop makes its "best guess" about where to create the selection boundary, based on color change and contrast. At the edges of the selection, background color is replaced with transparency so that the selected element can blend seamlessly into a new composition. Since anything in the band can become part of the transparent edge, it's best to stay toward the outside of your object when selecting.*

IF YOU'RE NEW TO PHOTOSHOP, this chapter is designed to give you some general pointers on using the program more easily and efficiently. But it won't replace the *Adobe Photoshop User Guide* or *Tutorial* as a comprehensive source of basic information. If you're experienced with earlier versions of the program, this chapter will help bring you up to date on some of the changes in Photoshop 5 and 5.5.

WHAT'S NEW?

Here's a quick look at some of the things that are new or different in Photoshop 5 and 5.5 and where in this book you can find out more about them. The new features of version 5.5 are described first, then the tools and other functions that were new with version 5, all of which were carried over to 5.5.

New in Version 5.5

Brand-new to Photoshop 5.5 are two advanced selecting tools — the **Extract** command and the **background eraser**, both of which can help you tackle hard-to-select image elements. Also, an old standard selecting tool — the **magic wand** — has been improved in version 5.5. You can now choose to have it select pixels of the color you click on even if they're not contiguous with the pixel you click. The wand's counterpart, the new **magic eraser,** is like a one-click magic-wand-and-Delete combination — it erases all pixels of the color you click on, either contiguous or not — it's your choice. All of these improvements to selecting are described in Chapter 2.

The program's painterly abilities have been expanded with the **Art History brush**, which can help convert photos to paintings by reproducing the lines and curves of the image with a variety of brush strokes. Another new addition is a set of **natural brushes** — you can see the individual bristle trails in each stroke. These painting enhancements are demonstrated in Chapter 6.

Photoshop 5.5's Type Tool dialog box, described in the "Type Layers" section of Chapter 2 (page 86), now lets you choose the degree of antialiasing you want, with options for **improved legibility of on-screen text.** But for those whose work is destined for the Web, the biggest improvement to Photoshop 5.5 has to be the inclusion of **ImageReady 2.0** in the package, and the new

continued on page 8

*The interactive interface of the **Save For Web** dialog box lets you see how your image will look under different JPEG, GIF, and PNG compression schemes.*

Save For Web functions built into Photoshop itself. It's now much easier than before to **optimize graphics for the Web** in GIF, JPEG, or PNG format using Photoshop 5.5's Save For Web command. You can preview as many as four versions of the image as treated with different **compression schemes** that you can choose yourself or have Photoshop choose for you.

To go beyond these built-in enhancements, you can click the **Jump To** button at the bottom of Photoshop 5.5's tool palette and move directly to **ImageReady** for more — **slicing** images into faster-loading sections, using **object-oriented drawing tools** to make buttons, adding hyperlinks to make **image maps,** and preparing **JavaScript rollovers** and **GIF animations.** The new Web-related functions of Photoshop and ImageReady are presented in Chapter 9.

Version 5.5's File, Automate submenu offers help in producing a **Web Photo Gallery** from a folderful of files. For output to paper, the File, Automate submenu also offers the **Picture Package** command, which lays out a page with multiple copies of a single image at the sizes you choose.

The tool palette for ImageReady 2.0, which comes in the box with Photoshop 5.5, houses many tools brought over directly from Photoshop. In addition, it has a rounded-rectangle marquee, object-oriented geometric drawing tools, and equipment for making, selecting and displaying or hiding slices of an image. ImageReady is covered in Chapter 9, "Photoshop and the Web."

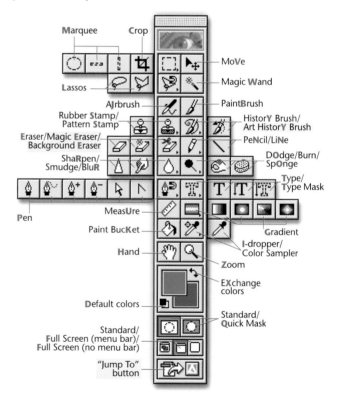

Shown here is the Photoshop 5.5 tool palette; tools that were added in version 5.5 are highlighted in yellow. In Photoshop 5 and 5.5 single-key commands (shown here in red) activate the tools. With the addition of the Shift key, they toggle between tools that share a space in the palette. A copy of this expanded palette is provided on the flap of the back cover of this book so you can cut it out and tape it to your monitor as a reminder.

Photoshop 5/5.5's History palette keeps track of the state of your image as you work, and lets you revert to, paint from, or delete a previous state in your current work session. When the History palette reaches the maximum number of states you've set (the default is 20), the oldest state is "pushed" off the top of the palette as a new one is added to the bottom.

ESSENTIAL TRANSFORMATIONS

Have you ever made or loaded a selection and then wanted to reshape the "marching ants" boundary before you actually selected any pixels? In Photoshop 5 and 5.5, the selection boundary itself (the marching ants) can be transformed by choosing Select, Transform Selection.

Also in Photoshop 5/5.5, paths can now be transformed directly.

R&R Fiji sunset 3.tif 2 @ 25% (RGB

25%   Doc: 5.24M/5.24M

New with Photoshop 5

One of the new features first included in version 5 is that Photoshop now **keeps track of everything you do,** storing the most recent steps — you determine how many steps — in the **History palette,** described in "The History Palette," on page 20. In conjunction with this palette, the new **History brush** tool lets you **recall an earlier stage of the image, one brush stroke at a time,** much like the From Saved or From Snapshot modes of the rubber stamp tool in earlier versions of Photoshop. Creative uses for this tool are described in Chapter 6, "Painting."

New features that make it **easier to select** the parts of a Photoshop image you want to work on are the Reselect command, the "magnetic" versions of the lasso and the pen tool, the freeform pen tool, and the ability to rotate, skew, and otherwise **transform paths and selection boundaries**.

- The **Reselect** command lets you **revive your last selection** after you've deselected it, simply by choosing Select, Reselect.

- The **magnetic lasso** and **magnetic pen** provide a **partially automated tracing** function for these two tools, automatically following the boundaries between areas of different colors to select a shape.

- With the **freeform pen** you can now drag this tool as you would the lasso, and it **automatically places points** to make a path.

- The **Select, Transform Selection** and **Edit, Transform Path** (or Points) commands let you **modify an active selection boundary** or **a path** (or selected parts of a path), changing only the "marching ants" or path **without rearranging any pixels.**

All of these new selecting features are covered in Chapter 2.

A NEW MODUS OPERANDI

Photoshop 5/5.5's new magnetic tools give you a new way to operate their cursors. You can move these automated cursors simply by "floating" them — moving the mouse without holding down the mouse button, clicking only when you want to force a new point.

LINING UP LAYERS

Photoshop's new Distribute Linked command from the Layer menu lets you align and distribute the contents of several linked layers. To line up buttons for a Web page, for instance, this is much quicker than hand-placing guidelines from the rulers and then aligning elements to the guides.

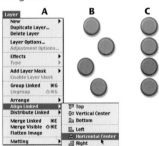

The Layer, Align Linked command (A) and Layer, Distribute Linked allow you to line up elements and space them evenly. If you have elements contained on several layers (B), you can align them by clicking to activate one of the layers, then clicking in the column next to the eye icon in each of the other layers to link them, and finally choosing Layer, Align Linked and selecting the type of alignment you want. The elements will be aligned according to your choice (C).

You'll notice that the lasso and pen aren't the only tools that have changed since Photoshop 4. Here are other changes to the way the toolbox looks and operates:

• The **pencil** and **line tool** share a spot in the toolbox, making room for the **measure tool**, described in "Precision" later in this chapter.

• Some of the **single-letter keyboard shortcuts have changed,** as shown in the toolbox illustration on page 8.

• **Switching between tools** that share a palette position, such as the marquees, now requires the use of the **Shift** key along with the tool's single-key shortcut.

• **Type** and **type selection** tools now include variants that let you set type **vertically.**

• The **pattern stamp** (described in Chapter 6) shares a palette niche with the rubber stamp, and the **History brush** took on the From Saved, From Snapshot, and Impressionist functions of the rubber stamp in previous versions along with its unique new functions.

• The gradient function was split into **five separate gradient tools** that share a place in the toolbox. In addition to the Linear and Radial gradients available in earlier versions, you can now produce an **Angle** (or conical) gradient, a **Reflected** (or mirrored) gradient, and a **Diamond** (or starlike) gradient. The use of these gradient fills is shown in Chapter 6.

The **Layer, Effects** commands make it easy to apply **simple, easily edited dimensional effects** to type and other elements. You can assign bevels, shadows, and glows to the contents of any layer. These features are covered in Chapter 8, along with the more sophisticated dimensional effects you can create with multiple layers and with the Lighting Effects and Distort filters.

The Layer Effects treatments, combined with improvements to the **type** function, give you the potential for **more sophisticated type treatments that stay editable** even after you've changed the color and applied bevels and shadows. The improvements to type begin with the ability to control the font, size, style, and spacing of type letter-by-letter as you set it. And once the type is set, you can keep it "live" until you're ready to save the file in a format for printing or Web use. The type tool is covered in Chapter 2, in "Type and Graphics Special Effects," on page 94. Its palette-mate, the type selection tool is covered with the other selection tools in Chapter 2.

Completely new in version 5.0 was the **3D Transform** filter in the Filter, Render submenu. This filter lets you **treat a two-dimensional image or type as if it were in three-**

Choosing Layer, Effects offers you a list of dimensional effects you can apply to the content of the active layer. Choosing one of these options opens the Effects dialog box, where you can apply and customize one or more effects. These effects will stay with the layer, even if the layer is edited or moved. And the effects themselves remain "live" so you can later change the direction of the lighting, the depth of a bevel, or the softness of a shadow, for instance.

To label this jar, the type and partially transparent white strip were merged on a layer above the photo of the jar. Then, with the label layer active, the Render, 3D Transform command was applied. A step-by-step description is provided in "3D Labeling" in Chapter 5.

dimensional space — you can treat it as a basically cuboidal, spheroidal, or cylindrical shape and rotate or resize it to view it from a different angle or viewpoint, to show more or less of its individual surfaces. Its use is described in Chapter 5 in "Filter Demos" on page 194 and in "3D Labeling" on page 182.

There were major **changes in color** introduced in Photoshop 5. These are described in more detail in "Color in Photoshop," on page 34, but here's a brief introduction:

- The **Gamma** utility, provided with Photoshop for calibrating monitors that don't have their own calibration hardware or software, **comes with assistance** to lead you through a simplified calibration process step-by-step. This makes it easier to keep basic color needs standardized for more reliable output, as described in "Getting Consistent Color," on page 40.

- Photoshop 5 also introduced **different RGB color spaces than previous versions**. As part of this change, by default the program makes assumptions about what you would like to do about files created under other color schemes. **You'll probably want to change the default** (see **"Coping with Color Change"** at the right and **"Choosing an RGB Color Space"** on page 42).

- Photoshop 5's introduction of **spot color** channels makes it much easier to prepare images for output in custom colors. The use of this feature is described in "Adding a Spot Color" and "Making a Three-Color Print," both in Chapter 3.

- Expanding the usefulness of the Info palette, as many as

OLD GAMMAS WON'T WORK

Photoshop 5 does not support Gamma settings saved in earlier versions. So if you've saved settings for specific purposes, you'll need to redo them with Photoshop 5's Gamma utility.

COPING WITH COLOR CHANGE

With Photoshop 5, Adobe made some very significant changes in the way the program manages color. These include the use of ICC color profiles and setting the sRGB color space as the default. While these changes provide certain advantages in color management, they also have several drawbacks. For instance, you can unwittingly and permanently change the colors in some image files simply by opening and resaving them in Photoshop 5 or 5.5.

Starting with version 5.0.2, Photoshop ships with a Color Assistant to help you avoid trouble. It loads automatically the first time you open a newly installed copy of Photoshop and leads you through the process of making decisions about color. If you want to use it again later, you can find it in the Help menu.

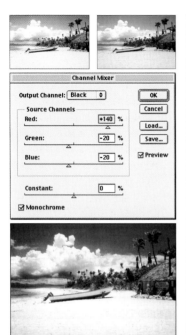

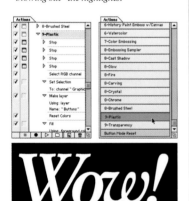

In Monochrome mode, using the Channel Mixer to boost the Red channel and reducing the contribution of the Blue and Green channels allowed more of the shadow detail in and around the hut to show, without "blowing out" the highlights.

Photoshop 5's Actions can be quite elaborate, like the one shown here. The Actions palette can be displayed in List mode (left) so you can see and edit the individual steps, or Button mode (right), which is more compact and can be organized with colors.

four **color samplers** can be positioned in an image so you can repeatedly **check color in exactly the same spots** as the image develops.

• The **Channel Mixer,** which can be applied either from the Image, Adjust submenu or as an Adjustment layer, lets you interactively mix color channels by percentages, viewing the effect of your changes as you make them. This mixing ability can be useful for getting the best possible grayscale image from a color file, or for imitating special photographic effects such as infrared photos. For more about the Channel Mixer, see "Channel Mix-and-Match" on page 115 and "Channel Mixer Presets" on page 148.

Another change in Photoshop's approach to color is the addition of **color sliders in the Hue/Saturation dialog box**.

An improvement to Photoshop's overall efficiency is that the program can now make **better use of available hard disk space,** as described in "Virtual Memory" later in the chapter. With the addition of the History palette, this ability to supplement the computer memory that Photoshop uses to carry out its operations is even more important than it was in earlier versions of the program.

Finally, the ability to automate complex multistep Photoshop procedures has been simplified. **Improvements in the Actions** allow more tools and palettes to be recorded in an Action than was possible in Photoshop 4. And the finished Actions can be organized into sets for easier management. These and other changes are described in "Automating with Actions" later in the chapter.

In addition to the automation provided by Actions, new **Wizards** (Windows) and **Assistants** (Mac) make it easier to work your way through complex tasks. You can fit an image to a particular height or width (File, Automate, **Fit Image**) or scale images for print or the Internet (Help, **Resize Image**) or prepare images so part of the image is masked out when the image is placed in a page layout program (Help, **Export Transparent Image**). Also in the File, Automate submenu is the **Contact Sheet** command, which produces a sheet of thumbnails of all the images in the folder you designate.

THE MAC'S "OTHER" MEMORY

On a Macintosh, the System software has its own version of virtual memory. But for Photoshop to run most efficiently, the System's virtual memory should be turned off: Choose Control Panels from the apple menu, open the Memory Control Panel, and turn off Virtual Memory.

To list Photoshop in the top level of the Start menu in Windows 95/98, drag its program icon or shortcut icon onto the Start button. Now when you press Start, the Photoshop (or shortcut) icon will appear in the list at the top of the pop-up menu.

On a Macintosh system you can put a Photoshop alias icon at the top of the apple menu: Working in the Finder, click once on the Photoshop icon to select it, and choose File, Make Alias (you can put a space in front of the name if you want it at the top of the list), and drag the new alias icon into the Apple Menu Items folder (inside the System Folder).

File   Edit   View

About This Computer

PS 5.5
Applications ▶
Control Panels ▶
Misc Apple Menu ▶
System Folder ▶
Utilities ▶

For large graphics files stored on a relatively unfragmented hard disk, the disk's *access time* (how fast it can find and begin to read a file) is generally less important than its *transfer rate* (how fast it reads a file once it's found). The goal is to buy the biggest and fastest drive or drives you can afford.

Some hard disks are composed of two drives linked in a dual array to double the speed of data transfer — it's kind of like using two fire hoses instead of one to put out a fire.

If you have a newer model computer, look for the new firewire drives, which are fast, flexible, and economical.

CPU, RAM, AND ACCELERATION

Photoshop files tend to be large — a lot of information has to be stored to record the color of each of the thousands or millions of pixels that make up an image. So it can take quite a bit of computer processing just to open a file (which brings that information into the computer's working memory, or RAM) or to apply a special effect (which can involve complicated calculations for evaluating and changing the color of every pixel in the image). Photoshop needs a lot of RAM to hold an image while it works on it, especially with the addition of improvements to efficiency such as the History palette's ability to keep track of earlier stages of the file. Although you can do good Photoshop work on a smaller, slower, less powerful computer system, the program works best if you have a fast computer, a great deal of RAM, a monitor displaying full 24-bit photorealistic color, and a very large, fast hard disk (or disks) with plenty of optimized free space.

The **minimum system *required*** for running Photoshop 5/5.5 under **Windows** is a Pentium-class or faster processor, the Windows 95 (or later) or Windows NT 4.0 (or later) operating system, an 8-bit (256-color) video card, a CD-ROM drive, a minimum of 32 MB of RAM, and at least 125 MB of free hard disk space. The **minimum system *recommended*** by Adobe for decent Photoshop performance, though, is at least 64 MB of RAM, a PostScript printer, and a 24-bit (millions of colors) video display card, although 16-bit color (thousands of colors) may be adequate for some color work. Also, if you want to run the *Adobe Photoshop Tour and Training* CD-ROM that comes with the program, you'll also need a sound card.

The **minimum system *required*** for running Photoshop 5/5.5 on a **Macintosh** system is a PowerPC or faster processor with a color monitor capable of 8-bit color (256 colors) or better and at least 32 MB of RAM available for running the program; that figure doesn't include RAM required for the operating system (which must be MacOS version 7.5 or later), or for other programs you might want to run at the same time. The system must also include a hard disk drive with at least 60 MB of free space (119 MB for version 5.5) and a CD-ROM. The **minimum system *recommended*** includes a PowerPC G3 or faster processor, MacOS version 8.1 or later, 64 MB of RAM, a PostScript printer, and a 24-bit (millions of colors) video display card, although 16-bit color (thousands of colors) may be adequate for some color work.

For either Windows or Mac, accelerator products are available, designed specifically to support some of Photoshop's calculation-intensive functions, such as running filters or resizing images. Look for the Adobe-Charged logo to be sure they will significantly improve Photoshop's performance.

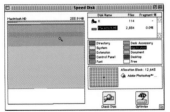
VIRTUAL MEMORY

If Photoshop doesn't have enough room to handle a file entirely in RAM, it can use hard disk space for memory — that's *virtual memory*, or in Photoshop parlance *scratch disk*. In that case, two factors become important. The first is the amount of empty hard disk space (beyond the 60 to 125 MB required, you'll want at least as much space as you have RAM and at least three to five times the size of any file you work on). The second factor is the transfer rate of the disk drive (the speed at which data can be read off a disk). Photoshop 5/5.5 can make use of as many as four scratch disks and can use up to 200 GB of hard disk space as virtual memory. Think about dedicating an entire fast hard disk as a scratch disk. Disk space is relatively cheap these days, and this will give Photoshop plenty of "elbow room." Also, because you won't be storing anything on the drive permanently, you won't have to defragment the disk.

WORKING SMART

Once your system is set up with lots of RAM and a fast hard disk drive, here are some other things you can do to make your "Photoshopping" time more productive:

Opening several files together. You can open several files at once from the desktop by Shift-clicking their icons or names to select them all and then dragging them onto the Photoshop icon or a Photoshop alias icon. The files need not be Photoshop files to be opened in this way, as long as they are in a format Photoshop can open.

Using Layer Effects. Applying special-effects treatments by means of the Layer, Effects command gives you tremendous flexibility. First, you can make repeated changes to the Effects themselves without degrading the image. Second, you can copy and paste the Effects to one or more other layers in the same file or even in other files. And third, you can even change the contents of the layer you've applied them to and the Effects will automatically and instantly "rewrap" themselves to fit the new contents of the layer. To learn how to put Layer Effects to work, see "Using Layer Effects" in Chapter 8, starting on page 272.

Working with Adjustment layers. If you store color adjustment information in Adjustment layers (as described in Chapter 3), you can readjust without having to start over and without degrading the original image by reworking it. Adjustment layers also let you save settings that you can't normally save, such as Color Balance.

Using Free Transform. When you want to perform some combination of scale, rotate, skew, distort, perspective, or flip, use the Free Transform command rather than making the individual transfor-

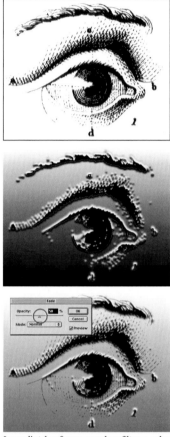

Immediately after you apply a filter, a color adjustment, or painting strokes, you can use the Filter, Fade command to reduce the effect or change the blending mode. Here we started with a scan of line art, then applied the Plaster filter and used the Fade command to change its Opacity to 50%.

mations with the Transform command (both commands are found in the Edit menu). This makes the transformation process much more interactive, since you can work back and forth between the different transformations until you get exactly what you want. Also, doing all the work in a single session keeps the image from being degraded by each separate transformation. To use Free Transform, press Ctrl/⌘-T to activate the Transform box. Then right-click (Windows) or Control-click (Mac) to bring up a context-sensitive menu from which you can choose the kind of transformation you want.

Mastering the art of selection. Knowing the ins and outs of making, cleaning up, storing and recalling selections is at the heart of successful montage and image editing. Take the time to make sure you understand how to choose and use Photoshop's many selection methods, especially the powerful additions — background eraser and Extract command — that arrived with version 5.5. These topics are covered in Chapter 2.

Saving selections and paths as you work. If you're using one of the selection tools or commands to make a complex selection, you may want to save the selection periodically by making it into an alpha channel. With a backup version of the selection saved with the file, if you accidentally drop the selection and it's too late to use the Reselect command, you won't have to start over completely. Having the selection stored in a channel also allows you to use the painting and editing tools to clean up the selection boundaries. Be sure to save the selection again when it's finished, so you can reselect exactly the same area if you need to later. If you're using the pen tool to create a selection outline, save the selection as a path rather than a channel. A path takes much less disk space. And as you create paths, be sure to convert each one from the Work Path to a saved path to store it individually.

Taking advantage of History. Understanding how Photoshop 5/5.5's History palette works can make your Photoshop sessions much more efficient. To get familiar with it, read "The History Palette," starting on page 20.

Blending a "processed" image with the original. To interactively adjust the effects of filters, color adjustments, and paint, use the **Fade** command, which is found in the Filter menu but which also applies to the Image, Adjust commands and to painting. When you choose Filter, Fade and then move the Fade dialog box's Opacity slider or change its blending mode, it's as though the effect had been applied to a copy of the image that was then stacked on top of the original; changing Opacity or blending mode produces the same result as it would in that top layer. But the Fade command is available only immediately after you apply an effect. Instead of

Actions

| Scan Color Fix |
| Convert to GIF |
| Convert to JPEG |
| Convert to TIFF |
| Make Really Cool |

Things that you're likely to do again and again, like correcting a color cast introduced by a scanner or converting files to GIF or JPEG for use on the Web are great candidates for Actions. The Actions palette can be stored in Button mode for one-click operation.

HANDY KEY COMMANDS

There's a complete list of the default keyboard shortcuts on the Adobe Photoshop Quick Reference Card that comes with the program, but here are some especially useful toggles for showing palettes or hiding them to free up some screen real estate:

Brushes palette F5

Color palette F6

Layers palette F7

Info palette F8

Actions palette F9

If a palette doesn't appear on the first press of the function key, try again. It may have been obscured behind another palette, so the first press turned it off, and the second will bring it back and place it in front of the others.

To **hide the currently open palettes** or to bring them back into view, press **Tab.**

To **hide all the open palettes** *except the toolbox* or to bring them back, press **Shift-Tab.**

using Fade, if you can afford the memory overhead, you may want to apply your effect to a copy in a separate layer, and then you'll be able to "fade" with the layer's Opacity slider long after you applied the effect. An Adjustment layer is a still better solution for those effects that can be applied that way; again, the Adjustment layer's Opacity slider and blending modes let you fade the effect anytime you want to.

Recording your actions. Any time you make changes that you think you might someday want to make to other images, record the process using the **Actions palette**. Recording doesn't take extra time or RAM, and it may very well produce a useful "macro." Actions work better for recording some processes than for others. Not everything you can do in Photoshop 5/5.5 can be recorded in an Action. For instance, brush strokes with painting and toning tools are left out. To get a start on recording and applying Actions, see "Automating with Actions" on page 27.

Building a file in stages. If you're planning to modify and combine images, do the modifications on the separate, smaller parts first, and then combine them into a larger file. Instead of having a separate layer for every piece of the image, consider building an illustration in "modules": Build one component of several layers, then copy those layers into a single layer (Ctrl/⌘-Shift-C copies all visible layers within a selection boundary); create other components the same way; then manipulate the combined copies to make the final image. (Chapters 2 and 4 tell more about copying and merging layers.)

Starting out in low resolution. For some images you can do your planning and "sketching" in a lower-resolution file than you will ultimately need for output. (See "Resolution, Color Depth, and File Size" on page 50 for tips on determining the resolution you need.) Working at low resolution will reduce processing time for changes you make to the image. Although you'll have to make the changes again on the higher-res file, some of the changes you make at the lower resolution can be saved as Adjustment layers and then dragged and dropped from the Layers palette of the low-resolution image into the bigger file. If an Adjustment layer includes a mask, however, the layer can't be successfully dragged and dropped to the higher-resolution file because the mask will be too small. To learn more about Adjustment layers, start with "Adjustment Layers: The Ultimate in Flexibility" on page 102. (Settings for some of the Image, Adjust commands that can't be applied as Adjustment

RESIZING LAYER EFFECTS

Since there are upper limits to the settings in Layer Effects (such as 50 pixels for Blur), you need to remember when you create a Layer Effect in a low-res comp to leave yourself some leeway to increase the settings in the final high-res file.

Working at low resolution saves time and disk space. Several designs for the Healthy Traveler *book cover were worked out at 72 dpi before one was chosen for development at high resolution.*

MAKE ME ANOTHER ONE

When you choose File, New, you can base the new file size on any document that's open in Photoshop: Instead of filling in the dimensions called for in the New File dialog box, pull down the Window menu and choose from the files listed at the bottom to open a new file with the same dimensions, resolution, and color mode as the one you chose. This trick also works with the Image Size and Canvas Size dialog boxes.

CAUTION BOX ESCAPES

Pressing the Enter/Return key is a well-known shortcut for "Save" in the caution box that appears when you close a file. But you can also use single-key shortcuts for the other options: Press "D" for "Don't Save" to close the file without changes, or "C" for "Cancel" to get out of the dialog box without closing the file.

layers, such as Variations and Replace Color, can be saved and loaded again later, using the Save and Load buttons in their dialog boxes.)

Like Adjustment layers, active Layer Effects from a low-resolution file can often be successfully transferred into the high-res version, in this case by copying and pasting. To successfully move Layer Effects from a low-res to a high-res file, you'll need to proportionally increase any settings that are expressed in pixel dimensions.

"Emptying" the clipboard and other caches. If you cut or copy something to the clipboard or use the Define Pattern command, the stored material is retained in RAM even after you've

KEEPING PALETTES HANDY

The palettes for Layers, Channels, Info, Tool Options/Brushes, and colors can be stored on-screen, ready to use, without taking up much space. Click the small box in the upper right corner of each palette to toggle between its collapsed version with only its tab showing and its expanded, functional version. (Some palettes have a two-stage collapse/expand function, and you have to Alt/Option-click to collapse the palette all the way down to its tab alone.) When you click to expand a palette, it pops *into* the window. So even if you store the collapsed palettes at the very bottom of the screen, they'll be fully visible when they expand. Shift-click on a palette's title bar to snap it to the nearest edge of the screen; or Shift-drag to move it around the edge of the screen. (For an uncluttered view with all palettes available, if you're running Photoshop under Windows 98 or on a Mac, consider an inexpensive second monitor for palettes alone.)

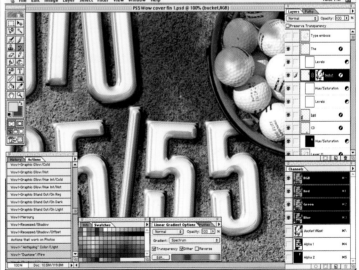

Here's one way to set up a 1024 x 768-pixel screen for working efficiently in Photoshop, with most of the palettes handy. The Actions palette is stretched along the edge of the screen so its buttons are always available and is nested with the History palette. The Channels and Layers palettes are separated so both can be open at the same time; the Brushes palette is nested with the Tool Options palette so it's available for use with any tool. The Info palette is present, nested with the Swatches palette. The Document Size/Scratch Size window in the lower left corner can show information about memory, file size, and image resolution.

Free Transform ⌘T
Transform ▶
Define Pattern
Purge ▶ | Undo
Clipboard
Pattern
Histories
All

You can purge any or all of Photoshop's various caches to free up RAM.

To save on storage space but still preserve access to all the blending mode, opacity, Adjustment layer, font, Layer Effects, and masking information that you used to build a montage, use the Image Size command to store a very small copy of the file before you flatten the original for printing. Sized at 2000 pixels wide, (top), this multilayered working file would occupy about 70 MB of storage space. But a small "thumbnail" version (center), reduced to 100 pixels wide, takes only about 50K and will remind you how the montage was put together.

pasted a copy in place, or used the pattern. In addition, Photoshop always remembers what the image was like before your last change, in case you decide to use Edit, Undo (Ctrl/⌘-Z) or use the History palette. Since some of Photoshop's commands can be carried out only in RAM (not in virtual memory), it's good strategy to release the RAM by clearing a large clipboard selection, a pattern, all History states, or a step you know you won't need to Undo. Photoshop 5/5.5's Purge command makes it really easy. Just choose **Edit, Purge**; any choices that aren't grayed out indicate that something is stored and can be purged.

Saving "thumbnail" files.
When you've finished a multilayered image, and you've flattened a copy and printed it, you may not want to store the original in its layered, memoryintensive form. Still, you'd like to be able to go back someday and see how you accomplished the look you got in the final printed piece — how the elements were layered and what blending modes, Opacity settings, type specifications, Effects, layer options, layer masks, alpha channels, Adjustment layers, and clipping groups you used — in case you want to get a similar effect in another image. To save all this information, use Image, Image Size to reduce a copy of the layered file to a small, low-res version. You could never use it for print, but it will store the layer information in much less space.

continued on page 20

If RAM is limited, there are several ways you can "copy and paste" a selection, a layer, a channel, or an entire image without using the clipboard, which requires RAM.

• **To duplicate a selection in the same file,** press Ctrl/⌘-J (for Layer Via Copy).

• **To duplicate the content of a layer,** drag its thumbnail to the New Layer icon. Or use Duplicate Layer from the Layer menu.

• **To duplicate a selected area or a layer from one file to another,** drag and drop with the move tool from one document to the other; to center the selection in the new file, press and hold the Shift key before you stop dragging. Or use the Layer, Duplicate Layer command.

• **To duplicate a channel from one image into another,** drag the channel from the Channels palette into the other image.

• **To copy an entire image as a new file,** choose Image, Duplicate.

• **To duplicate a Snapshot from one file to another,** drag its thumbnail from the History palette into the other file.

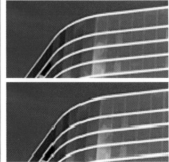

Remember, the views at 100% (top), 50%, 25%, 12.5%, and so on down look much smoother and are more accurate for on-screen editing than odd settings like 33.3%, 66.7%, or the 104% view shown here (bottom), which can give you the impression that your image has been somehow corrupted.

The small box in the lower left corner of the Photoshop window holds a lot of information:

• **How big is the file?** In Document Sizes mode the box shows the current open size of the file with all its layers and channels (right) and the size it would be if it was flattened to one layer with all alpha channels removed (left) — that is, the amount of data that will be sent to the printer or other output device.

• **Is the scratch disk being used?** In Scratch Sizes mode the box shows how much RAM is available for Photoshop to use (right) and how much memory is currently tied up by all open Photoshop files, the clipboard, Snapshot, and so on (left). If the left-hand figure exceeds the right-hand figure, it means Photoshop is using virtual memory to carry out its functions.

• **Would more RAM help?** You can watch the Efficiency indicator to see how much Photoshop is using RAM alone, rather than swapping data with the scratch disk. A value near 100% means the scratch disk isn't being used much, so adding more RAM probably wouldn't improve performance. A value less than about 75% means that assigning more RAM would probably help.

• **How long did that take?** In Timing mode the box tells how long the last operation took. So you can walk away from your computer leaving it to filter a large file, and find out when you return how long it took, so you'll know for future filtering.

• **What tool am I using?** With the ability to choose Brush Size or Precise cursors instead of picture icons (File, Preferences, Display and Cursors), and with the ability to hide all palettes, including the toolbox (press the Tab key), it can be hard to tell what tool is active. Before you click or drag and make a mistake you'll have to undo, you can check the Current Tool listing for the name of the active tool.

• **How will it print?** Pressing on the numbers themselves opens a box that shows the size of the image relative to the page size currently selected in File, Page Setup.

• **How is it organized?** Holding down the Alt/Option key while pressing the numbers shows the dimensions (in pixels and in the Rulers units, set with File, Preferences, Units & Rulers), the resolution (in pixels per inch or pixels per cm, as set with Image, Image Size, Resolution), the color mode, and the number of channels in the image file.

Holding down the Ctrl/⌘ key while pressing the numbers shows the number and size of the rectangular "tiles" that make up the image. The tiles are the blocks of information Photoshop uses to store the image. (In a large file you can see them appear one by one as the screen is redrawn when you work on a file.) The amount of additional memory required by each layer depends on how many of these tiles its pixels occupy. For instance, in a nine-tile file, a layer with a small circle of pixels at the center of each tile would require more memory than a layer with all the small circles aggregated in one tile.

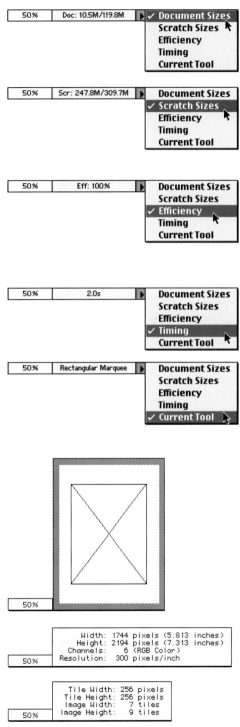

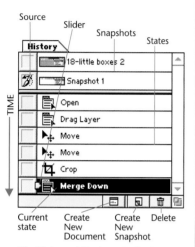

Choosing History Options from the History palette's pop-out menu opens a dialog box that lets you choose how many of the most recent changes to the file you want the palette to retain, from the present backward. You can also choose whether to bypass the default first Snapshot or Allow Non-Linear History (see "Linear or Non-Linear" on page 22).

The History palette stores step-by-step states at the bottom, recording everything you do to the file. Snapshots, made when you choose to preserve the file at a particular stage of development, are stored at the top of the palette. The History brush icon in the source column means that the state or Snapshot next to the brush icon will be the source if you paint with the History brush, the Art History brush, or the eraser in Erase To History mode, or if you use the Fill command with the History option turned on. The states are in order by time, with the most recent at the bottom, although in Non-Linear mode there can be extras states in the list (see "Linear or Non-Linear" on page 22).

Closing other applications. If your main goal is to work in Photoshop, open Photoshop first, before opening any additional applications. This gives Photoshop first claim on RAM. As you work, if you find that you need more RAM, close any other programs you've opened. Even if you aren't doing anything with them, open applications reserve their assigned amount of RAM, which may cut down on the amount available to Photoshop.

THE HISTORY PALETTE

Understanding how Photoshop 5/5.5's History works can make your Photoshop sessions much more efficient. The History palette (Window, Show History) lets you go back to a previous state of the image and work from there. You can return to a previous state of the entire image, or use the History brush or Art History brush to paint with a sample from a previous version of the file, one brush stroke at a time. The eraser tool and the Fill command can also use History as a source.

States

The History palette "remembers" the most recent *states,* or steps, of your current work session — the work you've done since you opened the file. This gives you the potential for multiple Undo's, since you can work backward state by state. However, once you finish your current work session and close the file, the History palette is emptied — it no long retains step-by-step information about what you did.

In practice, the History palette's "memory" can be quite limited. In order to keep from tying up too much RAM, by default the palette retains only the last 20 steps. You can increase the number of steps (increasing the amount of RAM used and potentially slowing down all Photoshop operations) or decrease the number of steps (making more RAM available for other operations, but limiting how far back you can go to restore a previous state).

The History palette automatically adds a state for every change you make to the image — every selection, every brush stroke, every filter application, and so on. When the list of states in the bottom section of the History palette reaches the number set in the History Options dialog box, the older states at the top of the list are deleted to make room for more to be added at the bottom.

You can **return to a previous state of the image** by highlighting an earlier state in the History palette; highlighting is done by clicking on the name of the state in the History palette or by dragging the palette's slider to the state. You can **delete a state** by dragging it to the trash icon at the bottom of the palette. In this case the image doesn't change, but the state you deleted is no longer available as a point to return to.

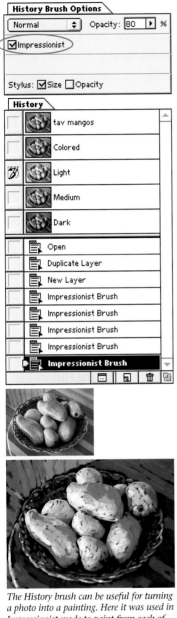

The History brush can be useful for turning a photo into a painting. Here it was used in Impressionist mode to paint from each of three Snapshots — Light, Medium, and Dark. For the Light Snapshot, the Levels command was chosen, the tonality was adjusted, a Merged Snapshot was taken, and the Levels adjustment was undone (Ctrl/⌘-Z) to restore the original tonality, which was used to make the Medium Snapshot. Then the Dark Snapshot was made like the Light one.

Snapshots

A *Snapshot* is a stored version of the file you're working on. You can **make a Snapshot** by choosing New Snapshot from the palette's pop-out menu. Or you can click or **Alt/Option-click the New Snapshot icon,** in the middle at the bottom of the palette. If you simply click the icon, the Snapshot will be made in **Full Document** mode, retaining all the layers, masks, and so on of the current state. But if you Alt/Option-click or choose from the menu, you also have the option of making a single-layer Snapshot: The **Merged Layers** option combines all visible layers into one to make the Snapshot. The **Current Layer** option makes a Snapshot that preserves only the layer that's currently active.

When you make a Snapshot, it will be added at the bottom of the upper section of the History palette. By default the History palette starts with a Snapshot of the file as it was when you opened it.

You can click in the source column to the left of a Snapshot's thumbnail to use it as a **source for painting** with the History or Art History brush or filling with the Fill command. This can be useful for certain **image-editing** tasks, as in "Fixing a Problem Photo" in Chapter 3, and for painting, as in "'Hand Painting' from History" and "Art History Lessons" in Chapter 6.

If you click on the Snapshot's thumbnail, the file **reverts** to that state of the image, eliminating any changes that you've made to the image since you created the Snapshot. This can be useful for eliminating changes you're not satisfied with.

Like the individual step-by-step states in the bottom part of the palette, Snapshots "evaporate" when you close the file. (For a workaround to preserve Snapshots, see "Holding onto History" on page 22.)

(For a workaround to preserve Snapshots, see "Holding onto History" on page 22.)

HISTORY TROUBLE

If you make a Snapshot from the Full Document, you can run into trouble later if you've added any layers in the meantime. If you try to paint on one of your new layers with the History brush or Art History brush from the Full-Document Snapshot, you'll see a warning:

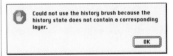

And if you try to use the eraser tool or the Fill command, the History option will be dimmed and unavailable.

You can **avoid** this problem by choosing Merged Layers when you make a Snapshot:

But if you've already made a Full-Document Snapshot and you get the "Could not use . . ." message or find the History option dimmed for the eraser or Fill, there's a way to **remedy** the situation: Click on the Snapshot's thumbnail to activate it, and take another Snapshot — merged this time — and then drag the old one to the trash icon at the bottom of the palette if you don't need it for anything.

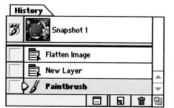
Linear or Non-Linear

By default the History palette operates in a **linear** way. That means that it keeps a kind of "straight line" record of how the image has developed. If you highlight a state or Snapshot, two things will happen: (1) all the changes you've made since that state or Snapshot will disappear from the image, and (2) the History palette will reflect this by dimming all the states from that version forward — to let you know that they will be completely deleted as soon as you make your next move. At this point, if you decide you've made a mistake in reverting, you can Undo by clicking on the most recent (bottom, dimmed) state in the History palette to restore all states to their undimmed glory. Even after you make your first change to the image, you still have a chance to change your mind: Press Ctrl/⌘-Z to undo what you did; this will restore the dimmed palette and you can then click on the bottom dimmed state.

If you choose the Allow **Non-Linear** History option in the History Options dialog box, the palette will work differently. Now if you highlight a state or a Snapshot, the file will revert to that version and the next thing you do will build from there, just as in Linear mode, with the current state added at the bottom of the list. The difference is that in Non-Linear mode the intermediate states are not dimmed or removed from the palette, though the actions they represent no longer contribute to the current version of the file.

Non-Linear mode has the advantage of retaining everything, so that no states are lost, even if they are no longer part of the development of the current image. This means, for instance, that you can go back and highlight one of these "off-line" states and make a Snapshot if you like. But the disadvantages of Non-Linear mode are that (1) you don't free up any memory and (2) things can get confusing, because there are now several "trails" through the History of the file instead of just one, and there's no way to tell by looking at the History palette which states are still part of the development of the current image. Instead of a single unbranching timeline, the History is more like a flow chart with no clear indication of which is the main flow or where the branches begin and end.

Using History Efficiently

An efficient approach to working with History is to **limit the number of steps to 20 or fewer** and **make a duplicate of any current state** that you think you might want to refer back to during the current work session. As described earlier, you can make a duplicate by creating a **Snapshot.** Or for even more safety, you can create a **new document,** which can be saved, from the current state of the image by clicking the leftmost icon at the bottom of the History palette.

Sometimes it can be helpful to see full-size "footprints" of the tools, including brushes you've defined yourself, so you can instantly visualize the brush size and shape. To see cursors up to 300 pixels in diameter, choose File, Preferences, Display & Cursors and then choose Brush Size in the Painting Cursors section of the dialog box. The cursor grows or shrinks as you increase or decrease magnification, so it's always the right size relative to the image. (If it gets too big to be practical, it switches back to the standard tool icon; if it gets too small to show up, it becomes crosshairs.)

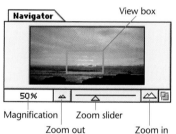

The Navigator palette provides all the tools you need for managing your view of an image. Click one of the two mountain icons to zoom in or out. Drag the View box to see another part of the image. Or enter a percentage in the Magnification box.

Palette Options, from the Navigator palette's pop-out menu, lets you change the color of the view box for good contrast with the picture.

CHANGING YOUR VIEW

When Photoshop 5/5.5 opens a file, it stores information for a number of standard views, such as 33.33%, 50%, 66.67%, 100%, and 200%, up to 1600%. The result is that you can zoom to those views or scroll around in them very quickly, since the program has already calculated all the screen pixels it needs in order to change the display. In addition, the Navigator palette makes it easy to move different parts of the image into the work window and to change magnification. You can also change magnification with keyboard shortcuts or with the zoom tool or hand tool.

What Percentages Mean

Changing the percentage (displayed in the file's title bar and the lower left corner of the Navigator palette) doesn't change the pixels in the image file — it just changes your on-screen view of them.

- When you view a Photoshop image at **100%**, it doesn't mean you're viewing it at the dimensions it will print. It means that every pixel in the image file is represented by 1 pixel on-screen.

- **Higher percentages** mean that more than 1 screen pixel is being used to represent 1 pixel of the image file. For instance, 200% means that each pixel in the file is being shown as a 2 x 2-pixel square on-screen; at 300% it's a 3 x 3-pixel square, and so on.

- **Lower percentages** mean just the opposite: 1 on-screen pixel represents more than 1 pixel in the image file. For instance, at 50% each pixel on-screen represents a 2 x 2 block of pixels in the image file; at 33.33% each on-screen pixel represents a 3 x 3-pixel block in the file, and so forth.

Zooming

To get the view you want, you can of course choose one of the Zoom functions from the Window menu. But you'll save time and mousing effort if you zoom with the Navigator palette as described at the left, or with keyboard shortcuts and the zoom tool.

To zoom from the keyboard:

- **Ctrl-Alt-+** (Windows) or **⌘-+** (Mac) **zooms in, enlarging the window** as well.

- **Ctrl-Alt-minus** (Windows) or **⌘-minus** (Mac) ("minus" is the hyphen key), **zooms out, shrinking the window** as well.

- To zoom in or out **without resizing the window**, press **Ctrl-+** or **Ctrl-minus** (Windows) or **⌘-Option-+** or **⌘-Option-minus** (Mac).

Here are two special cases:

- **Ctrl/⌘-0** enlarges the image to **fit the available screen space.**

To see your image in an uncluttered black window, press the "F" key twice to hide the menus and turn the background black, and press the Tab key once to hide the palettes (press again to restore the palettes). To hide all palettes except the toolbox, use Shift-Tab.

You can change the "window filler" from the default gray to the Foreground color by Shift-clicking the gray with the paint bucket You can change the color back to the default gray by clicking the Foreground square in the toolbox, then entering 191 for the R, G, and B values in the Color Picker, and Shift-clicking on the window filler with the paint bucket.

In a dialog box like Color Balance, where there are a number of settings that can be adjusted, use Ctrl/⌘-Z to undo the last slider setting or typed entry. You can also hold down the Alt/Option key to change the Cancel button to a Reset button, restoring the starting values for all sliders in the box.

- **Ctrl-Alt-0** (Windows) **or ⌘-Option-0** (Mac) sizes the view to **100%**.

The toolbox offers several ways to zoom in or out. **With the zoom tool** (the magnifier from the toolbox) you can pick the area you want to magnify:

- **Click to zoom in** to a new view centered on the clicked spot.
- **Alt/Option-click to zoom out.**
- **Drag diagonally** to **enlarge the area** you drag over to fill the window.
- **Double-click** the tool in the toolbox to get the **100%** view.

Whether the window is resized depends on whether Resize Window To Fit is chosen in the Zoom Tool Options palette.

With the hand tool, double-click the tool in the toolbox **to make the image as big as the available screen space.**

With any tool active, Ctrl/⌘-spacebar (held down) toggles to the **zoom-in** version of the zoom tool. Add the **Alt/Option** key to toggle to the zoom-out version.

Other Views

Other viewing possibilities include the opportunity to hide the clutter of the desktop and view your image centered on a black background, or on the color of your choice, as shown at the left.

RECOVERING

Photoshop's **Ctrl/⌘-Z** (for Edit, Undo) will undo your last operation, and the History palette's states and Snapshots can be set up to let you go much further back than the most recent single step in your work (for more, see "The History Palette," starting on page 20). In addition, Photoshop provides several ways to work backwards if you need to. Here are some suggestions:

Using the Reselect command. New in Photoshop 5/5.5, the Reselect command from the Select menu lets you recover a selection after you've deselected it. You can Reselect long after you've let the selection go, as long as you haven't selected anything else in the meantime.

Make changes to Adjustment layers. By applying the effects of the Image, Adjust menu through Adjustment layers, you can go back and change the settings, simply by double-clicking the layer's circular icon in the Layers palette to reopen the dialog box. And if you decide that a different type of adjustment would be better, you can drag the Adjustment layer to the trash can at the bottom of the Layers palette and add a new Adjustment layer in its place.

Starting with a scanned photo (top), a Color Balance Adjustment layer was added to brighten the gold tones. A masked Hue/Saturation Adjustment layer changed the color of the walls and ceiling. These modifications were made without permanently changing the photo, which remained intact in the Background *layer.*

When you copy a file by using the Image, Duplicate command or the History palette's Create New Document, the new file is named but not saved. As soon as you duplicate a file, it's a good idea to choose File, Save As (Ctrl/⌘-Shift-S) so you'll be able to rename and permanently save the file.

Record and play an Action. Besides letting you automate a multistep process so you can apply it to other files, recording an Action while you work can provide a way to go back and reapply the series of changes, modifying intermediate steps that would be unreachable with the Edit, Undo command or with History states that have been purged. Double-clicking a step in the Actions palette (or choosing Record Again from the palette's pop-out menu) opens up the step so you can change dialog box settings. Then run the edited Action on another copy of your original file. **Note:** Not all of Photoshop's many operations and settings are "actionable" (able to be recorded in an Action); for instance, strokes made with the painting and toning tools can't be recorded. Therefore, an Action may not include everything you need in order to backtrack and re-create an effect. For tips on how to work so that non-actionable operations are stored and available to be reused, see "Saving selections and paths as you work" on page 15.

Use "Undo" inside a dialog box or palette. When you're working inside a dialog box that has more than one entry box or slider, you can use **Ctrl/⌘-Z** (or Edit, Undo) to undo the last setting you changed. This also works for entry boxes — but not sliders — in tool palettes.

Reset a dialog box. In any dialog box that lets you enter at least one value and that has a Cancel button, holding down the Alt/Option key while you click Cancel leaves the box open but resets all the settings to the state they were when you first opened the box.

Save intermediate versions. By using the **Image, Duplicate** command or the **Create New Document From Current State** button in the History palette, you can save several intermediate versions of a file under different file names. If you use Duplicate, the file will be named the same as the original, but with "copy" added. If you use the History palette, the duplicate will be given the name of the selected state or Snapshot.

When you make a new file in either of these ways, the copy will become the active file. The original file will remain open on-screen as well, easily accessible (but also tying up RAM, of course). You can reduce the file size of the duplicate by choosing to merge the visible layers and discard the invisible ones.

Another way to make a copy of the active file is to use File, **Save A Copy** (**Ctrl-Alt-S** on Windows or ⌘-**Option-S** on Mac). The duplicate file is stored closed, thus not using any RAM. And you have several storage options: You can merge all the layers into one, save the file with or without its alpha channels, or save in a different file format.

Using the **File, Save As** command (**Ctrl/⌘-Shift-S**) and giving the file a new name is another way to save an intermediate version.

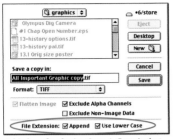

A big benefit of using Save A Copy is that you can copy the file in a format other than Photoshop without flattening it as a separate step. If you choose the "Ask When Saving" option for "Append File Extension" under Preferences, Saving Files, the three-letter extension to the filename will be added any time you Save A Copy but you'll be offered the option of turning it off or putting it in all caps, as shown here.

The History palette and Fill command can be used to restore part of a previous version of the image. This method was used here to focus attention on the face: First the image was blurred and the face area was selected with a feathered lasso. Then the original sharp version of the image (the Open state) was chosen as the source, and Edit, Fill, History was used to fill the selected area.

With this method the original file is closed and stored in the form that it was before you last saved, and the Saved As (current) version remains open and active.

Revert to the original version.

To keep the file open but eliminate all the changes you've made since you last saved it, choose **File, Revert** or click on the initial Snapshot in the History palette.

Restore part of a previous version of the image.

"NO-LOSE" REVERT

In Photoshop 5.5 when you Revert, all the Snapshots and the recent states of the file will be retained, so you'll still have access to them. The Revert operation simply becomes the most recent state in the History palette.

To choose the History state or Snapshot you want to use as the source for restoration, click in the source column next to its thumbnail in the History palette, to turn on the History brush icon. Then use either the **History brush** or the **eraser** in Erase To History mode (set in the Eraser Options palette). Both the History brush and the eraser give hand-held control of the restoration process. The History brush, however, has the added advantage of being able to change the painting mode if you want to.

Besides painting, another way to restore from a previous version is to make a selection of the area you want to restore and choose **Edit, Fill;** then choose History from the Contents list in the Fill dialog box.

With any of these methods, the changes are made to the active layer only. (See the "History Trouble" tip on page 21 for advice on how to avoid problems if the currently active layer wasn't present in the state or Snapshot you want to restore from.)

Duplicate a layer. Sometimes you may want to make changes to a particular layer but you want an "escape hatch" to get back to the previous version, or you want the flexibility of combining the changed version with the original. In that case, copy the layer and work on the copy. You can do this by dragging the layer name in the Layers palette to the New Layer icon at the bottom of the palette. We use this method throughout the book to allow for the greatest flexibility.

Make a "repairs" or "painting" layer. If you're using the sharpen/blur, smudge, or rubber stamp to make repairs to an image, you can add the repairs to a separate, transparent top layer, making sure that Use All Layers is selected in the tool's Options palette. That way the sharpening, blurring, smudging, or stamping strokes will use a composite of all layers of the image to make the repairs.

With a repairs layer the new work doesn't actually get mixed into the image. So if you want to undo part of your repair work, you can erase, or select and delete, that part from the layer, leaving intact the rest of the repairs, as well as the layers beneath.

After this image was rotated to level the horizon, a "repairs" layer was added and the rubber stamp tool was used in Clone (Aligned) mode to fill in the corners and to add plants to the beach. Turning on Use All Layers made it possible to keep the top layer active for repair work while sampling repeatedly from the image on the layer below.

To turn a flattened copy of the repaired photo into a painting, a transparent layer was added and the smudge tool was applied with Use All Layers turned on to pick up paint from the layer below.

Besides repairs, you can use a separate layer for adding brush strokes to a painting without messing up the work you've already done. When you're sure you like the new work, you can merge it with the layer below (Ctrl/⌘-E), then add another new layer and experiment with more brush strokes.

AUTOMATING WITH ACTIONS

The Actions palette offers a way to record a series of Photoshop operations and play them back in order, on a single file or a whole batch. In a nutshell the process is as follows: You turn on Photoshop's recording apparatus, carry out the operations you want to record, stop recording, save the Action, and play it back on another file whenever you want to.

In versions 5 and 5.5 many more commands and operations can be recorded as part of an Action than could be recorded in version 4. This makes Actions easier to understand and to use. Actions are also better organized now.

Action Organization

Actions are displayed by name in the Actions palette (opened by choosing Window, Show Actions). Within the palette they are grouped in sets, indicated by folder icons. Here are some important things about this organization:

- The **small triangle** to the left of the name of a set or an Action in the Actions palette is a toggle. Clicking it expands the set or Action to show all its components, or collapses it to hide them.

- An Action's position in a set can be changed simply by **dragging the Action's name to a new position** in the Actions palette.

- You can **play an entire set of Actions** by selecting the set in the Actions palette and clicking the Play (triangle) button at the bottom of the palette. This makes it possible to assemble sets of Actions as "toolkits" that are appropriate for particular jobs. You can include the same Action in several different toolkits if appropriate.

- **A set can (and should!) be permanently saved** with the Save Actions command in the Actions palette's pop-out menu.

- An Action can be **moved from one set to another** simply by dragging.

- An Action can be **copied,** either within the same set or to a different one, by Alt/Option-dragging to the position in the palette where you want the duplicate.

The Recording Process

The Actions recording process differs, depending on whether you want to make a clickable button to choose a single menu item or whether you want to record a multistep process.

- **To turn any Photoshop command into a clickable button** or an F-key that chooses a command, open the Actions palette and click the New Action icon at the bottom of the palette. Name the Action and assign a color or function key shortcut if you like; then click Record. Choose Insert Menu Item from the pop-out menu and select the command you want from a menu or submenu, or type in the command's name as it's listed in the menu. Then click the square Stop button at the bottom of the palette to complete the recording.

  Now whenever you play that Action in the Actions palette, Photoshop should respond as if you had chosen the command from its menu. And if the command includes a dialog box, the box should open so you can enter the settings you want, just as it would if you were choosing it from the menu.

- **To record a multistep operation** so you'll be able to apply the whole series of commands again, open a file like the ones you want to work on, and click the New Action icon at the bottom of the Actions palette. Name the Action, click Record, and start performing operations, tailoring your choices within the limitations of "actionable" operations mentioned in "What's 'Actionable'?" which follows this section. The round Record button at the bottom of the Actions palette will stay red (indicating that recording is in progress) until you press the square black Stop button to end the recording session

What's "Actionable"?

In Photoshop 5/5.5 many more commands and operations are "actionable" — able to be recorded as part of an action — than in Photoshop 4. And for many of the commands and operations that still can't be recorded directly, there are workarounds.

- Operations carried out with most tools can now be recorded, but **brush strokes made with the paint tools** (paintbrush, airbrush, eraser, background eraser, smudge), **the focus tools** (sharpen and blur), and **the toning tools** (dodge, burn, and

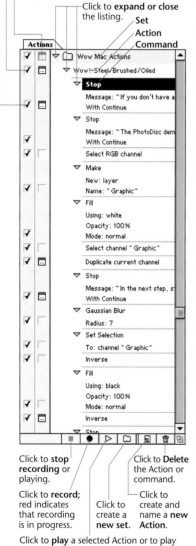

A **checkmark** next to a command indicates that it is active; if no checkmark appears, the command is currently turned off and will not be carried out when the Action is played.

A **checkmark** next to the Action name shows that the Action is active and will play as part of a set. A **red checkmark** alerts you to the fact that some commands in the Action are currently not active and won't play when the Action is played.

A red dialog box icon in the **modal control column** indicates that some steps in a set or Action will stop and wait for input via a dialog box or the Enter/Return key. If the icon is black, there will be a stop at *every* step where input is possible.

Click to **expand or close** the listing.

Set
Action
Command

Click to **stop recording** or playing.

Click to **record**; red indicates that recording is in progress.

Click to create a **new set**.

Click to create and name a **new Action.**

Click to **Delete** the Action or command.

Click to **play** a selected Action or to play from a selected command onward; Ctrl/⌘-click to play only the selected command and then stop.

When you choose Insert Stop from the Actions palette's pop-out menu so that your Action will stop running and display a message or give the user a chance for input, you have the opportunity to "Allow Continue." If you check this box, the message that's displayed when the Action stops will include a Continue button that the user can click to continue to run the Action. If you don't provide the Continue button, the user will have to click the Stop button and then click the Play button (the triangle at the bottom of the Actions palette) to continue the Action.

sponge) **aren't recorded.** Instead you can insert a pause, complete with directions for what to do during the pause, so the user can stop and paint. To put a pause in the Action, choose the Insert Stop command from the Actions palette's pop-out menu.

- Choices made in the **Layers, Channels, Paths,** and **History palettes can be recorded.**

- **Brush choices** made from the Brushes palette are recorded by *position in the palette.* As long as there is a brush in that position when the Action is played, that brush will be chosen, although it may be different from the one that was there when the Action was recorded. The commands from the Brushes palette's pop-out menu aren't recorded.

- Choices made in the **Options palettes for the tools aren't recorded.** Again, you can include the Insert Stop command and directions so the person playing the Action can make the appropriate settings.

- Paths themselves won't be recorded as you draw them, but you can include a path as part of an Action by drawing it, saving it in the Paths palette with a unique name, then selecting the path in the Paths palette and choosing the **Insert Path** command from the Actions palette's pop-out menu. When the Action is played on another file, the original path will be added to the new file's Paths palette, and further commands in the Action can use that path.

- Some commands, such as changing Preferences or Color Settings, showing a CMYK Preview or Gamut Warning, zooming your view, or turning Snap To Guides on or off, won't record directly as part of a multistep Action. Instead this kind of command has to be recorded by choosing **Insert Menu Item** from the Actions palette's pop-out menu. Then choose the command, or type the command's name into the Insert Menu Item dialog box, or type the beginning of the

BUTTON, BUTTON . . .

If you use a multicolumn layout for the Actions palette in its Button mode — which you can do just by dragging a corner to reshape the palette — the individual buttons get narrower, and the palette takes up less space per button.

WHEN YOU "INSERT". . .

Using the Insert Menu Item command as you record an Action will indeed add the command to the Action. But *it won't carry out the command during the recording session.* So if you need a nonrecordable command to be carried out in order for the rest of the Action to be recorded correctly, you'll have to both carry out the operation in its nonrecordable form (to get the job done in the file you're recording from) *and* use the Insert Menu Item command (to get the operation recorded so that it will be carried out when the Action is played later).

The Insert Menu Item command allows you to include a command in an Action without specifying exactly how that command's options will be set when the command is carried out. For instance, to make an Action for loading a selection, click the New Action icon at the bottom of the Actions palette, name the Action "Load Selection" and click Record to close the dialog box (A). Choose Insert Menu Item from the palette's pop-out menu, and then choose Select, Load Selection from the main menu so that "Load Selection" appears in the Insert Menu Item dialog box (B). Now when you play the Action (C), it will open the Load Selection dialog box (D), offering you the choice of whatever selections are available to load for the particular file you're working on — alpha channels, layer masks, or transparency mask, for instance — and whether you want to add it to, subtract it from, or create the intersection of the current selection if there is one.

command and press the Find button, which will supply the full name, correctly spelled.

- Of course, your Action will only work if the **conditions of the file** you're working on will allow it to work. For instance, if your Action includes a step to add a layer mask, you won't be able to do that if the layer that's active when that step is played is the *Background* layer, which can't have a mask, or if it's a transparent layer that already has a layer mask. Likewise, if the step requires an active selection (as the Select, Modify, Contract command does), it won't work unless something is selected when the step is played. So you have to be sure that you include in the Action all the steps necessary to prepare the file for each step of the Action to work — or a Stop step that explains the requirements so the user can pause and get the file ready.

- You can **nest an existing Action within the one you're currently recording** by playing it as you record. Click in the Actions list to select the Action you want to include, then press the Play button. This Action will be added as a step in the one you're recording.

Saving Actions

When you finish recording an Action, it remains part of the current Actions palette, even if you don't go through a saving process. Even if you quit and restart Photoshop, your new Action will still appear in the palette, unless

In an Action the effect of a toggle command like Snap To Guides or Show/Hide Guides will depend on the state of the file when the command is played as part of an Action. In other words, even though the command you recorded when you made the Action was Show Guides, if guidelines are already showing when the Action plays the Show Guides command, it will *Hide Guides* instead.

There are some things that are worth recording at the beginning of almost any Action:

- **Start the Action by making a copy of the file's "pre-Action" state** — either with the Image, Duplicate command, or by taking a Snapshot by clicking the New Snapshot icon (the middle button at the bottom of the History palette), or by clicking the New Document From Current State button (to the left of the New Snapshot button). That way you'll have a way to recover your original if you don't like the "actioned" file.

- For some Photoshop operations the file has to be in a certain mode. For instance, the Lighting Effects filter runs only in RGB Color mode. Also, you can't convert an RGB or CMYK file directly to Bitmap or Duotone without going through Grayscale mode first. If your Action requires that the file be in a specific mode, you can avoid problems by inserting the **File, Automate, Conditional Mode Change** command, which will change the mode if necessary.

If you click on the name of an Action in the Actions palette's list mode and then choose the File, Automate, Batch command, your Action will be applied to all the images in the folder you choose as the Source, and then the treated files will be saved. The Batch dialog box gives you the chance to bypass any Open and Save As commands that exist as part of your Action. You can run more than one Action at a time on a batch of files: Create a New Action, and then record the File, Automate, Batch command to play each of the Actions you want to run.

CROSS-PLATFORM ACTIONS

If you work on a Mac and you plan to share your Actions with someone using Photoshop 5/5.5 on a Windows platform, you'll need to add the appropriate three-letter filename extension to any files (including saved settings) that you supply to be loaded and used with the Action — for instance, settings for Curves. Here's a list of Windows extensions for settings that can be saved:

Action: *.ATN

Levels: *.ALV

Curves (pencil icon): *.AMP

Curves (curve icon): *.ACV

Hue/Saturation: *.AHU

Replace Color: *.AXT

Selective Color: *.ASV

Variations: *.AVA

Color Range: *.AXT

Lighting Effects (Filter, Render): none

Custom (Filter, Other): *.ACF

---

the **Actions Palette.psp** file (Windows) or the **Actions Palette** file (Mac) is deleted or corrupted. Replacing the file from the Photoshop CD-ROM will restore the Adobe default set of Actions but not any other Actions that have been added. For this reason, it's a good idea to always preserve a new set of Actions with a name of its own by choosing **Save Actions** from the palette's pop-out menu.

Actions have to be saved in sets. If you select an Action in the Actions palette and try to choose Save Actions, you'll find that the choice is dimmed. To make a set, choose New Set from the pop-out menu, name the set, and click OK. A folder icon will appear in the Actions palette. You can now drag any Actions you want to save into the folder. With the set assembled, even if it contains only a single Action, you can choose Save Actions from the pop-out menu.

Playing an Action

Once you've recorded an Action or loaded an Action that was recorded by someone else (see "Loading Actions" on page 33), you can play it back on a single file or on all the files in a folder.

- **To run an Action or set of Actions,** click its name in the Actions list and click the triangular Play button at the bottom of the palette.

- **To play an Action from a specific step** forward, select that step in the Actions list and then click the Play button.

- **To play a single step** of an Action, click on that step to select it, and then Ctrl/⌘-click the Play button.

- **To run an Action on a whole batch of files**, put the files into a folder and use the File, Automate, Batch command. On the Mac, to run an Action on files in more than one folder, create an alias (in the Finder choose File, Make Alias) for each of the folders you want to run it on; put these aliases into a single folder and run the Batch command on this folder.

PLAYING IT SAFE

The Undo command works only on the last executed step of an Action, not on the entire Action. So before you run an Action, make sure you have a way to get the "pre-Action" version of your image back, in case the originator of the Action didn't build in a safety net (see "Safety Nets" on page 30). One way to do this is to choose File, Save A Copy before you play the Action, or click the New Document From Current State button (on the left at the bottom of the History palette). Or take a Snapshot (click the New Snapshot icon in the middle at the bottom of the History palette); that way, if you don't like the results of the Action you can click on the Snapshot in the History palette to return the file to the state it was in before you ran the Action. Alternatively, you can undo only part of the action by clicking on one of the states that the Action generated in the History palette. (For more about how the History palette operates and about how to return an image to a previous state, see "The History Palette" on page 20.)

Editing Your Actions

After you've finished recording an Action and have tried playing it, you may need to go back and change its steps, especially in cases where some experimentation was involved while you recorded. For instance, setting the blending mode or Opacity for a layer may be a trial-and-error process. But since you probably don't want to repeat the experimentation each time you place the Action, you can go back and remove the experimental steps, leaving only the version you finally decided on. As usual in Photoshop, when it comes to editing an Action, there are several ways to do it. But here are some easy methods:

- **To remove a step** (or even an entire Action or set) from the Actions list, click its name and Alt/Option-click the trash icon at the bottom of the Actions palette; or drag it to the trash icon; or choose "Delete [Action's name]" from the palette's pop-out menu. (To get a good look at the contents of a set or Action, or at the settings for a command so that you're sure what you're deleting, you can click the little triangle in front of a command to see its settings.)

- **To change dialog box settings** for a step that opens a dialog box, double-click the command's name in the Actions palette, enter new settings, and click OK.

- **To insert a new command** (or commands) in the Actions list, click the command you want the new command to come after. Then click the round Record button, record the new command(s), and click the square Stop button.

- **To change the order of steps,** drag their names up or down to new positions in the Actions list.

- **To completely change a step,** first click on the step above it and choose Insert Stop from the pop-out menu. Start from a fresh copy of a file like the one the Action is meant to be used on, and play the entire Action from the beginning. The Stop you inserted will pause the Action when it gets to the step you want to replace. Then follow the directions above for inserting a new step. (The reason for playing the entire Action from the beginning when you want to re-record one or more steps is to ensure that you've given the Action a chance to create the conditions that will be needed — layers and channels, for instance — when you get to the step you're redoing.) Then remove the old version of the step, as described in "To remove a step," above.

- **To duplicate a step** in an Action, hold down the Alt/Option

You'll find the **Wow Actions** set on the CD-ROM that comes with this book. To use a Wow Action, load the entire set (choose Load Actions from the Actions palette's pop-out menu). The Wow Actions set will be added at the bottom of the Actions palette.

Click the triangle to the left of the set's name to expand its listing so you can see the individual Actions.

Most of the Wow Actions are designed to approximate one of the techniques presented in *The Photoshop 5/5.5 Wow! Book*. The first Stop command in each of the Actions tells you what kind of image file you need in order to run a particular Wow Action successfully. You can start the Action by clicking the Play button, and read the Stop message. Then, if necessary, click the Stop button in the message box and prepare your file. Then resume the Action by clicking the lit button if your actions are in Button mode or by clicking the Play button again if your actions are in List mode.

key and drag the step's name to the point where you want the copy in the Actions list.

- To make your Action **pause between steps** and provide instructions to the user, or to insert tips about settings for an upcoming dialog box, click the command in the Actions list that you want the pause to come after. Then choose **Insert Stop** from the palette's pop-out menu, and type the message. Select the Allow Continue option if you want the user to be able to proceed with the Action after reading the message. If you leave this box unchecked, the user will have to click the Stop button in the message box and then click the Play button in order to continue. Leave the Allow Continue box unchecked anytime that some input is required before the Action can proceed. When you've finished making entries in the Record Stop dialog box, click OK.

- To make the Action **pause within a step** so the user can choose whether to accept the settings in a dialog box or continue with its current settings (by pressing OK), click in the modal control column just to the left of the command's name. A dialog box icon will appear in the column to show that the command will pause with its dialog box open. Clicking again in this column toggles the pause function off.

  The modal control works not only for dialog boxes but also for operations that require pressing the **Enter/Return key** or double-clicking to accept the current settings, such as using the Free Transform command or cropping with the crop tool.

- To **temporarily disable a step** so it isn't carried out when you play an Action, without permanently removing the step from the Action (or to disable an Action without permanently removing it from the set), click the checkmark in the farthest left column of the Actions palette. Click in this column again to bring back the checkmark and re-enable the step.

Loading Actions

You can load a saved Actions palette either as an addition to the current palette (choose Load Actions from the palette's pop-out menu), or you can load it *instead of* the current palette (choose Replace Actions. **Note:** Before you replace Actions, make sure you've saved the current set so you'll be able to retrieve it again.

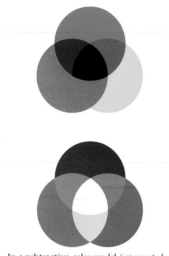

In a subtractive *color model* (represented by the top illustration), *cyan, magenta, and yellow inks* combine to make a dark, nearly black color. In additive *color (bottom), red, green, and blue light* combine on-screen to make white light.

UNPRINTABLE!

Photoshop's out-of-gamut warning lets you know if an RGB color you're looking at on the screen can't be printed accurately with CMYK inks. In the **Info palette**, the warning shows up as exclamation points beside the CMYK values, which represent the color mix closest to the specified RGB color. In other words, the CMYK values tell how the color will be printed if you convert from RGB to CMYK with the current Separation Setup. In the **Color Picker** and the **Color palette** the warning shows up as a caution sign with an accompanying swatch of the nearest CMYK match. Clicking the swatch changes the chosen color to the printable match. Note that Photoshop's out-of-gamut warning tends to be conservative, presenting some colors as unprintable when they may actually print OK.

COLOR IN PHOTOSHOP

Photoshop's interface for choosing and mixing color includes the Image, Mode submenu, the Foreground/Background color squares, the Color Picker, the color palettes (Color and Swatches), the eyedropper tool, and the gradient.

Color Modes

Photoshop uses several different systems of color representation. These systems — Bitmap, Grayscale, Duotone, Indexed Color, RGB Color, CMYK Color, Lab Color, and Spot Color — can be selected through the Mode menu. Each color mode has a different *gamut,* or range of colors that can be produced in that color system.

CMYK Color. In any color system the *primary colors* are the basics from which all other colors can be mixed. In *four-color process printing,* which is the type of printing most often used for reproducing the photos, illustrations, and other works created in Photoshop, the primaries (called *subtractive primaries*) are cyan, magenta, and yellow, with the addition of black to intensify the dark colors and details. Adding black makes dark colors look crisper than darkening with a heavier mix of cyan, magenta, and yellow. Darkening with black also requires less ink; this can be important because press has an upper limit to the amount of ink it can apply to the printed page before the ink will no longer adhere to the paper cleanly.

RGB Color. The CRT monitors used in computers and TV generate primary colors of light (called *additive primaries*) by bombarding the phosphor coating of the screen with electrons. The mix of red, green, and blue light that results is perceived by the eye as color. When all three colors are turned on at full intensity, the result is white light; when all are turned off, black results. Different intensities of energy excite the phosphors to different degrees, and the various brightnesses of the three colors mix visually to form all the colors of the RGB spectrum.

Because of the architecture of typical computer hardware and software, there are theoretically 256 different levels of energy that can be applied to each of the three primary colors of the computer's RGB system; this means that there are 256 x 256 x 256 (or more than 16 million) colors that can be mixed. This gamut provides enough colors to very realistically represent the world we see.

It takes 8 bits of computer data (a bit is a 1 or a 0, an ON or OFF signal) to represent 256 different energy settings ($2^8 = 256$), as needed for grayscale monitors, for instance; to represent three sets of energy settings takes 24 bits (2^8 x 2^8 x $2^8 = 2^{24} = 16.7$ million). So full color as displayed on the computer screen is called 24-bit color.

In Photoshop 5/5.5 the RGB Setup dialog box (opened by choosing File, Color Settings, RGB Setup) offers 11 different RGB *color spaces,* each with its own color gamut. The different color spaces are

Pantone's HexWrench plug-in for Photoshop can help prepare images for printing on six-color presses, with the option for two more ink colors in addition to C, M, Y, and K.

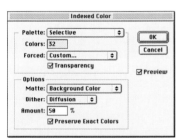

Photoshop's Indexed Color dialog box lets you choose from a number of indexed palettes, specifying the number of colors, the color space the colors are chosen from, whether transparency is included in the palette, and what kind of dithering to use to produce colors that are outside the chosen color table.

UNSAFE!

In addition to the out-of-gamut warning, Photoshop 5.5 also offers a "not Web safe" warning for colors that are outside the 216-color Web palette. The indicator is a small cube, accompanied by a swatch of the closest Web color. Clicking the swatch chooses the Web color.

The out-of-gamut warning and the "not Web safe" warning from Photoshop 5/5's Color Picker

described in Chapters 4 and 5 of *The Adobe Photoshop 5.0 User Guide.* "Getting Consistent Color" on page 40 of this book provides pointers on choosing how to manage the RGB Color Setup.

Indexed Color. Some computers aren't equipped to display 24-bit color. Instead, they can display a maximum of 256 colors at once, or 8-bit color. In such a system, 256 colors are stored in a *color look-up table* (or *CLUT*) whose storage addresses are identified by numbers between 0 and 255. The process of assigning 256 colors to represent the millions of colors potentially in a full-color image is called *indexing.* When you choose Mode, Indexed Color in Photoshop, the Indexed Color dialog box lets you choose a type of palette and offers a number of choices for narrowing the palette. The dialog box is now interactive — it lets you preview the effect of converting the palette. In the Palette section of the Indexed Color dialog box you can choose to index the colors to:

- An **Exact** palette (if the image includes 256 or fewer colors). Only the colors that occur in the image are preserved in the palette.

- A **System** palette (either **Macintosh** or **Windows**). The System palettes are the sets of 256 colors that are used on each of these platforms to represent all parts of the RGB gamut).

- The **Web** palette (a set of 216 colors that the most widely used Web browsers use to represent color). Every color in this palette is found in both the Macintosh and the Windows System palettes; colors that appear in only Mac or only Windows aren't included in the set. Using the Web palette helps ensure that the color in your image will stay the same — no substitutions will be required — regardless of whether it's seen on a Mac or a Windows machine, with Netscape or with Microsoft Internet Explorer.

- A **Uniform** palette (a set of colors sampled evenly from all areas of the spectrum). In a Uniform palette there are approximately equal numbers of reds, greens, blues, cyans, magentas, and yellows. The Uniform palette can be set for as many as 256 colors or as few as 2 by entering the number of Colors you want.

- **Perceptual, Selective** and **Adaptive** palettes (sets of 2 to 256 colors chosen to best represent the colors used in a particular image).

  An **Adaptive** palette is one that's adapted, or optimized, to reproduce the colors that occur most often in the image.

  A **Perceptual** palette is an adaptive palette that takes into consideration the parts of the spectrum where the human eye is most sensitive, assigning more of its palette spots to colors in those particular ranges.

  A **Selective** palette is an adaptive palette that's optimized to favor Web colors and colors that occur in large areas of flat color.

  For Adaptive, Perceptual, and Selective palettes, you can choose whether to **Force** the palette to include black and white, the

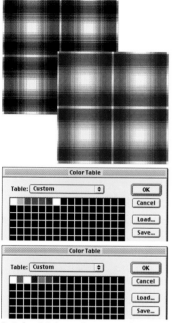

![Color Table dialog boxes]

In Indexed Color mode, you can change colors quickly by choosing Image, Mode, Color Table and clicking on the cells of the Color Table. This method can be used to try different colorways in fabric design, as shown here.

Photoshop's Duotone mode provides curves that store information for printing a grayscale image in one to four ink colors. The program comes with several sets of preset duotone, tritone, and quadtone curves. Or you can shape the curves yourself. By drastically reshaping curves as in this tritone, you can make different colors predominate in highlights, midtones, and shadows. A Preview checkbox lets you view the changes in your image as you experiment with curves and colors.

primary colors (cyan, magenta, yellow, red, green, and blue), the Web palette's colors (as long as the palette contains between 216 and 256 colors), or a set of custom colors that has been named and saved as a Color Table or as a set of Swatches.

- A **Custom** palette (a set of colors selected for some particular purpose). Choosing Mode, Indexed Color, Custom opens the Color Table dialog box, where you can choose one of several Custom palettes that are supplied with the program, or make your own color table by clicking the individual squares of the table and choosing new colors to fill them. As long as your file is in Indexed Color mode, you can choose Mode, Color Table and change the table.

- The **Previous** palette (the set of colors that was used the last time, within the current Photoshop session, that a file was indexed with a Custom or adaptive palette). This option is useful for converting a number of images so they share a single custom palette.

For those indexed palettes that can include **Transparency** — that is, palettes with fewer than 256 colors — the Indexed Color dialog lets you choose whether to maintain the Transparency or to convert it to the **Matte** color (or white if Transparency is not chosen and Matte is set to None). You can also choose whether to allow **dithering,** which is simulating a color by interspersing

"SHAPING" ADAPTIVE PALETTES

If you select an area of the image that contains the important colors before you choose Image, Mode, Indexed Color, the colors of the Adaptive, Perceptual, or Selective palette will be weighted in favor of the colors in that selection. For instance, you may want to preserve the skin tones in a portrait, giving less weight to the clothing or background colors.

Converted with skin tones selected　　*Converted without a selection*

INDEXED TO INDEXED

There are two ways to change a color file from one Indexed Color palette to another:

- If you know the existing color palette you want, choose **Image, Mode, Color Table** and Load the palette you want to change to.

- If you want to create a new Indexed palette — for instance, if you want to try reducing the number of colors — you first have to go back through the RGB Color mode.

In either case the best approach is to start with the original RGB version of the file, if you've saved it, and reconvert. No other option uses the original 24-bit source color as the target to shoot for. If the RGB original is no longer available, choose Image, Mode, RGB Color and then choose Image, Mode, Indexed Color. Keep in mind that choosing RGB Color after indexing merely changes the color mode — it does not restore the original RGB Color of the file, so you will be indexing from an already reduced set of colors.

The Overprint Colors button in the Duotone dialog box lets you make the on-screen display of your duotone look more like it will when it's printed. Clicking any of the color squares in the Overprint Colors dialog box opens the Color Picker so you can change the display of that color mix to match a printed sample that shows your ink colors overprinted solid. The color gradient bar at the bottom of the Duotone Options dialog box reflects the settings in the Overprint Colors dialog box. For color accuracy, you need to have a calibrated monitor (see "Calibration" on page 42).

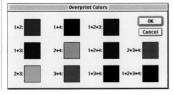

In Duotone mode you can't see the individual color plates that will be used for printing. To look at them, you can convert the file to Multichannel mode temporarily, open a second window, and view a different channel in each window. (If you want to see the plates in color, choose File, Preferences, Display & Cursors, Color Channels In Color). Follow these steps exactly: Open the Channels palette (Window, Show Channels) and open a second view of the image (View, New View). Then choose Image, Mode, Multichannel. Activate a different Channel (by clicking on its name in the Channels palette) for each window. View both plates, but don't try to edit or you won't be able to get back to Duotone. After you've looked at the plates, Undo (Ctrl/⌘-Z) to go back to Duotone mode.

pixels of other colors; whether to use a random, randomly patterned, or uniformly patterned dither (Noise, Diffusion, or Pattern); and how much dithering Photoshop should use to prevent banding between solid colors. Increasing the Amount of dithering improves color transitions in the image but also increases file size, since it reduces the degree of compression that's possible. Turning on and off **Preserve Exact Colors** may make a slight difference in the Diffusion dither pattern; you can toggle it to see if it produces a difference you like.

Lab Color. Instead of being separated into three colors (plus black in the case of CMYK color), color can be expressed in terms of a brightness component and two hue/saturation components. Photoshop's Lab Color mode uses such a system. So does Kodak Photo CD (its Photo YCC color system) and so does analog color television. Because its gamut is large enough to include the CMYK, RGB, and Photo YCC gamuts, Photoshop's Lab Color mode serves as an intermediate step when Photoshop converts from RGB to CMYK or from Photo YCC to RGB.

Grayscale. A Grayscale mode image, like a black-and-white photo, includes only *brightness* values, no data for *hue* or *saturation,* the other two components of color. Only 8 bits of data are required for storing the 256 shades (black, white, and grays) in the Grayscale gamut.

Duotone. Even though a Grayscale image can include 256 levels of gray, most printing processes can't actually produce that many different tones with a single ink color. But with two inks (or even one color of ink applied in two passes through the press) it's possible to extend the tonal range. By adding a second color in the highlights, for example, you increase the number of tones available for representing the lightest tones in an image. Besides extending tonal range, the second color can "warm" or "cool" a black-and-white image, tinting it slightly toward red or blue, for example. Or the second color may be used for dramatic effect or to visually tie a photo to other design elements.

In Photoshop's Duotone mode, a set of *gamma curves* determines how the grayscale information will be represented in each of the ink colors. Will the second color be emphasized in the shadows but omitted from the highlights? Will it be used to color the midtones?

If you do a lot of two-color printing, it's worthwhile to investigate the Powertone plug-in from Intense Software, a demo version of which comes on the Photoshop 5.5 Application CD-ROM. Using two colors, it does its best to match the full-color image.

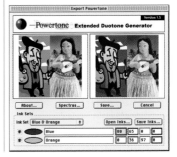

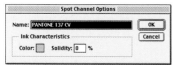

Choosing New Spot Channel from the Channels palette's pop-out menu opens the Spot Channel Options dialog box where you can click the color swatch to choose an ink color. You can also set the Solidity, which affects how the ink's coverage is approximated on your computer screen. Some inks are very solid, covering any inks they are printed over — for instance, pastel inks contain opaque white, and metallic inks are also opaque. Other custom colors are partly transparent. To find out what number to use for the Solidity setting for a particular ink, check with your printer. A Solidity setting of 0% is appropriate for a clear varnish.

When you add a spot color channel, it appears below color channels but above alpha channels in the Channels palette.

A spot color channel can be useful for adding a custom color to a CMYK printing job, as described in "Adding a Spot Color" on page 141.

Spot color channels can be useful for special printing applications such as screen printing; or for precise control of the printing plates in a CMYK project, as shown in "A Three-Color Print" on page 143.

The Duotone image is stored as a grayscale file and a set of curves that will act on that grayscale information to produce two or more separate plates for printing. Duotone mode also includes tritone and quadtone options, for producing three or four color plates.

Bitmap. The least "bulky" mode in Photoshop is Bitmap, which uses only 1 bit of "color" data to represent each pixel. A pixel is either OFF or ON, producing a gamut of two colors — black and white. Photoshop's several methods for converting Grayscale images to Bitmap mode provide useful options for printing photos with low-resolution, one-color printing methods, as well as some interesting graphic treatments (see Chapter 3, "Enhancing Photos").

Other Mode Choices

In addition to the color modes themselves, the Image, Mode submenu includes more choices: Multichannel, 8 Bits/Channel, 16 Bits/Channel, Color Table, and Profile To Profile.

Multichannel mode can be useful for viewing the plates of a Duotone image, as shown on page 37. Color images automatically become Multichannel files when one of the color channels is deleted.

The **8 Bits/Channel** and **16 Bits/Channel** choices let you choose the *color depth,* or how many bits per pixel are used to store color data. The standard is 8 Bits/Channel. Using the 16 Bits/Channel setting, Photoshop can perform some of its operations in files with 10, 12, or even 16 bits per pixel. So if you have a scanned image with more than 8 bits per pixel of color information, you can open it in Photoshop, and make tonal and color adjustments using this extra information — for instance, fine-tuning the shadow detail. Then choose 8 Bits/Channel so that you can use all of Photoshop's other functions, most of which won't work on files with "deeper" than 8-bit color.

Color Table lets you view and edit the colors in an Indexed Color image. You can also name and save the colors in the Color Table, and load previously saved Color Tables and Swatches files.

Profile To Profile lets you convert an image from its current RGB, CMYK, or Grayscale color space, or gamut, to the color space that's currently set in the RGB Setup, Grayscale Setup, or CMYK Setup dialog box. This can be helpful in getting predictable color (see "Getting Consistent Color" on page 40).

Spot Color

Spot colors, or custom colors, are special premixed ink colors, the most popular being the Pantone Matching System inks. They are used to print specific colors, instead of trying to produce these

The Gamut Warning (from the View menu) uses a medium gray to indicate colors that may change when the file is converted to CMYK mode. If gray doesn't work well for a particular image, you can change the indicator color by choosing File, Preferences, Transparency & Gamut, clicking the color square, and choosing a new color.

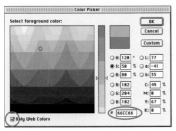

Photoshop's default Color Picker lets you simply click to choose a color by eye or enter numeric values to mix colors in the RGB, CMYK, Lab, and HSB (hue, saturation, brightness) modes. Or you can click one of the round buttons to switch between color models. Clicking on Custom lets you choose from several custom color matching systems. In Photoshop 5.5 the Color Picker also has a checkbox that lets you restrict the Color Picker's choices to those in the Web palette, as shown here, and a box that provides the hexadecimal code for the current color.

The Color palette has a color bar from which colors can be sampled. The color space of the bar can be changed by choosing Color Bar from the palette's pop-out menu or Command-clicking on the bar to open the Color Bar dialog box. Or Shift-click on the bar to toggle through the four color bar choices: RGB Spectrum (A), CMYK Spectrum (B), Grayscale Ramp (C), and Current Colors (Foreground To Background) (D).

colors by overlapping the tiny halftone dots of the standard CMYK process ink colors. In Photoshop 5/5.5 you can use spot colors in Duotones (described on page 37) or in spot color channels, added by choosing New Spot Channel from the Channels palette's pop-out menu.

Spot color channels can be used along with the CMYK inks, as described in "Adding a Spot Color" in Chapter 3, or instead of CMYK. A spot color channel can be used when an absolute color standard has to be met for a corporate color or logo — the ink is premixed to the standard, so that the printed color always looks the same. Or it can be used for colors that are outside the CMYK printing gamut, such as certain oranges or blues, flourescents, or metallics. Spot color channels can also be used to maintain control over the individual printing plates — for posters, T shirts, and so on. Photoshop's spot color channels can also be used for applying a clear varnish.

Color Views

The **CMYK preview** lets you see how an RGB image will look if you convert it to CMYK mode with the current CMYK Setup parameters. Opening a second view of your RGB file (View, New View) and choosing View, Preview, CMYK lets you see the file in both RGB (the original file) and CMYK (the new view) at the same time. Unlike choosing Mode, CMYK Color, the CMYK preview option doesn't actually make the conversion, so you don't lose the RGB color information and therefore you still have the full RGB color gamut to work with.

Gamut Warning, also chosen from the View menu, identifies the colors in your RGB image that will be adjusted to bring them inside the printable color range if you change to CMYK mode with the current CMYK Setup settings (File, Color Settings, CMYK Setup).

Using the Color Picker and Color Palettes

The **Foreground and Background color squares** in the toolbox show what color you'll get when you paint on any layer (the Foreground color) or erase on the *Background* layer (the Background color; but erasing on a transparent layer produces transparency rather than the Background color). You can choose Foreground and Background colors simply by clicking on one of the squares to open the **Color Picker** and then choosing or specifying a color.

Beyond the Color Picker, the two **color palettes** (Color and Swatches) can be left open on-screen and are ideally suited for certain ways of choosing colors: The **Color palette**, with its different modes and sliders, lets you mix colors scientifically (by reading the numbers as you move the sliders) or "by feel," or by sampling from the Color Bar at the bottom of the palette. By default the **Swatches palette** shows a set of 122 color samples. You can click a swatch to select a Foreground color or Alt/Option-click to select a Background

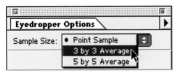

For the eyedropper tool the Sample Size, set in the Eyedropper Options palette, lets you pick up the color of a single pixel or the average color from a 3 x 3- or 5 x 5-pixel area around the cursor's "hot point." The Sample Size setting is shared by the eyedropper and the color sampler — changing the setting in the Options palette for either tool will also change it for the other. The sample size of the eyedroppers in the Levels and Curves dialog boxes is also controlled by this setting.

HEXADECIMAL COLOR CODES

In Photoshop 5.5 right-clicking (Windows) or Control-clicking (Mac) with the eyedropper tool opens a context-sensitive menu that lets you choose the sample size or copy a color's hexadecimal code — for instance, COLOR="#B80505" — so it can be inserted in an HTML document.

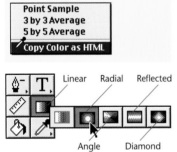

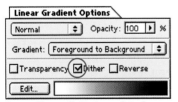

Photoshop's gradient tools allow you to apply ramps of multiple colors and transparencies. "The Gradient Tools" on page 228 in Chapter 6 provides examples of using gradients.

In a gradient tool's Options palette the Transparency checkbox can turn on or off the transparency feature for gradients that have transparency built-in. The Dither box introduces a little "noise" in the color transitions to prevent banding. And the Reverse box lets you apply the blend in the direction opposite of the way it was designed.

color. The palette can be expanded to hold a scrolling preset palette of colors, such as the System or Web-safe colors in the Color Palettes folder.

Other Color Tools

Photoshop 5/5.5's other tools for creating and sampling colors include the eyedropper tool, the gradient tools, the Info palette, and the color sampler. The **eyedropper** can sample color by clicking on any open file or palette; the sampled color becomes the Foreground color. Alt/Option-clicking sets the Background color.

The five **gradient tools** — Linear, Radial, Angle, Reflected, and Diamond — come with a stock supply of preset multicolor blends, some of which include transparency. In addition, you can create your own gradient combinations. Double-clicking any of the five tool icons opens the Options palette, where you can set blending mode to control the way the gradient interacts with color already in the image (described in "Blending Modes" on page 82) and the Opacity with which the gradient is applied. Clicking the Edit button opens the Gradient Editor, where you can change the color and transparency for any point you choose along the gradient.

The **Info palette** provides an interactive display of color composition — as you move the mouse, the color composition is shown for the pixel currently under the cursor. When you apply a color or tonal adjustment such as Levels or Hue/Saturation, while the dialog box is open and you are adjusting settings, the Info palette displays the color composition before and after the change. You can choose two color modes for the composition readout, set by choosing the Palette Options in the Info palette's pop-out menu.

In Photoshop 5/5.5 you can also set up to four "permanent" color sampling sites in your image, each of which will provide a separate readout in the Info palette. To set up the sites, choose the **color sampler tool** (it shares a position with the eyedropper in the toolbox) and click it in as many as four spots where you want the Info palette to provide readouts. Once the points are established, you can use the tool to drag them around, or Alt/Option-click on a point to remove it.

GETTING CONSISTENT COLOR

If you've done color artwork on the computer and then looked at it on another computer system or printed it out, you may have noticed some fundamental differences in the way color is represented on different monitors and on printed pages. There are several fundamental factors contributing to the differences between on-screen and printed color.

- **First of all,** transmitted (additive) **color from a monitor looks brighter** than the color produced by light reflected from ink on paper (subtractive color).

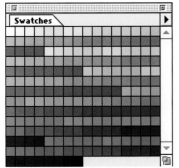

Choose Replace Swatches from the Swatches palette's pop-out menu to open a "swatch book" like this Web palette, which is one of the palettes included with Photoshop 5/5.5. If you want to add swatches to the existing palette instead of replacing the palette, choose Load Swatches. You can always reset to the default Photoshop Swatches palette by choosing Reset Swatches from the pop-out menu.

- Second, because the RGB gamut is bigger than the CMYK gamut, **not all the colors that can be displayed on-screen can be printed,** so it's possible to mix colors in RGB files that can't be reproduced on the printed page.

- Third, because you're moving from a three-color to a four-color system in which black can partially substitute for mixes of the other three colors, **there are many different ways to represent a particular RGB color in the CMYK system,** and because of the way ink pigments interact, the results of all these ways can look slightly different from each other.

- And finally, **variations** in halftone screen density (lines per inch), film separation processes, paper, ink, proof printers, presses, and press operators also affect the color in the final printed product.

Using The Adobe Color Management Assistant

As if the differences between on-screen and printed color weren't enough, there are also differences in the way various scanners record colors and the way monitors display them. To compensate for this variability, starting with version 5, Photoshop offers the **Adobe Color Management Assistant,** which helps you configure Photoshop to produce consistent color from scan to print or to the Web. The Assistant, opened automatically when you first install Photoshop, can also be opened later by choosing Help, Color Management.

In a perfect world — one in which every component of every computer graphics system was calibrated (adjusted so that its color stayed consistent over time and was standardized to a universal benchmark), and in which we knew each component's ICC profile (the characterization of the component's color space according to an international standard designed to help reproduce colors accurately) — the color management system built into Photoshop 5/5.5 could work perfectly, allowing files to look the same no matter what device or graphics program was used to display or print them. Unfortunately, the world isn't perfect yet in this regard.

Many Photoshop 5/5.5 users, especially **if they don't share their files during the Photoshop image-creation process,** prefer to turn off Photoshop 5/5.5's color management features. By working in the familiar Photoshop 4 color space, they can avoid any complications that might arise because color was changed by the color management system, or because the file was passed to another graphics program that doesn't include the same color management functions, such as most Web page applications and HTML editors. "Choosing an RGB Color Space" on page 42 tells how to choose the Photoshop 4 color space and "A 'Back-to-Front' Calibration System" on page 44 tells how to substitute a less technologically complex method for getting predictable printed color.

To get consistent color, not only the monitor but also the viewing environment has to be maintained constant, because changes in lighting conditions can change your perception of colors on the screen. Here are some ways to keep environmental color conditions from interfering with your on-screen color work:

• Position the room's light source above and in back of the monitor, and keep it dimmed and constant.

• If your room lighting is controlled by a rheostat, mark the knob and the base plate so you can always restore the lighting to the same level.

• The wall behind you should be neutral in color, with no bright posters or other images.

• Wear neutral colors when you sit in front of the monitor, to minimize color reflections from your clothes to the screen.

• Use a neutral desktop color (medium gray works well), with no bright colors or pictures.

If you choose Help, Color Management, clicking the Open Adobe Gamma button, and then clicking the Step-By-Step Assistant button as shown here, the Adobe Gamma Assistant will lead you through the process of calibrating your monitor.

Choosing to imitate Photoshop 4's color

On the other hand, **if the work flow involves passing files back and forth** from one person to another for different stages of the creative process, it may be worth trying to use Photoshop 5/5.5's color management system within the workgroup. Refer to "Choosing an RGB Color Space," below, for pointers on using the Adobe Color Management Assistant to help with the setup. Setting up and using the color management system will involve keeping each component in the work flow calibrated, searching out the technical specifications for each monitor and output device, and studying the recommendations in Chapter 5 of *The Adobe Photoshop 5.0 User Guide.* (For a thorough analysis of the color management system provided with Photoshop 5/5.5, see *Real World Photoshop 5* (Blatner and Fraser, Peachpit Press).

Calibration

In order for your computer monitor to show you consistent color, it has to be calibrated periodically. In Photoshop 5/5.5 when you choose Help, Color Management to open the **Adobe Color Management Assistant,** the Assis-

Since the color characteristics of monitors change as they warm up, turn your monitor on half an hour or more before calibrating or making critical color decisions.

tant encourages you to calibrate your monitor. If you haven't already done that, using special calibration software that came with the monitor or a special hardware-software combination package, you can click the Open Adobe Gamma button to do a simplified calibration. In the **Adobe Gamma** dialog box, choosing **Step By Step (Assistant)** will lead you through the monitor calibration process.

Choosing an RGB Color Space

With your monitor calibrated, the Assistant next helps you configure Photoshop's RGB working color space. **If you want to turn off the color management system** by choosing the "Imitate Photoshop 4.0 Color Handling" option in the Adobe Color Management Assistant configuration screen. This will ensure that files won't be markedly changed just by opening them on your system.

   If you want to use Photoshop's color management system, choose "Optimize for Web Use," "Optimize For On-Screen Presentations," or "Customize For Prepress And Other Uses" in the Adobe Color Management Assistant configuration screen. According to your choice the Assistant will show its recommended color space. For instance, the Adobe RGB (1998) color space, which is the default if you choose "Customize For Prepress And Other Uses," allows you to use a broader range of printable colors and tones in your images than sRGB color, the default for "Optimize For On-Screen Presentations."

The parameters for converting RGB to CMYK color are set in the CMYK Setup dialog box. Unless you understand the technical aspects of working with color separation curves and dot gain, use the default setting or get advice from your printer or from your imagesetting service bureau. Technicians there may be more familiar with Photoshop than the printer is. Better yet, have the printer and service bureau technician talk to each other and then let you know how to set the Dot Gain.

None   *Black plate*

Medium   *Black plate*

Maximum   *Black plate*

The results of converting from RGB to CMYK color using each of three different Black Generation settings in the CMYK Setup dialog box

In the next few screens the Assistant offers options about how to treat files produced on systems whose color space is different than the one you're using. Accept the defaults or make the appropriate choices for your workgroup situation, referring to Chapter 5 of *The Adobe Photoshop 5 User Guide.*

Making RGB-to-CMYK Conversions

If you're preparing an image for print, unless you use one of a few desktop color printers that can't handle CMYK files, the image will eventually need to be turned into CMYK separations. This can be done at several different stages in the development of the image. For instance:

- You can choose CMYK Color mode when you first create a new Photoshop file (File, New).

- Some scanning services (and even some desktop scanning software) can make the CMYK conversion for you. The quality of the result depends on the sophistication of the software and the suitability of its settings for the kind of printing you want to do, or on the skill of the professional scan operator. (For more about scanning, see "Setting Up a Scan" on page 53.)

- You can choose Photoshop's Mode, CMYK Color at any point in the development of an image. But **once you make the conversion you can't regain the original RGB color** by choosing Mode, RGB Color. (Instead, step back through the History palette's states, or choose a Snapshot made before the conversion, or choose File, Revert to go back to the last saved version of the file. (Using History is explained in "The History Palette" on page 20.)

- Or you can keep the file in RGB Color mode, place it in a page layout, and allow the page layout or color separation utility to make the separation.

When To Convert. How do you decide when to convert from RGB to CMYK? Here are some tips to help you choose when to convert:

- The single advantage of working in CMYK from the beginning is that it prevents last-minute color shifts, since it keeps the image within the printing gamut during the entire development process.

- But if you're working in CMYK mode and your printing specifications change (a different

As a CMYK file to use for back-to-front calibration, "Olé! No Moiré" (from the Photoshop 5/5.5 Application CD-ROM) provides fine-tuned color and good shadow detail so you can be confident about whether a printed proof is accurate. It also includes standard color swatches that your imagesetting service bureau can check with a densitometer. The seven gray levels in the black ink scale will show you what's happening to the highlight and shadow tones in your image.

paper may be chosen for the job, for instance), the CMYK specifications you chose may no longer apply. In that case, for the highest-quality separations you'll have to start over from an RGB version of the final image or compensate manually (see the tip "Keep an RGB Version" at the left.)

- Working in RGB and putting off the CMYK conversion to the last possible moment allows more freedom, so you can get just the color you want on-screen and then work with Photoshop's Hue/Saturation, Levels, or Curves adjustments to tweak out-of-gamut colors to get CMYK alternatives that are as close as possible to your original colors.

- Another, very significant advantage of working in RGB is that some of Photoshop's finest functions (for example, the Lighting Effects filter described in Chapter 5) don't work in CMYK mode.

- With CMYK Preview and Gamut Warning available, **it makes sense to work in RGB, preview CMYK in a second window, and do the actual RGB-to-CMYK conversion at the end of the process.**

- You may be able to bow out of the conversion process altogether for many jobs. **Your page layout program or** the **separation utility** used by your imagesetting service bureau **may do an excellent job of converting most of your RGB images to CMYK.** If that's the case, you can save yourself some time and angst by using this method, although there may be an additional charge. It's often worth the money to run a test file through film separation to laminate proof to check the result. Or if your files will be printed without film production — direct-to-plate or direct-to-press — a press test, though it can be expensive, may be the only reliable way to predict printed color.

At whatever point you make the conversion, the RGB Setup and CMYK Setup functions (under File, Color Settings) will affect the final result. Chapter 5 of the *Adobe Photoshop 5.0 User Guide* that comes with the program walks you through the process of producing a CMYK separation in Photoshop.

A "Back-to-Front" Calibration System

In order for your computer monitor to be as accurate as possible in showing how an image will look when it's printed, not only does your monitor have to be calibrated as described in "Calibration" on page 42, but all the parts of the system, each calibrated to its own standards, also have to be coordinated with each other. If you are in a workgroup that uses Photoshop's color management system to achieve this coordination, refer to "Calibrating the Screen Image to the Proof" in Chapter 5 of the *Adobe Photoshop 5.0 User Guide.*

If you aren't using a color management system, you can do a sort of "backwards calibration" to make sure your screen display is

SCANNING IN 3D

By placing a small object on a flatbed scanner, you may be able to capture its dimensionality. One or more sides of the object may show, depending on where on the bed you place it. The farther you move the object toward an edge or corner of the scan bed, the more of its sides will show.

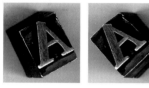

AVOIDING RAINBOWS

To reduce the rainbow sheen that can appear when you scan a 3D object, select the area and use Image, Adjust, Hue/Saturation to desaturate. In the pop-out list of colors at the top of the box, sequentially adjust only the Reds, Greens, and Blues (not Cyans, Magentas, or Yellows) by moving the Saturation slider. The color will remain but the rainbow glare will be lessened. Another option is to scan in Grayscale mode and colorize the image afterwards.

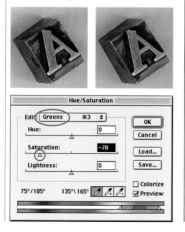

an accurate predictor of the color you'll get in a print or proof. Here's a way to do it:

1 Print or proof a color file; this could be an image of your own, but you may also want to include the "Olé! No Moiré" image from the Photoshop 5 or 5.5 Application CD-ROM. Either:

- print the file on the same system you'll use for final printing,
- print the file on a proofing printer that your press operator assures you will be a good predictor of final printed color,
- or produce film and a laminate proof that your printing press operators can check and assure you they can match on press.

Going all the way to press, rather than stopping at a proof, is even better, but often it isn't possible.

2 In your controlled-light environment (see "Your Color Environment" on page 42), open the file on-screen. Hold the print or proof up to the screen to compare color.

3 Readjust your monitor with the Adobe Gamma control panel (Help, Color Management, Open Adobe Gamma, Control Panel) until the on-screen image looks like the printed piece, and use the Save Settings button in the Gamma panel to save the settings for future use in projects that will use the same printing process. The back-to-front system calibration process depends on changing the display characteristics of the monitor, not the file itself at this point. So don't do any work in Photoshop during the process — that is, *don't change the file.*

Once your monitor has been readjusted so the on-screen image matches the print or proof, you can assume that for files you produce in the future, when the image looks the way you want it on-screen, the print or proof will look like the screen.

IMAGE INPUT

Scanners — desktop, mid-range and high-end — turn photos into image files that can be manipulated in Photoshop. An inexpensive desktop flatbed scanner can capture photographic prints, other hard copy, and even some three-dimensional objects to make files you can use for photo-illustration (for scanning tips see "Setting Up a Scan" on page 53). Desktop slide scanners and some transparency adapters for flatbed scanners make it possible to capture images from transparencies in sizes from 35 mm to 8 x 10 inches, though the quality of transparency adapters varies greatly.

Another input option is to **have your images scanned by a service bureau** using scanners with optical-mechanical systems that are more precise than those of desktop scanners. Keep in mind that the quality of a service bureau scan depends not only on the quality of the scanning equipment, but also on the operator's

OPENING PHOTO CD FILES

To get the best color you can when you open a Kodak Photo CD image in Photoshop, it pays to run a comparison test at one of the small file sizes:

First choose the number of the image you want — you can find the number by looking at the index print that comes in the Photo CD jewel case with the disc. Open the 768 x 512-pixel PICT for this image from the Photos folder. Leave it on-screen at 100% size.

Then open the Photo CD file for the same image from the IMAGES folder inside the PHOTO_CD folder. In the dialog box, choose the same resolution (768 x 512), leave the Destination setting at the default RGB setting, and click the Open button. Save and rename the file.

Then open the same Photo CD file from the IMAGES folder again, but this time click the Destination button and choose one of the "pslab" listings to open the file in Lab mode.

With all three files open, choose the one that looks best. If you need to work with a higher-resolution version of the file, open it using the method you chose.

Some digital cameras come with plug-ins for Photoshop that allow you to open images chosen from a "contact sheet."

willingness to calibrate and maintain it, and on his or her understanding of color, and skill in operating the machine.

Besides inputting images by scanning, you can also buy collections of photos and other artwork already scanned and provided on **CD-ROM**. Many stock images, patterns, and textures are now available on CD-ROM, with a variety of arrangements for use and payment (you can find examples in Appendix A).

Kodak Photo CD technology provides an easy and inexpensive way to have images from film (35 mm negatives or slides) stored on a compact disc. The easiest and least expensive way to get your images in Photo CD format is to take your film to a photofinisher who offers the Photo CD service. You'll get the disc back along with the finished prints or slides. The images on the disc are relatively high-quality scans, efficiently compressed, and stored in Kodak's Image Pac format, which provides each image in five different resolutions, or file sizes. Pro Photo CD discs include the five file sizes used for Photo CD plus a higher resolution for bigger enlargement. Pro Photo CD can also accommodate larger original film formats (up to 4 x 5 inches).

Kodak's FlashPix technology, which is an option you can choose when having images stored on Photo CD, is designed to compress images smaller and make opening them faster. Although Photoshop 5/5.5 is not optimized to take full advantage of the speedy FlashPix technology, it *can* open FlashPix files.

NEW INPUT POSSIBILITIES

Photoshop 5/5.5 can open layered files created in Adobe Illustrator 8, provided the files have been exported in Photoshop format.

Version 5/5.5 can also import multipage PDF files, with each page becoming a single Photoshop image. Single-page PDFs can be opened with the File, Open command. But to open a multipage PDF, choose File, Automate, Multi-Page PDF To PSD.

The first page of a multipage PDF document, imported into Photoshop with the Multi-Page PDF To PSD command

PHOTO CD COLOR

When an image is scanned for Photo CD, the workstation operator can choose either a *scene space* option or a *universal film terms* option for color. **Scene space** adjusts the color of the image in an attempt to provide realistic-looking color, correcting for the photographer's incorrect control of the exposure if necessary. **Universal film terms** saves the image as it was recorded on the film. You may have chosen a particular film for its color characteristics and used a nonstandard shutter speed, so you don't want a standard scene space correction. If that's the case, request that the film be scanned using universal film terms when you take it in for Photo CD processing.

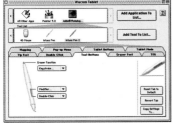

Especially for an artist accustomed to working with natural media, a pressure-sensitive tablet with stylus can take full advantage of Photoshop's painting tools.

OPENING A SECTION

The Quick Edit plug-in supplied with Photoshop 5/5.5 lets you open a selected part of any file saved in Photoshop 2.0 (a single-layer format), uncompressed TIFF, or Scitex CT format. To install the Quick Edit plug-in, drag it from the Adobe Photoshop CD-ROM into the Import-Export folder inside the Plug-ins folder and restart Photoshop. Now you can choose File, Import, Quick Edit to open the part of the file you want. After you've worked on the part, choose File, Export, Quick Edit Save to return it to exactly the same place in the larger file. The modifiable Grid makes it possible to open and replace non-overlapping sections of an illustration, one by one, so you can modify a large image with much less RAM than you would need to work with the whole image at once.

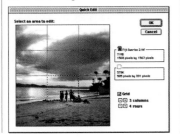

PHOTO CD FILE SIZES

The five file sizes in the Photo CD Image Pac (six sizes in Pro Photo CD) are as follows. Print sizes are for high quality at halftone line screens of 150 lines per inch. Many Photo CD files can be printed bigger than the sizes listed if the photo doesn't include hard edges or if the halftone line screen used for printing is lower than 150 lpi; the lower the line screen, the more the image can be enlarged.

Base/16	192 x 128 pixels	For thumbnail sketches
Base/4	384 x 256 pixels	For position only in layouts
Base	768 x 512 pixels	For TV, for on-screen computer presentation, or for high-quality print up to about 2 x 3 inches
4•Base	1536 x 1024 pixels	For HDTV or for print up to about 3½ x 5 inches
16•Base	3072 x 2048 pixels	For print up to about 7 x 10 inches
64•Base*	6144 x 4096 pixels	For print up to about 14 x 20 inches

* *Available with Pro Photo CD only*

Digital cameras, which bypass film altogether and record images as digital files within the camera, are another potential source of images for manipulation in Photoshop. Many come with Photoshop-compatible plug-ins for loading images directly into Photoshop. Some of these plug-ins are "actionable," so that files can be imported using a Photoshop Action and the File, Automate, Batch command.

Video — from video camera, videocassette, or videodisc — can be brought into Photoshop through the File, Import command, using a plug-in module provided with a *video frame grabber,* a hardware-software combination designed to acquire and enhance the video images.

The image quality that can be achieved with relatively inexpensive digital cameras or with video is not as good as film but is improving. If an image is to be extensively manipulated for a photo-illustration, is to be reproduced at a small size, or is to be used only at a fairly low resolution — for instance, for placement in a World Wide Web page — the convenience of having the "photo" instantly available may outweigh the quality difference.

For imitating traditional art media such as the paintbrush, pencil, airbrush, or charcoal, a **pressure-sensitive tablet** with stylus — for example, any of those in Wacom's Intuos line — has a more familiar feel than a mouse and also provides much better control. Photoshop's painting tools (see Chapter 6) are "wired" to take advantage of pressure sensitivity.

STORAGE AND TRANSPORT OF FILES

With Photoshop, of course, you can never have enough RAM — as soon as you get more, you want *even more.* But even if you have enough RAM so you rarely need to use virtual memory, a fast large-capacity hard disk will be vital. First of all, Photoshop requires that

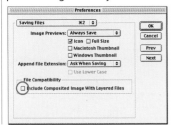
you have scratch disk space available, as described in "Virtual Memory" on page 14. And second, you'll need space to store the files you work with.

Zip and Jazz disks are popular for transporting large files. As desktop CD-ROM writers become less expensive, CD-ROM is becoming popular for transport and storage, since the medium is inexpensive and stable, and the format is well-established and widely readable.

FORMATS FOR SAVING FILES

Photoshop can save or export images in 20 different file formats. Here are some tips for saving files, depending on what you want to do with them:

For the most flexibility in what you can do with the file in the future, save in Photoshop format. It preserves all the layers, channels, and paths.

To save a very large flattened image in a format that will let you open a *part* of it with Quick Edit, one of the Optional Plug-ins supplied on the Adobe Photoshop 5/5.5 CD-ROM, save in Photoshop 2.0, Scitex CT, or uncompressed TIFF format. Although these formats all require flattening the file to a single opaque layer, the files *can* include alpha channels.

For files you can use with Adobe Illustrator, save as Photoshop EPS or TIFF, or simply drag and drop from an open Photoshop file to an open Illustrator file (see Chapter 7 for more about using Photoshop with Illustrator).

For files you can use with Macromedia FreeHand, save in TIFF format.

For files to be viewed with Adobe Acrobat Reader, save as PDF.

To place Photoshop images on pages in PageMaker or QuarkXPress for color separation to make film for printing, TIFF and EPS formats work well. But it's a good idea to check with your imagesetting service bureau to see how they suggest saving and placing the Photoshop files.

To save a Bitmap image whose white parts will be clear instead of opaque white when you place it in an application such as Illustrator, PageMaker, or QuarkXPress, save in TIFF or Photoshop EPS format, choosing the Transparent Whites option.

To save a Duotone file for placement in an application such as Illustrator, PageMaker, or QuarkXPress, save in EPS format.

To save a file for use on the World Wide Web, in both Photoshop 5 and 5.5 you can use the File, Save As command to save files in JPEG (as discussed below) or PNG format. Or use File, Export, GIF89a Export.

In addition to the Save As and Export commands, Photoshop 5.5 also provides the Save For Web interface, which lets you do

In most cases, when you save an image in GIF format for the Web, the size- and color-optimizing options offered by the File, Save For Web command make it a better choice than File, Export, GIF89a Export. There are two exceptions:

• If you want to use an alpha channel as a mask to establish transparency in the image, you'll need to use GIF89a Export, since this option isn't available in the Save For Web dialog box. A method for producing such a mask is presented in "Silhouettes, Shadows, and Transparency" in Chapter 9.

• If you want to weight a Selective, Adaptive, or Perceptual palette so that it gives preference to the colors in an important, selected, area of the image (see "'Shaping' Adaptive Palettes" on page 36), you can't do it in the Save For Web dialog box. Instead, working in the RGB file, select the important area and choose Image, Mode, Indexed Color and choose the Adaptive, Selective, or Perceptual palette. Then use the GIF89a Export command.

side-by-side comparisons of JPEG, PNG, and GIF formats and optimize the size and color of images for the Web. Chapter 9 tells about these formats and how to use them to best advantage for Web images.

The JPEG format is also useful **to compress a finished image** in order to send it by modem, to reduce its size for transport, or even to use it in some page layout applications. In compressing a file, the JPEG routines start by eliminating detail data that's likely to be lost in the printing process anyway. The reduction in file size that JPEG provides depends on the compression setting and the content of the image; a typical compressed size for a 900K image might be 59K for the Low setting and 169K for the Maximum setting. Compression at Photoshop's Maximum Quality level for JPEG usually produces acceptable results for emergency archiving or transmitting of CMYK images that will eventually go to print. The most compressed (Low Quality) shows the most image degradation.

Photoshop 5.5's **Save For Web** interface reduces the guesswork associated with the JPEG saving process. It lets you see the results of up to four different levels of JPEG compression at once so you can compare them. You can refine the Quality settings by typing a value between 0 and 100.

In contrast, when you choose File, Save As, JPEG — the only JPEG saving option available in Photoshop 5, since the Save For Web command isn't available — a JPEG plug-in provides a single preview and a sliding scale of compression.

JPEG compresses by averaging the color of blocks of pixels. The greater the compression, the more pixels per block. As a result, the color in JPEGged images can look "chunky," especially at the lower-quality compression settings. To cut down on chunkiness, choose Baseline Optimized, or Optimized, when saving in JPEG format instead of the default Baseline Standard, or with Optimized turned off. Another JPEG option, Progressive, is important for display of images on the Web. Instead of downloading the final image line by line while the viewer waits, it downloads the image in several stages, with a fuzzy, low-resolution image first, replaced by a better-looking version, and finally by the high-quality image.

Another compression option for storing and sending files is the lossless LZW compression option available when you save in TIFF format. It has the advantage of not degrading the image, but the compression is far less than with JPEG.

For images to be used for on-screen presentations other than on the Web, you may be able to save in PICT File format; check the documentation for the destination program (such as Macromedia Director or PowerPoint) to see what format is

Repeated JPEG compression noticeably degrades the image. So don't JPEG an image that has been stored in JPEG format and then opened.

In scans and screen displays, images are made up of pixels. The pixels are all the same size but vary in color, with over 16 million color possibilities.

Many printed images are composed of overlaid screen patterns of halftone dots. These dots vary in size, but the number of lines of halftone dots per inch remains constant. The number of ink colors is often limited to four: cyan, magenta, yellow, and black. The spectrum of printed colors results because the eye "mixes" the dots of color.

Stochastic screening is another way of using a visual mix to print color. The "cells" of the stochastic screen pattern, instead of containing halftone dots that vary in size, contain very tiny but uniformly sized dots that vary in number. The number of tiny dots within a region (or "cell") is what makes the color more intense (many dots) or less intense (few dots). Because the tiny dots within a cell are spread randomly instead of being clumped together to make larger dots, no halftone pattern is generated, and so more image detail can usually be seen.

recommended. Remember to set Resolution (in the Image Size dialog box) to 72 dpi to match the screen. PICT can accommodate one alpha channel, which many multimedia design and production programs can interpret as a mask.

To save files to be opened in paint programs on DOS- or Windows-based computers, the BMP, PCX, Amiga IFF, TIFF, and Targa formats work in many instances. Before choosing a file format, check to see what format(s) will work with a particular hardware-software-operating-system combination.

To pass files to other computer systems such as Scitex, Amiga, or Pixar, use the special format provided for that system. Pixar files can include an alpha channel, which can be used as a mask.

OUTPUT: PROOFING AND PRINTING

Like other desktop color files, Photoshop images can be printed on inkjet, thermal transfer, or dye sublimation printers, color photocopiers that can accept digital input, or film recorders (as negatives or positive transparencies). Typically, inkjet, thermal transfer, or dye sublimation printing is used to show generally how the image and the color will look when printed on an offset press, or to achieve a particular kind of art print quality.

Photoshop files can also be produced as color-separated film for making plates for offset printing, by using imagesetters or high-end color-separation systems such as Linotype-Hell or Scitex systems. And they can be output direct-to-plate (which bypasses film), or even direct-to-press, which bypasses both film and plates.

When color separations for offset printing are made by the traditional halftone screening method, the *contract proof,* which a printer and client agree is the color standard to be matched on the printing press, is usually a laminate made from the film that will be used to make the printing plates. However, as stochastic screening (shown at the left), direct-to-plate, and direct-to-press printing technologies replace halftone film for some printing jobs, the "soft" proof (often made by an inkjet or dye sublimation printer rather than from color-separated film) becomes more important.

RESOLUTION, COLOR DEPTH, AND FILE SIZE

Resolution is the term used to describe the **amount of data**, or color information, in a scan, a stored image file, a screen display, or a printed image. Typically, the more data, the larger you can print the image before it starts to look pixelated and lose detail.

Resolution is sometimes expressed as the number of dots, pixels, or ink spots per unit of measure (inch, centimeter, or pica, for example). Alternatively, resolution may be stated as pixel dimensions — 640 x 480 pixels, for instance — giving a more direct report of how much data is present, independent of the measured height and width of the image.

With stochastic screening it's possible to get good prints from smaller file sizes than with halftone screening. Because there's no halftone dot pattern with stochastic to interfere with the edges and detail in the image, these smaller files can produce sharper images.

But there are also some things to watch out for:

• Without extra dot gain compensation, images printed with stochastic screens tend to be darker overall and show higher contrast. This is because the dots used for stochastic screening are extremely tiny — much smaller than halftone dots — so dot gain can be much more significant. The "spread" of the dot can be a much bigger fraction of the original dot size than it is for the larger halftone dots, and so the change in color due to dot gain is more drastic than for halftone printing.

• The tiny size of the dots in stochastic screening also means that it's much harder for press operators to make the kinds of adjustments they can use to correct color during a print run.

• Since dot gain can be so important, and since an ordinary laminate proof doesn't accurately show dot gain, a special, alternative proofing method may be needed.

If you plan to use stochastic screening, be sure to get advice from both your printer and your imagesetting service bureau. The service bureau should have an imagesetter equipped with a *RIP* (raster image processor) that uses stochastic screens, such as Adobe Brilliant Screens, Agfa's Crystal Raster technology, or Linotype-Hell's Diamond Screening. Have the service bureau run a test on separated film, and then ask the printer to check the film to make sure it will work for printing.

The terminology used to discuss resolution is a hodgepodge of words from printing, computer graphics, and prepress services. For consistency and to reduce confusion, this book uses resolution terminology the same way it's used in the *Adobe Photoshop 5.0 User Guide*. Our discussion of resolution starts with *screen frequency* because that's the piece of information you need to know first, in order to figure out how much information to collect in a scan or build into an image file in order to get the best printed image at the size you want. If you can help it, you don't want to find yourself in the opposite position: faced with a finished file and wondering how big you'll be able to print it without losing image detail and quality.

Screen Frequency

The term *screen frequency* refers to the resolution or density of halftone screens, which are the patterns of ink dots used for printing most of the pages that come off presses today. Screen frequency is expressed in terms of how many rows of halftone dots there are per linear inch, called *lines per inch* (lpi). The higher the lpi, the less obvious the halftone dot pattern and therefore the more image detail you can see in the print.

In a printed image, the screen frequency (lpi, or number of rows of dots per inch) is the same in all areas of the image — it's the same where the color is pale as it is where the color is intense. The main characteristic that changes the intensity of the color is the *halftone dot size*. For example, in an image printed with a 150 lpi screen, an area of pale yellow is printed with 150 very small dots of yellow ink per inch, and perhaps no dots of cyan, magenta, or black, the other three process printing colors. Because quite a bit of bare white paper shows through between the tiny dots, the color looks pale. A bright red, on the other hand, might be made up of magenta and yellow dots, printed on top of each other and as large as the 150 lpi screen density allows. Since these larger dots fill up the space, no white shows through, and the color is intense. Screen frequency, along with height and width of the printed image, determines how much information is *needed* to print the image without its showing pixels.

Image Resolution

Set in the Resolution field of the Print Size section of Photoshop's Image Size dialog box, *image resolution* is expressed as pixels per inch or pixels per centimeter. Image resolution, along with the image Height and Width in the Print Size section, determine how much information is stored in the file.

• **The image resolution you need for an image that will be printed** depends on the screen frequency ("Getting Enough Information" on page 52 tells how to figure it out).

• **The image resolution you need for an image that will be displayed on-screen** (for the Web, for example) is typically

72 pixels per inch, which is the standard monitor resolution. Or it may be expressed directly as pixel dimensions — 640 x 480 pixels for instance.

Instead of being expressed as pixels per inch or pixel dimensions, **image resolution can be expressed as file size** (in K or MB), which also takes into account the height and width of the image. Both pixel dimensions and file size indicate how much information (or, relatively, how much image detail) is stored in the file.

Scan Resolution

Scan resolution is usually expressed as the number of *samples per inch, pixels per inch* (ppi), or sometimes *dots per inch* (dpi) recorded by the scanner. Scan resolution, along with the height of the scanned area and its width, determines how much information is *collected* for the image file. The more information the scan collects, the more image detail is recorded. With more image detail, the scan can be printed at a higher screen frequency or at a larger size. Like image resolution, scan resolution is sometimes expressed as file size (K or MB) or as pixel dimensions, which can be computed by multiplying the height and width of the image by the samples per inch.

Monitor Resolution

Also called display resolution, *monitor resolution* is determined only by the monitor itself and the software that runs it. Some monitors have more than one setting and can display at a higher resolution than the standard 72 pixels per inch. Whatever the display resolution, **when you view a Photoshop image at 100% magnification** (shown in the title bar of the image), every pixel in the image is represented by a pixel on-screen. So you're seeing it *not at the final printed size,* but at the monitor's display resolution, usually 72 to 85 pixels per inch.

Color Depth

Besides the dimensions (length and width) and the resolution (number of pixels per inch), *color depth* (or pixel depth) is the other factor that affects the amount of information stored in an image. Color depth is the amount of computer data required to store the color information for each pixel in the image.

- A **grayscale** image includes only brightness data; each pixel requires 8 *bits* (also called 1 *byte*) to store this brightness information.

- Typical **color scanners** pick up 8 to 12 bits of brightness information for each of the three colors of light in the additive color model — red, green, and blue. So **a color scan** requires 24 to 36 bits of information per pixel (8 x 3 = 24; 12 x 3 = 36).

Getting Enough Information

When you're trying to decide on a resolution for scanning or creating an image, the goal is to gather (or create) enough image

When your scanner shows you a preview of your image, use the scanning software's cropping tool to identify the area you want to scan.

For a color scan, set the type of scan to "Millions of Colors" or "24-bit color" (top) and adjust your scanner's Resolution and Scaling settings. (If you're using the checking method described in "Double-Checking" on page 54, the Image Size value in K or MB should now match or slightly exceed the Pixel Dimensions file size number that you get in step 4. At this point, if your scanner is capable of 30- or 36-bit scanning, choose "Billions of Colors" (bottom). The file size will go up automatically. Then complete the scan. (The interface shown here is for the Microtek ScanWizard desktop scanning software.)

information to print the image successfully — keeping the color transitions smooth and the details sharp. If your scan doesn't collect enough image information (or you create your artwork file too small), Photoshop's Image Size command can sometimes interpolate to increase the file size to the amount needed for printing. This may produce a better image than having the output device do the interpolation. But still, **an enlarged image won't look nearly as good as if you had collected (or painted) the right amount of information in the first place.**

Although you want to be sure to use a high enough scan resolution, you don't want to overdo it — because the higher the scan resolution, the bigger the file size. The bigger the file size, the more disk space you need to store it, the more RAM and scratch disk space you need to work on it in Photoshop, and the longer it takes to open, work on, save, and print. So the real goal in scanning is to capture enough information to make your final print or slide look great, but not significantly more.

SETTING UP A SCAN

In your quest to collect enough image data in a scan, the scan resolution setting (in pixels per inch) and the height and width (in inches or cm) or scale (in percentage) can all vary, as long as enough information is collected. Most scanners now allow you to prescan so you have an image on-screen and you can identify the area of this image that you want to scan. Then you can specify the color mode (color depth) and scan resolution (dpi) that you want, and enter a scale factor (a percentage) if the final printed size will be larger or smaller than the original.

To figure out the scan resolution to specify, you can multiply the print resolution (number of lpi in the halftone screen) by 1.5 or by 2. The 1.5 multiplier can work well for photos of natural scenery without geometric patterns, sharp color boundaries, or fine details; 2 works well for everything, including graphics and photos of man-made structures, which tend to have straight lines and sharp color breaks. Above 2, you increase file size without making the picture look significantly better.

Extra Color Depth

If your scanner offers 30-bit scanning (10 bits per color channel) or 36-bit scanning (12 bits per color channel), you can get more color depth in your scan than with 24-bit color (8 bits per color channel). Photoshop 5/5.5 can use the extra color depth to help make finer color and tone adjustments. For instance, you will have greater image detail to work with when you adjust Curves to optimize the shadows. Then, because most of Photoshop's commands and tools — even the basic ability to handle multiple layers — won't work on files with greater than 24-bit color depth, convert the file (Image,

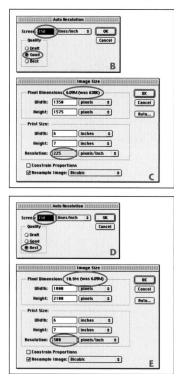

Step 1 *To figure out how big a scan file should be, start by opening a "dummy" file in Photoshop and setting the color mode. You don't have to worry about setting the Height, Width, or Resolution at this point.*

Steps 2, 3, and 4 *Open the Image Size dialog box, set the Print Size dimensions to the units and size you want, and click Auto. In the Auto Resolution box enter the halftone screen frequency that will be used to print, and choose either Good (which uses a 1.5:1 ratio) (B) or Best (which uses 2:1). Then click OK to return to the Image Size box (C). The Resolution value is set automatically, based on your entry in Auto Resolution. The Pixel Dimensions value tells how large (in K or MB) the scan file will have to be. Either a larger Screen value or a higher Quality setting (D) will increase the Resolution, which increases the Pixel Dimensions size (E).*

Mode, 8 Bits/Channel) before continuing with your image editing. However, if no editing is required beyond simple color and tone adjustments, save the file directly to TIFF or EPS format for printing, without converting to 8 Bits/Channel.

Double-Checking

If you plan to send a photo or artwork to a service bureau for scanning, or if you just want a way to check and make sure you're using the right scanner settings, you can use Photoshop to calculate the size of the file you need. Then check this calculated file size with the file size the scanner software comes up with. Here's a way to do it:

1 Setting the color mode. One of the things that will affect the amount of information collected is the color depth, determined by the color mode used for the scan. Open a new file (File, New). This "dummy" file will not be used to make an image, only to calculate scan resolution. The first step is to set the mode (see figure A at the left):

- For both color and grayscale images, the mode used for scanning should be RGB Color; grayscale images typically turn out better if you collect the color information in the scan and then convert to Grayscale in Photoshop. (See "Converting from Color to Grayscale" on page 108 for tips.)

- Use Grayscale mode for scanning black-and-white line art. Line art usually turns out better (with smoother, more consistent lines) if it's scanned in Grayscale mode and then perfected with Image, Adjust, Levels. ("Coloring Line Art" on page 234 demonstrates this method.) Then it can be left as Grayscale or converted to Bitmap mode, depending on how you want to use it.

With the mode set, click OK.

2 Setting the dimensions. The amount of scan data you need depends on the printed size and the halftone screen frequency. Choose Image, Image Size. In the Print Size section of the Image Size dialog box, make sure that the Constrain Proportions checkbox is unchecked. Then enter the dimensions (Height and Width) you want for the final printed image.

3 Factoring in the screen frequency. Now you'll account for the halftone screen. In the Image Size dialog box, make sure the Resample Image box is checked, so Photoshop will be able to adjust the Resolution without changing the final printed dimensions.

With the Height and Width already set by the entry you just made in step 2, to get the Resolution setting, click the Auto button. In the Auto Resolution dialog box set the Screen (halftone screen frequency) you and your printer agree on. Then choose Good (1.5 times the screen value, for natural, organic images) or Best (2 times the screen, for images with hard-edged elements or fine detail).

There are two potential problems with scanning something that has already been printed — for example, from a book or magazine: First, unless it's very old, it's probably copyrighted. That means that the right to reproduce it or make derivative works *in any form* belongs solely to the copyright holder (usually the originator), so you need that person's permission to copy it. Second, the halftone screen pattern used to print it will probably interact with the scanner's sampling pattern to produce an unwanted moiré pattern when you print.

Some scanners have built-in descreening algorithms for eliminating the moiré that can result from scanning a page that was printed using halftone screens. Shown here are scans made with Microtek ScanWizard desktop scanning software with (bottom) and without (top) the descreening function.

4 Reading the Resolution and file size. Back in the Image Size dialog box, note the new Resolution number in the Print Size section of the box. It should match the number you got if you did your own multiplication of screen frequency by 1.5 or 2.

Also look at the file size number in the Pixel Dimensions section of the box (write it down). This is the file size (in K or MB). In other words it's the amount of data the scanner will need to gather to support the size and halftone screen you've chosen. If you are doing a 24-bit scan, you can compare this number to the file size your scanner arrives at, to see if they are approximately the same. If they are very different, you may need to look at the problem again. You can also provide this number if you are having the scan done by a service bureau. If they offer you a number of standard file sizes (expressed in MB), you'll probably want to pick the one that is the same as the file size you calculated in Photoshop (in the Pixel Dimensions section of the Image Size dialog box), or the next higher size. You don't want a scan that's smaller than the calculated size, because it won't have enough information. But you don't want one that's too large, either. Typically, larger file sizes cost more, and they take more memory, disk space, and processing time.

Other circumstances. You may not always know in advance exactly how big to make your scan. Here are some approaches you can take if you don't have all the info you need for steps 1 through 4:

- **If you don't know the screen frequency for printing,** guess high. Enter the Screen value in step 3 as 150 lpi or higher.

- **If you don't know the final printed dimensions of the image,** go for the "optimal scan": Scan the image at its full original size either at the Resolution in the Print Size section of the Image Size box or the scanner's default, whichever is larger. If this would make the file too big to work with, scale it down to the biggest file size you can manage.

- **If the image you're scanning will be only a small part of a composite,** you can either: Estimate the final printed size of that element and use those dimensions in the Image Size dialog box in step 2. Or, if you really don't know how big you want to use the element, scan it at its full original size at the Resolution in the Print Size section of the Image Size box or at the scanner's default resolution (as above). Place the scanned element on its own layer in your composite file. If you need to size it up or down, use Layer, Free Transform to size it relative to the other components of the image.

RESAMPLING IN PHOTOSHOP

Regardless of how well you plan there are likely to be times when you need to *resample* — either resample down or resample up — in Photoshop. *Resampling down* means decreasing the file size. You

Increasing the file size (*resampling up*) by means of the Image, Image Size command "invents" the new pixels that make the file bigger. The colors of these new pixels are "averaged" from the colors of the old ones, which is likely to make the larger image look a little fuzzy. Other operations that can involve color averaging are the Edit, Free Transform and Edit, Transform commands (Scale, Rotate, Skew, Distort, and Perspective); the Image, Rotate Canvas command; and "sampling down" (shrinking the image size). After any of these operations, run Unsharp Mask to sharpen up the image (see "Sharpen" on page 172).

DOING IT ALL AT ONCE

Transforming — scaling, skewing, rotating, or distorting, for example — causes resampling. To avoid resampling several times and thus degrading the image, you can use Edit, Free Transform (Ctrl/⌘-T) and do several transformations with only one resampling, rather using the individual Edit, Transform commands, which will resample each time.

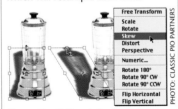

PHOTO: CLASSIC PIO PARTNERS

Here scaling (left) and skewing of the shadow layer were done with only one resampling. Pressing Ctrl/⌘-T brought up the Transform box; dragging the top center handle downward scaled the shadow; then with the cursor inside the box, right-clicking (Windows) or Control-clicking (Mac) brought up the context-sensitive menu so Skew could be chosen, and the top center handle was dragged to the left.

might do this because you have more information than you need for printing and you want to reduce the bulk of the file. *Resampling up* increases the file size. In a case where you can't rescan the original again at the correct settings, you might need to do this in order to have enough information to reproduce the image at the size and screen frequency or display resolution you want.

To resample, use the Image Size dialog box. Make sure that both the Constrain Proportions and the Resample Image box are checked and that Bicubic is chosen from the Resample Image popout list. Then:

- **To change the image dimensions,** enter a new value in the Height or Width field. The other dimension will change automatically and so will the file size. The Resolution will stay the same.

- **To change the image resolution,** set Height and Width units to anything but pixels. Then enter a new value in the Resolution field. The dimensions will stay the same but file size will change.

After you've resampled, remember to run the Unsharp Mask filter to "bring back" some of the detail lost along the way. Knowing how to establish the original file size, how to resample if necessary, and how to "clean up" after resampling, you'll be able to produce the right file sizes for anything from postage stamps to wall murals.

ELECTRONIC "GRAIN"

There may be some instances when you *want* a kind of "digital grain" in your final image. For that pixelated look, try Photoshop's Mosaic filter.

Choose **Filter, Pixelate, Mosaic** and enter the Cell Size you want. The larger the setting, the "lower-resolution" your filtered image will look. For instance, if you set the Cell Size at 10, each 10 x 10-pixel area of your image will be replaced with 100 pixels of a single color, averaged from the original colors in that 10 x 10 area. Because all 100 pixels are now the same color, the area looks like a single large square pixel.

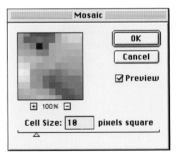

Designer **Wayne Rankin** created *Planet Ocean* as a special souvenir stamp sheet for Australia Post's Stamp Collecting Month and also to commemorate the United Nations International Year of the Ocean. The sheet features six stamps, each highlighting a sea creature native to the waters surrounding Australia. The animals were generated from 3D models provided by Viewpoint Datalabs (**www.viewpoint.com**). These models (top left) were then customized in 3D Studio Max using photographic reference and advice from marine experts to match the characteristics of the Australian species (center left). The texture and bump maps applied to make the 3D models look realistic were created both from photographic sources and by painting directly in Photoshop.

To cast ocean water shadows on the creatures when they were rendered in the 3D program, Rankin used an imported black-and-white image as a lighting gel (bottom left). This mottled image was created in Photoshop by drawing white lines and swirls over a solid black background with the airbrush tool, then applying a slight Gaussian blur to further soften the lines, and finally extending the texture by duplicating parts of the drawing and flipping and rotating the copies.

The background for *Planet Ocean* was created directly in Photoshop using the airbrush tool and the Motion Blur filter to blend together scanned photos and painted areas. The type for each stamp and the layout of stamp outlines were created in Illustrator. The Illustrator line work was rasterized into the Photoshop file as a separate layer (File, Place), to help with positioning each creature over the background. For final output, visibility for the line work layer was turned off before the flattened file was made, and the final layout was assembled in Illustrator.

Gordon Studer created *Abstract Angel* for an "Arts for AIDS" auction to benefit the San Francisco AIDS Foundation. Studer scanned a hand-drawn sketch and used it as a guide for making the graphic's many separate shapes, each of which was dragged and dropped into its own layer.

Studer used many sources for the components: The floral texture was derived from a scan of Japanese paper; the wings from a PhotoDisc photo collection on CD-ROM called *Retro Relics;* the hair, mouth, nose, ear, and hands from Photodisc's *Retro Americana* and *Retro Americana 2* collections; and the breasts came from a photo he had taken.

He converted the grayscale images to RGB and added the initial color by clicking the Colorize box in the Hue/Saturation dialog box. He then used the Variations dialog box to try out different versions, choosing the ones with the most pleasing color.

In many cases the photo element was "shaved away" to fit the shape of the "puzzle piece" it would fill by selecting the parts to be deleted with various selection tools.

For the auction, the piece was produced as an Iris print on watercolor paper and framed.

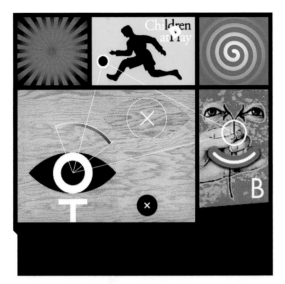

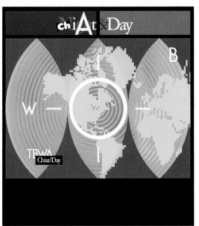

Louis Fishauf created the *TBWA Chiat/ Day window murals* for a ground-floor all-purpose space that housed reception, employee lockers, lunch tables and meeting areas at the company's headquarters in Toronto. The 7-foot-high door (above right) shows the scale of the murals; the black areas outline the mostly rectangular panes of glass.

The murals were assembled in Photoshop from scanned imagery from Fishauf's clip art collection, with type set in Adobe Illustrator. Where exact placement was critical, Fishauf saved his Photoshop image in EPS format, opened it in Illustrator, and created crop marks to exactly fit the outline of the image. After setting the type to fit and saving the Illustrator file in EPS format, he used Photoshop's File, Place command to render the type, aligned automatically by the crop marks, exactly in position in the Photoshop file. For type whose placement

was less critical, he dragged and dropped from Illustrator to Photoshop.

The large-format inkjet process that was used to print the window-covering film introduced a dithering effect that allowed the images to be printed from relatively low-resolution files. Fishauf kept the files as small as possible, varying the resolution depending on the content of the panels and using smaller files for soft-focus images like the woman's face shown at the upper right. The largest file — the girl riding the fish — was only 70 MB.

Files were output in 54-inch-wide strips, first as proofs on paper and then on a thermal transfer material that was laminated onto three different kinds of window-marking film. From inside the building some parts of the mural are visible and others look like clear or smoked glass. From the outside, all parts of the mural are visible, as shown at the right.

The white curves, generated in Adobe Illustrator, were applied in a highly reflective opaque material, produced with a computer-driven cutting machine.

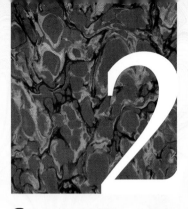

SELECTIONS, MASKS, LAYERS, AND CHANNELS

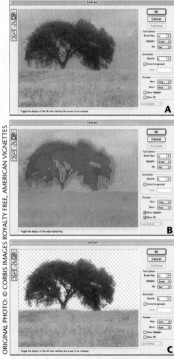

Perhaps the most time- and labor-saving addition to Photoshop 5.5's selecting capabilities is the Extract command, added to the Image menu. It's now much easier to isolate subjects with complex or poorly defined edges, like a portrait with wisps of hair, a tree with masses of leaves (A), or a subject on a background that's partly similar in color and partly contrasting. If you roughly define the edge of the subject (green) and its interior (red) (B), the Extract command can remove the background (C).

WHETHER YOU'RE WORKING ON GRAPHICS for the World Wide Web or for print, creating images with Adobe Photoshop almost always depends on isolating some part of the image so you can paint it, filter it, move it, adjust its tone or color, or make it part of a montage. Isolating part of an image this way is called *selecting*. To work effectively with Photoshop, you need to know about selections: how to make them, how to store them, how to activate them again from storage, how to combine them, and how to modify them.

Selections can be made with choices from the **Select menu**, with **selection tools,** with the **path tools** or **type mask tools,** or by modifying a copy of one of the file's **color channels** — for instance, the Red, Green, or Blue channel of an RGB image. Selection options new to Photoshop 5 are the **magnetic lasso** and **magnetic pen. Photoshop 5.5** also adds the **magic eraser,** the **background eraser,** and the **Extract command.**

The magic eraser, background eraser, and Extract command automatically make their selections permanent by isolating the subject on an otherwise transparent layer. But with the other selection tools, when you make a selection, a flashing boundary (sometimes referred to as "marching ants"), lets you see what part of the image is selected. The selection boundary disappears if you click outside it with a selection tool or press Ctrl/⌘-D or choose Select, None. Photoshop 5/5.5 provides a safety net in case you need a selection back after you've deselected. You can restore the most recent selection, even after you've made changes to the image — as long as you haven't made another selection — by choosing Select, **Reselect.**

A more permanent way to preserve a selection is to store it permanently as an **alpha channel** (page 75), a pen **path** (a very economical way to store a hard-edged selection, as discussed on page 68), a **layer** of its own (since many Photoshop illustrations are constructed by stacking up layers of image material, as described on page 79), a **layer mask** (which limits how much of a particular layer contributes to an image, as shown on page 84), or an **Adjustment layer** (which lets you target a color or tone change to a particular part of an image; Adjustment layers are discussed on page 88).

MAKING SELECTIONS

In general, selections that are made *procedurally* — that is, by using information like color or brightness that's intrinsic to the image —

continued on page 62

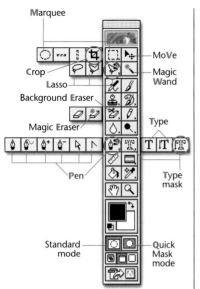

Marquee
Crop
Lasso
Background Eraser
Magic Eraser
MoVe
Magic Wand
Type
Pen
Type mask
Standard mode
Quick Mask mode

The most important changes in the selecting tools in Photoshop 5.5 are (1) improvements that allow the magic wand to select all pixels of the same color, not just contiguous ones, (2) the magic eraser, which can provide a one-click version of using the magic wand and then pressing Delete, and (3) the background eraser tool, a hand-guided tool that erases to transparency according to how you set its options. These are in addition to Photoshop 5's "magnetic" lasso and pen tools, the improved crop tool, which can expand as well as reduce the canvas size of an image, and a new vertical type mask tool that makes type-shaped selections with characters arranged from top to bottom instead of left to right.

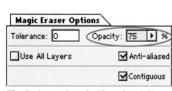

The Options palette for Photoshop 5.5's new magic eraser tool is very similar to that of the magic wand. The addition of an Opacity slider lets you control how "clear" the transparency will be in the erased areas. It's a bit counterintuitive, but the higher the Opacity setting, the more transparent the result.

rather than by drawing a selection boundary by hand, are often faster and more accurate. But the tool or command that works best for making a selection depends on what you want to select. Each of the selection tools and commands has its own advantages and disadvantages. To decide which to use, you need to analyze the area you want to select — Is it organic or geometric? Is it fairly uniform in color, or is it multicolored? Does it contrast with its background or blend into it, or do some parts of it contrast and others blend in? Then you can choose the tool, command, or combination of techniques that will do the job. The three sections that follow, "Selecting by Color" (below), "Selecting by Shape" (page 65), and "Selecting by Shape *and* Color" (page 71), tell how to choose and use the appropriate selection methods.

Sometimes the best way to select is to use one selection method and then add to the selection, subtract from it, or transform it by moving or reshaping the selection boundary. The "Modifying Selections" section (starting on page 76) tells how to accomplish these changes.

SELECTING BY COLOR

Cleanly silhouetting a subject by color can help you grab elements such as a purple flower among pink ones, or a brown dog on a green lawn. Selecting by color is a *procedural* method. It uses the image's hue, saturation, or brightness information (or some combination of these) to define the selection. To make a selection of all the pixels of a similar color, you can use the magic wand tool or the Select, Color Range command, or develop a selection from one of the color channels — for instance, the Red, Green, or Blue channel of an RGB image.

Using the Magic Wand

One advantage of the **magic wand** tool is that it's quick and easy. It's good for selecting one uniformly colored area or a small number of similarly colored areas in an image where there are other spots of the same color but you don't want to select them all. By default, magic wand selections are **antialiased,** or smooth-edged (see "Antialiased Selections" on page 67).

- **To make a selection with the magic wand,** just click it on a pixel of the color you want to select. By default the wand is in **Contiguous** mode, so it selects the pixel you clicked and all similarly colored pixels for as far as that color continues without interruption.

- In **Photoshop 5.5** you can use the wand to **select *all* pixels of the same color,** whether they're contiguous or not, by turning off the default Contiguous feature in the Magic Wand Options palette (you can open the palette by double-clicking the wand in the toolbox). In **Photoshop 5,** without the ability to turn off Contiguous, you can add to the color-based selection by

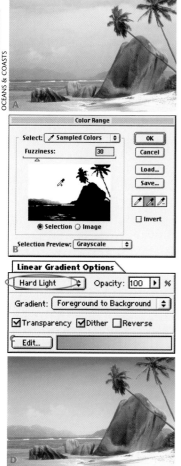

A

Color Range

Select: [✎ Sampled Colors ▼]   [OK]

Fuzziness: [30]   [Cancel]

[Load...]

[Save...]

[✎] [✎] [✎]

☐ Invert

◉ Selection ○ Image

B

Selection Preview: [Grayscale ▼]

Linear Gradient Options

[Hard Light ▼]   Opacity: [100 ▶] %

Gradient: [Foreground to Background ▼]

☑Transparency ☑Dither ☐Reverse

[Edit...]

D

Use the Select, Color Range command in Sampled Colors mode to select a broad expanse of closely related colors. Here the challenge was to add drama to the sky without having to make a manual selection in a photo (A) with a subtle gradation at the hazy horizon and complex shapes (the palms) that had to be excluded. The Color Range eyedropper was dragged across the sky to select a range of blues. Then the Alt/Option key was held down and the eyedropper was clicked on the colors we wanted to exclude. Fuzziness was adjusted between 15 and 30 — a good range for Fuzziness in general — to antialias the selection around the palms and "feather" the horizon area (B). The selection was stored as an alpha channel for safekeeping (Select, Save Selection). With the selection active, the gradient tool was used in Hard Light mode (C) to add a color ramp while retaining some of the subtle cloud structure from the original sky (D).

Shift-clicking similarly colored areas with the magic wand.

- **To specify how broad a range of color the magic wand should include in a selection,** set the Tolerance value in the Magic Wand Options palette to a number between 0 and 255. The lower the number, the smaller the range of colors. (The magic wand's Tolerance setting also controls the color range used by the Grow and Similar commands from the Select menu; see "Modifying Selections" on page 76.)

- **To control whether the selection is based on the color of only a single layer or of all visible layers** combined, turn Use All Layers off or on in the Magic Wand Options palette.

Using the Magic Eraser

Often, the goal of making a selection is to isolate the selected subject on a layer of its own, so you can use it in a layered composition. When the subject you want to select appears on a contrasting background, Photoshop 5.5's magic eraser is ideal for silhouetting it by removing that background. When you use the magic eraser, the result is not the ephemeral marching ants that you get with the magic wand, but instead **a subject isolated on an otherwise transparent layer.**

- **To make a selection with the magic eraser,** click it on a pixel of the color you want to make transparent. By default, the magic eraser, like the magic wand, is in Contiguous mode, and the edge of the transparent area is antialiased.

- **To allow the transparency to replace every occurrence of the color you clicked on,** turn off the Contiguous setting before you click on the color you want to eliminate.

- **To specify how broad a range of color** the magic eraser should include in a selection, set the Tolerance value as described for the magic wand above.

The Color Range command makes it easy to "subselect" by color criteria, sort of like searching a database using several key words: "Select everything *red* that's *in this one area of the image* so I can change the color to green." The key to subselecting is that Color Range makes its selections *within the current selection.*

To select within a color family *and* within a particular area of the image, use a selection tool to surround the general area you want to change (A). Then choose Select, Color Range; choose the color family from the "Select" list (Reds in this case) (B). (If the color family you need doesn't appear in the list — like orange, for example — leave the Select setting on Sampled Colors.) Click OK to close the dialog box, and press Ctrl/⌘-H to hide the "marching ants" selection border so you can see what you're doing. Then use Image, Adjust, Variations or Hue/Saturation to adjust the color (C).

ORIGINAL PHOTO: © CORBIS IMAGES ROYALTY FREE, GLAMOUR & ROMANCE

• **To control the degree of transparency,** use the Opacity slider — the higher the Opacity setting, the greater the erasing effect and therefore the more transparent the area will become.

Selecting by Color Range

The **Select, Color Range** command is complex, but it's well worth learning to use. In some cases it offers more control of what's selected than the magic wand does, and it **shows the extent of the selection more clearly.**

The little preview window in the Color Range dialog box shows a grayscale image of the selection. White areas are selected; gray areas are partially selected, with the degree of selection decreasing as you go toward black, which indicates areas that are completely deselected. With its many levels of gray, this picture is much more informative than the marching ants you see when you use the magic wand.

The **Fuzziness** is like the magic wand's Tolerance setting, but it's easier to work with, since the entire range is spread out on a slider scale and the preview window instantly shows the effect of changing it. Keeping the setting above 16 to 32 will usually prevent jagged edges in the completed selection.

The **"Select" field** at the top of the box lets you choose the color selection criteria:

• **To select based on colors sampled from all visible layers of the image as if they were merged,** choose Sampled Colors, then choose the dialog box's leftmost eyedropper tool and click on the image, just as you would with the magic wand. The selection extends throughout the image (or the existing selection, if there is one), as if you had made a magic wand selection in Photoshop 5.5 with Contiguous turned off.

• **To select based on color sampled from a single layer,** first make all other layers invisible by clicking off their "eye" icons in the Layers palette (see "Layers" on page 79 for more about the Layers palette). Then choose Select, Color Range and click with the eyedropper.

• **To extend or reduce the range of colors in the current selection,** click or drag with the + or – eyedropper to add new colors or to subtract colors. Or click or drag with the plain eyedropper, with Shift (to add) or Alt/Option (to subtract). You can also expand or contract the selection by adjusting the Fuzziness, but pixels whose colors are at the extremes of the selected color range are only partially selected.

• **To select a family of colors,** choose from the color blocks in the "Select" list. The color families are predefined — you can't change the Fuzziness or use the eyedroppers to expand or shrink the range.

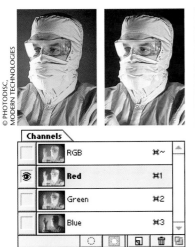

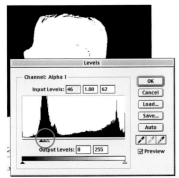

To start a mask to select the surgeon, we found that the Red channel showed good contrast between the subject and the background. So we duplicated it to make an alpha channel.

Contrast was increased in the alpha channel by adjusting the Input Levels (Image, Adjust, Levels). The airbrush and paintbrush tools were used to touch up the alpha channel with black and white paint, getting rid of unwanted gray pixels.

The completed alpha channel was loaded as a selection, and Image, Adjust, Variations was used to change the overall color and lighting.

- **To Select only the light, medium, or dark colors,** choose Highlights, Midtones, or Shadows. Again, there's no opportunity to make adjustments to these ranges.

- The **Invert box** provides a way **to select a multicolored subject on a plain background:** Use the Color Range eyedropper to select the background, and then click the Invert box to reverse the selection.

Using a Color Channel as a Starting Point

Photoshop stores color information in individual color channels, such as the Red, Green, and Blue values of an RGB image. Often the contrast between a subject and its surroundings is a lot more pronounced in one of the color channels than in the others.

To use a color channel as a starting point for making a selection, look for a channel where the subject is very light and the surrounding area very dark, or vice versa. Then copy that channel to make an alpha channel and use the Levels command to increase the contrast between the areas you want to select and those you want to leave unselected. (This technique is illustrated at the left.)

SELECTING BY SHAPE

If the subject you want to select is not distinctly different in color from its surroundings, then using the magic wand, the magic eraser, the Color Range command, or a color channel won't be effective, so you may want to select it by shape. In that case the marquee tools, the lassos, and the pens are the tools you'll need to choose from. (Since the magnetic lasso, magnetic pen, background eraser, and Extract command employ both color and shape, they are covered in "Selecting by Shape *and* Color" on page 71, rather than here with the completely "hand-operated" tools.)

Selecting Geometric Shapes — The Marquees

To "frame" a selection, use one of the marquee tools: the rectangular marquee or the ellipse. The marquee tools offer a variety of options for selecting.

- The default mode for the marquee tools is to start the selection from the edge. But many times you have better control of exactly what you select if you draw the selection from the center out. **To start a selection at its center,** press and hold the Alt/Option key at any time while you're drawing the marquee.

- **To select a square or circular area,** constrain the rectangular or elliptical marquee by holding down the Shift key as you drag.

- **To make a selection of a particular height-to-width ratio,** double-click on either of the marquee tools to open the Marquee Options palette, choose Constrained Aspect Ratio for

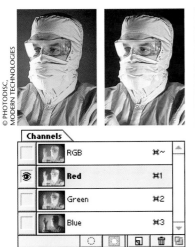

For a vignette effect with a hard or soft (feathered) border, use the rectangular or elliptical marquee.

To select an area that has a complex outline and shares colors with its surroundings so it's hard to select by color, use the lasso tool.

Holding down the Alt/Option key lets you switch between dragging the lasso in its freeform mode and clicking it as a polygon lasso.

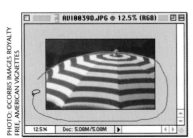

With the Alt/Option key held down, you can click or drag the lasso outside the boundaries of the image, to make sure your selection doesn't miss any pixels at the edges.

the Style, and set a particular height-to-width ratio. Now the marquee will make selections of those proportions.

- **To make a selection of a specific size:** If you want to make a selection of a specific measurement **in pixels,** choose Fixed Size for the Style, and enter the Width and Height measurements in pixels.

To size the selection **in inches or centimeters,** build the selection boundary in the upper left corner of the image: Choose Normal for the Style in the Marquee Options palette. Turn on the rulers (Ctrl/⌘-R), drag Guides into the image from the rulers, and align them at the measurements you want. For instance, if you want a horizontal 3 x 2-inch selection, drag a Guide from the top ruler and align it with the 2-inch mark on the vertical ruler; drag a guide from the side ruler and align it with the 3-inch mark on the horizontal ruler. Turn on Snap To Guides (View, Snap To Guides) and drag the marquee from the upper left corner of the image until it snaps to the Guides. Now turn off Snap To Guides and move the selection boundary (put the cursor inside it and drag) until it surrounds the area you want to select.

- **To make a soft-edged selection,** you can set the Feather in the Marquee Options palette before you make the selection, or make the selection and then apply the Select, Feather command (see "Feathering a Selection" on page 67 for more information).

- You can **adjust the position of a selection marquee** either while you're drawing it or afterwards. If, for instance, you start to draw a marquee from the middle but find that it's developing a little off-center, you can **hold down the spacebar** while you drag to move it, and then release the spacebar and continue to drag to finish the selection.

To reposition a completed selection boundary without moving any of the pixels inside it, put the selection tool's cursor inside the selection and drag.

Selecting Irregular Shapes — The Lassos

To select a multicolored area with a complex boundary, especially if the thing you want to select shares colors with its

SELECTING WITH THE GRID

Photoshop's nonprinting Grid makes it easy to create geometric selections that were once difficult. For instance, with the Grid it's easy to draw a set of same-size, aligned selections by using marquee tools: Choose View, Show Grid to display the grid, and View, Snap To Grid to make the Grid "sticky," so the motion of the tools will be controlled by the grid. Choose a marquee tool, line up its cursor with a grid point, and drag to draw a boundary starting from an edge, or Alt/Option-drag to draw from the center. To add another selection, line up the selection tool with another grid point, hold down the Shift key so the old selection will also stay active while you add this new one, and drag again.

Antialiasing smooths a selection's edge without softening it as feathering does, making the edge pixels partly transparent so you don't get "stairsteps" that would be caused by fully opaque pixels along curves and angles in the selection border. When the antialiased selection is pasted into its new surroundings, these partly clear pixels pick up color from the ones they're pasted on top of, so they make a smooth transition between the colors on the two sides of the selection border.

The rectangular marquee, with its straight-sided selections, doesn't need antialiasing. For the other selection tools, you can turn antialiasing on or off.

Antialiasing (right) looks blurry close up, but it smooths the appearance of edges.

To make a selection that's partly sharp-edged and partly feathered, set the Feather in the selection tool's Options palette and make the feathered selection first; then set the Feather to 0 and add the unfeathered selection by holding down the Shift key as you select. (If, instead, you make the sharp-edged selection first and then the feathered, the feather softens the junction of the two selections.)

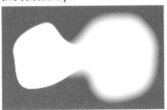

The feathered selection was made first; then the sharp-edged selection was added.

surroundings, you may have to hand-draw the selection border with the plain lasso tool or the polygon lasso.

- Clicking a **series of short line segments with the polygon lasso** is often an easier and more accurate way **to define a smooth curve** than trying to trace the edge by dragging the lasso.

- Holding down the **Shift key** as you use the **polygon lasso** restricts its movement to **vertical, horizontal, or 45° diagonal.**

- Holding down the **Alt/Option key** lets you **operate the tool as either** the lasso or the polygon lasso, switching back and forth between them.

There's another advantage of holding down the Alt/Option key: Holding down the key **keeps the selection from closing up** if you accidentally let go of the mouse button before you've finished selecting. If you make a mistake, you can **"unravel" the selection boundary** you're drawing, holding down the Delete key as well as the Alt/Option key until you get back to the "good part." And if you want to **make sure your lasso selection extends all the way to the edges** of the image without missing any pixels, you can hold down the Alt/Option key and click the tool outside the image.

A feathered edge can be useful for making a "seamless" change when part of an image is selected, modified, and then released back into its original unmodified surroundings. Feathering extends the selection outward but at less than full opacity so that some of the surrounding image is included. At the same time the opacity of the image is also reduced for a distance inside the selection border. It's the Feather Radius that determines how far into and outside of the selection border this transition extends.

- **To feather a lasso or marquee selection as you make it,** first double-click the tool in the toolbox to open its Options palette so you can enter a Feather setting. Then make the selection.

- If you forget to set the Feather ahead of time, or if the selection method you used didn't have a Feather option, **you can feather the selection after you've made it** (but before you move or change it): With the selection active choose Select, Feather and set the Feather Radius.

The Type Mask Tools

Photoshop 5/5.5's type tools provide access to fonts, so you can incorporate type into images. There are two main kinds of type tool, each with horizontal and vertical forms:

- The **plain type tools** let you set type horizontally (the way it's typically set) or vertically. The type appears on a new layer, and it stays "live" and editable until you decide to render it.

- The **type mask,** or **type selection, tools** — the two "T's" made of dashed lines in the tool palette — make type-shaped

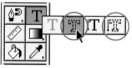
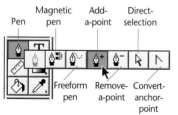

Photoshop 5/5.5's type mask tools let you select type-shaped areas of an image. The tool with the downward-pointing arrow sets the type in vertical columns instead of in the typical horizontal format.

The pen tools' pop-out toolbar includes seven tools. From left to right they are the pen (for drawing a path by placing anchor points to define a Bezier curve), the magnetic pen (for automatically drawing a Bezier path around an item that contrasts with the background), the freeform pen (for drawing a Bezier path by dragging), the add-a-point tool (for adding an anchor point between existing points to reshape a curve), the remove-a-point tool (for deleting an anchor point), the direct-selection tool (hollow arrow; for moving anchor points or curve segments) and the convert-anchor-point tool (for changing the nature of the joint at an anchor point).

selections horizontally or vertically. (See "Type Layers" on page 86 for pointers on Photoshop 5/5.5's new typesetting abilities for both the type mask tools and the plain type tools.)

For most type tasks, using one of the plain type tools to make an editable Type layer will produce better results than using the type masks. However, there are at least two jobs for which a type mask tool can be more efficient than starting with a Type layer:

- **To cut type shapes out of a texture** or other image, set type with the type mask tool to make the selection.

  To turn the selection into **type-shaped holes** in the layer, simply press Delete.

  Or, to keep the type and **remove the part of the image that's outside the type,** select the inverse (Ctrl/⌘-Shift-I) and press Delete.

  To preserve the image layer intact and put the **image-filled type on a layer of its own,** press Ctrl/⌘-J (for Layer, New, Layer Via Copy).

  To **cut the type to a new layer,** leaving a type-shaped hole in the original layer, press Ctrl/⌘-Shift-J (for Layer, New, Layer Via Cut).

- **To make a layer mask** for the active layer, use a type mask tool to set your characters and then click the Add Layer Mask icon on the left at the bottom of the Layers palette to make a white-type-on-black-background mask.

  To make a **reverse mask** that hides the type shapes and lets the surrounding image show, Alt/Option-click the layer mask icon. (For more about how to use layer masks, see the "Layer Masks" section of this chapter, starting on page 84.)

Selecting with Curves — The Pen Tool

The pen tool has a pop-out toolbar for choosing from the seven path-drawing and path-editing tools. Pressing the "P" key cycles through these seven tools. The Paths palette (opened by choosing Window, Show Paths) includes everything necessary to name these smoothly curving paths (called Bezier curves), and to save them, to fill or stroke them, turn them into selections, combine one with an existing selection, or turn a selection into a path. The filling, stroking, and selecting functions are found in the icons at the bottom of the palette, along with icons for creating a new path from a selection and for removing a path. Everything you can do on the palette itself you can also do by choosing from the palette's pop-out menu; in addition, the menu lets you designate a **clipping path** for "clipping" away the surrounding image to silhouette the selection for export to a page layout program, for example.

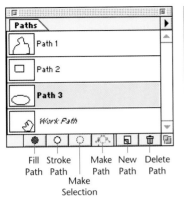

The Paths palette, for storing and stroking paths, converting selections to paths and vice versa, and making clipping paths (via the palette's pop-out menu)

Clicking to make corner points

Dragging to make smooth points

Closing a path

Adding a point

Deleting a point

Changing the type of point

STOPPING

The **freeform pen** ends a path as soon as you release the mouse button.

With the standard **pen tool**, you can end a path before closing it by holding down the Ctrl/⌘ key to toggle to the direct selection tool, clicking, then releasing the key to toggle back to the pen.

With the **magnetic pen**, as with the magnetic lasso, end a path by pressing the Enter/Return key.

The shape of the Bezier curve drawn by the pen tool is controlled by the positions of **anchor points** and **direction lines,** or "handles," which direct the curve as it comes out of the anchor points. The **freeform pen** tool, added in Photoshop version 5, lets you operate the tool as you would a pencil, by dragging to draw a path; control points are placed automatically. Tips for using the **magnetic pen tool** can be found in the "Selecting by Shape *and* Color" section, in the tip "How the Magnetic Tools Work" on page 71. Here are some quick tips for drawing with the standard Bezier pen tool and for editing any path, no matter how it was drawn:

Drawing a path (either an open-ended path or a closed shape) with the pen tool is done by placing a series of anchor points:

- **To place a corner point** where the line can change direction abruptly without a smooth curve, click with the pen. Placing two corner points one after another draws a **straight line**.

- **To create a smooth (curve) point,** position the pen tool's cursor where you want the point and then hold the mouse button down and drag to position the handles that control the curve as it approaches and leaves the point.

- **To constrain the position of the next corner or smooth point** to any 45° or 90° angle, hold down the Shift key as you place the point.

- **To close a path,** move the pen icon close to the starting point; when you see a little circle to the right of the pen icon, click.

To reshape a path after it's drawn, you can:

- **Move a point:** Drag it with the direct-selection tool (the arrow).

- **Select a control point or a curve segment so you can move it:** Click with the direct-selection tool. Shift-click to select more.

- **Add a point:** Click on the curve with the pen+ tool.

- **Remove a point:** Click on that point with the pen– tool.

- **Turn a corner into a smooth point or vice versa:** Click it with the convert-anchor-point tool (the caret).

STAYING AHEAD OF THE CURVE

To be able to see the next segment of the pen path as you're drawing it, you can put the pen tool into "rubber band" mode: Double-click the pen in the toolbox to open the Pen Tool Options palette; click the Rubber Band checkbox (A). Now when you draw you'll be able to see how the curve is shaping up before you click to place the next point (B). If you're just learning how Bezier curves work, this can be a big help.

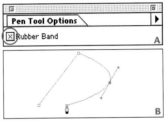

- Turn any path tool into the **direct selection arrow** by holding down the **Ctrl/⌘** key.
- Press **Shift-P** to toggle through the path tools.

SETTING PATH TOLERANCE

Whether you're adept with the pen tool or not, sometimes it's easier to use a selection tool or command. Use the selection as the starting point for a path, moving or adding points to make the path precisely fit the shape you want.

With a selection active, choosing Make Work Path from the Paths palette's pop-out menu brings up a dialog box that lets you set Tolerance. This will specify how closely the Bezier curve will trace the selection boundary when the selection is converted to a path. A tolerance of "0" makes a very accurate and tight-fitting, though possibly "jaggy" and complex path. The higher the Tolerance value, the looser and smoother the path, but the less likely it is that the path will create a limitcheck error on output if it's exported to another program. As a rule of thumb:

- To draw a path to store a **selection,** use a tight setting (**0–1**) unless the shape is geometric or is composed of smooth curves.
- If the path is being created as a **clipping path,** use a setting of **2.**

```
┌─────────────────────────────┐
│      Make Work Path         │
├─────────────────────────────┤
│  Tolerance: 2.0  pixels  ┌──────┐  │
│                          │  OK  │  │
│                          └──────┘  │
│                          ┌──────┐  │
│                          │Cancel│  │
│                          └──────┘  │
└─────────────────────────────┘
```

- **Reshape a curve by moving one handle independently of its mate:** Drag on the handle with the convert-direction-point tool. If you then want to move the other handle, use the direct-selection tool.

You can **Copy** (Ctrl/⌘-C) or **cut** (Ctrl/⌘-X) a path to the clipboard and then **paste** it (Ctrl/⌘-V).

To duplicate a path, hold down the Alt/Option key, and drag with the direct-selection tool to position the copy where you want it. Hold down the Shift key as well to constrain the motion.

To activate a path, click its name in the Paths palette.

To move a path, with the path active (click it with the direct-selection tool or click its name in the Paths palette to make it active), Alt/Option-click with the direct-selection tool to select all the points in the path. Then release the Alt/Option key and drag the path to move it without duplicating it or changing its shape.

To save a Work Path so that it can be stored individually and can be made into a clipping path, double-click its name in the palette.

To convert a selection to a path, click the Make Work Path icon, third from the right at the bottom of the palette.

To convert a path to a selection (or add it to or subtract it from an existing selection), use one of the shortcuts in "Fingers and Thumbnails" on page 77.

To stroke a path with the Foreground color, choose a painting tool and press the Enter key or click the Stroke Path icon, second from the left at the bottom of the Paths palette.

To fill a path with the Foreground color, click the Fill Path icon, farthest left at the bottom of the Paths palette.

ROUNDED RECTANGLES (V. 5)

The pen tool snaps to the Grid — both for placing points and for positioning direction lines. This makes possible elements like symmetrical scalloped and wavy borders and the elusive round-cornered rectangle that's so popular for navigational buttons. For each corner, click to place the first point where you want the curved corner to begin and drag to the matching around-the-corner point to make the curve. You can control the roundness of the corners by setting the Grid size (File, Preferences, Guides & Grid). Use a larger grid for bigger, rounder corners, a smaller grid for tighter, squarer ones.

ROUNDED RECTANGLES (V. 5.5)

When you need a rounded rectangle in a Photoshop 5.5 file, you can call on ImageReady 2.0: Use Photoshop's Jump To button at the bottom of the toolbox to move the file to ImageReady. Then use the rounded rectangle tool to draw the figure and the Edit, Free Transform command to scale and otherwise modify it. (In Image-Ready the rectangle is stored as vector information rather than pixels, so distorting doesn't deteriorate its edges.) When you click ImageReady's Jump To button to return to Photoshop, the layer will be pixels, not a path.

Magnetic Pen Options

Curve Fit: 2 pixels

Pen Width: 10 pixels

Frequency: 20   Edge Contrast: 10 %

Stylus: ☑Pressure

CBU0022D/1k.TIF @ 100% (RGB)

100%   Doc: 4.3M/4.3M

The magnetic pen (shown here) and magnetic lasso automatically find edges to help you create a path or selection boundary. In Photoshop 5.5 a "+" marks the center of the cursor, to help you center the tool on the edge you want to trace. The Options palette for each tool lets you tell the tool how tightly to fit the curve, how distinct the edge is, and how often to anchor the path or selection boundary. You can change the settings as you work, and you can override the automatic tracing and operate the tool by hand where it's necessary for a good fit.

SELECTING BY SHAPE *AND* COLOR

The original lasso and pen tools were designed to manually draw a selection boundary around an element that didn't have good color contrast with its surroundings and thus couldn't be selected by color. Photoshop 5/5.5's **magnetic lasso** and **magnetic pen** were designed to allow you to take advantage of the color contrast anywhere it exists, but to also substitute manual selection in areas where the contrast breaks down. Photoshop 5.5 became even more intelligent about selecting by shape and color with the addition of the **Extract** command and the **background eraser.**

How the Magnetic Tools Work

To operate a magnetic tool — lasso or pen — click the center of the circular cursor somewhere on the edge you want to trace and then "float" the cursor along, moving the mouse or stylus without pressing its button. The tool will automatically follow the "edge" created by color contrast. The way the tool performs depends on the settings in its Options palette, which can be opened simply by choosing the tool and pressing the Enter/Return key. Parameters that can be set in the Options palette for both the magnetic lasso and the magnetic pen include Width, Frequency, and Edge Contrast.

Width is the radius of the area where the tool looks for the edge as you float it along. The smaller the Width, the more discriminating the tool is about where the edge is, but the slower the tool operates and the more eye-mouse coordination is required.

- If you're tracing a **well-defined edge,** use a large Width and move the tool quickly.

- To avoid confusing the tool **if there are other edges** or distinct objects near the edge you want to trace, use a small Width and keep the cursor centered on the edge you want to trace.

- For a **soft edge** with little contrast, use a smaller Width and trace carefully. Click to add points when there's *no* contrast.

- You can **change the Width** by typing a number into the Options palette, or use your free hand to operate the "[" and "]" keys while drawing, to lower and raise the Width setting as the nature of the edge changes.

Frequency specifies how often a **fastening point** is laid down. With either tool, if you run into an area where the tool can't do a good job automatically, you can **force a point** by clicking, and with the magnetic lasso you can also **hand-draw the boundary** by dragging. *Fastening points* are not exactly the same as the final *anchor points* in the path in the case of the magnetic pen. For both the magnetic pen and the magnetic lasso they simply fasten the path or boundary and determine how far it will be "unraveled"

When you use the magnetic pen or lasso, it's important to have good contrast at the edge you're tracing. If the image you're working with doesn't offer good contrast — either the contrast is poor overall, or the contrast varies along different parts of the edge, here are some things that can help:

• Boost the contrast by adding a Levels or Curves Adjustment layer. You can turn the visibility of the Adjustment layer on and off as needed, and when you've finished the tracing, you can delete it, leaving the contrast of the image unchanged. (For info on how to use Adjustment layers, see "Adjustment Layers: The Ultimate in Flexibility" on page 102.)

• Inspect the color channels to see if one of them shows better edge contrast. You can look at a channel by pressing the Ctrl/⌘ key and the number for the channel — for instance, 1 for Red, 2 for Green, and 3 for Blue in an RGB file. If you find one with good contrast, use the magnetic tool on it. Then press Ctrl/⌘-tilde (that's the "~" key) to return to the main (color composite) channel.

if you decide to undo your work. For both tools, pressing the **Delete** key will **"unravel,"** backing up the cursor in one-fastening-point increments.

• For **complex, detailed edges,** use **more fastening points** (strangely, you use a lower Frequency setting for the magnetic pen but a higher setting for the magnetic lasso).

• For **smooth edges** you can use **fewer fastening points** (a higher Frequency for the magnetic pen, a lower setting for the magnetic lasso).

Edge Contrast specifies how much contrast the tool should look for in finding the edge.

• Use a **high setting** to select a subject that **contrasts strongly** with its surroundings.

• Use a **low setting** if the edge is **soft.**
    For the magnetic pen you can also set the **Curve Fit** (see the "Setting Path Tolerance" tip on page 70). For the magnetic lasso you can set the **Feather,** or softness of the selection boundary (see "Feathering a Selection" on page 67).

Extract

Unlike most other selecting tools, the Extract command doesn't produce marching ants. Instead it isolates a part of an image by erasing all other pixels on that layer, leaving transparency in their place. (The nature of layers and transparency is discussed later in the chapter, in the "Layers" section, starting on page 79.)

Choosing Image, Extract opens a dialog box that lets you set the stage for Photoshop to do its "intelligent masking." The Extract interface can be confusing, but here's one fairly direct way to proceed:

1 With the **edge highlighter** tool selected, set the Brush Size in the Tool Options section. Choose a size that's big enough so you can easily drag it around the edge of the area you want to isolate (the subject). But keep in mind that anything within this edge is fair game for Extract to make fully or partially transparent. Try to keep this transition area tight. And try to keep most of the highlight on the *outside* of the object. You don't want to give the Extract command permission to encroach *into* the subject you're selecting. This kind of mistake will be much harder to repair than if you have extra background left outside the edge, where the extra material can be removed with the background eraser tool, as described on page 73.

2 Drag the highlighter around the edge to enclose the subject. If the area you want to select extends to the edge of the image, you can draw just to the edge — you don't have to drag around the border. You can use the bracket keys as described in "Two-Handed Selection" on page 71 to change the tool's footprint as you drag.

The Extract command gives you several options for viewing the silhouetted subject. In addition to the default transparent background (shown on page 60), you can choose black, white (shown here at the top), or 50% gray, or view the selection as a black-and-white mask (bottom), or choose your own color for a contrasting background that lets you better inspect the edge.

A COPY FOR SAFEKEEPING

Using the **Extract** command, the **background eraser,** or the **magic eraser** is a "destructive" process — that is, it changes the layer by eliminating pixels. Therefore, before you start to use one of these isolation methods, it's a good idea to preserve an intact copy of the layer you'll be working on, so that you have an untouched original if you need to go back to it for some reason. The best way is to duplicate the layer: In the Layers palette, drag the layer's thumbnail to the New Layer icon in the center at the bottom of the palette.

3 Choose the dialog box's **fill tool** and click inside the highlight-bordered subject area.

4 Click the **Preview** button to see the extracted subject. You can zoom in for a closer look at the edge with the dialog box's **magnifier** tool. To check the quality of the edge, you can change the preview's background color by choosing from the pop-out **Show** list in the Preview section of the dialog box; this is a good way **to check the integrity of the edge.** You can also compare the extracted subject with the original by choosing from the **View** settings.

NO PREVIEW BUTTON?

The Preview button in the Extract dialog box is dimmed and inoperable unless one of two conditions is met:

- Both a highlight (green by default) and a fill (blue by default) are visible in the image.
- Or a highlight is visible and Force Foreground is turned on in the Extraction section of the dialog box; in this case, Extract uses the highlight as both highlight and fill, extracting anything covered by the highlight and eliminating everything else.

If the Preview shows that the extracted subject isn't to your liking, you have several choices for making corrections:

- If the Extract process has left **problems at the edge** — extra pixels outside the edge, or semitransparency where the subject's edge should be solid — you may be able to fix it by smoothing or narrowing the highlight: With the **edge highlighter tool, click on the edge** of the subject to show the existing edge highlight. Now you can increase the **Smooth** setting in the Extraction area of the dialog box. Or to add to the highlight, use the **edge highlighter** tool. To take away from the highlight, use the edge highlighter tool with the Alt/Option key held down, or use the **eraser.** When your edge repairs are complete, **use the fill tool again,** and then you'll be able to click the **Preview** button again to take another look.

- If the edge looks so sloppy that you want **to start over** completely, hold down the Alt/Option key to change the Cancel button to **Reset,** click the button, enter a **new Brush Size,** and start again.

- If the edge itself looks good but there are areas that are completely inside the edge but that need to be eliminated — such as **small patches** of sky showing through the leaves of a tree you've selected — you don't need to highlight the edge of each patch. Instead, click OK to close the Extract dialog box and then use the **background eraser** as described next.

Background Eraser

Photoshop 5.5's background eraser tool, which shares a spot with the other erasers in the toolbox, is sort of like the Extract command

If the area you want to Extract is small, fairly uniform in color, and has an intricate boundary, cover the entire subject with highlighter instead of using a fill. Then click the Force Foreground option in the Extraction area of the Extract dialog box, and click the eyedropper tool on the subject. (Even though it's covered with the highlight color, go ahead and click it.) The highlighter will act as both edge and fill.

Ultimatte KnockOut is a stand-alone image extraction and masking program that goes beyond the selecting capabilities of Photoshop 5.5. For silhouetting subjects with difficult edges, like a photo of a glass or of gauze or anything else that you can't successfully isolate with Photoshop's Extract command, KnockOut is definitely worth a try.

With Ultimatte KnockOut, you define what's definitely inside and what's definitely outside the part of the image you want to isolate, and the program very successfully deals with the "border area" in between. It provides tools for identifying and selecting complex color transitions and soft edges such as shadows.

in a wand. It erases the pixels you drag it over, leaving transparency instead. A versatile tool, it's good for "cleaning up" after an extraction. If you choose the tool, you'll see a "+" in the center of a brush footprint. The "+" indicates the tool's "hot spot," and the footprint around it defines the tool's "reconnaissance area." The footprint you see is determined by what brush tip is selected in the Brushes palette. Pressing the "[" or "]" key changes the brush tip, stepping toward the beginning or the end of the Brushes palette.

When you click the background eraser tool, it samples the color under the hot spot. And as you drag the tool, it evaluates the color of pixels within the reconnaissance area, to see which ones should be erased. Which pixels get erased depends on how you customize the settings in the Background Eraser Options palette, opened by pressing the Enter/Return key:

Tolerance affects the range of colors that are erased:

- A **high Tolerance** setting erases a **broader range of color** than a low setting.
- With a setting of **0,** pixels of only a **single color** are erased — the specific color under the hot spot when you click.

For the type of **Sampling,** you can choose Continuous, Once, or Background Swatch.

- **To erase every color you drag the eraser's hot spot over,** choose **Continuous** sampling, which repeatedly updates the color to be erased.
- **To erase only the color that's under the hot spot when you first push the button down** on your mouse or stylus, choose **Once.** When you push the button down, the eraser will choose the color to erase. It will erase this color as you drag, until you release the mouse button. When you push the button down again, it will resample and choose the new color that's now under the hot spot.
- **To set a single specific color or color family to be erased,** regardless of when you press and release the mouse button, choose **Background Swatch.** Set the Background color by clicking the Background square in the tool palette and either specifying a color in the Color Picker or clicking in your image to sample a color. This type of sampling, combined with adjustments to the Tolerance settings, provides a great amount of control.

For the **eraser type,** you can choose Discontiguous, Contiguous, or Find Edges.

- **To erase any occurrence of the color anywhere within the brush's footprint** as it moves along, choose **Discontiguous.**
- To erase **only pixels whose color continues uninterrupted** from the pixel under the eraser's hot spot, choose **Contiguous.**

The Options palette for the background eraser tool is complex, but knowing how to mix and match the settings makes the tool a very powerful and flexible one. The Protect Foreground Color option lets you sample and protect one color at a time as you erase.

- **Find Edges** is like Contiguous, but it pays special attention to **preserving sharp edges.**

STORING SELECTIONS: ALPHA CHANNELS

Paths aren't the only way to store a selection in a stable form. While paths are good for storing hard-edged selections, Photoshop's alpha channels provide out-of-the-way storage for either hard-edged selections or soft-edged masks. And the Quick Mask is a simple way to quickly stabilize and store a selection temporarily so you can edit it.

Alpha Channels — For Permanent Storage

Alpha channels provide a kind of subfile for storing selection boundaries so you can load them back into the image and use them later. A selection stored in an alpha channel becomes a mask, with white areas that can be loaded as an active selection, black areas that protect parts of the image where changes shouldn't apply, and gray areas that expose the image to changes proportionally to the lightness of the gray.

An alpha channel is more versatile than a path because it can store soft-edged as well as hard-edged masks. But for hard-edged selections, a path is more efficient because it takes much less memory than an alpha channel.

A Photoshop file can have as many as 24 color and alpha channels in total. So an RGB file, for example, since it has three channels tied up in the three individual colors, can have up to 21 alphas, each providing a way to recall or create a particular selection independently of any other selection.

To make an alpha channel from a selection:

- With a selection active (marching ants) click the Save Selection As Channel icon, second from the left at the bottom of the Channels palette. To name the channel as you make it, Alt/Option-click the icon to open the Channel Options dialog box.

- Or choose Select, Save Selection.

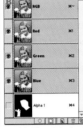

In this "hand-tinting" project we saved the skin selection (A) in an alpha channel (B). Then we could make a rough selection of the dress, without tracing the neck or arm (C). We Ctrl-Alt-clicked (Windows) or ⌘-Option-clicked (Mac) the alpha channel in the Channels palette to subtract it from the rough selection so we could color the dress (D).

To load an alpha channel as a selection:

- Ctrl/⌘-click on its name in the Channels palette. You can also add it to or subtract it from a currently active selection using the techniques described in "Fingers and Thumbnails" on page 77.

- Or choose Select, Load Selection and choose the document and channel you want to load. This command gives you the added ability to load an alpha channel from any open document of the same pixel dimensions as the one you're working on.

Quick Mask — For "Painting" Selections

By making a selection and then clicking the Quick Mask icon (on the right side near the bottom of the toolbox), you can turn an active selection into a clear area in a semitransparent mask. You can see both image and mask, so you can do some fairly subtle mask modification. As you edit it with painting tools or filters, the Quick Mask remains stable — like an alpha channel or layer mask. When you've finished modifying the mask, you can turn it back into a selection boundary by clicking the Standard mode icon (to the left of the Quick Mask icon). The use of Quick Mask is demonstrated in step 3 of "Retouching a Photo" on page 135 and step 1 of "Casting a Shadow" on page 280.

MODIFYING SELECTIONS

Photoshop provides several ways to make a selection larger or smaller, or change its position or shape. In addition to the techniques presented in "Adding to a Selection" and "Subtracting from a Selection" (below) be sure to see the **"Fingers and Thumbnails"** tip on page 77 for quick, easy-to-remember shortcuts.

Adding to a Selection

You can enlarge a selection in any of the following ways:

- **To make a "hand-drawn" addition to the current selection,** hold down the **Shift key** and use any selection tool to surround the area you want to add.

- **To expand a selection outward,** picking up more pixels at the edge, use **Select, Modify, Expand.**

- **To add pixels that are similar in color and adjacent to the current selection,** you can choose **Select, Grow.** Each time you use the command, the range of colors selected gets larger. The amount that the color range grows is controlled by the Tolerance setting in the Magic Wand Options palette.

- **To add all pixels in the image that are similar in color** to the pixels in the current selection, choose **Select, Similar.** The Tolerance setting in the Magic Wand Options palette determines how similar the additional pixels have to be. A setting of

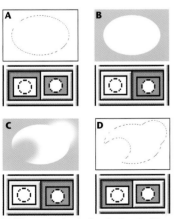

Making a selection in Standard mode (A) converting to Quick Mask mode (B), changing the selection mask by adding to the mask with black paint and removing from the mask with white paint (C), and turning the altered mask back into a selection (D)

"0" adds only pixels that are exactly the same colors as pixels in the existing selection.

Subtracting from a Selection

- **To remove part of the current selection,** hold down the **Alt/Option key** and use any selection tool to surround the area you want to remove.

- **To contract a selection inward,** dropping the edge pixels, choose **Select, Modify, Contract.**

- **To deselect part of a selection — or some parts of a multipart selection —** hold down the **Alt/Option and Shift keys** and use the lasso or marquee to surround the parts you want to keep. This is called selecting an **intersection,** the area where an existing selection and the new selection overlap.

Cleaning Up a Selection

Sometimes, despite the most careful selecting, the selected part of the image retains a tinge of background color, visible around the edge. To get rid of this unwanted "fringe," you can use the commands of the Layer, Matting submenu. Note that these commands work only after the selected material is separated from its surrounding pixels, by being made into a layer of its own, for instance.

- **To eliminate an "edging" picked up by an image selected from a black (or white) background,** choose Layer, Matting, Remove Black Matte (or Remove White Matte). Photoshop lightens dark pixels (or darkens light pixels) that it finds at the edges.

- **To remove edging in a color other than black or white,** try the Layer, Matting, Defringe command. This will "push" color from the inside outward into the edge pixels. Be careful, though — using a Defringe setting of more than 1 or 2 pixels can create "spokes" or "rays" of color at the edge.

- Besides the Layer, Matting command, **another way to remove color edging** is to **"choke"** the layer, to shrink the edges in just slightly, so what's causing the edging is excluded. Load the layer's transparency mask as a selection by Ctrl/⌘-clicking its thumbnail in the Layers palette. Next choose the Select, Modify, Contract command to shrink the selection, then invert the selection (Ctrl/⌘-Shift-I) and press Delete to remove the troublesome edge.

Moving Selections

Selection tools both create and move selection boundaries. The move tool is what moves pixels. It can move the selected pixels if there's a selection active. Or it can move an entire layer — or a set of linked layers — if there's no active selection.

Sometimes you don't notice a "fringe" of background pixels surrounding a silhouetted subject until you've layered it on top of a new background (left). But it isn't too late to remove it. Choose Layer, Matting, Defringe before you merge the layer with the composite. The Defringe command pushes color from the inside of the selection outward to replace the edge pixels, thus eliminating the fringe.

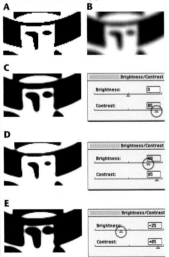

- **To move the selection boundary (the marching ants) without moving any pixels,** with any selection tool active, put the cursor inside the selection boundary and drag. (For moving a marquee selection while you're in the process of drawing it, hold down the spacebar as you make the move, then release the spacebar to continue forming the selection.)

- **To move the selected pixels,** regardless of what tool is active at the moment, press the "V" key to switch to the move tool, and drag. Or hold down the Ctrl/⌘ key to toggle to the move tool temporarily, drag to move the selected pixels, and release the Ctrl/⌘ key to switch back to the tool you were using.

- **To constrain the movement of the selection border or selected pixels to horizontal, vertical, or a 45° diagonal,** use the Shift key. This technique works with either a selection tool or the move tool. But if you use it with a selection tool, you have *wait to press the Shift key until after you start the dragging process.*

- **To move a selection boundary or selected pixels 1 screen pixel at time,** choose the move tool or a selection tool and use the arrow keys on the keyboard. Hold down the Shift key with the arrows to move a selection **10 screen pixels at a time**.

Transforming Selections

Starting in version 5, Photoshop added the ability to scale, rotate, skew, and otherwise distort selection boundaries (marching ants). To transform a selection boundary without disturbing any pixels, choose **Select, Transform Selection.** You can now:

- Shift-drag a corner handle of the Transform box to **scale the selection boundary proportionally.**

- Drag one of the handles to **scale disproportionately.**

- Drag in a clockwise or counterclockwise direction outside the Transform box **to rotate.** (To change the center of rotation, drag on the target circle in the middle of the box.)

- Access the **Skew, Distort, Perspective, Flip,** and **Numeric** transformations by

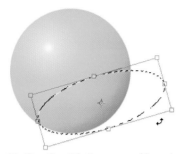

The Transform Selection command is great for angling and skewing selections. Here it's used in the process of shaping a shadow. We Ctrl/⌘-clicked the layer's thumbnail to load the transparency mask for the sphere. Then we chose Select, Transform Selection. Dragging inside the transform box moved the selection, dragging handles inward and outward scaled it, and dragging outside a corner handle rotated it. It's also possible to skew or otherwise distort the selection: Right-click (Windows) or Control-click (Mac) to open a context-specific menu, where you can choose the transformation you want. When you've finished, double-click inside the Transform box to accept the changes.

BIG DATA

If an image element extends beyond the frame of the image, the part that "hangs out" will be retained, even if you make other changes to the image or close the file. It stays intact until you crop the image or flatten the file. This provides a great deal of freedom to experiment with image composition, since you don't have to worry about losing the parts you can't see.

But having pieces of images sticking out will add to the file size. So when you've settled on a final arrangement for your montage, select all (Ctrl/⌘-A) and choose Image, Crop to trim off the outlying pixels to reduce the file size but keep the layers intact. Or choose Flatten Image from the Layers palette's pop-out menu to trim and flatten in one step.

moving the cursor inside the Transform box, right-clicking (Windows) or Control-clicking (Mac), and choosing from the context-sensitive menu that appears.

You can make as many transformations as you like. When you've finished, press **Enter/Return** or double-click inside the Transform box to accept the changes. Or press **Ctrl/⌘-period** or the **Escape** key to close the Transform box without implementing any of the changes.

LAYERS

A Photoshop image file can have as many as 100 *layers,* unless it's limited to a lower number by the RAM in your computer. Layers act like a stack of transparent plastic sheets, ready to accept pixels. (Adjustment layers are different. They hold masks and instructions about color or tone. They are described separately on page 88.)

Layers let you keep individual parts of an image separate — and manipulate them singly — as you build a composite image. Once you're sure you like the image, you can combine the layers into a single layer. Although layers can be "memory-hungry," they provide amazing flexibility in building composite images. A layer can have several parts:

- **Nontransparent (opaque or partly opaque) pixels,** where there is image information

- **Transparent areas,** where there's no image information

- A **transparency mask,** which is the invisible mask information that defines edges between transparent and nontransparent areas of the layer (described on page 83)

- A **layer mask,** which is a mask that affects how the pixels of only that layer contribute to the composite (described on page 84)

- "Live" **type** that remains object-oriented and editable (described on page 86)

    (Transparency masks, layer masks, and type can also define the edges for adding dimensional and lighting treatments with Layer Effects, described on page 87.)

To help you manipulate and keep track of the layers in an image, the Layers palette (Window, Show Layers) shows them in their stacked order.

Working with Layers

Here's a quick summary of what you can do with a layer.

- **Change it independently** of other layers by clicking on its name in the Layers palette to designate it as the active layer and then painting on it or filtering it or otherwise modifying it. Only one layer can be active at a time.

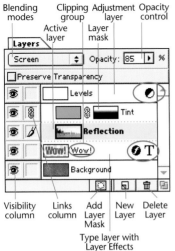

Blending modes — Clipping group — Adjustment layer — Opacity control
Active layer — Layer mask

Layers

Screen | Opacity: 85 | %

☐ Preserve Transparency

Levels

Tint

Reflection

Wow! (Wow!) T

Background

Visibility column | Links column | Add Layer Mask | New Layer | Delete Layer

Type layer with Layer Effects

The Layers palette provides many options for controlling how the layers of an image interact, including the blending modes list, the Opacity setting, visibility icons, and link icons. Within a clipping group, the bottom layer acts as a mask for the layers above. The Type layer's "T" icon lets you double-click to reopen the Type Tool dialog box to edit live type. A Layer Effects icon — the "f" symbol — lets you double-click to open the Effects dialog box to change the special effects settings. Double-click an Adjustment layer's circular icon to change the adjustment settings.

LAYERS SHORTCUTS

Here are some tricks for managing layers by using the Layers palette:

• **To hide a layer or make it visible** (it's a toggle operation), click in the visibility (eye) column.

• **To hide all layers except one,** Alt/Option-click in that layer's eye column; Alt/Option-click again to make all layers visible.

• **To make a layer the active layer,** click on its name or thumbnail.

• **To make a layer active and turn off visibility for all other layers,** Alt/Option-click the layer's name.

• **To make the next layer up (or down) the active layer,** press Alt/Option-] (or Alt/Option-[ ).

• **To change a layer's name or use compositing controls on it,** double-click its name or thumbnail to open the Layer Options dialog box.

• **Make it visible or invisible** by turning on or off its eye icon in the visibility column. Any or all layers can be visible at once.

• **"Slide" it around independently** of the rest of the image by dragging with the move tool in the image window.

• **Link it to other layers** so they move together, by clicking in the column to the right of the eye column.

• **Control its overall transparency** with the Opacity slider (described on page 81).

• **Control how its colors blend** with the layers below by choosing a blending mode (see page 82).

• **Include or exclude pixels from the blend** based on their colors and the colors of the pixels in layers below with the composite controls in the **Layer Options** dialog box (for more about Layer Options, see pages 155 and 156).

• **Hide parts of it** by creating a layer mask (see page 84).

• **Scale, rotate, skew or otherwise distort it** by using the Edit, Transform command, which operates like the Transform Selection command described on pages 78 and 79.

• **Turn it into a mask** for layers above it by including it as the bottom layer in a **clipping group** (described on page 85).

• **Add special effects** such as bevels, shadows, and glows with Layer Effects, introduced on page 87.

• **Combine it** with some or all of the other layers in the stack by merging or flattening (see page 83).

Creating Layers

There's more than one way to add a layer to an image:

• Make a blank (completely transparent) layer by **clicking** or **Alt/Option-clicking the New Layer icon**, in the middle at the bottom of the palette.

• Duplicate an existing layer by dragging its Layers palette **thumbnail to the New Layer icon.**

• Create a layer from the contents of the clipboard with the **Edit, Paste** command (Ctrl/⌘-V).

• Add a layer that's a merged copy of all visible layers by turning on the eye icons in the Layers palette for the layers you want to copy, clicking the New Layer icon to add a new empty layer above them, and choosing **Merge Visible** from the palette's pop-out menu.

• Use the move tool to **drag a layer in from another Photoshop file.**

• Set type with a **type tool**, as described in "Type Layers" on page 86.

You can drag a copy of a selection boundary, a selection, or a layer across your screen from one open Photoshop window to another.

- **To copy a layer from the *active file* into another file,** use the move tool. Start the drag either from the active image's working window (in which case you'll be dragging the *currently active* layer) or from its Layers palette (in which case you can drag any layer you want). Drop the layer into the other file. It will appear in the stack above the currently active layer, and it will become the active layer.
- **Linked layers** will be dragged and dropped *together* if you drag from the working window, but *alone* if you drag from the Layers palette.
- **To copy selected image material from the *active file* into another file,** use the move tool. When you drop the selection into the other file, it will become a new layer.
- **To copy *a selection boundary* into another file,** drag with any selection tool.

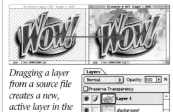

Dragging a layer from a source file creates a new, active layer in the target file

When a selection tool, the move tool, or a type tool is active (selected in the toolbox), pressing the number keys on the keyboard changes the opacity of the active layer (1 is 10%, 2 is 20%, and so on, with 0 being 100%). If you type the numbers quickly, you can be more specific: 56%, 43%, 39%, and so on.

- Copy or cut a selected part of an existing layer by choosing Layer, New, **Layer Via Copy** (Ctrl/⌘-J) or Layer, New, **Layer Via Cut** (Ctrl/⌘-Shift-J).
- **Render** a set of **Layer Effects** into separate layers (see "Layer Effects" on page 87).
- **Drag and drop** an object from an open Photoshop or Adobe Illustrator file or **import** an EPS graphic using File, Place (see Chapter 7).

The tools and commands you need for adding and removing layers, and changing the way they blend with the other layers in the composite are found in the Layers palette itself or in the palette's pop-out menu, or in the main Layer menu. "Exercising Layers," starting on page 90, will give you an opportunity to apply the basics of layer operations before tackling the techniques presented later in the book.

Transparency

Transparency is the essence of layers. Except for the *Background*, an opaque layer at the bottom of the stack, all layers automatically start out transparent. (Even the bottom layer can start out transparent if you set it up that way when you start the New file, or if you open an EPS file that has no background.)

You can see a representation of transparency if you view any transparent layer by itself (by Alt/Option-clicking its eye icon to turn its visibility on while turning off visibility for the other layers). The transparent parts of the layer, represented by a checkerboard pattern, let the layer underneath show through unmodified. If there are no transparent (checkerboard) areas in a layer, it blocks underlying layers from view, or at least modifies the way they look.

When you paint on a layer, the transparent pixels are replaced by ones that have color and opacity values. If the Opacity for the layer is set at less than 100, the pixels are partly transparent. Or if the edge of the element is antialiased or feathered, the pixels at the edge are partly transparent.

The Opacity for the layer as a whole can be controlled with the pop-out **Opacity slider** at the top right side of the Layers palette. The effect of the Opacity setting is cumulative with whatever opacity is already built into the pixels in the layer. For example, if you

By default Photoshop represents transparency on-screen with a gray checkerboard pattern so you can differentiate a transparent background from a solid white one. But you can change the color, size, and tone of the pattern by choosing File, Preferences, Transparency & Gamut.

Normal

Dissolve, 75% Opacity *Multiply*

Screen *Overlay*

Soft Light *Hard Light*

Color Dodge *Color Burn*

Lighten *Darken*

Difference *Exclusion*

Hue *Saturation*

Color *Luminosity*

Photoshop's blending modes are available in the Layers palette, the Options palette for the painting tools, and the dialog boxes for Layer Effects, Fade, Fill, Calculations and Apply Image.

paint a stroke with the Opacity slider in the Paintbrush Options palette set at 50% and then set the layer's Opacity at 50% also, the stroke will have an effective Opacity of 25%. (Chapter 6 tells more about paintbrush controls.)

Blending Modes

Along with the Opacity slider, the blending modes affect how a whole layer interacts with the layers below it in the stack.

If a layer is in **Normal** mode, the color stays normal-looking and doesn't interact with color in the layers underneath.

At full opacity, **Dissolve** mode is just like Normal. But reducing the Opacity setting, instead of pushing all the pixels toward transparency, makes a dither (randomized dot) pattern, with some pixels completely transparent and others at full opacity. The lower the Opacity setting, the more pixels disappear.

The effect of **Multiply** mode is like putting two slides together in the same slide projector and projecting them. Where both of the slides have color, the projected color is darker than either. White is neutral in Multiply mode; that is, the white parts of a layer are like the clear parts of a slide — the white has no effect on the layers below. Multiply mode is good for applying shadows without completely eliminating the color of the shaded areas in the layers underneath and for layering line work over color, as in "Coloring Line Art" on page 234.

Screen mode is like projecting two slides from separate slide projectors onto the same spot on the wall, or like overlapping colored spotlights. The result is to lighten the composite. Black is a neutral color in Screen mode, causing no effect. Screen mode is good for applying highlights to an image.

Overlay, Soft Light, and **Hard Light** provide three different complex combinations of Multiply and Screen, acting differently on dark colors than on light colors. For all three, 50% gray is neutral, which makes them work well for layers treated with the Emboss filter, since the flat surfaces of an embossed image are 50% gray, and therefore only the highlighted and shadowed edges will show up in the composite. These modes are useful in general for applying special effects; you'll find examples in Chapter 8.

Color Dodge and **Color Burn** increase contrast of the image underneath, intensifying the color by changing the hue and saturation. Color Dodge lightens as it brightens, and Color Burn darkens. With Color Dodge, light colors affect the composite more. With Color Burn, dark colors have more effect.

If you want **to limit changes to the nontransparent areas of a layer** — for instance to blur within the element on the layer but not blur beyond its outline — use the **Preserve Transparency checkbox** at the top of the Layers palette.

Or to preserve transparency as you **replace the color** in a layer with the Foreground or Background color, hold down the **Shift key** as you Alt/Option-Delete (to fill with the Foreground color) or Ctrl/⌘-Delete (to fill with the Background color). Transparent areas will stay clear, and partially transparent pixels will stay partially transparent.

In Photoshop 5/5.5 if you turn on Auto Select Layer and use the move tool, the tool will operate on the topmost layer that has pixels — rather than transparency — under the cursor. The move tool "sees" any pixels that are 50% opaque or more, regardless of blending mode. To select a layer beneath the topmost layer, hold down the right mouse button (Windows) or Control key (Mac) to choose from a list of all the layers with pixels under the cursor.

New Layer...
New Adjustment Layer...
Duplicate Layer...
Delete Layer

Layer Options...

Merge Down
Merge Visible
Flatten Image

Palette Options...

The Merge commands available in the Layer menu or in the Layers palette's pop-out menu vary depending on which layers are active and visible.

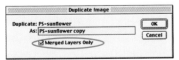

The Duplicate command (in the Image menu) lets you make an open copy of the current file. If you want to reproduce only the layers that are visible (and therefore contributing to the image as it currently looks), turn on Merged Layers Only.

Lighten mode compares pixels in the overlying layer and the image underneath, channel by channel — that is, it compares the Red channels of both, the Blue channels, and the Green channels — and chooses the lighter channel component in each case.

Darken mode makes the same comparison as Lighten does, but chooses the darker channel component in each case.

Difference mode does a complex calculation to compare the overlying layer and the image underneath. Black results if there is no difference in the pixel colors, and black is also the neutral color for Difference mode, causing no change in the image underneath. Since Difference mode usually results in more intense colors, it's good for creating psychedelic color effects. It's also good for comparing two images to see if there is any difference between the two. **Exclusion** is like a subdued, grayed-back version of Difference.

Hue, Saturation, and **Luminosity** modes each apply only one of the three attributes of the pixels in the overlying layer. Hue is good for shifting color without changing brightness or value. Luminosity is the mode to use if you want to transfer the light-and-dark information from a texture onto an image underneath.

Color mode is like a combination of Hue and Saturation modes. The layer contributes all the information except Luminosity (the brightness information).

Transparency Masks

If you create a new layer, it will consist of nothing but a transparent sheet. But as soon as you paint on it or otherwise add something, the layer will have three components — transparency, pixels, and a transparency mask.

The **transparency mask** is a stored selection boundary that defines the edge between a layer's opaque pixels and its transparent ones. Where there are semitransparent pixels — for instance, at the antialiased edge — the mask will be semitransparent also. If you move an element around on its layer, its transparency mask moves with it. If you change the element by scaling it, blurring it, or painting on it, for instance, the transparency mask changes to fit.

You can make a layer's transparency mask into an active, visible selection by Ctrl/⌘-clicking the layer's thumbnail in the Layers palette. The transparency mask is also what the Layer, Effects command uses for forming a glow, shadow, bevel, or color fill, as described in "Layer Effects" on page 87. Unlike a layer mask, a transparency mask can't be viewed independently.

Merging and Flattening

When you've finished working on a set of layers and it produces exactly the effect you want, you may decide that you no longer need to keep all the parts of the image on separate layers. Reducing the number of layers reduces the amount of RAM needed for the image and can make Photoshop work faster. To reduce the number

Here are some tricks for managing layer masks by using the layer mask thumbnail in the Layers palette:

To make changes to a mask, click the mask thumbnail. A heavy outline around the thumbnail and a little mask icon to the right of the eye column shows that the mask is active. You'll still be viewing the image rather than the mask, but any painting, filtering, or other functions you do will affect the mask, not the layer.

To make the *mask* visible instead of the layer, Alt/Option-click the mask thumbnail.

To turn the mask off temporarily so it has no effect, Shift-click the mask thumbnail. A red "X" on the thumbnail shows that the layer is turned off. Shift-click again to turn the mask back on.

To load the layer mask of the active layer as a selection, press Ctrl/⌘-Option-\, or Ctrl-⌘-click the mask's thumbnail.

of layers, you can merge or flatten them. *Merging* combines visible layers of a file into one layer. But there are at least six different possibilities for merging. Four of them — Merge Down, Merge Visible, Merge Linked, and Merge Group — can be found in the Layers palette's pop-out menu and the Layer menu, and the others in the File, Edit, and Image menus. **A "merger" has to include the active layer.** If the active layer isn't visible, you won't be able to merge layers.

- **Merge Down** combines the active layer with the layer just below it in the stack shown in the Layers palette. Both must be visible.
- **Merge Visible** combines all visible layers (those with their eye icons showing in the Layers palette) and also keeps invisible ones.
- **Merge Linked** combines the active layer and any visible layers linked to it, discarding any hidden linked layers.
- **Copy Merged** (from the Edit menu; Ctrl/⌘-Shift-C) makes a copy of the selected area of all visible layers. Then Edit, Paste (Ctrl/⌘-V) can be used to turn the copy into a new layer.
- **Duplicate** (from the Image menu) and **Save A Copy** (from the File menu) offers the Merged Layers Only option, which makes a copy of the file with invisible layers discarded and visible ones merged into a single layer. **Save For Web** (from Photoshop 5.5's File menu) automatically flattens the file it creates.

When layers are merged, the new combined layer takes its blending mode and opacity from the bottom layer of the merging group.

Flattening not only combines all visible layers into a single layer, discarding the invisible ones, but it also takes away the option for transparency, making a *Background* layer. Any areas that were transparent in the combined layers become white in the flattened file.

- **Flattening discards the hidden layers** in the process of combining the visible ones. (A dialog box warns you about this so you can reconsider.)
- When you merge or flatten, **layer masks and Layer Effects are applied** (their effects are made permanent) and then discarded from the file.
- **Alpha channels are retained** in merging or flattening.

LAYER MASKS

Besides its pixels, its transparent area, and its built-in transparency mask, each transparent layer you create can also have its own non-destructive layer mask, which you add by clicking the mask icon (the circle inside the gray square) at the bottom of the Layers palette. A layer mask provides a way to affect how the layer contributes to the composite image, without permanently changing the layer itself. For instance, instead of erasing part of the layer, you can

The gradient tool can produce a graduated layer mask that lets you apply any change in a gradual way.

To transition a photo into a painting or graphic, start with two identical layers, make a gradient-filled layer mask for the top one, and apply a filter to this layer.

© PHOTODISC, THE PAINTED TABLE

To protect a central part of an image from a change, apply the change to the upper of two identical layers and also add a Radial gradient mask to this layer.

© CORBIS IMAGES ROYALTY FREE, ACTIVE LIFESTYLES

To combine two different images, make a gradient layer mask for the upper layer, so that it gradually fades out.

© CMCD, JUST HANDS

leave it intact but block it with a layer mask. (An opaque *Background* at the bottom of a stack can't have a mask.)

When a layer mask is created, three things happen in the Layers palette to tell you how the mask relates to the image in the layer:

- A **mask icon** appears in the narrow column next to the "eye" column to let you know that whatever you do will be done to the mask instead of the image. (The mask icon replaces the paintbrush icon, whose job is to tell you that the image, not the mask, will be the target of whatever you do next.)

- A **mask thumbnail** appears beside the image thumbnail.

- A **link icon** appears between the two thumbnails, to show that if you move the layer or the mask, the other one will move along with it. (To move one without the other, you can unlink by clicking the link icon.)

A layer mask is a grayscale entity that can have up to 256 shades of gray, from white to black, like an alpha channel. Where the mask is white, it's transparent, and it allows the image on its layer to show through and contribute to the composite. Where the mask is black, it's opaque, and the corresponding portion of the image is blocked (masked out). Where the mask is gray, it's partly transparent — the lighter the gray, the more transparent — and the corresponding pixels in the layer's image make a semitransparent contribution to the composite. A layer mask affects only its own layer — it doesn't mask the layers above or the layers below, unless it's the bottom layer of a clipping group (as described below). Layer masks are important in making montages, covered in Chapter 4.

CLIPPING GROUPS

Another nondestructive compositing element, a *clipping group* is a group of layers, the bottom layer of which acts as a mask. The bottom layer clips all the associated layers so only the parts that fall within the shape of its own transparency mask can contribute to the image.

You can make a clipping group by Alt/Option-clicking on the

With a selection active, adding a layer mask by clicking the Add Layer Mask icon makes an opaque mask with the selected area transparent. Alt/Option-clicking makes a mask with the selected area opaque and the rest of the mask transparent. You can also make either kind of mask by choosing Layer, Add Layer Mask.

Add Layer Mask ▶	Reveal All
Enable Layer Mask	Hide All
Group with Previous ⌘G	Reveal Selection
Ungroup ⇧⌘G	Hide Selection

To duplicate a layer mask from one layer to another, Ctrl/⌘-click on the existing mask's thumbnail in the Layers palette to load it as a selection. Then activate the layer you want to add it to by clicking the layer's thumbnail in the palette. Finally, click the Add Layer Mask icon at the bottom of the Layers palette to turn the selection into a mask for this layer.

Turning on ATM is essential for getting smooth-looking PostScript type in Photoshop. To minimize problems with Mac OS 8.5, turn on Preserve Line Spacing and turn off Disable Smoothing At Screen Font Point Sizes.

Photoshop 5.5's Type Tool dialog box gives you a better view and more control of typesetting than in previous versions. In both version 5 and 5.5 the type Color can be specified in the dialog box, without changing the overall Foreground color in Photoshop's toolbox. In version 5.5 type can also be "faux"-styled, which means you can make bold, italic, and underlined forms of type without having fonts especially designed for that purpose. Also in 5.5 you have four antialiasing options.

borderline between the names of two layers. The lower of the two layers is the clipping mask. Its name is now underlined in the palette and the borderline becomes dotted. The other layer is clipped. Working your way up the palette clicking more borderlines adds clipped layers to the group. To be members of a clipping group, layers have to be together in the stack.

A clipping group can also be set up or added to when a layer is first added to the stack, by checking the Group With Previous Layer box in the New Layer dialog box.

Clipping groups are "high-overhead" items. They take more computation than layer masks or alpha channels. So if you can think of another way to accomplish the "clipping" you want, you might be better off doing that instead of making a clipping group.

DOUBLE MASKING

If the bottom layer of a clipping group has a layer mask, that mask will also affect all the other layers in the clipping group.

MERGING A GROUP

When the bottom layer of a clipping group is the active layer, the Merge Group command (from the Edit menu) combines all visible layers of the group, discarding the file's hidden layers.

TYPE LAYERS

Photoshop 5 and 5.5 have added some important new typesetting capabilities. **Fonts, styles,** and **sizes** can be mixed in a single type block, and **type can be kerned** automatically or by hand. Perhaps the most important changes are that type remains "live" — editable and object-oriented. That means that it can be edited, and that scaling, rotating, or otherwise distorting it won't degrade its edge quality. In addition, any special effects you add with Layer Effects (described on page 87) will also be adjusted to fit if you edit or transform the type.

When you choose a type tool and click in an image, the Type Tool dialog box opens. There you can specify typeface, style, size, color, and spacing, and enter the text you want to set. By default the Preview option is checked so you can see the type in your image as well as in the preview area at the bottom of the box. You can also reach outside the Type Tool box and drag to reposition the type.

By selecting and styling individual characters, you can mix fonts, styles, and sizes, though you can use only a single color and alignment for the type block (see step 8 on page 97 for a workaround for coloring individual lines of a multi-line type block).

Clicking OK in the Type Tool dialog box returns you to the image. The type appears as a layer of its own in the Layers palette, identified by a "T" icon, which shows that the type is live and object-oriented. Here are some tips for using type in Photoshop:

• If you're using PostScript fonts, make sure you have **Adobe Type Manager** installed so Photoshop has access to smooth PostScript-based type outlines. If it's installed but you're still

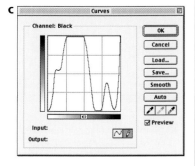

Dramatic "inline-outline" type effects can be accomplished in Photoshop by setting type (A), blurring it to get a full range of gray tones (B), and then putting a number of "switchbacks" into the Curves dialog box (C,D). Colorizing the type with Image, Adjust, Hue/Saturation before adjusting Curves gives even wilder results (E).

An "f" icon in the Layers palette indicates that one or more Layer Effects have been added. In this case they have been added to a live Type layer, indicated by the "T."

having problems with jagged type, open the ATM control panel and increase the size of the Font Cache.

- Unless you want stairstepped, jaggy type for some reason, always select an **Anti-Alias** option other than **None** in the Photoshop 5.5 Type Tool dialog box: Use **Smooth** if your artwork is destined for print; **Crisp** and **Strong** are especially useful for on-screen display. In Photoshop 5 your choices are limited to Anti-aliased or not.

- **Auto Kern** uses a font's built-in kerning information to space letter pairs as you set type. You can also **kern by hand:** Insert the cursor between the two letters whose spacing you want to change; deselect Auto kerning, hold down the Alt/Option key, and press the left arrow key to tighten the space or the right arrow key to expand it. (Another way to kern is to enter a value in the Kerning box. Values are in thousandths of an em space; use negative numbers to tighten, positive values to expand.)

  Tracking, which is tightening or loosening space for a *group* of selected letters, can also be done with Alt/Option and the arrow keys, or by entering values.

- To shift the **Baseline** for selected characters, click in the Baseline box and then use Alt/Option with the up or down arrow key.

  If you don't click in the Baseline box before pressing an arrow key, the Alt/Option-arrow combination will change the **Leading** for the lines containing the selected letters.

- Choosing **Fit In Window** at the bottom of the Type Tool dialog box lets you see your entire type block in the preview window. Or click the "+" or "–" button to enlarge or reduce the view. At the same time, you can see the type in context by looking at the artwork in the Photoshop working window.

- You can **reposition your type** in the image, even while you're working in the Type Tool dialog box. Just move the cursor into the image and drag the type.

- Because of the Preview option, which allows you to see type in position as you set it, and the ability to move your cursor out of the Type Tool dialog box and drag the type around, you can come quite close to **sizing type to fit your image**. Because Type layers store outline information rather than pixels, after you close the dialog box you can use the Free Transform command (Ctrl/⌘-T) to do any final scaling necessary for an exact fit.

- Type set on its own transparent layer can be used to **mask several layers at once**, as described in "Clipping Groups" on page 85.

LAYER EFFECTS

Photoshop 5/5.5's Layer, Effects commands can add shadows, bevels, and glows to any transparent layer, including Type layers.

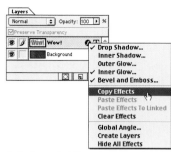

In the Layers palette each of a layer's thumbnails (image and mask) and icons (Adjustment layer circle, Layer Effects "f," and Type layer "T") produces a different context-specific menu if you right-click (Windows) or Control-click (Mac) and press the mouse button. For instance, as shown here, choices in the "f" icon's menu include the ability to change the Layer Effects, copy them from one layer so you can paste them into to another, or separate them into layers of their own.

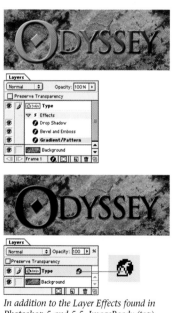

In addition to the Layer Effects found in Photoshop 5 and 5.5, ImageReady (top) has Gradient/Pattern. When a file with these effects is opened in Photoshop (bottom) a triangle over the "f" icon shows that there are additional Effects that don't show but that will be there if you reopen the file in ImageReady.

(Version 5.5 can also add a color fill as a Layer Effect, and Image-Ready adds Gradient/Pattern.) The Layer Effects you add will exactly fit the edges of the contents of the transparent layer, as defined by the transparency mask, type, or layer mask. Since the Layer Effects are stored as instructions rather than pixels, they can be changed easily and without degrading the artwork until you need to flatten the file or render them as separate layers in order to work on them separately. The Layer Effects are covered in "Using Layer Effects" on page 272 in Chapter 8, "Graphics Special Effects." Examples of their use can be found throughout the book, but especially in Chapter 8.

ADJUSTMENT LAYERS

Adjustment layers are layers without any image pixels. They can carry two kinds of information. First, they store directions for color and tonal adjustments; second, they can include a mask. An Adjustment layer's mask can be completely clear, in which case the layer's adjustments are applied to visible pixels in the layers beneath it in the stack. Or, like a layer mask, it can contain gray-scale information that restricts its adjustments to certain areas. An Adjustment layer can also be part of a clipping group, affecting only the layers in the group. Like layer masks, Adjustment layers are nondestructive. That is, their effects can be applied without permanently changing any pixels in the image. "Adjustment Layers: The Ultimate in Flexibility" on page 102 in Chapter 3 tells how to put Adjustment layers into action. *Wow!*

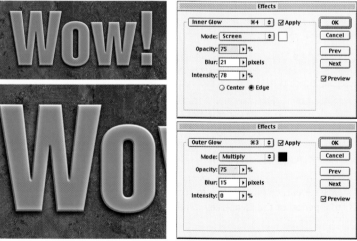

In addition to Bevel And Emboss effects and an offset Drop Shadow, the Layer Effects applied to this type include a light Inner Glow in Screen mode and a dark Outer Glow in Multiply mode, so that the lighting and dimensionality look less flat and mechanical. Many tips and techniques for using Layer Effects are presented in Chapter 8.

CROPPING: A "SPECIAL CASE" SELECTING TASK

Cropping is trimming an image to the size and proportions you want. In Photoshop, cropping is done by selecting the part of the image you want to preserve, and then removing everything outside the selected part. You can use either the rectangular marquee or the crop tool.

If you have an **active, unfeathered rectangular selection** and you choose **Image, Crop,** the image will be cropped to that shape.

For some situations the **cropping tool** provides an advantage over using the rectangular marquee because you can move the cropping borders in, out, up, or down by dragging on the side or corner handles; you can rotate the cropping frame to straighten a crooked image by dragging just outside the cropping frame; and you can trim and resample an image in one step.

Double-clicking the cropping tool in the toolbox opens the Cropping Tool Options palette. If you click on Fixed Target Size and then on Front Image, the palette shows the Width, Height, and Resolution of the image.

- If you **set the Width and Height values** but delete the number in the Resolution field so the field is blank, and then drag the crop tool, the cropping frame will hold the proportions you set in Width and Height. When you click inside the selected area to accept the crop, the Resolution will be set at a value that won't cause resampling (adding or averaging pixels).

- If you leave the Height and Width fields empty but **set the Resolution,** you can drag the cropping frame to any proportions you want. And when you click to accept the crop, the dimensions will be adjusted and no resampling will occur.

- But if instead you set the **Width and Height** *and* **enter a value for Resolution,** the image will be resampled as it's cropped, so that it will come out to the dimensions and resolution you specify. Then you'll probably need to apply the Unsharp Mask filter to repair the fuzziness that resampling will have introduced.

In Photoshop 5/5.5 you can also use the cropping tool to quickly add as much "canvas" as you want around an image. First shrink your view by pressing Ctrl-hyphen (Windows) or ⌘-Option-hyphen (Mac) until you can see gray around your image. Drag the Crop tool across the image and then grab a corner handle of the crop box and drag outward. The advantage of enlarging your canvas this way rather than with the Image, Canvas Size command is that you can proportion the new space exactly as you want it at the top, bottom, and sides of the image.

When you've finished your cropping, Press the Enter key or double-click inside the crop box to accept the crop, or press Ctrl/⌘-period or the Escape key to release the crop box without cropping the image.

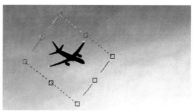

A one-step crop and rotation of a selection

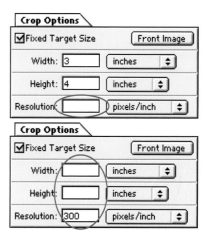

Two ways to crop without resampling

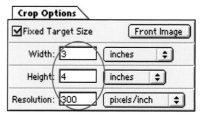

Cropping with resampling

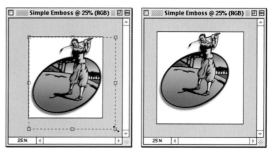

Adding "canvas" with the crop tool

Exercising Layers

Overview *Duplicate the Liz and Elaine files from the **Dressup** folder on the Wow! CD-ROM. Work with the Layers palette to learn its functions.*

 **IMAGE** "**Liz**" and "**Elaine**" files

1

Liz (left) and Elaine (holding Buster) as you find them in **Dressup**

2a

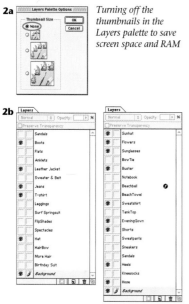

Turning off the thumbnails in the Layers palette to save screen space and RAM

2b

Layers palettes for Liz and Elaine in their original condition; refer to these if you accidentally turn off layers and need to reset visibility or stacking order.

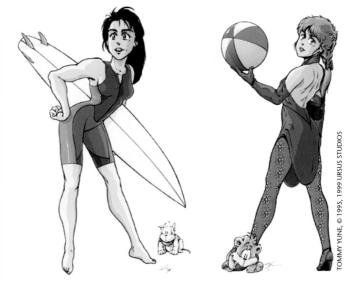

INSPIRED BY A LAYERS DEMO featuring "Barbie/GI Joe" and presented by Russell Brown of Adobe Systems, Inc., we asked Tommy Yune, creator of the *Buster the Amazing Bear* comic books (see more of his work in Chapter 6), to put together a file that could be used for an elementary demo of how layers work. On the Wow! CD-ROM find the **Dressup** folder with two Photoshop files — Elaine (above on the right) and Liz, two heroines from the *Buster* series. Then follow the steps on these four pages to get the hang of turning layers on and off, linking them, adjusting Opacity, trying out blending modes, preserving transparency, making clipping groups and layer masks, and experimenting with Adjustment layers and Layer Effects.

1 Making a duplicate. Before you start, copy the **Liz** and **Elaine** files from the Wow! CD-ROM to a hard disk. Then open both files and open the Layers palette (Window, Show Layers).

2 Reducing palette size. Choosing Palette Options in the Layers palette's pop-out menu lets you choose the size of the thumbnails that appear in the palette, or choose no thumbnails at all. Large thumbnails let you see more detail. But they can also slow down your work, since redrawing them occupies RAM. To fit the entire Liz and Elaine Layers palettes on a small screen, you can turn off their preview thumbnails: Choose Palette Options and click the None button. Yune, who often works with the Layers thumbnails turned off because it can improve Photoshop's speed, has named the layers by their content, so you don't need the icons to know what's what. Also, in Photoshop 5 with the Auto-Select feature turned on in the move tool's Options palette, you can activate the layer for a particular element simply by clicking on that element in the image.

3 Hiding layers: Organizing Elaine. To get Elaine ready for an evening out, click to turn off the eye icons for these layers to hide them: Sunhat, Flowers, Sunglasses, and Sweatshirt.

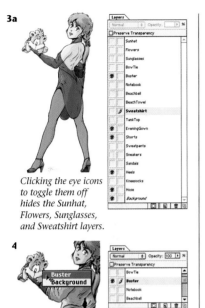

3a

Clicking the eye icons to toggle them off hides the Sunhat, Flowers, Sunglasses, and Sweatshirt layers.

4

Right-clicking/Control-clicking on an image element with the move tool brings up a list of all layers under the cursor so you can choose the layer you want.

5

Linking Buster and his bow tie allow them to be moved together. To link a layer to the active layer, simply click in its links column.

6

If you drag-and-drop layers from one file's image window to another, any linked layers come along. But to move linked layers up or down the stack within a file, they have to be dragged one by one.

4 Activating a layer: Selecting Buster. You can activate a particular layer in the stack by clicking its name in the Layers palette. Or with Auto-Select turned on you can click with the move tool to activate the topmost layer that has pixels directly under the cursor. If you want to activate some layer other than the topmost one, you can right-click/Control-click on the image with the move tool to bring up a context-sensitive menu that lists all currently visible layers with pixels under the cursor. Then you can then drag through the list to choose a layer. Try selecting Buster, first with the Auto-Select method and then, just for practice, by right-clicking/Control-clicking on him with the move tool; you can toggle to the move tool from any tool but the pen by holding down the Ctrl/⌘ key.

5 Linking layers: Putting Buster on the floor. Clicking in the links column in the Layers palette (next to the "eye" column) will *link* any layer to the *currently active layer*. A chain symbol appears in the links column of any layer that you link. In the Elaine file, activate the Buster layer and then click in the links column of the BowTie layer to link it to Buster; note the chain icons in the palette. Also click the BowTie eye column so you can see the tie. Now activate the Evening Gown layer and link the Heels layer to it; again note the link mark. Now link the Hose to this group also. Then activate the BowTie layer, and notice that the link marks no longer appear for the Heels or Hose — only for the layer (Buster) that's linked to the *currently active layer* (BowTie).

When layers are linked, moving one layer with the move tool also moves any linked layers. With Buster linked to his bow tie, use the move tool to slide him to the floor. (To give Elaine something to do with her hands now that Buster is on his own, click in the eye column of the Beachball layer to make it visible.)

6 Dragging and dropping: Cloning Buster. With more than one Photoshop file open, you can use the move tool to copy a layer from one file into another. It's quick and easy, and it bypasses the clipboard, saving RAM. With both the Liz and Elaine files open, activate the Buster layer of the Elaine file and the Leather Jacket layer in the Liz file, put the move tool on the bear in the Elaine image, and drag him into the Liz window. Buster, with his linked bow tie, will end up approximately where you drop him in the Liz image. Drag him to Liz's shoulder, and then drag the Buster and BowTie names to the top of the Layers palette so he's *on* the shoulder rather than behind it.

GOING SOLO

Dragging a linked layer with the move tool from one image to another brings its linked layers along with it. But to move one of a set of linked layers without moving the others, drag it from its Layers palette instead of from the image itself.

7 Trying out blending modes: Stockings to tights. The blending mode (set by choosing from a pop-out list at the top left

7

Hard Light mode can create a transparent plastic look.

8

When you fill a layer, Preserve Transparency restricts color to nontransparent areas.

9

The bottom layer of a clipping group limits the contribution of the upper layers of the group; the result is shown at the top of page 90.

10a

Adding a layer mask

10b

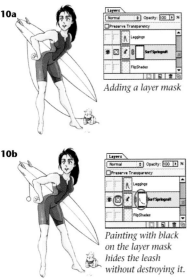

Painting with black on the layer mask hides the leash without destroying it.

of the palette) controls how the pixels of a layer interact with the layers underneath. To see the effect of Multiply mode, in the Elaine file activate the Hose layer. Switch the layer's blending mode from Multiply to Normal and back again; you'll see the change as the muscle contours and skin color of the Background layer disappear and reappear.

Leather to plastic. For a "plastic" look with exaggerated highlights, choose Hard Light mode for the Jacket layer.

8 Preserving transparency: Expanding a wardrobe. The Preserve Transparency checkbox at the top of the Layers palette keeps color "inside the lines" by activating a layer's built-in transparency mask. In the Liz file, activate the Jeans layer. Click the checkbox to turn on Preserve Transparency. Then choose a bright color (click the Foreground color square in the toolbox) and choose Edit, Fill, Foreground Color, Normal. The Jeans will change color but the folds of the cloth will be lost. Press Ctrl/⌘-Z to Undo, and try the Fill operation again; but this time choose Edit, Fill, Foreground Color, *Multiply*. Although the layer stays in Normal mode, the color is applied in Multiply mode, allowing the detail of the Jeans to show through.

9 Using a clipping group: Making patterned stockings. To add a pattern to the Hose, you could use a pattern fill with Preserve Transparency turned on, as in step 8. But if you use a separate pattern layer and make a clipping group so you can use the shape of the stockings from the Hose layer to mask the pattern, you'll be able to move the pattern to adjust its position within the masked area. To help you see how the clipping group works, choose Palette Options from the pop-out menu and choose the smallest thumbnail size.

In the Elaine file turn on visibility for the Flowers layer alone by Alt/Option-clicking its eye icon. Use the rectangular marquee with the Shift key to surround a flower; choose Edit, Define Pattern; then click eye icons to turn on visibility for Hose and other layers and turn off visibility for Flowers. Activate the Hose layer and create a new layer above it by clicking the New Layer icon in the center at the bottom of the Layers palette. Choose Edit, Fill, Pattern, Normal to fill the new Layer 1 with flowers.

To use the Hose layer to "clip" the pattern-filled layer so the flowers appear on the stockings only, in the Layers palette Alt/Option-click the border between the pattern-filled layer and Hose. The border will become a dotted line, showing that the two layers are "clipped" together, and the Hose name will be underlined, showing that it's the bottom layer of the clipping group. You should now see flower-patterned Hose. To shift the pattern, drag with the move tool.

10 Using a mask: Unleashing the dog. A layer mask lets you remove part of a layer from the image, without necessarily making the removal permanent. The image on the layer stays intact so it can

11a

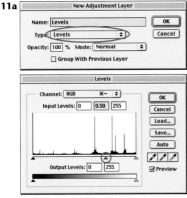

Adding an Adjustment layer and moving the gamma slider (gray triangle) darkens the skin tones.

11b

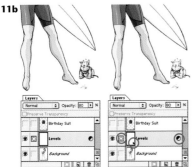

With Levels adjusted, Liz and her dog sport suntans (left). But painting the built-in mask in the Adjustment layer blocks the Levels effect, leaving Liz tanned but the dog pale (right).

12a

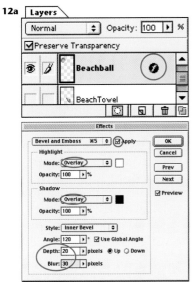

Double-clicking the "f" will open the Effects dialog box, where Effects can be edited.

12b

An Inner Bevel applied to the Beachball layer makes the ball look rounded (left). Large Blur and Depth settings create the soft "sphere" shading; the Highlight and Shadow fade as they reach inward from the ball's edge. In Overlay mode the Highlight doesn't interfere with the black line work, and the Shadow darkens the ball's colors without dulling them. Click the Apply checkbox to toggle the effect off (right).

be restored later by turning off or deleting the mask. In the Liz file, Alt/Option-click the Surf Springsuit name to activate that layer and hide all others. Click the eye icon for *Background* to turn its visibility back on.

Now you'll make a layer mask for the Surf Springsuit layer that will remove the leash from the picture. Click the Add Layer Mask icon on the left at the bottom of the palette. The mask icon to the left of the Surf Springsuit thumbnail shows that the mask is active, so anything you do now will be done to the layer mask, even though you're looking at the image. Make sure that black is the Foreground color. Then choose the paintbrush tool. Open the Brushes palette (Window, Show Brushes; or the default shortcut is F5). Since you'll want to have good control of the paint when you get to the point where the leash meets the surfboard, choose a fairly small, hard brush tip. Now when you "paint" the leash, the black paint will actually go onto the layer mask, opaquing that part of the mask to make the leash disappear from the composite image.

11 Adding an Adjustment layer: Cultivating a tan. An Adjustment layer adds no pixels to the image. Instead it contains instructions for performing one of the modifications available in the Image, Adjust submenu. To make an Adjustment layer to "tan" Liz, activate the *Background* layer and then Ctrl/⌘-click the New Layer icon. In the New Adjustment Layer dialog box, choose Levels from the Type list. In the Levels dialog box, move the gamma slider (the gray triangle in the Input Levels controls) a little to the right. Click OK to close the dialog box. In the Layers palette, note that the new layer has a black-and-white circle to the right of its name, indicating that it's an Adjustment layer. Like any other layer, an Adjustment layer's contribution to the image can be reduced: To lighten the tan, reduce the Opacity for the layer.

The thumbnail for the Adjustment layer represents a mask (note the mask icon next to it) that controls where the Adjustment layer's effects are applied. Adding black to the mask restricts the effect of the Adjustment layer. To prevent canine sunburn, with the Adjustment layer active, airbrush with black over the dog.

12 Applying Layer Effects: Inflating the ball. When you apply Effects to a layer, it's the Transparency mask (or the layer mask if there is one) that determines where the effects will happen. Double-click the "f" symbol on the Beachball layer in the Elaine file so you can see how the ball was rounded.

Applying Type and Layer Effects

Overview *Lighten a pad for type; create and add special color effects to large display type; set a block of smaller type and "clip" color inside it.*

ACTION **IMAGE** "Text Panel" image and Action

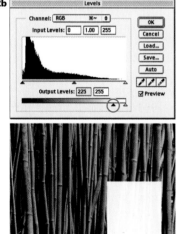

The original photo of bamboo

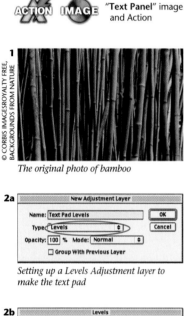

Setting up a Levels Adjustment layer to make the text pad

Lightening an area by adjusting Output Levels

WITH THE IMPROVED TYPE HANDLING and editable Layer Effects of Photoshop 5/5.5, it's now possible to design and produce any simple page layout that consists entirely of images and display type. Here we've put the largest type directly over the image and also created a lightened panel area that allows the image to show through but provides good contrast for the smaller display type.

1 Preparing a background. Choose File, New to open a new Photoshop file the size and resolution you need for your layout. When you set the Width and Height, be sure to include the edge area you need for any bleed (usually 0.125-inch on the final print job). For Resolution for an image that has high-contrast, hard geometric edges like this one, use a number that's twice the halftone screen resolution at which the job will be printed. (For our postcard mockup we were able to use a 1000-pixel-wide file.)

Now open your photo file and drag and drop the photo into your layout. Use Ctrl/⌘-T (for Free Transform) to scale the image up or down, but keep in mind that you can't scale it up more than about 10% and still have it look good. If scaling makes the image look slightly fuzzy, choose Filter, Sharpen, Unsharp Mask and experiment with settings until it looks like the original (see "Sharpen" at the beginning of Chapter 5 for tips on settings).

Be sure the Layers palette is open so you can use it in the steps that follow (choose Window, Show Layers to open it if necessary).

2 Making a pad for type. Drag with the rectangular marquee to select the area you will lighten as a pad for the type. To create an Adjustment layer so you can lighten the type pad area, Ctrl/⌘-click on New Layer, the middle icon at the bottom of the Layers palette. In the New Adjustment Layer dialog box, choose Levels from the Type list, name the layer if you like, and click OK.

When the Levels dialog box opens, move the black point on the Output Levels slider to lighten the selected areas. Image detail will

3a

Opening the Effects dialog via the context-sensitive menu for the Adjustment layer

3b

When a drop shadow is added to the Adjustment layer and its mask, it appears only around the edges of the text pad.

4a

Adding a large "G" with the type tool

4b

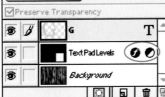

The type tool automatically creates a separate layer above the currently active layer. The "T" icon indicates that the type is live. The "f" on the layer below indicates editable layer effects.

be maintained, but contrast will be reduced so the image won't interfere with the type you'll be putting on the pad.

There are many other ways you can make a lightened pad for type. However, using an Adjustment layer not only produces a pad that can be moved around if you want to, but also automatically masks the shadow that you'll create in step 3, so it shows only beyond the edges of the pad and doesn't darken the pad itself.

3 Adding a shadow. To add a drop shadow, open the Effects dialog box by right-clicking/Control-clicking on the Adjustment layer's name in the Layers palette. This will open a context-sensitive menu of the options available for that layer. Choose Effects from this menu to open the Effects dialog box.

When the Effects dialog box opens, offering you the Drop Shadow effect, you can choose the kind of shadow effect you want. To make a "dark halo" rather than an offset shadow, we set the Distance to 0 and set a large Blur. Notice that the shadow effect appears only outside the pad.

4 Setting the largest type. Three type elements were used for the postcard: the large "G," the "green gold," and the block of type on the lightened pad. These had to be set separately so they could be individually positioned.

To set a large letter like the "G," choose the type tool and click on the image to open the Type Tool dialog box. Choose the Font and style you want, and enter a value for the Size. If the letter that appears on the image is too small or too big, enter a new Size value. Even with the dialog box open, you can drag the letter around in your image window to move it into position where you want it.

The Color swatch displays the current Foreground color. You can change the color used for the type, without changing the Foreground color, by clicking the swatch to open the Color Picker. We chose a pastel orange color, knowing that we would be applying layer effects and adjusting the blending mode to bring the color to life later (in step 6).

Clicking on the Fit In Window box at the bottom of the dialog box ensures that you'll be able to see all of the type you've set, even if it's very large. This is less important for a single letter like the "G" than for blocks of type like those you'll set in steps 5 and 7.

When the type is set, sized, colored, and positioned the way you want it, click OK to close the dialog box. If you want to change the type later, just double-click the "T" symbol for its layer in the Layers palette to reopen the dialog.

5 Setting type to a specific line length. We wanted the "green gold" type to sit on the platform created by the "G" and to extend as far as the right edge of the text pad. To set type to a specific line length like this, first click with the type tool to open the Type Tool dialog box and start a new type layer. Then set the type and adjust

As part of the process of fitting the type into the postcard design, a negative Tracking value was entered to pull all the letters closer together.

The Free Transform command was used to make final size adjustments for "green gold."

A diffuse yellow Inner Glow in Screen mode added interest to the "G." A Drop Shadow was added with a 50% Opacity, a Distance offset of 30 pixels at an Angle of 135°, and a 15-pixel Blur.

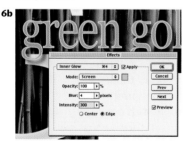

An Inner Glow in green with a much smaller Blur setting and a high Intensity created an outline effect for "green gold."

its size, position, and color as described in step 4. With Fit In Window chosen, work with the type in the dialog box as you check the width of the type block in your image. Get as close as you can to the right line length, including any letter-pair kerning and multiple-letter tracking you need:

- To **kern**, or adjust the space between a **pair** of letters for a more visually pleasing result, click the I-beam type cursor between those letters in the type on-screen, hold down the Alt/Option key and use the arrow key. (left to tighten the space between letters and right to expand it). Using the arrows turns off the automatic kerning so the space between the two letters can be adjusted. Note that kerning is controlled separately for each pair of characters. (Kerning can also be done in the preview area of the Type Tool dialog box: Click the check mark next to Auto Kern to turn off this feature, which uses the kerning values built into the font. Enter a value in the Kerning box — a negative number to pull the letters closer together, a positive number to spread them apart. To kern another pair of letters, click between that pair, turn off Auto Kern, and enter a Kerning value.)

- To adjust **tracking**, which means uniformly adjusting spacing between **all** the letters in a selection or block of type, enter a Tracking value (negative to tighten the spacing, positive to increase it).

When the line length is close to what you want, click OK to close the Type Tool dialog. Now you can use Free Transform (Ctrl/⌘-T) to finish scaling the type block to exactly the right width. The type layer remains "live" — an editable, *object-oriented* entity — so applying transformations such as rotation, skewing, and scaling won't affect the quality of the edges. (Transformations *can*, however, affect the aesthetics of the type. That's why it was important to get the size and spacing close using the Type Tool dialog box, rather than depending on the Transform functions to scale from body copy to heading size. Big changes in type size require adjustment in the spacing relationships between characters in order to look good; proportions that look good small don't necessarily look good big, and vice versa. Also, scaling a block of type horizontally or vertically to make it fit a certain space can differentially distort the thick and thin strokes, ruining the proportions designed into the characters.)

6 Applying shadows and color variation to the type. The glow in the large "G" and the outline on "green gold," as well as drop shadows, were applied with Layer Effects. For each layer we opened the Effects dialog box (right-click/Control-click on the layer's name in the Layer's palette and choose Effects from the context-sensitive menu). After applying Drop Shadow as we had for the text pad in step 3, we constructed the glow. To get the tonality we wanted for the "G," we applied an Inner Glow, softened with a large

6c

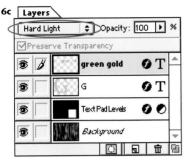

The Layers palette after Layer Effects were applied to both type layers

7

Several lines of black type were added as a single text block. The preview in the Type Tool dialog box was enlarged to give a better view of the kerning operation.

8

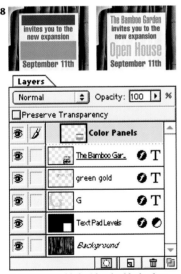

A layer was added with color blocks that covered the type; then this layer was clipped to the type layer below it.

Blur setting. To outline "green gold" we used an Inner Glow again, but this time with a low Blur setting and a high Intensity.

Three blending modes — Screen, Overlay, and Hard Light — can be especially useful for allowing glowing color to interact with the image in layers below. We had colored our type and glows with Hard Light mode in mind. Hard Light created a transparent effect and exaggerated the colors. The "green gold" type was just a little lighter than 50 percent gray, which is the neutral (invisible) color for Hard Light mode. So the Hard Light setting simply lightened the overall color of the background image under the type slightly, and it was the color and intensity of the Layer Effects that added impact.

7 Setting several lines of centered type. To set the type for the invitation, we clicked with the type tool to open the dialog box. We set the Color to black, clicked the Center alignment button, and typed the words for one line, then pressed Enter/Return to get to the next line, and so on.

By clicking the "+" sign in the lower left corner of the Type Tool dialog box, we could zoom up to see kerning details while also viewing the type at its real size in the layout. After clicking OK to close the dialog box, we set the Opacity for this new type layer to 75% and applied a bright Outer Glow (yellow in Screen mode with a 10-pixel Blur and an Intensity of 300).

8 Coloring individual lines in a block of type. The workaround we used to color the individual lines of type in the invitation block can also be used to apply textures or even photos to type. With the invitation type layer active, we clicked the New Layer icon to create a layer above it. We used the rectangular marquee to create selections just big enough to surround the pieces of type we wanted to color, then filled them with color so the color patches hid the type below. (Pressing Alt/Option-Delete fills an active selection with the Foreground color; click the Foreground color square if you want to choose a new Foreground color).

To restrict the color to the type, in the Layers palette Alt/Option-click on the border between the layer with the color-filled panels and the type layer below it. This creates a clipping group based on the outlines of the letters in the type below. The result will be color-filled editable type with the Layer Effects intact! *Wow!*

TYPE TOOL CAUTIONS

Photoshop 5/5.5's Type tool shows big improvements, but here are some limitations to keep in mind:

• Although you can vary the Size, Baseline, Font, and style for each character individually, the **Color and alignment have to be the same for the entire block of type.**

• When you choose Center or Right alignment, you need to leave out the between-word space at the end of each line. Unlike object-oriented drawing programs and page layout software, **Photoshop doesn't automatically wrap type or drop any end-of-line spaces.**

Beneath was produced by **Phil Saunders** as a pre-production visualization for a game concept. Saunders used a Wacom tablet and hard-edged brushes to duplicate the look of a gouache rendering. Photoshop's ability to organize image elements in layers and to save selections in alpha channels was important in assembling this hand-painted image. Saunders created layers for the foreground, midground, and background, as well as for some individual elements. This allowed him to control the contrast and color balance of each layer separately to achieve the sense of depth he wanted, and to adjust the perspective of the individual elements with Free Transform (Ctrl/⌘-T).

To simulate atmospheric perspective, he worked from dark to light, filling in the darkest values at each level of depth first, so that he could build up detail and texture with highlights later. In the background layers the darkest "darks" are lighter than those in the foreground layers, producing the illusion of distance. To paint the midground and foreground structures, Saunders used a scanned sketch as a guide.

To create the character, he used the pen tool and lasso to define separate areas for the pants, shirt, skin, and so on. As soon as it was made, each selection was filled with a shadow value of the base color for that element (Alt/Option-Delete fills the selected area with the Foreground color). Each selection was also saved in an alpha channel (Select, Save Selection). Later each stored selection was loaded (by Ctrl/⌘-clicking its name in the Channels

palette) and used as a frisket for painting the highlights and darker shadows, to keep the painted colors from going outside the shapes. The wings were created on a separated layer, also by selecting and filling.

The tone of each layer was fine-tuned (Image, Adjust, Levels) before a flattened copy of the image was saved for printing (File, Save A Copy). ▶ *Using Adjustment layers to apply color and tone adjustments and keeping them "live" in a layered file lets you make further adjustments after you've seen a color proof of your image.* ▶ *The File, Save A Copy command is the quickest way to flatten and save a copy of a file for printing without flattening the layered file.*

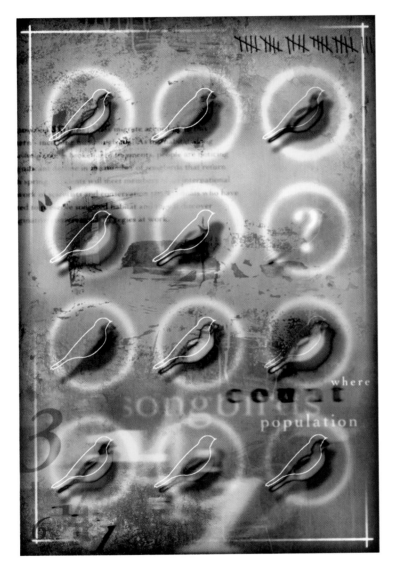

Alicia Buelow created *Songbirds* as an illustration for *Audobon* magazine. The background started with a scanned photo of a wall, and the color was altered with a Hue/Saturation Adjustment layer. Photoshop's blending modes, layer masks, and selection tools were important in building the image on top of this background.

Buelow created an image of a bird using several different orioles as sources, since the magazine's editor didn't want to highlight a particular species. The bird was copied to the clipboard and pasted 10 more times in a gridlike arrangement. All the birds were merged into a single layer. Buelow used a hand-painted layer mask to dim or partially hide some of the birds and created a drop shadow layer in Multiply mode for the birds. ▶ *If you use Photoshop's Layer Effects Drop Shadow on a layer that has a layer mask, the mask affects the shape of the shadow. To make a Drop Shadow that is unaffected by the layer mask, Shift-click the layer mask's thumbnail in the Layers palette to turn the mask off; make the shadow (Layer, Effects, Drop Shadow); separate it into a layer (Layer, Effects, Create Layer); and then turn the mask back on.*

The birds layer was assigned the Difference blending mode. This made each bird unique, its color depending on the density of the shadow below it and the color of the background image (some of the shadows had been made partly transparent with a layer mask).

Buelow created an outline for each bird by loading the transparency mask of the birds layer as a selection (Ctrl/⌘-click the layer's name in the Layers palette), adding a new layer (click the New Layer icon in the middle at the bottom of the palette), and stroking the selection with black (Edit, Stroke, Center). She used the move tool to offset the outlines layer a little up and to the left. Putting the outlines layer in Color Dodge mode brightened the colors in the image underneath to produce white outlines.

Buelow added the bright circles by introducing a transparent layer at the top of the stack, defining a circle with the elliptical marquee with the Shift key held down, feathering the selection (Select, Feather) and then stroking with black as she had for the bird outlines. With the layer in Color Dodge mode, the circles brightened the colors underneath to produce light rings but left the white bird outlines unaffected.

3

ENHANCING PHOTOS

THIS CHAPTER DESCRIBES SEVERAL TECHNIQUES for enhancing photos — from emulating traditional camera and darkroom techniques such as mezzotinting, soft focus, solarization, and duotones, to retouching, hand-tinting, and using Photoshop 5/5.5's new **spot color** and **channel-mixing** capabilities. But much of the day-to-day production work done with Photoshop involves simply trying to get the best possible print reproduction of an unretouched photo — a crisp and clear print with its full range of gray or color values.

The Photoshop functions most often used for improving a photo are chosen mainly from the Image, Adjust and the Filter, Sharpen submenus. The dialog boxes for two of the choices from Image, Adjust — **Levels** and **Curves** — look very "techy," and one — **Variations** — looks quite friendly. It's precisely these characteristics that make them so useful. Levels provides a lot of information about the image, and both Levels and Curves provide a great deal of control. But Variations lets you see in advance what will happen to the image with each of the several color and tone changes you can choose from (pages 127 through 129 show examples).

Another choice in the Image, Adjust submenu — **Brightness/ Contrast** — is easy to understand and relate to, unlike Levels and Curves. But the Brightness/Contrast control has a restricted set of functions that can compromise the color or tonal range of an image if they're applied alone. If using Levels and Curves on an image is analogous to tuning up all the sections of an orchestra so it can play harmoniously, then using Brightness/Contrast is more like the brass playing loud to cover up problems in the woodwinds section.

The **rubber stamp, History brush, sharpen/blur/ smudge,** and **dodge/burn/sponge** can be useful for correcting local flaws in an image. The History brush and rubber stamp can be used to cover unwanted blemishes or details by painting with a modified version of the image or with detail from another part of the picture. The sharpen and blur tools apply the same functions as some of the Sharpen and Blur filters (described in Chapter 5), but with hand-held precision. The smudge tool is really a painting tool that allows you to smear colors together (you can find an example of using this tool to blend a shadow effect with its background in "Casting a Shadow" in Chapter 8.)

The dodge and burn tools together can be thought of as Levels-in-a-wand — varying contrast, brightness, and detail, with independent

continued on page 102

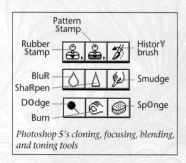

Photoshop 5's cloning, focusing, blending, and toning tools

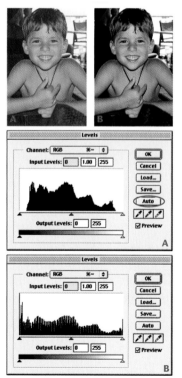

To add an Adjustment layer, Ctrl/⌘-click on the New Layer icon at the bottom of the Layers palette. In the New Adjustment Layer dialog box (top), choose the Type of adjustment; you can also choose the blending mode or make a clipping group (Group With Previous Layer) at this point, or you can do it later in the Layers palette. In the next dialog box that appears, make your changes. To edit the changes later, double-click the layer's little circle icon in the Layers palette (bottom).

Choosing Image, Adjust, Levels, Auto to adjust tonal range; before (A) and after (B)

control in the highlights, midtones, and shadows through the Options palette. The third phase of the tool — sponge — gives pinpoint control of the Saturation function from Image, Adjust, Hue/Saturation, again in highlights, midtones, and shadows. With all their power, these toning tools can be difficult to control; for pointers on other methods for pinpoint toning, see "'Nondestructive' Retouching" on page 105.

ADJUSTMENT LAYERS: THE ULTIMATE IN FLEXIBILITY

When you want to make tone and color changes to an entire layer or a selected area, you can apply the commands of the Image, Adjust submenu either directly to the image or indirectly, by means of an **Adjustment layer.** You can add an Adjustment layer by Ctrl/⌘-clicking the New Layer icon at the bottom of the Layers palette and choosing the Type of image adjustment you want. This opens the dialog box for that kind of adjustment so you can make changes just as if you were applying them directly to the individual layers. Adjustment layers provide so much flexibility that it's almost always worthwhile to use them:

- It's easy to reopen the dialog boxes and **change the settings later** to fine-tune the image without degrading the image by changing your original changes.

- You can **target the corrections** with each Adjustment layer's **built-in mask,** which can be edited like any layer mask, and modified later if you like.

- An Adjustment layer applies to all nontransparent areas below it in the Layers stack. But it's possible to **restrict the effect to particular layers.** Either move the Adjustment layer below any layers you don't want it to affect, or if that isn't possible, make it part of a clipping group: Alt/Option-click between the Adjustment layer and the layer below it to restrict the adjustment to that layer only. (See "Clipping Groups" on page 85 for more about clipping groups.)

You'll find many examples of using Adjustment layers in this chapter and throughout the book.

MAKING GOOD PHOTOS LOOK BETTER

If you ask an expert where to start in correcting a black-and-white or color photo, you're almost certain to hear, "It depends on the photo." That's certainly true. But here are some tips that may be generally helpful, especially if you apply them through Adjustment layers so you can easily make further adjustments if you need them. (Remember that for your printed image to match your screen display, your monitor and output system need to be calibrated and matched, as described in "Getting Consistent Color" in Chapter 1.)

Adjusting Levels and Curves overall and using dodge/burn techniques on local areas can restore information that seems to be lost. Where damage is really severe, the rubber stamp can be used to paint missing features, such as the ivy in the upper right quadrant of this photo.

Extending Dynamic Range

In a typical image, you'll want to get the broadest range of tones (and thus the largest amount of detail possible) by lightening the lightest area in the image to the lightest printable "white" and darkening the darkest area to the darkest printable "black." (For printing the images, the full tonal range often needs to be restricted so it doesn't exceed what the printing process can produce.)

To see whether an image uses the full tonal range that's available, you can choose Image, Adjust, Levels and inspect the *histogram*, which is the graph that shows what proportion of the image's pixels (the vertical measure) are in each of 256 tones (spread along the horizontal axis, from black on the left to white on the right). The darkest pixels in the image are where the leftmost vertical bar of the histogram shows up; the lightest pixels are represented by the bar at the right end. If the histogram doesn't extend all the way across the horizontal axis, it means the full range of tones is not being used in the image — the blacks are not really as black as they could be and the whites are not pure white.

Using Auto Levels. Working in the Levels dialog box, you can expand the tonal range (and thus increase the contrast) by simply clicking the **Auto** button. The effect of clicking the Auto button is to tell the program to make the darkest pixels in the image black, make the lightest ones white, and spread the intermediate ones over the full range of tones in between.

The Auto Levels adjustment works well for images that just need a boost in contrast. Sometimes the Auto button can even correct color, because a color cast can be the result of the way brightness values in the image are distributed among the colors (red, green, and blue, or cyan, magenta, and yellow), and the Auto correction takes into account the histograms for the individual colors. Always worth a try because it's so quick, the Auto correction can easily be undone if it doesn't do what you want: Just hold down the Alt/Option key to change the Cancel button to Reset, and click the button.

Setting Levels by hand. If the one-click Auto Levels method doesn't work for correcting overall tonal problems, set the black point, white point, midtones, and neutral color. You can accomplish this as follows:

1 Choose the black eyedropper from the lower right corner of the Levels dialog box and click it on the lightest spot in the image that should be black.

2 Choose the white eyedropper and click it on the darkest spot that should be white.

3 At this point you'll have a full range of tones from black to white. But if most of the intermediate tones in the image are still

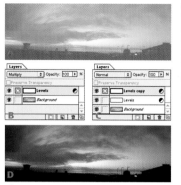

If you treat an overexposed photo (A) by adding a "blank" Levels Adjustment layer in Multiply mode (B) and then adding another Levels layer in Normal mode and making Levels adjustments here (C), you may be able to achieve a surprisingly good result (D).

Sometimes treating an image (A) with Auto Levels, applied here through a Levels Adjustment layer, can expand the tonal range as desired but at the same time cause an unwanted color shift (B). Changing the blending mode of the Adjustment layer to Luminosity eliminates the color effect (C). (Alternatively, if you want to keep the color correction produced by Auto Levels but don't want the change in tone, change the blending mode of the Levels layer to Color.)

too light or too dark, move the middle (gray) Input Levels slider to the right to darken or to the left to lighten.

4 To correct a color cast, choose the gray eyedropper and click it on a color in the image that should be a neutral gray, with no color. If this overcorrects the original color cast so that you now have a different color cast, click on other should-be-neutral spots until you find one that solves the problem. In general, choosing a spot that should be medium gray (rather than very light or very dark) works best.

Correcting "Exposure"

One of the most common problems with photos is incorrect exposure — the image is too dark overall (underexposed) or too light (overexposed) or the shadows have lost their detail. If adjusting the black and white Input Levels doesn't solve a photo's color problems, it may be that they can be corrected by fixing the exposure. To increase or decrease the amount of detail you can see in the highlights, midtones, or shadows, choose Image, Adjust, Curves. To change the tonal range, click on the curve to create a point; then drag the point to change its position. The rest of the curve will change shape to make a smooth transition from the black point to the white point through the new point.

You can make general corrections by reshaping the curve so it bulges toward the black side to lighten an underexposed image (by default this is to the left and upward for RGB images and to the right and downward for Grayscale or CMYK images, but you can reverse this by clicking on the grayscale bar that runs across the bottom of the Curves dialog box). Conversely, reshape the curve to bulge toward the white side to darken an overexposed photo.

One of the most commonly needed image corrections can be made with an **"M" adjustment** to the curve. With the Curves dialog set up so the dark ends of the tone bars are at the bottom and left, anchor the middle of the curve by clicking to make a midpoint. Then raise a point in the lower quarter of the curve to lighten the shadow tones and also raise a point near the upper end of the curve to slightly lighten the highlights.

Overall exposure corrections can also be made with the gamma (gray, middle) Input Levels slider in the Levels dialog box. But the advantage of using the Curves dialog box is that you can adjust particular values. If you move the cursor out of the Curves dialog box, it turns into an eyedropper. Click on a particular value in the image to identify its position on the curve, or Ctrl/⌘-click to automatically add the point to the curve. Then you can lighten or darken that part of the tonal range by moving that point on the curve, either by hand or by using the arrow keys, while you preview the result (see pages 127 and 134 for examples).

Making a slightly "M"-shaped Curves adjustment to bring out shadow detail and boost highlights; before (top) and after

VINTAGE / SEATTLE SUPPORT GROUP

Removing a Color Cast

If the image still seems to have color problems after you've expanded the dynamic range and corrected for exposure, try zooming in on some part of the image that should be neutral gray — that is, without color. Then select the gray eyedropper in the Levels or Curves dialog box and click it on the neutral spot. Unlike the black and white eyedroppers, the gray one has nothing to do with the overall brightness or contrast. Instead, it adjusts the color balance of the entire image based on the fact that you've told it what neutral should be.

If you can't fix the color cast with the Levels or Curves dialog box, try Image, Adjust, Color Balance, dragging the sliders to add the opposite of what your image has too much of. For instance, if it shows a blue cast, move the Blue/Yellow slider toward the Yellow end.

Retouching

Once the general tone and color corrections have been made, individual problems can be addressed. Some examples of common problems are listed on page 106.

"NONDESTRUCTIVE" RETOUCHING

Even with the option of using the History brush to fix significant goofs, using the retouching tools — rubber stamp, smudge, focus, and toning tools — involves "hand-painting," which can be tricky, especially if you have to go back later and correct a several-stroke mistake. Here are some ways to apply these tools so you don't permanently damage the image if you make a mistake, and so individual corrections can be easily seen and removed or repaired:

• Use the rubber stamp, smudge, or sharpen/blur on a transparent layer above the image (to add a transparent layer, click the New Layer icon in the middle at the bottom of the palette), first setting the tool to Use All Layers in its Options palette.

• The dodge and burn tools don't offer a Use All Layers option, but you can "fake" a merged dodge-and-burn effect as follows: Add a new layer in Overlay mode filled with 50% gray, which is neutral in Overlay mode. (If you Alt/Option-click the New Layer icon to open the New Layer dialog box, you can set the mode and fill when you first make the layer). Then work on this layer by using black paint (to dodge) and white paint (to burn) with a soft airbrush or paintbrush, with Opacity set very low. As you paint, be careful not to oversaturate the image.

• With the sponge tool it can be hard to pinpoint the saturation changes you want without also changing contrast or affecting more of the image than you want. Instead, add a Hue/Saturation Adjustment layer (Ctrl/⌘-click the New Layer icon). Make a Saturation adjustment that cures the particular problem — for the moment, ignore what happens to the rest of the image. Then fill the Adjustment layer with black, which will completely mask the Saturation change. And finally use a soft airbrush or paintbrush to paint with white in the problem areas, to let the saturation changes come through.

• Make an overall change to the image with a command from the Image, Adjust submenu or the Filter menu. Store a copy of the changed image by choosing Snapshot From Merged from the History palette's pop-out menu. Undo the change (Ctrl/⌘-Z), and use a soft-edged brush tip with the History brush to "paint" from the Snapshot where you want to apply the change.

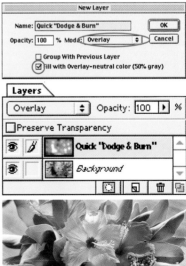

Using a separate 50%-gray-filled layer in Overlay mode for "dodging" and "burning"

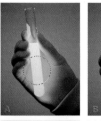

You can remove a color cast by adding the opposite of what you have too much of. Here a blue cast in the highlights was removed by adding yellow.

Making a selection (A) and changing the color balance can lead to harsh color breaks (B). But feathering the selection before making the adjustment helps the new colors blend in (C).

- **To correct the color of a particular area,** make a feathered selection and use Image, Adjust, Variations or Color Balance to adjust it. (Chapter 2 has tips on selecting and feathering.)

- **To correct only one particular color or family of colors throughout the image,** you can use the Select, Color Range command (see the "Selecting by Color" section on page 62 in Chapter 2) or use Replace Color or Selective Color from the Image, Adjust submenu. To constrain the color change to one area, make a selection that includes the region you want to change before you apply Color Range or Replace Color or Selective Color.

- **To remove dust and small scratches,** use the Dust & Scratches filter along with the History palette, as follows. The Dust & Scratches filter works by finding a distinct color break, such as you see when film has dust or scratches on it, and blurring the surrounding color into it to hide the blemish. To minimize the blurring of the rest of the selected area, start by setting the Dust & Scratches Threshold and Radius low. Increase the Radius just enough to fix the blemish, and then raise the Threshold as high as you can without eliminating the fix.

  In the History palette, choose New Snapshot from the pop-out menu to store a copy of this blurred image in the palette. Then Undo the Dust & Scratches filter (Ctrl/⌘-Z) to restore the nonblurred image. Now you can use the History brush to paint over the dust and scratches (this method is presented in detail in step 3 of "Fixing a Problem Photo" on page 123).

- **To remove larger blemishes,** use the rubber stamp, especially in Clone (Non-aligned) mode with a soft brush tip. Alt/Option-click to pick up neighboring color and texture, and click to deposit it.

Sharpening

Running the Unsharp Mask filter almost always improves a scanned photo. Usually it's the last thing that should be done to an image before it's prepared for the press, because the synthetic effects of sharpening can be magnified in other image-editing processes, such as increasing saturation of the colors. Sharpening is discussed more extensively in Chapter 5, "Using Filters."

MAKING BAD PHOTOS LOOK GOOD

There are times when a particular photo *must* be used in a project, but the photo just can't be redeemed by the normal correction processes. Here are some ideas for those kinds of photos:

- **To simplify and stylize an image,** use a filter to hide defects. Filter, Artistic, Cutout creates a posterized effect. You can choose a number of colors or shades of gray and also control the smoothness and fidelity of the color breaks. Or try Filter, Blur, Smart Blur as described in Chapter 5 on page 176.

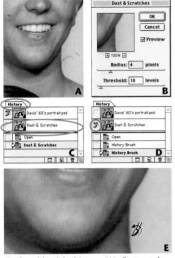

To fix a blemished image (A), first run the Dust & Scratches filter on the entire image, with settings high enough to hide all the problems (B). Then take a merged Snapshot of the filtered image (C). Undo the filter and set the new Snapshot as the source for the History brush (D). Paint with the smallest soft brush tip that will paint out the defects (E).

© CORBIS IMAGES ROYALTY FREE, BUSINESS & INDUSTRY

Posterizing an image with the Cutout filter

© CORBIS IMAGES ROYALTY FREE, MEN, WOMEN & ROMANCE

Removing unwanted detail

© PHOTODISC, HOLIDAYS & CELEBRATIONS

Blurring the background (right) can eliminate detail that competes with the subject.

- **To restore color to a severely overexposed (washed-out) photo,** add an Adjustment layer above it (by Ctrl/⌘-clicking the New Layer icon at the bottom of the Layers palette). In the New Adjustment Layer dialog box choose Levels for the Type and Multiply for the mode, and click OK. When the Levels dialog box opens, click OK without making any adjustments. Now that this "blank" Levels layer has given you a better range of tones to work with, add another Levels Adjustment layer, this time in Normal mode, and make typical Levels adjustments (beginning with Auto). (This trick won't work well with an image that's blemished or that shows obvious film grain, because these artifacts will also be multiplied, so it's a good idea to fix these problems first.)

- **To silhouette a subject against a bright background,** select the subject and fill it with black.

- **To get rid of unwanted detail in the background**, select the background and blur it as described in "Blurring for Attention" on page 130. Or use the rubber stamp in a Clone mode to paint over distracting background objects with other background texture.

- **To get rid of a background altogether,** select it and fill it with white or with a color. Another option is to make a clipping path that will silhouette the subject and mask out the background when you export the photo to another program: Press the "P" key to choose the pen or magnetic tool, and outline the subject. Or make a selection by other means and save it as a path. (Refer to Chapter 2 for the specifics of operating the pen and selection tools). Open the Paths palette (Window, Show Paths), choose Save Path from the palette's pop-out menu, then choose Clipping Path from the same menu, and select your named path in the Clipping Path dialog box. Enter a higher Flatness value if the path is very long and complex. Now you'll be able to save the file in EPS or TIFF format to be imported into another program and printed. Before you save it in TIFF format, make sure the page layout program and separation software you plan to use can handle TIFFs with clipping paths. And if you save it in EPS mode, you may need to convert it to CMYK mode (choose Mode, CMYK Color) in case the other programs can't separate RGB EPS files.

- **To piece together a problematic panorama,** you can remove and replace the original sky. Blending the part of the scene that continues from one photo to another — often this is the sky — is usually the hardest part of making a panorama sequence into a single image. One solution is to remove the sky, and then replace it with a sky from a different photo, a stretched version of the sky from one of the montaged images, or a synthetic sky (see page 157 for tips on assembling panoramas).

Silhouetting a subject with a clipping path allows it to be exported without its background

Starting with a color image (A), in most cases the simplest and best method for conversion to grayscale is to choose Image, Mode, Grayscale and then adjust Levels (B). Choosing Image, Adjust, Channel Mixer and loading the Grayscale Standard.cha preset (from the Presets folder in Goodies on the Adobe Photoshop 5 Application CD-ROM) can provide another good starting point for conversion to Grayscale (C), especially for low-contrast images.

CONVERTING FROM COLOR TO GRAYSCALE

Photoshop provides several ways of converting a color photo to black-and-white. Each method produces a somewhat different result. The method you choose will depend on what you want to do with the image, and you may need to do some experimenting and compare the results. With any of these methods you can try using Image, Adjust, Levels, Auto to optimize the dynamic range.

- The **quickest way** to convert a color file to grayscale is to choose Image, Mode, Grayscale. The intense grays produced by this method may yield the best results if your image will be output to a film recorder to make a photo negative or slide.

- Often you get a **crisper grayscale image for print reproduction,** where dot gain may be a factor, by converting from RGB Color to Lab mode (Image, Mode, Lab Color) and then deleting the "a" and "b" channels by opening the Channels palette (Window, Show Channels) and dragging these channels' names to the trash can icon at the bottom of the palette. Convert the resulting Multichannel file to Grayscale for export. This method can produce a lighter image than if you go directly from RGB to Grayscale.

- For a photo that will be reproduced in black-and-white with a printing method that uses a low halftone screen density, like a **laser print** or a newspaper, you can sometimes get a better result by converting to Bitmap mode using a diffusion dither as described in step 2 of "Making a Mezzotint" on page 109.

- For **special photographic effects,** such as simulating an infrared photo, you can produce a grayscale version of the image by selectively mixing the individual color channels. Choose Image, Adjust, Channel Mixer; turn on the Monochrome option; and move the sliders to try different mixes. Use the Constant slider to lighten or darken the image overall. For more about channel mixing, see "Channel Mix-and-Match" on page 115.

- For **special artistic effects,** most of the filters found in the Filter, Sketch submenu produce black-and-white results, although they don't actually make the mode change (you can do that afterwards with Image, Mode, Grayscale).

> **MINIMIZING NOISE**
>
> When you use the Channel Mixer for conversion of a scanned image to Grayscale, be careful of using too much of the Blue channel, because most of the noise (film grain and so on) is in that channel.

- If you'll need **to add color back to selected parts** of the image once you've removed it, use the Image, Adjust, Desaturate command, and then apply Image, Adjust, Variations (as in "Hand-Tinting an Image" on page 127) or Image, Adjust, Hue/Saturation with the Colorize box checked.

Making a Mezzotint

Overview *Experiment with the Mezzotint filter, Bitmap mode, and the Andromeda Series 3 filter.*

Filter, Pixelate, Mezzotint, Medium Dots

Mode, Bitmap, Diffusion Dither

Mode, Bitmap, Pattern Dither, Mezzotint-shape (from the PostScript Patterns folder)

Filter, Andromeda, Standard Mezzo, 85 lpi

A TRADITIONAL MEZZOTINT is produced with a halftone screen made up of custom dot shapes. (Halftone screens convert photos into patterns of tiny dots for printing.) Before experimenting with several ways to create a mezzotint from a grayscale image, choose Image, Image Size and set the Print Dimensions of your file. If you don't want to be able to see pixels, use a Resolution above 300 dpi. The exception is for the Diffusion Dither method (see step 2), where the Resolution should be set at 300 dpi or less.

1 Using Photoshop's Mezzotint filter. Choose Filter, Pixelate, Mezzotint; pick a dot, line, or stroke pattern in the Mezzotint dialog box's pop-out menu. (Unlike the other native Photoshop methods in steps 2 and 3, this treatment can also be applied to a color photo.)

2 Using a diffusion dither. Convert the image by choosing Image, Mode, Bitmap and choosing Diffusion Dither as the Method.

3 Using a pattern dither. Choose a pattern from the PostScript Patterns folder that comes with Photoshop 5/5.5 and open the pattern document. Or paint with black on white to create your own pattern. If you make your own pattern, keep the balance between black and white fairly even, and then blur the file slightly to get a full range of grays.

When the pattern tile is ready, Select All (Ctrl/⌘-A) and choose Edit, Define Pattern. Now in your grayscale photo file choose Mode, Bitmap. Enter an Output resolution, click the Custom Pattern button, and click OK. (The higher the resolution, the smaller the mezzotint "grain" will be and the less visible the pixels. But be careful you don't create a dot pattern too fine to print well.)

4 Using Andromeda Software's Screens filter. For a variety of well-crafted mezzotint effects, you may want to buy the Andromeda Series 3 filter (see "Filter Demos" in Chapter 5). Install it in your Plug-ins folder and choose Filter, Andromeda, Screens. Select from the Preset menu, or enter your own settings. We used a Mezzotint for the image at the left and a Mezzogram for the image above.

Using an Image as a Halftone Dot

Overview *Use a grayscale image to make a custom "halftone dot" pattern; apply it to a photo.*

Image to be "halftoned"
(834 x 995 pixels)

Image to be used as the halftone dot

"Dot" image scaled down to 75 x 88 pixels

Defining the scaled and selected photo as a pattern

3a

Bitmap	
Resolution	OK
Input: 300 pixels/inch	Cancel
Output: 600 pixels/inch	
Method	
○ 50% Threshold	
○ Pattern Dither	
○ Diffusion Dither	
○ Halftone Screen...	
● Custom Pattern	

Converting the grayscale photo to Bitmap

Close-up of the Bitmap image

WORKING WITH A RECOGNIZABLE IMAGE as a "halftone dot" rather than a random, seamlessly tiling pattern can produce an interesting mezzotint effect.

1 Choosing images. Choose the photo file that you want to "halftone" with your custom dot pattern. Also choose a grayscale image, or a selection from an image, with a broad range of tones — black, white, and a full range of grays — to use as your halftone dot.

2 Defining the pattern. Reduce the "dot" image or selection to the relative size you want it to appear when it's used as a custom halftone dot. For instance, if you will use 600 pixels/inch for the final image (as described in step 3) and you want to see about 8 of your dots per inch (as we did), you should reduce the dot image to about 75 pixels wide (600 dpi ÷ 75 pixels = 8 "halftone dots"). You can do this by using Layer, Transform, Numeric on a selection or by choosing Image, Image Size. Then surround this small version with the rectangular selection marquee and choose Edit, Define Pattern.

3 Applying the pattern. "Halftone" your large photo by choosing Image, Mode, Bitmap (if the photo is in color, choose Image, Mode, Grayscale first and then Image, Mode, Bitmap). To convert the 256 tones of your grayscale photo to the black-and-white-only Bitmap, click the Custom Pattern button and enter an Output Resolution value (we used 600 pixels/inch). The value you enter here will determine how small your "halftone dots" will be relative to the image (the higher the number, the more dots) and whether you'll be able to see the pixels (lower resolutions) or not (higher resolutions).

"Artistic" Noise

Overview *Apply a Noise filter in Monochromatic mode; Despeckle.*

 "Artistic Noise" image and Actions

Original image

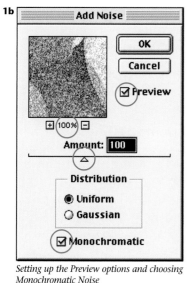

Setting up the Preview options and choosing Monochromatic Noise

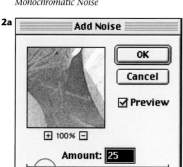

Experimenting with the Amount setting for Monochromatic Noise

AN EXAGGERATED FILM GRAIN EFFECT for a color image can be achieved quickly and simply with the Add Noise filter, applied so that it causes a random brightness pattern at the pixel level without introducing the color speckles of random hue variation.

1 Choosing hue-protected Noise. Open a color image in RGB mode. Choose Filter, Noise, Add Noise and choose Uniform. Click to select the Monochromatic option to produce *hue-protected noise*. Within the dialog box, set the preview size (the line with the + and − boxes) at 100% for the most accurate view of the effect. If you want to see the effect on the image overall, not just in the preview box within the Add Noise dialog box, make sure Preview is selected.

2 Experimenting with the amount and kind of Noise. Use the pointer (which turns into the scrolling hand) to move the image around in the Preview box until you see an area that will give you a good view of the changes, especially the lights and darks.

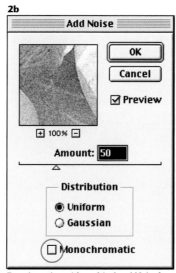

Experimenting with multicolored Noise by turning off Monochromatic

Adjust the Amount slider until you see the effect you want in the preview window. When the preview looks good, move the Add Noise dialog box out of the way so you can see the effect on the image overall. Finally, click OK in the dialog box to accept the Noise settings and close the dialog box. We tried settings of 100, 50, and 25 for this 900-pixel-wide image, and also tried turning off Monochromatic.

3

The Despeckle filter softens the grain, as shown here. Despeckle was applied to the image after filtering with Uniform Monochromatic Noise at a setting of 100.

3 Trying more variations. For a larger but softer and more "painterly" grain, apply the Despeckle filter (Filter, Noise, Despeckle) to the image after applying the Monochromatic Noise. The result shown at the top of the previous page was developed by running the Despeckle filter on an image filtered with a Uniform Monochromatic Noise setting of 50.

FILTER SETTINGS AND IMAGE SIZES

When you apply a filter or other special effect that operates at the pixel level of an image, the setting to use will depend on the degree of effect you want *and on the resolution* of the image you're working on. The larger the absolute size of the image — indicated by the dimensions of the image in pixels or the size of the flattened file (in K or MB) — the higher the setting will need to be to produce the effect. In the examples shown below, note that a low setting has a much stronger effect on a smaller image than on a larger one. For the larger version, the setting has to be increased quite a bit to get a similar-looking result. So if you see a filtered image and want to create that particular effect on an image of your own, you need to know not only the filter settings that were used, but also the size of the image that was filtered.

Image size: 250 pixels wide (157 K); Uniform Monochromatic Noise, Amount setting: 20

Image size: 500 pixels wide (625 K); Uniform Monochromatic Noise, Amount setting: 20

FADING THE EFFECT

Photoshop's Filter, Fade command provides a way to "soften" the effect of a filter immediately after applying it, without completely undoing it and starting over. The Fade command isn't necessarily equivalent to using a lower filter setting. Instead, it's as if you had run the filter on a copy in a layer above the original and you were now reducing the Opacity of this top layer, varying the contribution of the filtered and nonfiltered images to the final effect. The Fade command can also be used with the commands of the Image, Adjust submenu and with painting.

Image size: 250 pixels wide (157 K); Uniform Monochromatic Noise, Amount setting: 40

Image size: 500 pixels wide (625 K); Uniform Monochromatic Noise, Amount setting: 40

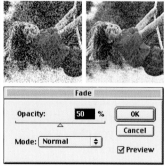

Image size: 250 pixels wide (157 K); Uniform Monochromatic Noise, Amount setting: 40, Despeckle

Image size: 500 pixels wide (625 K); Uniform Monochromatic Noise, Amount setting: 40, Despeckle

Before (top left) and after applying the Filter, Fade command after Noise, Add Noise

Dithering

Overview *Convert the image to Bitmap mode with a low-resolution Diffusion Dither; convert the Bitmap image to RGB color; select and copy the black pixels only to a separate transparent layer; replace black with a color gradient; replace the color in the Background layer with another gradient.*

 "Dithering" Action

CONVERTING IMAGES TO BITMAP MODE with Photoshop's Diffusion Dither pattern can be useful for making the plates used for silkscreen printing or for adding a distinctive texture to a color illustration. If you start out by putting the black and the white elements of the dithered image on two separate layers of an RGB file, it's easy to experiment with color until you have exactly the result you want.

1 Converting a photo. Start with a color or grayscale image. Convert it to Bitmap through the Mode submenu: If the image is in Grayscale mode to start with, choose Image, Mode, Bitmap. If it's in color, you'll have to choose Image, Mode, Grayscale first, because you can't convert directly from a color mode to Bitmap or vice versa. When you make the conversion, specify a low resolution in the Bitmap dialog box. We used 123 dpi, but you can use any resolution low enough to show a pleasing pattern. The resolution that looks best to you may vary, depending on your printing specs, how large you want to print the image, and what its particular content is.

2 Making a layer for the black pixels. To convert the dithered image to RGB mode so you can add color, choose Image, Mode, Grayscale and then Image, Mode, RGB.

Now you'll select all the black pixels: Double-click the magic wand in the toolbox to open its Options palette. Turn off Anti-aliased, and **if you're using Photoshop 5.5**, turn off Contiguous. Since there are only black and white pixels in the image — no intermediate colors — the wand's Tolerance can be set to anything but 255 and still pick out only black pixels when you click on a single black pixel. (To get a closer view so you can pick out a pixel, hold down the Ctrl/⌘-spacebar key combination to turn the magic wand into the magnifier temporarily.) **If you're using version 5**, once

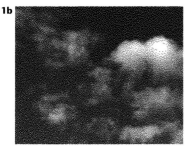
Converting a Grayscale photo to Bitmap

The Bitmap image converted to RGB

2

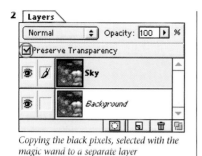

Copying the black pixels, selected with the magic wand to a separate layer

3a

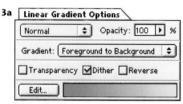

Setting the Linear gradient options

3b

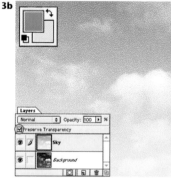

Black pixels filled with a gradient

4

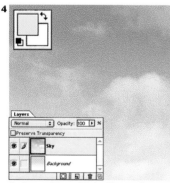

Background layer filled with a gradient

5

Gradients replaced with other gradients (left) and with two solid colors (right)

you've clicked on a black pixel, choose Select, Similar to add all the rest of the black pixels to the selection. Copy the selection to make a new layer (Ctrl/⌘-J) that includes the black pixels only; we named our layer "Sky." Turn on Preserve Transparency (click the check box at the top of the Layers palette) to ensure that when you color the layer the existing pixels, but not the transparent areas, will be colored.

3 Coloring the black pixels. With the new layer active, double-click on the Linear gradient tool to open its Options palette; set it for a Normal mode, Foreground To Background, and 100% Opacity. Then, in the toolbox, click on the Foreground and Background color icons in turn and choose colors for the extremes of the color gradient you'll use to replace the black pixels. We used a blue for the Foreground color and a lighter blue for the Background color. In the image, drag the gradient tool from where you want the color to start changing to where you want the transition to end (we dragged from top to bottom). The black pixels will be replaced with the color gradient.

4 Adding the second color gradient. Activate the Background layer by clicking on its name in the Layers palette. You can now apply your second gradient — the one that will color the white pixels — to the entire Background layer. Set the Foreground and Background squares in the toolbox to new colors (we used a pink and white), and use the Linear gradient tool again to apply the color (we applied this gradient vertically also, this time dragging from about a third of the way from the top to about a third of the way from the bottom). Although this operation will color both the black and the white pixels in the Background layer, the layer above (Sky in our example) will allow only the pixels that used to be white (the clouds in our example) to show through its transparent areas.

5 Experimenting with other color schemes. Now you can try new color gradients by repeating the coloring instructions in steps 3 and 4 with different colors. Or you can use a multicolor gradient or a solid color for either or both of the layers. Or, instead of using the gradient tool in steps 3 and 4, use the Edit, Fill command (or Alt/Option-Delete and Ctrl/⌘-Delete) to refill the pixels in the two layers. Whichever method you use, be sure to keep Preserve Transparency turned on when you fill the top layer.

Combining resolutions. To combine the look of a low-resolution dither with a higher-resolution element as we did for the eye-in-the-sky image, you can use Image, Image Size, Resample Image: Nearest Neighbor on the dithered image, increasing the Resolution to an even multiple (2, 4, 6, or 8 times) of the current resolution to reach print resolution. Then drag and drop your original high-resolution element into the file.

Channel Mix-and-Match

Overview *Experiment with color and grayscale effects with a Channel Mixer Adjustment layer.*

"Channel Mix" image and Actions

Original photo

1b

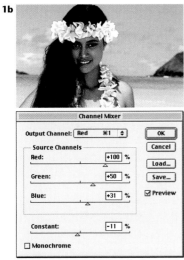

*Loading Adobe's **RGB Pastels.cha** preset provides a good start toward a hand-tinted look by adding to all color channels to lighten the colors in the image.*

2

*Adobe's **RGB Swap Red&Blue.cha** preset*

JHD / ORIGINAL PHOTO: © CORBIS IMAGES ROYALTY FREE, AMERICAN DESTINATIONS

EVERYTHING FROM SUBTLE COLOR ADJUSTMENTS to radical colorizing, to sepia tones, to optimized grayscale conversions can be produced with the Channel Mixer command. And if you apply the channel mix by means of an Adjustment layer, you have the makings of a very practical image manipulation tool.

Because it would take a great deal of space to show the settings for all the variables in the Channel Mixer dialog box, for this example we've used the presets that Adobe supplies with Photoshop. One way to learn how to work this complex dialog box, with as many as 20 variables to set, is to apply a preset and study the settings that produce the result you see. Then experiment with the settings and watch the changes in the image. (Printed examples of Adobe presets are provided in "Channel Mixer Demos" on pages 148 and 149.)

1 Starting with pastels. Open an RGB image, open the Layers palette, and Ctrl/⌘-click the New Layer icon at the bottom of the palette to add an Adjustment layer. From the Type list, choose Channel Mixer. In the Channel Mixer dialog box, click the Load button and find and load the RGB Pastels preset (it's on the Adobe Photoshop Application CD-ROM: Presets, Special Effects, **RGB Pastels.cha**). Inspect the settings in the Channel Mixer box for each Output Channel: Red, Green, and Blue. Notice that the dialog box tells you that the new Red channel now includes all the brightness information it originally contained (Red, 100%) plus 50% of the brightness information from the Green channel and 31% of the brightness information from the Blue channel. The brightness in the other Output Channels is similarly boosted. The effect of adding brightness to all three Output Channels (R, G, and B) is to

3

Wow RGB Hula Color.cha (from the Wow CD-ROM)

4a

Blocking the effects of the Channel Mixer Adjustment layer with a painted mask

4b

*Starting with the **Wow RGB Hula Color.cha** preset in step 4, we adjusted Layer Options to allow part of the original blue sky to show.*

lighten the colors, producing pastels. Reducing the Constant setting to –11% balances the lightness somewhat by slightly darkening image tone overall.

2 Swapping channels. While you're working in the Channel Mixer, try another option. Load Adobe's **RGB Swap Red&Blue.cha** preset to produce a color reversal. Because the Green channel stays intact, the image stays positive rather than becoming a negative.

3 Heading toward fluorescent. Still in the Channel Mixer, load the **Wow RGB Hula Color.cha** preset (from the Wow Channel Presets folder on the Wow CD-ROM). Click OK to close the Channel Mixer dialog box.

4 Restricting Channel Mixer effects. Now you can paint the Adjustment layer's built-in mask so it blocks the Wow RGB Hula/ Color Channel Mixer effect from the flowers and skin tones, as follows. With the Channel Mixer layer active and with black as the Foreground color, choose the paintbrush tool. Press Enter to open the Options palette, set the tool's Opacity low, and paint.

Another way to "drop out" the effect of the Channel Mixer layer from some parts of the image is to choose Layer Options from the Layers palette's pop-out menu and adjust the "This Layer" and "Underlying" sliders. To split the sliders so color transitions are gradual rather than abrupt, hold down the Alt/Option key as you move one half of the slider. (For a more thorough explanation of how these sliders work, see page 155). Move the righthand slider in This Layer inward so that light colors of the channel mix don't contribute to the image. Move both Underlying sliders inward to restrict the channel mix to the midtones, so part of the original blue sky shows through.

Experimenting with grayscale. Try some conversions from RGB to Grayscale with Monochrome chosen in the Channel Mixer box.

4c

The image at the top of page 115 was produced with the layer mask shown in figure 4a and with the Layer Options settings above, which protected the lightest colors, such as the white in the bathing suit, from change.

*A grayscale conversion made with the **Wow RGB Hula Grayfx.cha** preset. See page 139 for other grayscale conversion methods.*

Duotones and Other Tint Effects

Overview *Apply each of four subtle coloring techniques: (1) preparing a Duotone, (2) colorizing a gray version of the image, (3) combining color and gray versions, and (4) changing the color scheme of the composite.*

  "Duotone" image and Actions

1a

1b

Original image with type added and rotated

Converted to grayscale

1c

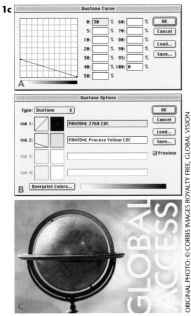

The curve for the yellow ink was adjusted to color the highlights (A). The Overprint Colors bar in the Duotone Options dialog box (B) predicts how the ink mix will look throughout the full range of tones, with yellow dominating in the highlights and purple shadows in the duotone image (C).

IF YOUR PRINTING BUDGET LIMITS YOU to two-color design, Photoshop's Duotone mode can deliver a sophisticated look that's quick, easy, and flexible. Even for a four-color print job, the subtle coloring of a duotone or a soft tint may be just what you're looking for. Here are four ways to achieve subtle color; you can start with a color image, as we did, or start with a Grayscale file and convert to the mode you need — Duotone for the technique in step 1, or RGB for the methods in steps 2, 3, and 4.

1 Making a duotone. Through the curves for Ink 1 and Ink 2 in the Duotone Options dialog box, Photoshop's Duotone mode gives you precise control of how each of your two colors is applied to the range of tones in your image. To set up your Duotone, if your image is RGB, convert it to Grayscale, since a Photoshop Duotone is actually a grayscale image with Curves information stored with it. We used Image, Mode, Grayscale to convert this image; other conversion methods are described in "From Color to Gray" on page 139.

Now you can convert to Duotone mode (Image, Mode, Duotone) and choose Duotone from the Type pop-out menu. You can then set up your two color curves, as described in the next paragraph, or click the Load button and select one of the

2

Using the Colorize option in a Hue/Saturation Adjustment layer to tint an image

3

Toning down a color image by adding a Hue/Saturation Adjustment layer in Color mode

4

Changing the Hue to go from a warm to a cool color scheme

Duotone color sets supplied in the Duotone Presets folder on the Photoshop 5/5.5 Application CD-ROM.

To make your own set of curves as we did, click the color squares for Ink 1 and Ink 2 in turn and choose a color from the color sets offered when you click the Custom button in the Color Picker dialog box. Once the colors are chosen, if you click the Curves box next to each color square in the Duotone Options dialog box, dragging to change the curve will modify the color treatment. You can watch the image change as you adjust the curves. For this example, we left the dark purple (Ink 1) at its default setting and changed the curve for the yellow (Ink 2) so that a 30% tint of yellow was applied to the highlights, fading to 0% at the dark end of the tonal scale, so that the deepest shadows would remain pure purple.

2 Colorizing. To create a sepia or other subtle tinting effect, start with a grayscale image converted to RGB (Image, Mode, RGB) or with a color file desaturated (Image, Mode, Desaturate) as described in "Preserving Luminosity" at the right. Then add an Adjustment layer by Ctrl/⌘-clicking the New Layer icon in the Layers palette and choosing Hue/Saturation as the Type. In the Hue/Saturation dialog box, click the Colorize box and experiment by moving the Hue and Saturation sliders until you get the color you like.

3 Desaturating a color image. Start with an RGB image and add an Adjustment layer by Ctrl/⌘-clicking the New Layer icon in the Layers palette. Choose Hue/Saturation as the Type, and be sure to choose Color as the Mode (see "Preserving Luminosity" at the right). Move the Saturation slider in the Hue/Saturation dialog box to the left to reduce the color; we set it at –75.

4 Changing the tint. For the image shown at the top of page 117 we simply moved the Hue slider in the Adjustment layer added at step 3. This shifted the color from its original warm tones to cool, but maintained the range of subtle color differences. 🖉

PRESERVING LUMINOSITY

You can protect the original tonal range and contrast when you apply Image, Adjust, Desaturate in order to convert a color image to "black-and-white" but still have the potential for adding back color: Just choose Filter, Fade and choose Color for the Mode in the Fade dialog box.

Likewise, you can also preserve tonal range when you desaturate a color image by adding a Hue/Saturation Adjustment layer: When you add the Adjustment layer, choose Color as the Mode in the New Adjustment Layer dialog box.

WARNING!

Anytime you're working with the sliders in the Hue/Saturation dialog box and preparing an image for printing, it's a good idea to turn on the Gamut Warning (Ctrl/⌘-Shift-Y) so you don't get carried away.

Gamut Warning uses a medium gray to show colors that fall outside the printable range and thus can cause unpredictable results on press.

"Popping" an Image

Overview *"Ghost back" the* Background *layer of an image to make the subject "pop."*

"Popping Color"
image and Actions

Further **Up**, and Further **In.**
America's National Parks in 2000.

A POPULAR EFFECT IN BOTH PRINT AND VIDEO is to isolate the subject of an image by de-emphasizing the background. This effect can be used to make the subject stand out, to simplify the background for overprinting type, or to tie an image to others in a publication.

1 Isolating the subject. Use the appropriate selection tool or command to select the subject (see the beginning of Chapter 2 for tips on choosing and using the right selection method), and then save the selection. We used the pen tool (activate it by pressing the "P" key) to outline the hiker because the shape consisted largely of smooth curves. When the path was finished, we saved it by double-clicking the Work Path name in the Paths palette. Then we converted it to a selection by Ctrl/⌘-clicking its name in the palette.

1

Selecting the subject and saving the selection

2

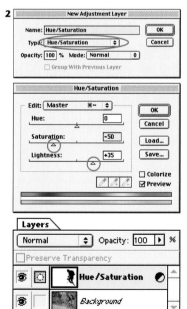

Adding a Hue/Saturation Adjustment layer to ghost back the background, with a mask to protect the subject from change

2 Ghosting the background. Switch your selection from the subject to the background (choose Select, Inverse, or press Shift-Ctrl/⌘-I). Create a Hue/Saturation Adjustment layer by Ctrl/⌘-clicking the New Layer icon at the bottom of the Layers palette and choosing Hue/Saturation from the Type list in the New Adjustment Layer dialog box. The active selection will create a mask in the Adjustment layer that will protect the subject from the adjustment. We reduced Saturation and increased Lightness.

Trying another variation. For the image at the right we selected the Colorize box, adjusted the Hue slider to the desired color, and then desaturated the color to 15%. (When Colorize is off, the Saturation scale goes from –100 to +100; when it's on, the range is 0 to 100.) Finally, we added type to the image using a method like that described in "Applying Type and Layer Effects" on page 94. *wow*

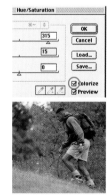

Turning Colorize on, adjusting Hue, reducing Saturation, and leaving Lightness at the default is another way to make the subject "pop."

Softening the Focus

Overview *Duplicate an image to an another layer; blur this layer; recombine it with the original.*

ACTION **IMAGE** "Soft Focus" image and Actions

JHD / PHOTO: © CORBIS IMAGES ROYALTY FREE, FOOD

SINCE THE END OF THE 19TH CENTURY, photographers have used haze and fog effects to impart a soft quality to an image that hides the detail in the highlights, or in both highlights and midtones, or in the image overall. With a camera, the effect can be achieved by smearing petroleum jelly on a filter in front of the lens, by breathing on the filter, or by placing fine nylon mesh over the enlarging lens in the darkroom. These techniques are often used to hide small skin blemishes, to make hair look softer, or to add a romantic, diffuse halo around the highlights of an image. In Photoshop you can get a similar effect with the Gaussian Blur filter and layers.

1a

Original image

1b

Image copied into a new layer

1 Making a duplicate of the image on a new layer. Open an image and open the Layers palette (Window, Show Layers). Drag the *Background* layer's name to the New Layer icon in the center at the bottom of the Layers palette to make a copy of the image.

2 Blurring the duplicate layer. Choose Filter, Blur, Gaussian Blur to make the new layer look out-of-focus. We used a setting of 10 pixels for this 1000-pixel-wide image.

3 Adjusting mode, Opacity, and Layer Options to make haze. Now make one of the following changes to the Layers palette settings for the top layer:

- **To reduce the haze** effect but still apply it to all the tonal values in the selected area, choose Normal and change the Opacity.

- To refine the haze effect **to soften the highlights only**, choose Lighten and adjust the Opacity to control the strength of the haze effect. (We used this technique for the opening image.)

- **To create a painted look**, reducing the number of colors and softening them, choose Darken and reduce the Opacity.

Other haze effects can be achieved by using the "This Layer" and "Underlying" sliders in Layer Options, chosen from the Layers palette's pop-out menu. To soften the image only within a particular

2a

Blurring the image

2b

The duplicate layer, blurred

3a

Reducing the opacity of the blurred layer

3b

Softening the highlights with Lighten

tonal range, hold down the Option key and drag the Underlying black and white sliders. Holding down the Alt/Option key as you drag will allow you to split each slider triangle, so you can smooth the transition by defining a range of colors that are to be only partially composited. Experiment with the slider positions, moving the two parts of each triangle apart slightly to avoid harsh color breaks. The settings that work best will depend on the colors in the image and the effect you're trying to achieve. (For tips on using the Layer Options sliders, see page 155.)

Saving the file. When you have an effect you like, click OK to close the Layer Options dialog box. If you think you may want to do some more experimenting with the image in the future, save it in Photoshop format to preserve the layers. If not, you can make the haze effect permanent by combining the file's layers into a single *Background* layer (choose Flatten Image from the Layers palette's pop-out menu). Flattening saves file space and also lets you save the file in a format — EPS or TIFF, for example — that can be imported into a page layout program. An alternative that allows more flexibility is to use File, Save A Copy to save a renamed, closed copy in any file format that Photoshop supports, leaving the current version of the file intact and open. ◗◗

3c

3d

Creating a painted effect with Darken

Softening only part of the tonal range

To add a "healthy glow" to a portrait or still life, you can use the color channels of an RGB file rather than an entire blurred layer: As shown at the right, activate only the Red channel but turn on the eye icons so you can view all three channels together; apply the Gaussian Blur filter. The image is softened and a small amount of the Red component is blurred outward, creating a glow. The unblurred Green channel maintains the detail so that the blurring effect is not too strong.

Fixing a Problem Photo

Overview *Adjust overall tonality; lighten or darken specific areas; eliminate blemishes*

"Problem Fix"
image and Action

JHD

1a

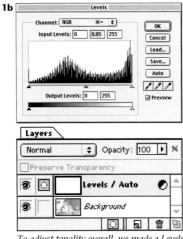

Original photo

1b

To adjust tonality overall, we made a Levels Adjustment layer named "Levels / Auto."

FIRST THINGS FIRST

In making color and tone adjustments to a photo, tackle the worst problem first. For instance, if the main problem is that it's too dark or too light overall, start with a Levels adjustment. But if it looks distinctly green, for example, fix the color cast first.

THERE ARE MANY APPROACHES TO FIXING a "problem photo." But the goal is to use a method that results in the highest quality and is at the same time fast, and flexible enough so it's easy to make changes, if needed, after a test print. While specific problems vary from photo to photo, some of the most common difficulties are an overall darkening, lightening, or a loss of tonal range in the midtones; particular areas that are either in shadow or are "washed out"; and blemishes caused by scratches on the film or print, or dust on the enlarger when the photo was printed. Our original, a family photo from the 1960s, showed all three problems. The fixing process began with restoring the tonal range, since this "quick fix" was likely to solve many of the photo's problems. The blemish repair was done last, since any slight artifacts caused by the repair might have been exaggerated by tonal adjustments if the repairs had been done first.

1 Adjusting overall tonality. The first step in bringing back the full tonal range in this faded photo was to use Photoshop's Auto Levels, applied in an Adjustment layer. To start the repair, open the Layers palette (Window, Show Layers) and make an Adjustment layer by Ctrl/⌘-clicking the New Layer icon at the bottom of the palette. Choose Levels as the Type, and click Auto Levels in the Levels dialog box.

Auto Levels makes the "best guess" at correcting tonality by redistributing the brightness information for all the color channels. Although this is often a good fix, it can sometimes exaggerate or even introduce a color cast. If that happens, or if the tonality still doesn't look good after you've run Auto Levels, you can click the Cancel button in the Levels dialog box and set the Levels manually, as described in "Making Good Photos Look Better" on page 102.

2 Dodging and burning. Photoshop's dodge and burn tools were designed to provide the digital equivalent of those two darkroom

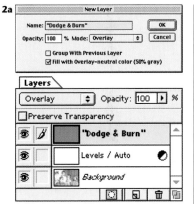

A "Dodge & Burn" layer was set up in Overlay mode, filled with Overlay-neutral 50% gray.

Because 50% gray in Overlay mode has no effect on the image underneath, you can look directly at the image (top) as you "burn" with black paint and "dodge" with white. (The "Dodge & Burn" layer is also shown here in Normal mode, at the bottom.)

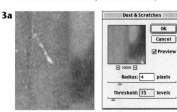

Applying the Dust & Scratches filter, increasing the Radius until the blemishes disappear

techniques, lightening and darkening specific areas of the image. But with three different options for each tool (Highlights, Midtones, and Shadows) set in the Options palette, the dodge-and-burn process can be slow and a bit confusing. For many images it's simpler to try what we call a special "Dodge & Burn" layer, set up in Overlay mode and filled with 50% gray.

When a layer is in Overlay mode, its dark tones darken the image underneath and its light tones lighten the image. Because 50% gray is neither dark nor light, it's neutral in Overlay mode — it has no effect.

With the top layer active, Alt/Option-click the New Layer icon to not only add a new layer but also open the New Layer dialog box. Now you can name the layer, set the Mode to Overlay, and then fill the layer with "Overlay-neutral" 50% gray. When you click OK to leave the New Layer box, you'll see that your image doesn't look any different than before you added the gray-filled layer.

Now you can use the airbrush or a soft-edged paintbrush to paint on the new "Dodge & Burn" layer. Double-click your painting tool in the toolbox to open its Options palette, and set the Pressure or Opacity setting very low (5–10%). Use black paint where you want to burn, or darken, the image underneath and white paint where you want to dodge, or lighten. With your painting tool at a low setting, you can go back and forth over the area you want to change until it looks right. Just don't overdo it — in a color image, too much burning can oversaturate the color. For this image black paint was used to tone down the white in the shirts, the light streaks in the wall in the background, and "hot spots" in the highlights on the faces. White paint brought out detail in some of the dark areas of the hair.

3 Getting rid of blemishes: Applying a filter with a brush.

Photoshop's Dust & Scratches filter is designed to hide thin lines and small spots that are very different in color from their surroundings. It does this by blurring the surrounding colors into the lines or spots. There are two problems with running the Dust & Scratches filter on an entire photo to get rid of imperfections: First, it can "fix" things that aren't broken — removing the highlights in the eyes of a portrait, for instance. Also, since the filter works by blurring, the degree of blurring that's needed to fix the worst spots may be more than you need to fix others, and it can result in the image looking blurred overall.

Now with the History palette it's easy to fix the problem spots without degrading the rest of the image: Choose Filter, Noise, Dust & Scratches, using Radius and Threshold settings that fix most

PRESERVING FILM GRAIN

In the dialog box for the Dust & Scratches filter, the Threshold setting controls how different from its surroundings a speck or scratch has to be before the filter will recognize it as a blemish and blur the image to cover it. To avoid eliminating the film grain in a scanned image, first set the Radius as high as you need to fix the problems. Then increase Threshold as high as you can without eliminating the fix.

3b

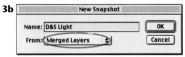

Taking a merged Snapshot of the filtered image after the first application of Dust & Scratches

3c

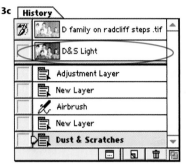

The History palette after taking the first merged Snapshot

3d

The History palette after undoing the first application of the Dust & Scratches filter

3e

The Dust & Scratches filter was run again, another merged Snapshot was taken, and Undo was applied again. The History brush was set up to paint over the blemishes, first using the D&S Light Snapshot and then the D&S Heavy Snapshot as shown here.

of the problem areas over the entire image, but at this point don't worry about the worst ones. Create a merged Snapshot of the image in this slightly blurred condition (Alt/Option-click the New Snapshot icon in the History palette to open the dialog box, where you can choose Merged Layers and name the Snapshot "D&S Light"). Then undo the filter (Ctrl/⌘-Z) and rerun it at a higher setting that gets rid of *all* the dust-and-scratches problems, including the worst ones. Take another Merged Snapshot, naming this one "D&S Heavy." Once again, undo the filter.

Now you have your photo in its original state and two Snapshots with different degrees of "fixing." Create a new empty layer above your image (click the New Layer icon in the Layers palette). Choose the History brush from the toolbox, and in the History palette click in the brush column to the left of the D&S Light Snapshot. "Paint over" the easier-to-fix problems, using the smallest soft brush tips that will eliminate them (Window, Show Brushes). Then click in the brush column for the D&S Heavy Snapshot and paint over the worst spots. After you've finished, survey the repairs. Because you've made a separate "repairs" layer, if you see spots that look too blurry or obvious, you can use the eraser and try again.

3f

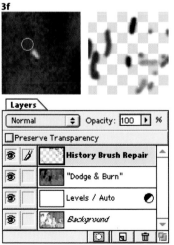

Painting on an empty "Repair" layer with the History brush lets you look directly at the image (top left) as you eliminate blemishes. Looking at the Repair layer by itself (top right), you can easily locate and erase any mistakes.

FIXING DOUBLE TROUBLE

For photos in which the sky is overexposed and the foreground underexposed, you can use two Levels or Curves Adjustment layers, each one with a mask that limits the change.

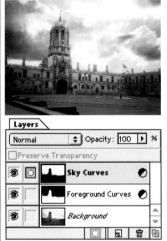

In this example the sky was selected using Select, Color Range. A Curves Adjustment layer was added by Ctrl/⌘-clicking the New Layer icon at the bottom of the Layers palette, and the selection automatically became a mask that limited the Curves change to the sky. The Curves layer was then duplicated by dragging its thumbnail to the New Layer icon, and the new layer's tonality was inverted (Ctrl/⌘-I) to create a mask that limited the effect to the foreground. Double-clicking the new layer's black-and-white circle reopened the Curves dialog, where the settings could be changed.

Simulating Motion

Overview *Isolate the subject of an action photo on a layer of its own; copy the original photo to another layer; motion-blur the copy; adjust the blurring of the image by masking the subject or changing the opacity of the blurred layer.*

1a

Original image

1b

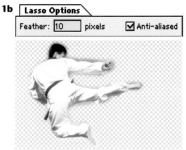

Subject isolated on a new layer made from a feathered selection

2a

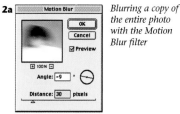

Blurring a copy of the entire photo with the Motion Blur filter

2b

Motion-blurred copy of the original image

ADDING A SENSE OF MOTION to a photo can draw the viewer into the excitement of the scene and give a good static image the added drama to make it great. Using blurring techniques in Photoshop, you can simulate the effect of a camera panning to follow the subject (as shown above) or of a stationary camera with the subject in motion. With layers, layer masks, and the Motion Blur or Radial Blur filter, you have an amazing amount of flexibility in localizing the motion effect to a particular area of the image if you like — a waving hand, for example. And the Opacity control in the Layers palette lets you interactively reduce the blur until you see exactly the effect you want.

1 Isolating a sharp copy of the subject. You'll need a way to keep the moving subject in focus when you blur the background. First open your image file, and then open the Layers palette (Window, Show Layers). Now select the subject: We made a rough selection, using a feathered lasso. (We set a 10-pixel feather for this 900-pixel-wide image. We kept the selection border just far enough away from the subject so the feathering didn't encroach on its outline. A rough, feathered selection can be used if the background image lacks detail, as this one does. But if the background is busy, you'll need a tighter, less feathered selection.) Turn the selection into a layer of its own (Ctrl/⌘-J).

2 Blurring the picture. To give yourself more options later (as described in step 3), make a duplicate copy of the full image in a new layer by dragging the *Background* label in the Layers palette to the New Layer icon in the middle at the bottom of the palette. Apply a blur to this new layer. We used Blur, Motion Blur at an angle of –9° and a distance of 30 pixels.

At this point, the blurred image in the "Background Copy" layer entirely hides the original in the *Background* layer underneath it. But the sharp copy of the subject (in the top layer) keeps the subject in focus; and the feathered edge of the sharp subject blends seamlessly into the blurred image below it.

2c

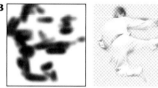

The result of layering the sharp subject and blurred Background Copy

3

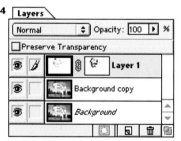

The dark parts of a painted layer mask (left) hide the corresponding parts of the subject. This will allow the blurred layer below to show through.

4

Layers palette for the image shown at the top of page 125, with the top layer and its mask offset to produce a strobe effect

An alternate approach: To simulate a photo taken with a stationary camera, the subject is isolated and blurred over the sharp background image.

3 Tailoring the blur effect. Now you can add a little "blur detail" to the subject by masking out some areas of the top layer. With the top layer active, click the Add Layer Mask icon on the left at the bottom of the Layers palette. Now the mask will be active but the subject itself — not the mask — will be visible. You can see the blur start to show through as you use a soft airbrush to apply black paint where you want to see more of the blur — for instance, at the trailing edge of the moving subject. The dark areas of the mask will prevent the sharp layer from contributing to the composite. If you "erase" too much of the sharp image, just paint the mask with white to bring back detail. Also, if the blur effect on the background seems too strong, you can sharpen the entire image by adjusting the Opacity slider of the blurred Background Copy layer to let the sharp original show through.

4 Simulating a strobe. To get the effect of a panning camera with a strobe (a flash that freezes part of the subject in focus while the slower shutter speed records the motion), you can offset the sharp copy of the subject. Working in the top layer, use the move tool to slide the subject a short distance in the direction of motion. Because by default the layer mask is linked to the image, as shown by the chain icon between them, the mask will move with the subject.

Trying a variation. To simulate a stationary camera photographing a moving subject, you can blur the subject and keep the background in focus: Select and copy the subject to its own layer as in step 1, and then apply a blur filter to this layer only.

More variations. Here are some other ways to tailor the blur to the image: You can show more motion in some parts of the subject than others by copying the subject onto two layers, blurring one more than the other, and then painting masks to allow more or less blur to show in different areas. And you can use a Radial Blur to show swinging or zooming motion. *Wow!*

A Radial Blur with a Spin setting was used to show the motion of the swing. Extra height was added with the Image, Canvas Size command so the blur center could be defined outside the image — above, where the chain is fastened to a tree limb. Then the final image was cropped. For the photo of the runner, the Background Copy layer was treated with a Radial Blur in Zoom mode, centered in the lower right corner of the image, to bring the runner forward.

"Hand-Tinting" a Portrait

Overview *Convert the black-and-white image to RGB mode; select areas and colorize with Variations.*

1a

Original grayscale image

1b

Converted to RGB

SECRETS OF THE CURVES BOX

The Curves dialog box offers several ways to customize your operations:

- Click the bar below the graph to toggle between 256-gray-level and 0-to-100% scales.

- Ctrl/⌘-click on the image to add a control point to the curve.

- Press the arrow keys to move the active point on the curve 2 out of 256 gray levels at a time, adjusting the shape of the curve.

- Alt/Option-click the grid for a finer scale (10% increments) so you can place and move points more precisely.

THE COLORING OF BLACK-AND-WHITE PHOTOS with paints and dyes began very early in the history of photography, and its popularity persisted until color photography became widespread. Today the look is popular again — not a technicolor imitation of a color photo, but a subtle coloring reminiscent of the early hand-tinting process.

1 Correcting the tonality of the image. Whether you start with a color or a grayscale scan of the black-and-white image, you can use Photoshop's Levels (Ctrl/⌘-L) and Curves (Ctrl/⌘-M) adjustments to spread the tones in the image over the full range of possibilities and to bring out the shadow and highlight detail. For this image, which seemed a little dark to begin with, we used Image, Adjust, Curves to lighten the three-quarter tones, thus increasing the shadow detail.

To find where to adjust the curve, move the cursor out of the Curves dialog box and onto the image. The cursor will turn into an eyedropper. If you click to pinpoint a tone that you want to adjust, a small circle will appear on the diagonal line in the Curves dialog box to show which part of the curve corresponds to the tone currently under the eyedropper. If you drag the eyedropper, the circle will move to reflect the current tone. When you've identified the tone you want to adjust, Ctrl/⌘-click at that spot on the image and a control point will be added to the diagonal line.

We identified a dark area of the image with the eyedropper and Ctrl/⌘-clicked on it to create a point at an Input value of about 15 on the diagonal line. Dragging upward on the point raised the entire curve. Clicking directly on the curve to form another point at an Input value of about 128 (halfway in the 0 to 255 range of the curve) and dragging downward closer to the center of the grid

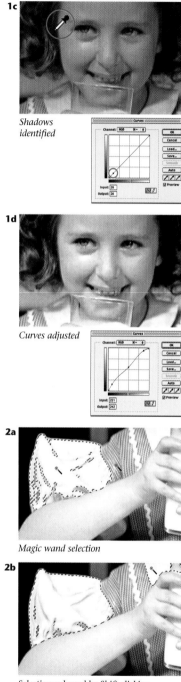

1c

Shadows identified

1d

Curves adjusted

2a

Magic wand selection

2b

Selection enlarged by Shift-clicking

returned the midtones, quarter tones, and highlights to values close to their original settings.

When making these kinds of Curves adjustments, it's important to maintain a smooth curve shape, without drastic changes in direction. Otherwise you can accidentally flatten the color or produce a sort of solarization effect with harsh tonal breaks.

LOCAL TONE ADJUSTMENTS

If you want to lighten or darken the three-quarter tones in only certain parts of an image, use the dodge and burn aspects of the dodge/burn/sponge tool instead of Image, Adjust, Curves. In the Brushes palette choose a soft brush tip of an appropriate size. In the Toning Tools Options palette choose a tonal range (Highlights, Midtones, or Shadows) and choose Dodge or Burn, depending on whether you want to lighten or darken.

To reduce the intensity of the dodge/burn tool's effect, lower the Exposure setting before you start using the tool. To reduce the effect even more, choose Midtones or Highlights to work on the shadow tones. At any of the three settings, these tools work on the entire range of tones but they have a more pronounced effect on the part of the range that matches the setting you choose.

If you overdo the lightening or darkening, you have at least two options for reducing the effect: You can use the Fade command (Filter, Fade) to reduce the "opacity" of the last stroke you applied. Or you can undo as many strokes as necessary by stepping back through the History palette, clicking on the most recent step and working backwards until you have undone your mistake.

2 Making selections. Next you'll select various parts of the image so you can make color adjustments. Select one area, change it by the method in step 3, then select another, and so on. For this image the dress was selected by clicking on it with the magic wand tool with a Tolerance setting of 32 (double-click the magic wand in the toolbox to open the Magic Wand Options palette to change the setting). Additions to the selection were made by Shift-clicking on other parts of the dress. When the selection was complete, it was assigned a 5-pixel feather for this 1155-pixel-wide image. (To open the Feather Selection dialog box so you can set the Feather Radius, choose Select, Feather.)

The skin was selected with the lasso, feathered 5 pixels (double-click the lasso to open Lasso Options to set the Feather). This selection was drawn loosely to imitate the old hand-tinting process, which often involved soft overlapping of colors.

ADDING COMMANDS

You can add any of Photoshop's commands to any Actions palette: Choose New Action from the palette's pop-out menu, then choose Insert Menu Item. Choose your command, click OK, and press the square button at the bottom of the Actions palette to stop recording.

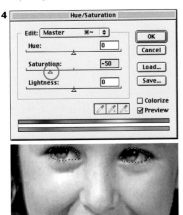

Adjusting color balance in the midtones

Desaturating white areas

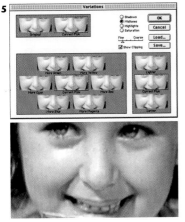

Adding color details

3 Coloring the selections.

Once selections have been made, choose Image, Adjust, Variations to open the Variations dialog box. (Unlike many other commands in the Image, Adjust menu, Variations can't be applied as an Adjustment layer; it has to be applied to an image layer directly.) The hue adjustment in the Variations box is especially helpful for creating skin tones — it's an electronic cosmetologist's dream that lets you preview the tinting possibilities at a glance. Starting with fairly coarse adjustments (set with the slider near the top right corner of the dialog box), you can clearly see what color changes you're selecting. As you zero in on the changes you want, move the slider left to make finer adjustments. Then click on the desired preview to make it the "current pick."

4 Desaturating neutral areas.

Areas that have been colored too much can be desaturated or recolored by selecting them with a very slightly feathered lasso (we used a 1-pixel feather) and choosing Image, Adjust, Hue/Saturation. For example, selecting the eyes and teeth and then moving the Saturation slider to the left tends to take away most of the tint, while still maintaining the overall warm color cast that makes these features "at home" in this tinted image.

5 Adding color details.

After hard-edged areas (such as the chair, butter, bread crust, and wrapper in this image) have been selected with a 1-pixel-feathered lasso and colored by using the Hue slider in the Hue/Saturation dialog box, subtle color variations can be added to the face. For instance, the cheeks in this image were selected with the lasso feathered to 5 pixels, and the Variations dialog box was used again to apply More Red in the Midtones.

AVOIDING HARSH BREAKS

For the most part, when you colorize parts of an image, change only the *hue* of the *midtones*. Changing the highlights or shadows or the brightness or saturation of selected areas tends to make selections look unnaturally distinct from their surroundings.

SAVING TIME ON IMAGE ADJUSTMENTS

If you hold down the Alt/Option key as you choose certain Image, Adjust commands, the dialog box will open with the last settings used, rather than with the built-in defaults. (Threshold and Posterize do this even without the Alt/Option key.) If you're working through a series of images, layers, or channels that all need the same kind of adjustment, holding down the key as you choose the Image, Adjust function and then clicking OK can be quite a bit faster than using the dialog box's Save and Load buttons.

Better yet, the first time you make the change, record an Action, and then play it on a batch of files (see "Automating with Actions" starting on page 27 in Chapter 1). Or make an Adjustment layer and drag-and-drop it from one file's Layers palette into your other files.

Blurring for Attention

Overview *Select the part of the image you want to remain sharp — the subject — and cut it out of the background; blur either the background alone or both background and foreground; add noise to simulate film grain in the blurred areas.*

"Background Blur"
image and Action

1a

Original image

© CORBIS IMAGES ROYALTY FREE, ARMED FORCES

IHD

1b

Channels		
RGB	⌘~
Red	⌘1
Green	⌘2
Blue	⌘3
Alpha 1	⌘4

The selection of the two men was stored in an alpha channel for safekeeping.

2a

Layers		
Normal	Opacity: 100 %
Preserve Transparency	
Background	
Original Image	

The original image was duplicated and the two layers were renamed.

THE TECHNIQUE OF ISOLATING THE SUBJECT and keeping it in focus as you blur other parts of the image can be used to remove uninteresting or distracting detail from an image, or as in this case to focus attention on the subject. The Photoshop technique presented here imitates the effect you get with a *shortened depth of field,* traditionally achieved by opening up the camera's iris (setting the f-stop low). The blurring can be limited to the background (follow the step-by-step process below, stopping after step 3), or as shown here the sharp subject can be sandwiched between blurred background and blurred foreground (continue through step 5 or 6).

1 Making and saving selections. Select the subject using the appropriate Photoshop tools or commands. (For help in choosing a selection method, see "Making Selections," "Selecting by Shape," "Selecting by Color," and "Selecting by Shape *and* Color," starting on page 62.) For this image we used the lasso to make the selection, then stored the selection as an alpha channel by choosing Select, Save Selection and clicking OK. (The stored selection would be useful later in making the selection of the sailor alone.)

2 Making a separate subject layer. At this point, to avoid confusion later in the process, we double-clicked the *Background* thumbnail in the Layers palette to open the Make Layer dialog box. There we could rename it "Original Image," since the next steps in the process would involve making a layer to isolate the background, and we wanted to be able to name it accordingly.

To make separate layers for the subject and the background, first duplicate the image by Alt/Option-dragging its thumbnail in the

2b

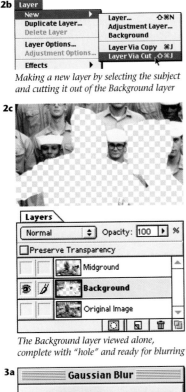

Making a new layer by selecting the subject and cutting it out of the Background layer

2c

The Background layer viewed alone, complete with "hole" and ready for blurring

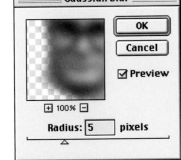

The Background layer viewed alone, complete with "hole" and ready for blurring

3a

Applying the Gaussian Blur filter

3b

All layers viewed together after the Background has been blurred

Layers palette to the New Layer icon at the bottom of the palette; this creates the layer and also lets you name it. We named the new layer "Background," since this is what it would soon contain.

Next cut the subject out of the Background layer as follows: Load the alpha channel for the subject by Ctrl/⌘-clicking its thumbnail in the Channels palette. To cut the subject to a layer of its own, choose Layer, New, Layer Via Cut or press Ctrl/⌘-Shift-J. Then double-click the new layer's thumbnail in the Layers palette to open the Layer Options dialog box, where you can name the new layer. We named ours "Midground," in anticipation of adding a blurred foreground later at steps 4 and 5.

You now have a top layer with the subject and no background, and a layer beneath it with the background and a "hole" where the subject used to be. This hole will prevent a "halo" from appearing around the subject when this Background layer is blurred. (If instead you were to layer a copy of the sharp subject over a blurred version of the entire original image, the blurring would bring some of the subject material outward into the surrounding area, causing an unwanted halo.) Now click on the Background layer's thumbnail to make it the active layer so you can blur it in the next step.

EXTRACTING THE SUBJECT

Photoshop 5.5's Extract command can be very useful in isolating a subject from its background, especially if there is strong contrast between the two. In the image used in "Blurring for Attention" the background includes patches of color that are very similar to the subject where they touch it, which makes the Extract command tedious to use — you'll spend more time fixing the mask than you would using the magnetic lasso or pen to make the selection.

However, for an image with more consistent contrast between background and foreground, Extract can be invaluable. You can follow this procedure (refer to "Extract" on page 72 if you need more information on how to use Extract): To make the subject into a layer of its own (as in step 2), start by duplicating the image to a new layer by Alt/Option-dragging its name in the Layers palette to the New Layer icon at the bottom of the palette. Then choose Image, Extract to open the Extract interface. Use the Edge Highlighter tool to outline the subject and click the Fill tool inside the painted border. Click the Preview button to see how the selected subject will look with the background removed, and click OK to complete the removal.

ORIGINAL PHOTO: © CORBIS IMAGES ROYALTY FREE, HOME IMPROVEMENT

3 Blurring the background. To blur the background, choose Filter, Blur, Gaussian Blur. We used a Radius setting of 5 pixels for this 1000-pixel-wide image to get the degree of blurring shown at the top of page 130. When this layer is blurred, the hole keeps the subject from being blurred outward, as described in step 2. The

4a

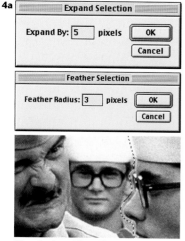

Expand Selection	
Expand By: 5 pixels	OK
	Cancel

Feather Selection	
Feather Radius: 3 pixels	OK
	Cancel

The selection of the sailor was expanded by 5 pixels so that blurring would not make his profile partly transparent. Feathering the expanded selection ensured that there would not be a visible edge between the blurred foreground and the midground and background behind it.

4b

	Blue	⌘3
	Alpha 1	⌘4
👁	Alpha 2	⌘5

A new alpha channel created from the expanded and feathered selection of the sailor in the foreground

4c

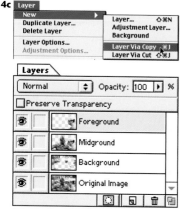

Layer
New ▸ | Layer... ⇧⌘N
Duplicate Layer... | Adjustment Layer...
Delete Layer | Background
Layer Options... | Layer Via Copy ⌘J
Adjustment Options... | Layer Via Cut ⇧⌘J

Layers
Normal | Opacity: 100 %
☐ Preserve Transparency
👁 | Foreground
👁 | Midground
👁 | Background
👁 | Original Image

Selecting the sailor from the Original Image layer and copying it to a new layer produced a separate layer for blurring.

edge of the hole becomes semitransparent as the hole blurs outward. But this semitransparency is hidden because the sharp Original Image layer below shows through to fill the narrow semitransparent fringe.

For many purposes the image-editing would be complete at this point, with a sharp subject — in this case the interaction between the officer and the sailor — emphasized against an out-of-focus background. Steps 4 and 5 change the focus of attention to the officer alone by blurring the sailor also. And step 6 adds back the film grain that was lost when parts of this grainy image were blurred.

4 Selecting the foreground for blurring. To select the sailor we loaded the alpha channel made in step 1 and subtracted from the selection (holding down the Alt/Option key as you use any selection tool subtracts what you select from the existing selection).

Before the new selection was saved as an alpha channel and then used to make a new foreground layer, the selection had to be modified further so that the blurred foreground would look right in the composite. We knew that blurring would make the edge semitransparent, as described in step 3. To make sure the edge of the foreground layer with the sailor didn't become semitransparent, allowing the more blurred Background layer to show through in some areas and the sharp Midground layer to show through in others, we expanded the selection at this point. That way the semitransparent transition edge would be outside the sailor's profile rather than cutting into it. We did this by expanding the selection by a few pixels more than the blur we would use on the sailor, so that some of what's behind the sailor in the photo would fill in the transparent places in the blurred transition. To do the expansion, we chose Select, Modify, Expand, 5 pixels. We softened the transition by choosing Select, Feather, with a Radius of 3 pixels. For safekeeping, the modified selection was then saved in a new alpha channel, which we named "Foreground" (Select, Save Selection, New).

5 Blurring the foreground. We activated the Original Image layer and used the selection we had just made of the sailor to create a new layer by copying (Layer, New, Layer Via Copy, or Ctrl/⌘-J). Then we moved this new copy to the front of the image by dragging its thumbnail to the top of the stack in the Layers palette. We applied a 3-pixel blur (Filter, Blur, Gaussian Blur), so that the foreground was blurred less than the background, as if the camera had been focused on the officer with a very short depth of field.

6 Restoring film grain. At this point the blurred background and foreground had succeeded in focusing attention on the officer, but our trickery was obvious because the blurring had smoothed out not only the details of the image but also the pronounced film grain in this photo. To replace the grain in the blurred areas, we decided to add two "noise" layers, one associated with the Foreground layer and one with the Background.

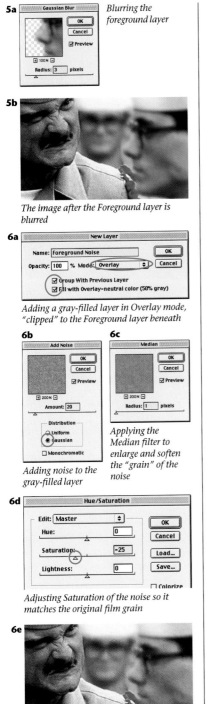

5a *Blurring the foreground layer*

The image after the Foreground layer is blurred

6a *Adding a gray-filled layer in Overlay mode, "clipped" to the Foreground layer beneath*

6b *Adding noise to the gray-filled layer*

6c *Applying the Median filter to enlarge and soften the "grain" of the noise*

6d *Adjusting Saturation of the noise so it matches the original film grain*

6e *The completed image focuses the viewer's attention on the officer, as shown here close-up and at the top of page 130.*

We started by Alt/Option-clicking the New Layer icon at the bottom of the Layers palette to add a new layer and to open the New Layer dialog box. There we chose Overlay for the Mode, and then turned on Fill With Overlay-Neutral Color (50% Gray); we also turned on Group With Previous Layer so that the new layer's effect would be limited to the Foreground layer immediately below it.

With the new layer in place we simulated film grain by adding noise: First we chose Filter, Noise, Add Noise, Gaussian, viewing the image and experimenting with the Amount setting until our experience told us that the speckling pattern we saw with Amount set at 20 would produce a graininess that would match the image once we applied the Median filter to soften the noise. (By not selecting Monochromatic, we kept color in the Noise treatment. Keeping the color would give us the freedom to adjust Hue and Saturation until our manufactured noise matched the original grain.)

Next, choosing Filter, Noise, Median, with a Radius setting of 1 pixel, produced a degree and quality of graininess that matched the original quite well. The only thing that remained was to modify the color in the added noise. We chose Image, Adjust, Hue/Saturation and moved the Saturation slider to the left until the manufactured grain matched the original.

To add film grain to the background we simply duplicated the Foreground Noise layer by dragging its thumbnail to the New Layer icon at the bottom of the Layers palette and then dragged the duplicate layer's thumbnail down to a position just above the blurred Background layer. *Wow!*

6f

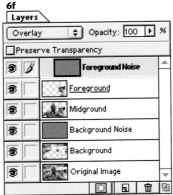

The finished image file includes the blurred Foreground, sharp Midground, blurred Background, Noise layers for the Foreground and Background, and the Original Image, which shows through only in the semitransparent edge areas of the Midground and Foreground layers.

FRAMING FOR FOCUS

A quick and easy way to focus attention on a subject is to simply select it with the rectangular marquee tool, copy the selected area to make a new layer (Ctrl/⌘-J), and then blur the *Background* layer. For added emphasis, add a barely noticeable dark "halo" around the sharp area using Layer Effects (step 3 of "Applying Type and Layer Effects" on page 95 tells how to apply this kind of Layer Effect).

Retouching a Photo

Overview *Scan the image; use Curves to adjust shadow and highlight density if necessary; roughly select any large, mostly uniform area that contains details that need to be removed; turn the selection into a mask that can be edited and then reloaded as a selection; replace the selected area; make repairs to other parts of the image using duplicated portions and cloning.*

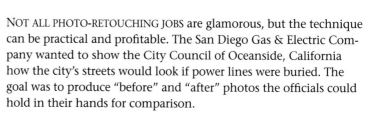

PHOTO: ROY ROBINSON

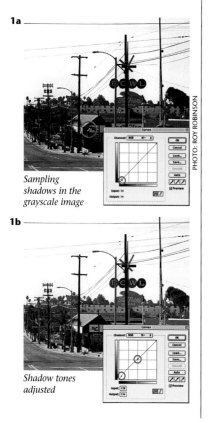

1a

Sampling shadows in the grayscale image

1b

Shadow tones adjusted

NOT ALL PHOTO-RETOUCHING JOBS are glamorous, but the technique can be practical and profitable. The San Diego Gas & Electric Company wanted to show the City Council of Oceanside, California how the city's streets would look if power lines were buried. The goal was to produce "before" and "after" photos the officials could hold in their hands for comparison.

1 Adjusting "exposure." Before retouching begins, the tonality of the original image may need correcting. We applied Image, Adjust, Curves to bring out shadow detail in the scanned photo without changing midtones and highlights.

The Curves function provides a way to isolate contrast and brightness changes to specific tonal ranges, such as quarter tones or three-quarter tones. Move the cursor out of the Curves box and onto the image (it becomes an eyedropper) and Ctrl/⌘-click to establish a point on the Curve for the tone you want to change; drag or use arrow keys to adjust its position. Then move other parts of the Curve back toward their original positions. (For more about operating the Curves dialog box, see page 127.)

2 Selecting the background. It can be very hard to seamlessly remove elements like power lines from a background texture like the sky, which can extend over a large area with subtle color changes. Sometimes it's easier to select the background, turn the selection into a mask, edit the mask to remove the extraneous elements, and then replace the entire background with a new one. For

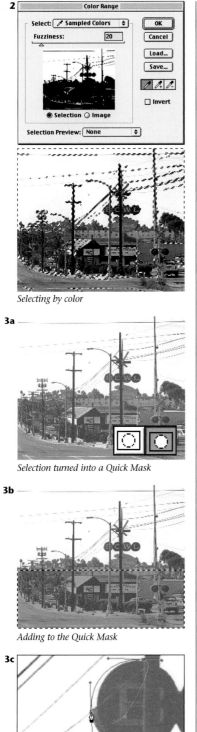

2

Selecting by color

3a

Selection turned into a Quick Mask

3b

Adding to the Quick Mask

3c

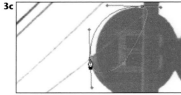

Repairing the mask

instance, instead of trying to remove the power lines by using the rubber stamp to paint sky over them, we decided to select the sky by color, add the power lines to the sky selection, and replace the entire selected area.

To select the sky by tone, we chose Select, Color Range. We wanted to make a selection that included all the grays in the sky. With Selection chosen for the display in the Color Range dialog box and starting with a Fuzziness of 20, we began by clicking with the Color Range eyedropper tool on a light part of the sky. To extend the range of selected tones, we held down the Shift key (the cursor turns to a "+," indicating that it will add to the current selection) and clicked on what seemed to be the darkest part of the sky. We continued to Shift-click, widening the range of selected tones, until the entire sky showed up as white in the preview box. Our selection included some light spots among the buildings, and it had missed the poles and wires. But now that the selection by Color Range had done most of the work, we could correct these omissions in the mask.

CHOOSING THE RIGHT FUZZINESS SETTING

When you select by Color Range it's a good idea to set the Fuzziness no lower than 16, to provide antialiasing. With a lower Fuzziness setting you get a very hard-edged selection and risk abrupt color breaks at the edges of the selected area. To select a specific area by color with a smooth, antialiased (but not feathered) edge, Shift-click with the Color Range eyedropper to expand the selection until it includes the area you want, and try to keep the Fuzziness setting between 16 and about 32. For soft-edged selections, set the Fuzziness higher. As the Fuzziness setting goes up, you tend to get a feathered effect, making the selected area partly transparent.

---

3 Using Quick Mask. When the selection is as complete as you can get it with the Color Range eyedropper and Fuzziness slider, click OK and then click on the Quick Mask icon in the toolbox. Then use the selection tools, eraser, and paintbrush to edit the mask.

The goal was to create a mask to protect everything but the sky and power lines. With black and white set as the Foreground and Background colors, respectively, we started by selecting a large rectangular area at the bottom of the mask, pressing Alt/Option-Delete to fill it with black and thus add to the mask, and then deselecting (Ctrl/⌘-D). To repair the few remaining white spots that were outside the sky, we painted with a paintbrush. We used the eraser to remove parts of the mask that covered the power lines.

Still in Quick Mask mode, we clicked and drew with the pen tool (press "P" to select the pen) to surround geometric areas that had been only partially included in the selection by color, such as parts of the "BOWL" sign. Opening the Paths palette (Window, Show Paths), we filled in the area surrounded by each path as we built it by clicking the Fill Path icon (at the bottom left of the Paths palette) to fill it with black and thus make it part of the protective mask.

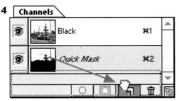
Saving the mask as an alpha channel

Replacing the sky with a gradient fill

Cloning to cover the power pole

Copying elements from the image

Copying and flipping

Trimming away hard-to-replace details

4 Saving the selection. Since your mask will probably be a complex one, store it in an alpha channel for safekeeping: Open the Channels palette (Window, Show Channels) and drag the Quick Mask channel icon to the New Channel button at the bottom.

5 Replacing the background. Next make the Quick Mask selection active by clicking the Standard Selection icon (next to the Quick Mask icon in the toolbox). You can now replace the background. We used a Linear gradient fill between two shades of gray from the existing sky: With the main Black channel active (clicked in the Channels palette) and the sky selection loaded (in the Channels palette, Ctrl/⌘-click its thumbnail), we started by clicking the eyedropper tool on the top of the sky to set the Foreground color; then we held down the Alt/Option key and clicked near the skyline to set the Background color. Next we double-clicked the Linear gradient tool in the tool palette to open its Options palette and set the tool to Normal, Foreground To Background, with the Dither check box turned on. We dragged the tool from the top of the sky selection to the bottom. To simulate the grain of the original photo, we added Noise (Filter, Noise, Add Noise) at a very low Gaussian setting.

6 Completing retouching tasks. Use the rubber stamp, lasso, and other tools and functions to retouch smaller areas of the image. We used the rubber stamp in Clone (Non-aligned) mode to grab (Alt/ Option-click) textures to paint over the power pole. We also lassoed and copied (Ctrl-Alt-dragged/⌘-Option-dragged) parts that could be reused, such as the "e" in the "Blue Palette" sign. For the "O" in "BOWL," we selected and flipped the intact half of the letter (press Ctrl/⌘-T for Free Transform, then pull up the context-sensitive Transform menu by right-clicking [Windows] or Control-clicking [Mac], and drag to choose Flip Horizontal).

Knowing what elements *not* to restore completely can save you a lot of time. For example, rather than trying to paint the missing part of a palm frond, we shortened the frond by rubber-stamping the roof texture over it.

Printing the picture. So that city officials could compare "before" and "after," prints were made of both versions.

Solarizing an Image

Overview *Prepare the image; add Adjustment layers, trying dramatic Curves settings.*

 ACTION "Solarizing" Actions

1a

Original image

1b

Blurring a duplicate of the image (bottom) softened the fine lines in the face.

SOLARIZATION WAS FIRST OBSERVED BY SABBATIER in 1860 and later discovered accidentally by Lee Miller and Man Ray in 1929. The partial reversal of positive to negative in a photographic print is caused by a brief exposure to light in the darkroom, often with dramatic effect. Today's photographic materials are much faster, though, which makes it difficult to solarize a photo in the darkroom. But you can get similar effects by manipulating Photoshop's Curves.

1 Preparing the scan. Both color and black-and-white (grayscale) images can be solarized. Open a scanned photo. If necessary, eliminate fine detail that might be undesirably exaggerated by the solarization process. The portrait shown here was duplicated (choose Window, Show Layers to open the Layers palette and drag the *Background* layer to the New Layer icon at the bottom of the palette). The copy was blurred slightly. We used Filter, Blur, Gaussian Blur with a Radius of 2 pixels to soften this 675-pixel-wide image. Then we reduced the Opacity of the blurred layer to about 50% to let some of the detail of the original image show through.

2 Making Curves Adjustment layers. To experiment with solarization without permanently changing your image, add an Adjustment layer: With the top layer active, Ctrl/⌘-click the New Layer icon in the middle at the bottom of the palette. In the New Adjustment Layer dialog box, choose Curves for the Type. When the Curves dialog box opens, select the pencil icon. Experiment by Shift-clicking with the pencil at the end points of the straight line segments you want to draw. At this point you can tell whether your combination

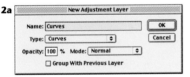
2a

Adding a Curves Adjustment layer

2b

Before adjusting Curves

2c

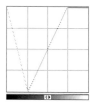

Drawing this "V" produces the same effect as the Solarize filter.

2e

Leaving midtones intact and pushing the lightest highlights to white

2d

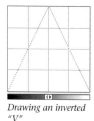

Drawing an inverted "V"

2f

Using a four-point curve

2g

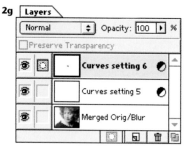

The image at the top of page 137 was made by stacking two Curves layers (2e and 2f above) with a small masking stroke of black over the nose in the 2e layer.

of blurred and original image works well for solarizing. If it does not, you can adjust the Opacity of the blurred layer or delete it altogether by dragging its name to the trash can icon at the bottom of the Layers palette. Start over by making a new duplicate layer for blurring at a different setting. When you have the result you like, merge the two layers (activate the upper image layer and press Ctrl/⌘-E to Merge Down).

Try new Curves settings by duplicating the Adjustment layer and then double-clicking the black-and-white circle icon on the duplicate layer and resetting the curve. View alternate settings by clicking the eye icons to turn your various Curves layers on and off. Try mixing and matching the Curves layers with different blending modes and Opacity settings. You can also apply black paint to a Curves layer to mask out the solarizing effect in particular areas.

When we had the effect we wanted, we flattened the file (by choosing Flatten Image from the Layers palette's pop-out menu) and applied Filter, Blur, Smart Blur to tone down pixel artifacts in the color without interfering with edge detail.

Trying other approaches. Convert a copy of your image to grayscale (Image, Mode, Grayscale) and apply solarizing curves. To colorize, add an Adjustment layer for Hue/Saturation, click the Colorize check box, and adjust Hue and Saturation.

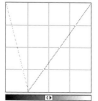

Solarizing a grayscale version of the file

Colorizing the solarized grayscale image with a Hue/Saturation Adjustment layer

From Color to Gray

Overview *Convert an RGB image using one of four methods.*

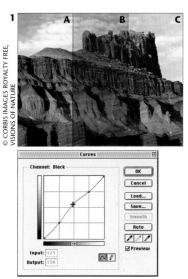

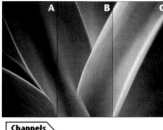

The RGB photo (A) was converted to Grayscale (B), and the midtones were lightened with a Curves Adjustment layer (C).

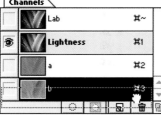

The RGB image (A) was converted to Lab color. Then the two color channels were removed and the file was converted to Grayscale (C). The direct RGB-to-Grayscale conversion (B) is shown for comparison.

IN PHOTOSHOP THERE ARE MANY WAYS to convert a color image to grayscale. The method you choose will depend on the characteristics of your original RGB image and whether you simply want to optimize the image for the best reproduction in one ink, or whether you want to achieve a particular photographic effect. In each case making the conversion to gray may be only part of the process. You may want to do some fine-tuning afterwards.

1 Making a "straight conversion." When your original RGB image shows good detail and tonal distinction, you can start with a direct conversion to grayscale and then fine-tune by adjusting Levels or Curves. For an image of canyon country we started by choosing Image, Mode, Grayscale. Then we lightened the midtones by adding an Adjustment layer. By saving the file with the Adjustment layer as well as a flattened copy for printing, we would be able to make changes to the Curves adjustment if a proof showed they were needed. To add a Curves Adjustment layer, Ctrl/⌘-click the New Layer icon, in the middle at the bottom of the Layers palette.

In the Curves dialog box you can "peg" the areas of the curve that you want to remain the same, and then make your adjustments. We wanted to preserve the highlights and shadows, so we clicked on the diagonal line at 25% and 75% of its length. Then we lightened the midtones by dragging the 50% point slightly up and to the left. (Fine-tuning with Curves or Levels can also be applied if needed after carrying out the techniques described in steps 2, 3, and 4.)

2 Reducing noise. If the image you start with is "noisy" with film grain or you simply want a softer look, you can do the conversion to grayscale by going through the Lab Color mode. To reduce the

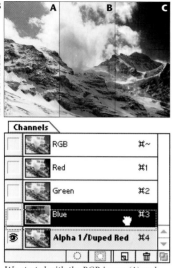

3

Channels

RGB ⌘~
Red ⌘1
Green ⌘2
Blue ⌘3
Alpha 1/Duped Red ⌘4

We started with the RGB image (A) and duplicated the Red channel as an alpha channel (here we've named it Alpha 1/ Duped Red). Then the three color channels were deleted and the file was converted to Grayscale (C). The direct RGB-to-Grayscale conversion (B) is shown for comparison.

4

Channel Mixer

Output Channel: Black

Source Channels
Red: 25 %
Green: 100 %
Blue: 25 %

Constant: 0 %

☑ Monochrome

OK
Cancel
Load...
Save...
☑ Preview

To make the poppies "pop" when this RGB image (A) was converted to black-and-white, we used a channel mix that included a 100% contribution from the Green channel and just 25% from the Red and Green (C). The direct RGB-to-Grayscale conversion, shown for comparison (B), lacked contrast, since the oranges in the poppies varied in hue but not much in tone.

film grain in this RGB image as we converted it to grayscale, we first chose Image, Mode, Lab Color. Then we removed the two color channels ("a" and "b") by dragging their names to the trash icon in the Channels palette, leaving only the Lightness channel. The image was now in Multichannel mode, which happens when you remove one or more of the color channels of an RGB, CMYK, or Lab file. Next we chose Image, Mode, Grayscale to finish the conversion.

3 Creating special photographic effects. To imitate the look of a photo taken with infrared film or with a color filter and black-and-white film, you can try picking your favorite grayscale version from the color channels of the RGB file. For this mountainscape, we opened the Channels palette of the RGB image and clicked in the eye column to turn the visibility of the channels off and on so we could view each channel alone as a grayscale image. (If your single-channel images are in color, you can switch to a grayscale display by choosing File, Preferences, Display & Cursors, and clicking the check box to turn off the Color Channels In Color option.) We duplicated this channel as an alpha channel by dragging it to the New Channel icon (next to the trash icon at the bottom of the palette). Then we deleted the three color channels by dragging each one to the trash icon. This left only the alpha channel, with the file in Multichannel mode. So we chose Image, Mode, Grayscale to complete the conversion. (Instead of making an alpha channel, you can simply delete the color channels you don't want by dragging each one to the trash icon. But this process can become confusing, since the color names of the channels change from the RGB system to the CMYK system as soon as the first color channel is removed. When the names change, Red always becomes Cyan, Green becomes Magenta, and Blue becomes Yellow, but the color display and name changes can be visually confusing. If you use an alpha channel, your grayscale choice will be displayed throughout the entire channel-deleting process.)

4 Mixing channels. In an image whose colors have distinctly different hues but similar values, the Channel Mixer can be used to good advantage. With your image in RGB Color mode, add an Adjustment layer as described in step 1, but this time choose Channel Mixer as the Type. In the Channel Mixer dialog box, turn on the Monochrome option by clicking the check box and make sure the Preview box is checked. Then move the Red, Green, and Blue color sliders to experiment with different contributions from each channel, keeping in mind that film grain and scanning noise are found mostly in the Blue channel. When you have a mix that you like, make a flattened duplicate of the image (Image, Duplicate, Merged Layers Only) so the Channel Mixer adjustment will be retained in your original when you convert your copy to grayscale (Image, Mode, Grayscale).

Adding a Spot Color

Overview *Import type or graphics into an RGB file; fill with white to make a knockout; create a spot color channel, allowing for trap; convert to CMYK; save in DCS 2.0 format.*

IHD/PHOTO: © CORBIS IMAGES ROYALTY FREE, DESTINATION TROPICS

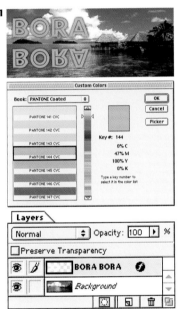

To create this clothing tag, the logo was dragged and dropped into an RGB file containing the background image. The logo was then filled with Pantone 144 CV for approval.

COMPUTING THE TRAP

Your printer can give you the size of the trap in mm or as a fraction of an inch, and you can convert that number to pixels:

Trap (in pixels) = Trap (in mm or inches) x Width of image (in pixels) ÷ Width of image (in mm or inches)

WHETHER YOUR GOAL IS TO EXACTLY MATCH a standard corporate color or to get that brilliant orange, blue, or metallic look that you know you just can't achieve with CMYK inks, Photoshop 5/5.5's ability to add spot colors can make the process easier than it was in earlier versions. Because of the difficulty of printing spot color on desktop color printers, producing a color file with an additional custom ink color starts with creating a layered file that looks like what you want to see in print. After approval of the color comp, you then create knockouts so that your custom ink can print directly on the paper rather than overprinting the other inks. Then make a special channel for the spot color. Somewhere in the process of making the knockout and producing the spot channel, you'll need to build in some *trap*, or overlap of the ink colors. That way if the paper shifts as it's going through the printing press, there won't be white gaps at the edges of the spot color elements.

1 Preparing a layered file for approval. Assemble your background image and spot elements in a layered RGB file, with the spot color elements on a layer of their own. (Starting in RGB Color mode provides the most color flexibility. For a discussion of the pros and cons of converting early or late in the file development process, refer to "Making RGB To CMYK Conversions" starting on page 43.) We started with a background image and dragged-and-dropped a logo that we had prepared in Adobe Illustrator. We added a "dark halo" to help the type stand out (Layer, Effects, Drop Shadow, with a Distance setting of 0 so the shadows are centered under the letters).

For on-screen or printed comp approval, activate the Layer with your spot color elements by clicking its name in the Layers palette, and then fill it with the custom color you plan to use for printing, as follows: Click the Foreground color square in the toolbox to open the Color Picker, click the Custom button, and choose your ink (we chose Pantone 144 CV from the PANTONE Coated set). Click OK to close the Color Picker and press Alt/Option-Shift-Delete to fill only the nontransparent areas with the custom color.

2 Preparing the knockout for print. After approval, you'll replace the stand-in spot color on your graphic layer to create a knockout so your custom ink will print directly on the paper rather than on top of the other inks. Simply change the Foreground color

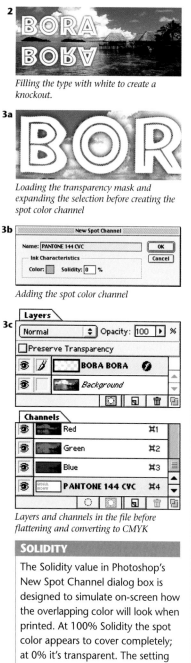

2

Filling the type with white to create a knockout.

3a

Loading the transparency mask and expanding the selection before creating the spot color channel

3b

New Spot Channel

Name: PANTONE 144 CVC   OK

Ink Characteristics   Cancel

Color: [ ] Solidity: 0 %

Adding the spot color channel

3c

Layers

Normal ⊕ Opacity: 100 ▶ %

☐ Preserve Transparency

👁 ✎ BORA BORA 🌀

👁 [ ] *Background*

Channels

👁 Red   ⌘1

👁 Green   ⌘2

👁 Blue   ⌘3

👁 PANTONE 144 CVC ⌘4

Layers and channels in the file before flattening and converting to CMYK

SOLIDITY

The Solidity value in Photoshop's New Spot Channel dialog box is designed to simulate on-screen how the overlapping color will look when printed. At 100% Solidity the spot color appears to cover completely; at 0% it's transparent. The setting doesn't actually affect the density of the printed ink; it's just to give you a preview. Generally, pastel colors (which contain opaque white) and darker shades (which contain black) are more opaque, and purer colors are more transparent.

to white (press "D" for the default colors and then "X" to switch the colors) and again press Alt/Option-Shift-Delete.

3 Adding the spot color channel, allowing for trap. The overlap needed for preventing gaps in ink coverage can be built by one of two methods — either by shrinking the knockout or by expanding the spot color elements. The method to choose will depend on the opacity of your custom ink. For instance, if the custom color is quite opaque, you should shrink the knockout, because any expansion of the elements will make them look "fatter." But if the ink is quite transparent (as is usually the case), you should expand the spot color elements, because shrinking the knockout will make them look too "thin." Your printer or the ink manufacturer can provide information about ink opacity. Also, your printer can tell you how large to make the trap, based on experience with press alignment.

To start the actual spot color plate and to build the trap, in the Layers palette Ctrl/⌘-click the knockout layer to load its transparency map as a selection. Then if you want **to expand the spot color elements** rather than shrink the knockout, you can do it as we did: Expand the selection by choosing Select, Modify, Expand and entering a value in the "Expand By" box (see "Computing the Trap" on page 141). With the selection active, open the Channels palette (Window, Show Channels) and choose New Spot Channel from the palette's pop-out menu. In the New Spot Channel dialog box, choose the custom color you used in step 1, set the Solidity, and click OK. The selection will automatically be turned into the new spot channel.

On the other hand, if you want **to shrink the knockout,** you can do it this way: With the selection active, open the Channels palette and choose New Spot Channel from the palette's pop-out menu. In the New Spot Channel dialog box, choose the same custom color that you used in step 1, set the Solidity, and click OK. Then go back to the Layers palette and click the knockout layer's name to make it the active layer. Ctrl/⌘-click its name to load its transparency map as a selection, and shrink the selection by the trap amount (Select, Modify Contract). Then trim off the edges of the knockout by inverting the selection (Ctrl/⌘-Shift-I) and pressing Delete.

Saving for output. Before you convert the file from RGB to CMYK (Image, Mode, CMYK), get your printer's advice about the settings in the CMYK Setup dialog box (File, Color Settings, CMYK Setup).

Unless your image will be output directly from Photoshop, Adobe Illustrator 7 or later, or Adobe PageMaker 6.5, choose File, Preferences, General and turn on the Short Pantone Names option. Next, for output via a page layout program, save the file in DCS 2.0 format (File, Save A Copy, Photoshop DCS 2.0); in the DCS 2.0 Format dialog box, turn off the Include Halftone Screen option and the Include Transfer Function option, and exclude the alpha channels. 🖌

A Three-Color Print

Overview *Prepare a grayscale image; create alpha channels to be used to control the spot colors; add spot color channels; load the alpha channels as selections in the spot color channels and fill them with black, white, and grays, trapping where necessary.*

 IMAGE "3-Color" image

1

The original digital photo

Levels adjusted and background removed

2

Adding a painted background in light and medium gray tones

3

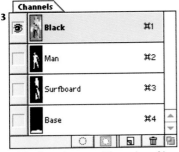

Channels		
👁 ▓ **Black**	⌘1
▓ Man	⌘2
▓ Surfboard	⌘3
▓ Base	⌘4

Alpha channels prepared for use in making selections for coloring the spot color channels later

CUSTOM (OR SPOT) COLOR IS THE CHOICE TO MAKE if you want more intense hues than CMYK inks can produce, if you want absolute control over the printing plates, or if you want to use a specialty ink such as a metallic, a fluorescent, or a varnish. Because of these attributes, spot color is often used for printing posters and for applying graphics to T-shirts and other nonpaper items.

One approach to this three-color project would be to choose the custom yellow and the custom red that you want to see in your printed image, and mix screens of these colors where orange is needed. If your project is riding along with a process color job, as of course ours was for the book, spot color allows you to take advantage

4

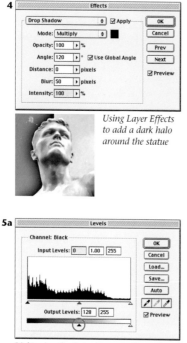

Using Layer Effects to add a dark halo around the statue

5a

Lightening the darkest tones in the surfboard and base to limit the black ink in the print

5b

Before (A) and after (B, C) adjusting Output Levels to reduce the darkest tones in the area controlled by the mask in the Adjusted layer

of the available colors and still have precise control of the printing plates. We used a mix of the process yellow and magenta to create red, with process black used for detailing, shading, and halo effects.

1 Preparing the photo. Our spot color project begins with a grayscale file. We started with a photo, taken on an overcast day, of a well-known statue in Santa Cruz, California, by Brian Curtis and Thomas Marsh. We adjusted the tonality (Image, Adjust, Levels) and used the Dust & Scratches filter globally to reduce noise in the image. Then the statue was traced with the magnetic pen, chosen because of the smooth, hard edges of the elements to be selected. The resulting path was saved by choosing Save Path from the Paths palette's pop-out menu and was turned into a selection by clicking the dotted circle icon at the bottom of the Paths palette. The selection was inverted so that the background could be removed by pressing the Delete key, isolating the statue on the transparent layer.

2 Adding the background. A new airbrushed background of abstract clouds was then added below the statue layer. First a new layer was added by clicking the New Layer icon in the middle at the bottom of the Layers palette, and it was filled with 50% gray (Edit, Fill, 50% Gray). The layer's thumbnail was dragged down to the bottom of the Layers palette to put the background behind the statue. Then this gray-filled layer was painted with soft-tipped brushes of different sizes with the airbrush tool, to create the amount of black detail that we wanted to see in the final image.

3 Making alpha channels. We started with the path saved in step 1 and made selections for the parts of the statue — surfer, surfboard, and base — and saved them in alpha channels, selecting the base and the surfer and then subtracting them from the overall selection to leave the surfboard (for tips on subtracting one selection from another, see the "Alpha Channel Efficiency" on page 76).

4 Adding a dark edging. To produce a soft, dark outline around the statue, we used a Layer Effects Drop Shadow, as follows: In the Layers palette we chose Layer, Effects, Drop Shadow and set the Drop Shadow parameters. To produce the dark edge we wanted, we used a large Blur setting, a high Intensity, full Opacity, and a Distance of 0 (for no offset).

5 Adjusting the maximum amount of black. To increase the impact of the large flat areas of the surfboard and base, we added a Levels Adjustment layer to lighten the black component of the image: We Ctrl/⌘-Shift-clicked on the thumbnails of the surfboard and base layers in the Layers palette to load them as a combined selection. Then we Ctrl/⌘-clicked the New Layer icon to add an Adjustment layer and chose Hue/Saturation as the Type. In the

6a

Type set and filled with 75% black

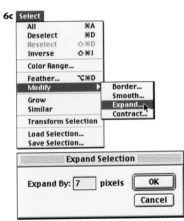

6b

Effects

Inner Shadow | ☑ Apply | OK
Mode: Multiply | ■ | Cancel
Opacity: 100 ▸ % | Prev
Angle: 120 ▸ ° ☑ Use Global Angle | Next
Distance: 0 ▸ pixels | ☑ Preview
Blur: 25 ▸ pixels
Intensity: 25 ▸ %

*Shading the interior of the letters with an
Inner Shadow Layer Effect*

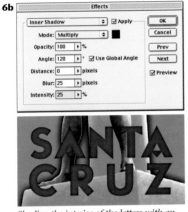

6c

Select

All	⌘A
Deselect	⌘D
Reselect	⇧⌘D
Inverse	⇧⌘I
Color Range...	
Feather...	⌥⌘D
Modify ▸	Border...
	Smooth...
Grow	Expand...
Similar	Contract...
Transform Selection	
Load Selection...	
Save Selection...	

Expand Selection

Expand By: 7 pixels | OK
| Cancel

*Expanding the selection made by loading
the type layer's transparency mask*

6d

*Filling the expanded selection to create an
outline for the type*

Levels dialog box we moved the Output black slider until the Output Levels value on the left read "128." That meant that 50% would be the highest density of black in the surfboard and base.

6 Preparing the type. To create the color-outlined type, we started by setting type in the Epic Gothic font and filling it with 75% black. (For information on setting type in Photoshop, see steps 4 and 5 of "Applying Type and Layer Effects" on page 95.)

To create an edge effect inside the type, we used an Inner Shadow Layer Effect on the type layer with a fairly large Blur setting and no offset (Layer, Effects, Inner Shadow).

To create the outline of the type — actually expanded letters behind the originals — we first loaded the type layer's transparency map as a selection (Ctrl/⌘-click the layer's thumbnail in the Layers palette). Then we added a new layer (click the New Layer icon) and dragged the new layer's thumbnail down in the palette to a position just below the type layer. Next we expanded the selection (Select, Modify, Expand), using an "Expand By" value of 7 pixels for this 1000-pixel-wide image. Finally we filled the selection with white (with white as the Background color, press Ctrl/⌘-Delete to fill).

To add the same dark halo to the outline of the type as we had used for the other elements, we copied and pasted the Layer Effects from the statue layer to the type outline layer, as follows: With the shadowed layer active, right-click (Windows) or Control-click (Mac) on its "f" icon and choose Copy Effects from the context-sensitive

6e

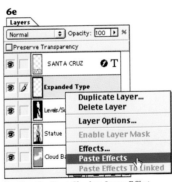

Layers

Normal | Opacity: 100 ▸ %
☐ Preserve Transparency

👁 | SANTA CRUZ | ⌀ T
👁 🖌 | **Expanded Type**
| Duplicate Layer...
| Delete Layer
👁 | Levels/S | Layer Options...
| Enable Layer Mask
👁 | Statue | Effects...
| **Paste Effects**
👁 | Cloud Ba | Paste Effects To Linked

*Pasting the Drop Shadow Layer Effect
copied from the statue layer into the*

6f

*The Drop Shadow added
to the expanded type layer*

6g

The finished grayscale image

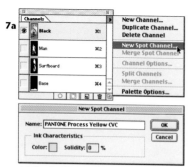

7a

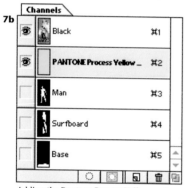

Adding the Pantone Process Yellow spot color channel

7b

7c

Adding the Pantone Process Yellow spot color channel

The image viewed with the Process Yellow spot channel added (left) and with both Yellow and Process Magenta (right)

menu. Then activate the layer you want to apply the shadow to and right/Control-click on the *name,* not the thumbnail, and choose Paste Effects.

7 Adding spot colors. As you add and manipulate spot colors as described in these next two steps, some advice from your printer can help you preview your developing design (read "Previewing Spot Colors," below).

PREVIEWING SPOT COLORS

Your printer can provide information about your spot color job that will help you set up your file for an accurate on-screen preview. For instance, you should be able to get a Solidity value (see "Solidity" on page 142), for how opaque each of your chosen ink colors is. Metallic inks are fully opaque, pastels and very dark colors are usually less transparent than brilliant hues, and varnish is completely clear. Entering this value when you add each spot color channel by choosing New Spot Channel from the Channels palette's pop-out menu will make your on-screen preview a more accurate predictor of what you will get when you print.

Also, your printer can tell you, based on the spot colors you've chosen, in what order the plates will be printed. The on-screen preview of spot colors assumes that the inks will be printed in the order in which they appear in the Channels palette. You can either add the spot colors with the first-to-print color added first, followed by the others, or you add the spot colors in any order and then re-order them by dragging their channels up or down in the Channels palette.

If you are using the Black channel of a Grayscale file as one of your printers, you won't be able to move the Black channel below the spot colors as long as the file remains in Grayscale mode. To be able to move the Black channel down the stack, convert to Multichannel mode (Image, Mode, Multichannel).

With the black channel complete, we opened the Channels palette and chose New Spot Channel from the palette's pop-out menu. In the New Spot Channel dialog box we clicked the Color square and chose Pantone Process Yellow CVC, then clicked OK to close the box. We wanted this spot color to print as solid yellow, so we filled the spot color channel with solid black (Edit, Fill, Black).

We followed the same procedure to add and file a second spot color channel, this time choosing Pantone Process Magenta CVC. Then we edited the Magenta spot channel to produce the desired color mixes in the surfboard and base by using the selections we had stored in the alpha channels.

7d

The channels palette with the original Black channel, two spot color channels, and alpha channels

7e

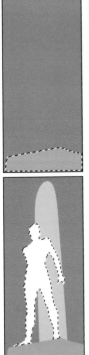

Loading and filling selections in the Magenta spot color channel: The base was filled with 75% black and the surfboard with 50% black. The surfer was knocked out of the Magenta plate by filling with white.

7f

The previewed image with all modifications to the Magenta channel complete, except the type outline

With the Magenta channel active, first we loaded the selection of the base by Ctrl/⌘-clicking on its alpha channel's name in the Channels palette. We filled it with 75% black by making this gray the Foreground color (see "Specifying Grays" at the right) and pressing Alt/Option-Delete to fill. When combined with the yellow in the other spot channel, this magenta coverage would produce a reddish orange.

Similarly, we loaded the surfboard selection and filled it with 50% gray, which would make the surfboard a yellower orange. We loaded the selection for the surfer and filled it with white (Edit, Fill, White). This would eliminate all color from the surfer in the Magenta channel, leaving him yellow in the final composition.

8 Coloring the type. To make the type outline red, we loaded its transparency mask as a selection by Ctrl/⌘-clicking on its name in the Layers palette. But instead of simply filling it with 100% black in the Magenta channel, we built in some trap so that a misalignment on-press wouldn't leave a thin yellow line at some edges of the letters. To build the trap we expanded the selection by 1 pixel (Select, Modify, Expand, 1 pixel) before filling. (For more about trapping, see step 3 of "Adding a Spot Color" and the "Computing the Trap" tip on page 141.)

8a

Loading the type as a selection in the Magenta channel (shown here is the bottom of the "A")

8b

The expanded selection filled with black in the Magenta spot channel. The expansion creates the overlap needed for trap.

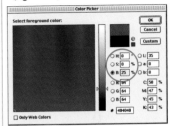
Saving files for output. Unless your file will be included in an Adobe Illustrator 7 (or later) file or in an Adobe Page-Maker 6.5 file, you'll need to open the General Preferences dialog box (File, Preferences, General) and select Short Pantone Names. Save a flattened copy of the file in DCS 2.0 format (File, Save A Copy, Exclude Alpha Channels), deselecting Include Halftone Screen and Include Transfer Function.

Channel Mixer Presets

Shown here are some of the Channel Mixer presets, found in the Presets folder on the Photoshop 5.0/5.5 Application CD-ROM. A preset can serve as a starting point for color change as in "Channel Mix-and-Match" on page 115. And if you use an Adjustment layer to apply it, you can change the Opacity or add a mask to target the effect, and you can go back and make changes to the channel mix later by double-clicking the black-and-white circle icon.

Original photo

*The Red Output channel of the **RGB Pastels.cha** preset*

Channel Mixer applied as an Adjustment layer

Channel Swaps: RGB Swap Green&Blue.cha

Channel Swaps: Swap RGB Red&Blue.cha

Channel Swaps: RGB Swap Red&Green.cha

Grayscale: CMYK to Gray.cha

Grayscale: Grayscale Standard.cha

Grayscale:Grayscale Yellows2.cha

Special Effects: RGB Blacklight.cha

Special Effects: RGB Blueprint.cha

Special Effects: RGB Burnt Foliage.cha

Special Effects: RGB Easter Colors.cha

Special Effects: RGB Holiday Wrap.cha

Special Effects: Inverted Warm Brass.cha

Special Effects: RGB Over Saturate.cha

Special Effects: RGB Pastels.cha

Special Effects: RGB Sepiatone subtle color.cha

Special Effects: RGBSepiatone subtle color2.cha

Special Effects: RGBSepiatone subtle color3.cha

Special Effects: RGB Warmer.cha

Special Effects: RGB yellows&blues.cha

YCC Color: RGB -> YCrCb.cha

Even with a strobe, **Eric Hanauer's** photo of the *Cormoran,* a World War I German merchant ship scuttled in Guam's Apra Harbor, lacked contrast and impact (above). Photoshop's Auto Levels brought out colors that hadn't been detectable in the murky water and brought to life a flat image. Hanauer also used Curves, working in the Green channel to reduce the cast in the water. ▶ *Photoshop's Adjustment layers, added by Ctrl/⌘-clicking the New Layer icon at the bottom of the Layers palette, make it possible to experiment with several changes to Levels and Curves, without permanently modifying the image until you have exactly the result you want.*

Hanauer used the Unsharp Mask filter to sharpen the image. He sometimes runs the Despeckle filter on the Green or Blue channel of an underwater photo before sharpening, to reduce the film grain so it won't be exaggerated by the sharpening process. But in this case the image detail he wanted to sharpen would have been blurred along with the film grain, and the graininess didn't really detract from the image, so he didn't use Despeckle.

Eric Hanauer's *Clown Triggerfish,* seemed lost against a bright, sharp background (lower left). There was also too much backscatter — lit, out-of-focus particles in the water, a common problem in underwater photography (lower right). Applying the Dust & Scratches filter to the entire image would not only remove backscatter but also eliminate much of the color variation in the ocean floor. So instead, the white flecks had to be removed by hand. ▶ *One way to remove blemishes is to start by running Dust & Scratches at a Radius high enough to hide the problems, and a Threshold high enough to preserve film grain. Then click the New Snapshot icon in the middle at the bottom of the History palette to make a Snapshot of the filtered image. Press Ctrl/⌘-Z to Undo the filter. Then click in the column next to the Snapshot's thumbnail to make it the source, and use the History brush to paint over the individual spots.*

Hanauer isolated the fish on a layer of its own and adjusted Input Levels to brighten the fish layer; he used Output Levels to darken and reduce contrast in the background layer. Finally, he used the Gaussian Blur filter to soften the background so the fish would stand out. ▶ *Photoshop 5/5.5's Image, Extract command can be useful for isolating a distinct subject so it can be treated separately from the rest of the image. First duplicate the*

image to a new layer. Then you can use Extract on the copy to isolate the subject. After treating the subject and background

separately, you can use the background eraser to fine-tune the edge of the subject where it blends into the image below.

Darryl Baird's *Aqueous Humor #14* is part of a series of humorous commentary on our culture. The image is composed of five black-and-white elements—three silhouetted vintage 1940's photos, a diagram, and reverse typography — each in a separate layer over an abstract background that was painted in watercolor and scanned.

To add subtle color tinting to each of the black-and-white elements, Baird created a layer filled with solid color just above each image layer, mimicking the hand-tinting done in the era when the photos were taken. Then each of these five pairs of image-plus-color layers was combined as a clipping group. In this way the bottom layer of each pair (containing the grayscale information) acts as a mask for the solid color layer above it. Three of the color layers were set to Soft Light mode (those for the swimmer, reverse type, and chorus line) and two were set to Multiply mode, so that they could tint the layers below without covering up the image detail. In addition, the tonality of the layer containing the black-and-white diagram was reversed (Image, Adjust, Invert) and the layer was set to Screen mode (at 60% opacity), which allowed the white type and lines to become part of the image but made the dark background of the layer almost invisible. Baird used a Color Balance Adjustment layer to warm the yellow of the lines and a Curves layer to darken the dark parts of the layer, which had the effect of darkening the entire image slightly.

MONTAGE AND COLLAGE

If you want to mask a copied and pasted element inside part of an existing image, you can select that part of the image and then choose Edit, Paste Into. The pasted element will come in as a new layer, complete with a layer mask that lets it show only within the area you selected.

If you hold down the Alt/Option key as you choose Paste Into, the effect will be to Paste Behind instead. Keyboard shortcuts are Ctrl/⌘-Shift-V for Paste Into and Ctrl-Alt-Shift-V (Windows) or ⌘-Option-Shift-V (Mac) for Paste Behind.

Typically, when you add a layer mask, the image and mask are linked, so moving the image moves the mask too. But when you use Paste Into or Paste Behind (above), the mask and image are unlinked by default. That way you can move the image around and still keep it "inside" or "behind" the area that was selected when it was pasted.

IN TRADITIONAL PHOTOGRAPHY and photo-illustration, *montage* is a method of making a single photographic print by superimposing several negatives. *Collage* is the assembly of separate photos mounted together, sometimes with other nonphotographic elements, to form another picture. With Photoshop, since photos, illustrations, and original painting can be combined in a single image, and since the "print" is likely to be output as part of a complete page layout, the distinction between montage and collage breaks down. But whatever you call it, the process becomes much easier when you don't need darkroom or glue.

Some of Photoshop's most useful compositing techniques involve feathered selections, gradient selections applied in layer masks, blending modes, clipping groups, alpha channels, Paste Into (and Paste Behind) from the Edit menu, and the composite controls provided in the Layer Options dialog box, which is available through the pop-out menu in the Layers palette. In addition to reading about the montage/collage projects described in this chapter, check Chapter 2 for more about the selecting, layering, and masking techniques that are so important for combining images.

CHOOSING AND PREPARING COMPONENTS

One essential element of making a successful "seamless" photo montage, when that's your goal, is choosing the right kind of selection and compositing techniques — like using a feathered lasso or marquee to create a soft, blending edge for the selection, or getting rid of background pixels at the edge of an image to get a clean silhouette, or using Gaussian Blur on the Background layer to create a realistic shortened-depth-of-field effect. Another requirement for a seamless blend is making sure that the component images match in several respects. For example, the light should be coming from the same direction, the color and amount of detail in the shadows and highlights should be the same, and the "graininess" of the images should match.

Highlight and shadow detail can be manipulated by using Image, Adjust, Curves and Image, Adjust, Levels. The color cast of a shadow, for instance, can be identified with the RGB or CMYK readings in the Info window (you can choose Window, Show Info to open it, or use the F8 default keyboard shortcut); then the color cast can be adjusted — with Image, Adjust, Curves or Levels or

continued on page 154

The hand, silhouetted on a transparent layer above the sky Background, before masking

Using a gradient layer mask made with the Linear gradient tool

Color Balance, for instance. And the Add Noise filter can be used to simulate film grain (see step 6 of "Blurring for Attention" in Chapter 3).

Changing the direction of the light, on the other hand, can be much more difficult than managing shadow detail or color cast. If the elements you want to blend are fairly flat (like pictures on a wall), the Lighting Effects filter may be helpful. For example, if the final effect you're looking for will tolerate it, you may be able to "overpower" the varied "native" lighting of the elements of a composite image by applying the same lighting effect to all the parts. You can see an example of this in "Combining with Light" on page 181 and in Lisa Cargill's *Your Ship Comes In* on page 219. You can also dodge and burn to create highlights and shadows for flat subjects (a nondestructive "dodging and burning" method is described in step 2 of "Fixing a Problem Photo" in Chapter 3). But if quick Lighting Effects or dodging and burning fixes won't work, you'll generally get better results if you continue your search for photos whose lighting matches, rather than trying to make further adjustments to correct the lighting.

MAKING SEAMLESS TRANSITIONS

Photoshop's Layers palette makes it easy to combine images:

- Elements on different layers can be moved around as separate objects with the **move tool** until you're happy with the arrangement. Photoshop's **"Big Data"** feature even preserves the parts that extend outside the margins of the canvas. So if you change your mind, the entire element will still exist and you can move it back into the image frame.

- The **blending mode** for each layer can be set to control how that layer is composited with the image beneath — by color, saturation, or brightness values, independently or in combination.

- The **Opacity** of a layer can be adjusted to give an entire element an "only partly there" or "ghosted" look.

- To make an element fade into the rest of the image gradually, you can create a **gradient layer mask,** as follows: With the layer active, click the mask icon at the bottom of the Layers palette. The new layer mask will be active. Use one of the gradient fill tools to make a black-to-white transition, using white where you want the image on that layer to show through at full strength and black where you want it to be completely absent from the composite, as shown at the left.

- You can make a **custom-fitted blurred mask** for the object you want to composite: With the object's layer active Ctrl/⌘-click its name in the Layers palette to load its transparency mask as a selection. Then click the Add Layer Mask icon at the bottom of the Layers palette. This will add a layer mask with the selected

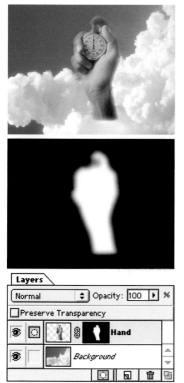

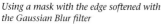

Using a mask with the edge softened with the Gaussian Blur filter

Adding a gradient to a blurred-edge layer mask

area white and the surrounding area black, so the mask just fits the object. Deselect (Ctrl/⌘-D) and then blur the edges: Choose Filter, Blur, Gaussian Blur, and view the composite image as you experiment with settings for blurring the mask until you get the amount of edge softness you want, as shown at the left.

- A **gradient** can also be **combined with another kind of mask** — for instance, a mask that blurs the object at its edges (below, left). Make the edge mask first and then add a black-to-white gradient to the mask by opening the Linear Gradient Tool Options palette and setting the blending mode for the gradient to Multiply, and then dragging the tool to make the gradient.

- With a **hand-painted layer mask** (below) you can control exactly which parts of the active layer are composited with the image below it and which parts are "ghosted" out of the picture. If you use black paint and the airbrush with Pressure set low in the Airbrush Options palette, you can paint and repaint, viewing only the image as you paint on the mask, until you get exactly the degree of ghosting you want. Painting the mask with white brings back the hidden parts of the image.

- With the sliders in the **Layer Options** dialog box, you can control how the pixels of the active layer (called "This Layer" in the

Using a hand-painted mask to "ghost" the hand

dialog box) and the image underneath (called "Underlying") will combine in the composite. The sliders of the **Underlying** bar define the range of colors in the underlying image that are made available to be affected by the active layer. So if you wanted to protect light or dark pixels, you would move the Underlying sliders inward to eliminate these tones from the available range.

The sliders of the **This Layer** bar determine what range of colors in the active layer will be allowed to contribute pixels to the composite image. These pixels will *replace* the corresponding underlying pixels if the active layer is in Normal mode, or will blend with them if the active layer is in a different blending mode. So if you want to use only the dark

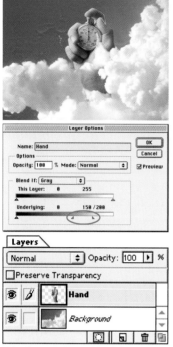

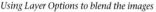

Using Layer Options to blend the images

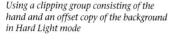

Using a clipping group consisting of the hand and an offset copy of the background in Hard Light mode

pixels, move the white slider for This Layer inward to exclude light pixels from the range of contributing colors.

Together, the two sliders set up a sort of "If . . . then" pr oposition for each pixel in the underlying image: "If the pixel falls within the range established in the Underlying slider bar *and* the corresponding active-layer pixel falls within the range established in the This Layer slider bar, then replace (or blend) the underlying pixel with the active one. Otherwise, leave the underlying pixel as it is, ignoring the active one." Holding down the Alt/Option key as you drag allows you to split each slider, so you can smooth the transition by defining a range of colors that are only partially composited.

- A **clipping group** can limit a layered element so it appears only inside the boundaries of a particular shape that's below it in the Layers palette. To create a clipping group, Alt/Option-click on the horizontal line in the Layers palette that separates your "cookie cutter" lower layer from the layer above it. The boundary line between the layers will become a dotted line, the name of the cookie cutter layer will be underlined to show that it's the bottom of the clipping group, and the thumbnail of the layer above will be indented to show that the layer is "clipped." Once you've established a clipping group, you can add the next layer up by Alt/Option-clicking the horizontal line between it and the clipping group, and so on.
- To blend images, you can also **rubber-stamp** from one part of the composite into another, or Alt/Option-drag **feathered selections**.

Although you'll often have to go back and do a more sophisticated masking job later, the Layer Options sliders can help eliminate backgrounds so you can quickly see how the parts of a montage will go together. If the default Gray setting for "Blend If" doesn't produce the blend you want, try a color channel.

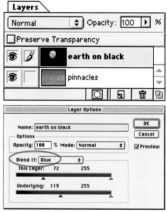

For this comp for a montage, the sky and pillars are very different in color, especially in their blue content, but they are similar in brightness. That meant that the default Gray setting in the "Blend If "section of the Layer Options dialog box wouldn't distinguish between the sky and pinnacles. So the Blue channel was chosen. The "This Layer" slider was set to mask out the black background of the earth-from-space image. And the Underlying slider was used to limit composition to the blue sky, protecting the reddish-brown pinnacles from compositing.

• To piece together a **panorama,** you can stack overlapping images (10–25% is a useful amount of overlap to shoot for when you take a sequence of photos for a panorama). Then use layer masks to blend the overlapping edges.

Blending the part of the scene that continues across all the photos — often this is the sky — is usually the hardest part of making a panorama sequence into a single image. One solution is to make tonal and color adjustments with a "dodge and burn" layer after piecing the panorama, as in the sunset scene below. Another approach is to remove the sky altogether and then replace it with a sky from a different photo, or a stretched version of the sky from one of the montaged images (if it has no clouds), or a synthetic sky, using stand-alone software such as MetaCreations' Bryce or a plug-in such as Rayflect's Four Seasons (see page 217).

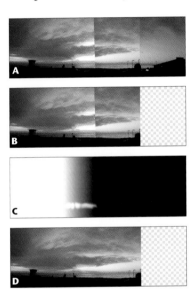

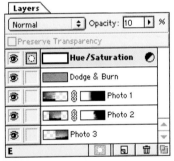

The different lighting in the sky in the three overlapping sunset images was the primary problem that needed to be solved in assembling them into a panorama. First the images were layered in a single Photoshop file. To align the three overlapping parts (A), the Opacity of each of the top two layers was temporarily reduced so the layer below could be seen. To solve the lighting problem, we used layer masks to make gradual transitions between the images: First the lefthand and middle photos (B) were blended using a layer mask on the layer with the lefthand image. The mask was first given a Linear gradient fill with a wide transition zone between black and white. Then hand-painted details were added to the mask with an airbrush (C) to control exactly where each of the two images would predominate in the composite (D).

A similar mask was added to the middle image to blend it into the righthand photo. Then a gray-filled layer in Overlay mode was used to "dodge and burn" certain areas of the composite image, using the method presented in step 2 of "Fixing a Problem Photo" in Chapter 3. A Hue/Saturation Adjustment layer, added to boost the color overall, completed the panorama (E, F).

Making Montages

Overview *Open a background image file; add collage elements by selecting, dragging, dropping, and creating layer masks.*

Background image after applying Variations and inverting the color of the right half

Original Couple image

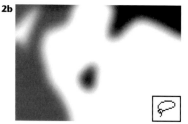

Layer mask for Couple: feathered selections filled and adjusted with Levels

Masked Couple image over background

THERE ARE PROBABLY ALMOST AS MANY WAYS to merge photos as there are Photoshop artists. The montage shown here was put together using several different methods of blending images. It began with a number of black-and-white photos that were composited in RGB mode so that subtle coloring could be added throughout. The elements were layered, mostly in Normal mode and at full Opacity.

Second only to choosing the right elements and composition to communicate your idea, the most important factor in making a successful photo montage is what happens at the edges where the parts blend. A smooth but dynamic merging of images can make the difference between a unified, effective collage and an awkward "cut-and-pasted" look.

1 Making a background. Open the image you want to use as a background. This collage began with two group photos — one of women and one of men. Much of this side-by-side image composite would be hidden, but it would act as a "texture" that conveyed the idea of human relationships. We reduced the contrast with Image, Adjust, Levels, moving the black point slider of the Output Levels to the right. The color change — a shift toward the cool (blue-violet) end of the spectrum — was accomplished with adjustments to the midtones via Image, Adjust, Variations, as were all the other changes used in making this collage. The right half of the composite image was selected with the rectangular marquee and turned into a negative (Ctrl/⌘-I) for contrast with the other images in the collage.

2 Using a feathered, freeform layer mask. The first blending method we used involves making a layer mask to hide part of an overlaid image. To follow our method, open the second image of your collage and use the move tool to drag it into the background file.

Add a layer mask by clicking the Add Layer Mask icon, on the left at the bottom of the Layers palette. The mask will be active (indicated by the mask icon in the column to the left of the layer's

3a

Diver masked with airbrushed layer mask

3b

Layers palette after adding the main couple, the divers, and the man and woman running on the beach

4a

Selection made with the elliptical marquee with a Feather

4b

Selection dragged into the montage file

5a

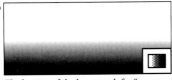

Square images added

5b

The bottom of the layer mask for Squares

5c

The Squares layer, masked into the montage

thumbnail in the Layers palette) but you'll be looking at the image itself. Use a feathered lasso to surround the parts of the image you want to mask out (the Feather can be set in the tool's Options palette, opened by pressing Enter or Return after you choose the tool). We used a Feather of 75 pixels for this 1100-pixel-wide image to get a very soft blending edge. Hold down the Shift key to add new lassoed areas to the selection. To completely mask out certain areas, make sure the Foreground color is set to black and press Alt/Option-Delete. Once the mask is made you can reselect and lighten some areas to let the image show partially. We selected the area to the left of the couple, again with a feathered lasso, chose Image, Adjust, Levels (or press Ctrl/⌘-L), and moved the black Output slider to lighten this area of the mask to dark gray. (A 50% gray in the mask will make the layer 50% opaque in that area.)

3 Softening the edge of the mask. We used a method similar to step 2 to import and mask the two diving board images and the man and woman running on the beach. But to further soften the edges of each layer mask, we painted the edge of the mask with a fairly large, soft airbrush with white paint so these images would fade into the background image more gradually.

4 Making a traditional vignette. Framing an image by selecting it with a rectangular or round shape is another collage technique. To create a "world of their own" effect for the boy and girl running on the beach, a feathered elliptical marquee was used to select them, along with part of their background. (You can select the elliptical marquee from the marquee tool's pop-out palette; set the Feather in the Options palette.) With the move tool, the selection was dragged and dropped into the collage file, where it became a new layer.

5 Using a graduated mask. Another way to blend collaged images is to build a gradient layer mask, going from black to white. This was the method used to add the square images at the bottom of our collage and also to add the type. To make a square selection, the Shift key was held down while dragging with the rectangular marquee. The selection was dragged and dropped into the collage file with the move tool. Then each of the other squares was selected, dragged into the file, and "merged down" with the Squares layer below it (Ctrl/⌘-E).

To make a black-to-white gradient like ours, add a layer mask (click the Add Layer Mask icon), choose the Linear gradient tool in the tool palette to open its Options palette, and choose Foreground To Background for the Style. Make sure your colors are black and white; you can restore these default colors by pressing the "D" key.

With the layer mask active, drag the gradient tool from where you want that layer to be completely hidden to where you want it to show fully. Remember — images show through the white parts of the layer mask and are blocked by the black parts. We used a gradient mask for the Squares layer and also for the Type layer; we adjusted

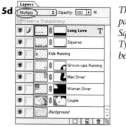

The Layers palette after Squares and Type layers have been added

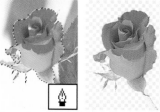

Rose selected from its background (left) and imported into its own layer and desaturated

Rose in place; all layers visible

Close-up of hand-painted mask for Rose layer

Rose "ghosted" through its layer mask

the Output slider in the Levels dialog box (Ctrl/⌘-L) on the Type layer mask so the lightest part of the mask was gray instead of white and all the type would at least be partially transparent. The mode for the layer was set to Multiply so the type would darken the image underneath, rather than cover it up.

6 Silhouetting with the pen tool. If you want to add a crisp-edged element to the collage, choose the pen tool (press the "P" key). Clicking to place points and dragging curve-shaping handles, outline the element. Save the path: Open the Paths palette (Window, Show Paths) and double-click the Work Path name so you can save the path. Then convert the path to a selection (Ctrl/⌘-click the path name), and drag the selected area into the collage with the move tool. After selecting and dragging the rose into the collage, we used Image, Adjust, Desaturate to turn it gray, and then used Image, Adjust, Variations to warm up the gray. (If the Desaturate command causes the image to lose its contrast, you can fix it by choosing Filter, Fade and changing the Mode to Color.

7 Painting a "ghosting" mask. A hand-painted mask can make it look like a collage element is partly in front of another element and partly behind it. To make the rose appear both in front of and behind the type, we added a layer mask on the Rose layer and used the airbrush with black paint and various Pressure settings in the Airbrush Options palette to paint a mask.

We used a similar technique to bring the couple's faces to the front: We copied the original Couple layer by dragging its name in the Layers palette to the New Layer icon at the bottom of the palette and then dragging the new "Couple Copy" thumbnail up to the top of the palette. We used Image, Adjust, Variations to give this layer a warm brown tone, added a layer mask filled with black (Alt/Option-click the Add Layer Mask icon), and airbrushed with white to add parts of the brown image back into the collage. Opacity was adjusted to 90% and a Hue/Saturation Adjustment layer was added to the top of the stack for final color tweaking. 🔲

Sepia-toned Couple Copy layer

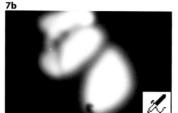

Mask for the Couple Copy layer

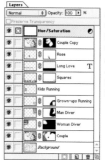

Layers palette for the completed montage, including the Hue/Saturation Adjustment layer for final color tweaking

7c

Blending with Layer Masks

Overview *Silhouette, color-correct, and enhance the individual components of the montage; bring each element into the compositing file, position it, and create a layer mask to composite it with a softened edge.*

1a

Monitor image silhouetted by removing the background

1b

Screen color adjusted with Color Balance and Levels

1c *Highlights mask*

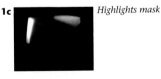

1d *Highlights enhanced and glow added*

PHOTOSHOP'S LAYER MASKS provide an excellent way to fade the layered elements of a montage into one another. This cover illustration for the packaging of TurboTax software started with a comprehensive sketch from Harold Sweet Design. Four separate photographs were scanned on a drum scanner and saved in CMYK color. Starting with the back element (the monitor), each piece was color-corrected and enhanced in its own file to keep RAM requirements low and working speed high. Then the pieces were layered into the final composite. For all but the back element, layer masks were created, and the edges of the masks were softened to accomplish the transitions as the fingers typed, the keyboard faded into the monitor, and the finished tax form emerged. The blending of images could have been done by deleting feathered selections from the elements on the individual layers. But using layer masks instead left these elements intact so that when the client wanted a minor change in the position or softness of some element, the change could be made easily.

1 Preparing the back element. It's a good idea to do as much of the basic color correction and enhancement of the separate pieces as you can (with Adjustment layers) before you begin to put them together. Once they're combined, the process of making changes can become slower because of the ballooning file size.

We began with the photo of the monitor. In the Layers palette we double-clicked the *Background* label in the palette to open the Make Layer dialog box, and renamed the layer "Monitor." We used the pen tool (press "P" to choose the pen) to draw a path around the monitor, and opened

AVOIDING SURPRISES

If you're going to drag and drop from one image to another, display both files at the same magnification on-screen (50% or 100%, for instance) so you get an accurate view of the size relationship between the parts. After you drag and drop, you can scale the parts by pressing Command-T (for Layer, Free Transform) and Shift-dragging a corner handle.

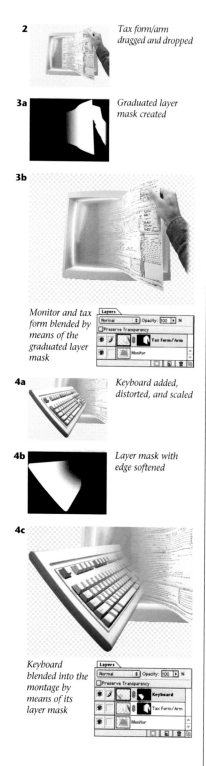

2
Tax form/arm dragged and dropped

3a
Graduated layer mask created

3b

Monitor and tax form blended by means of the graduated layer mask

4a
Keyboard added, distorted, and scaled

4b
Layer mask with edge softened

4c

Keyboard blended into the montage by means of its layer mask

the Paths palette. The path was saved (double-click the Work Path label in the palette) and then converted to an antialiased, unfeathered selection (Ctrl/⌘-click the path name). Inverting the selection (Ctrl/⌘-Shift-I) and pressing the Delete key removed the background.

Another path was drawn to isolate the monitor's screen; the path was saved and turned into a selection. With this selection active, Color Balance and Levels adjustments were used to "colorize" the screen.

To make a grayscale mask for selecting the highlights, the still-selected screen interior was copied (Ctrl/⌘-C) and saved in an alpha channel (open the Channels palette and click the New Channel icon at the bottom of the palette; then paste — Ctrl/⌘-V). In this highlights alpha channel, Image, Adjust, Levels was chosen and the Input Levels sliders were adjusted to increase the contrast. This mask was then used to select the highlights on the screen (click the RGB channel's name in the Channels palette and then Ctrl/⌘-click the alpha channel's name) so they could be brightened by adjusting Levels. A glow was added at the edge of the screen (methods for creating glows are described in Chapters 8 and 9).

More space was added around the monitor with Image, Canvas Size. The result was a 1700-pixel-wide file.

2 Starting to build the montage. The next step is to isolate the other elements from their backgrounds and assemble them into the montage. We added a hand holding a tax form. To get the stretched and skewed shape needed for the illustration, the PostScript illustration of the rectangular form had been distorted using CorelDraw's Envelope function and printed out on paper. The photographer then positioned this prop so that it was curving away from the hand, and the curve and distortion worked together to create the exaggerated perspective needed for the photo. The element (arm and tax form) was outlined with the path tool like the monitor in step 1, and the path was saved for use later. To blur the left edge of the form, the edge was selected by clicking with the polygon lasso with a 50-pixel feather, and a motion blur was applied (Filter, Blur, Motion Blur). Softly feathered selections were made within the form and Image, Adjust, Levels was used to exaggerate its shadows and highlights. The path was now loaded as a selection (Ctrl/⌘-click the path name), and the selected object was dragged and dropped with the move tool to make a new layer in the monitor file.

3 Making a layer mask. To make a gradual transition from one element to another, you can create a layer mask and apply a gradient to it: With the upper layer active (the tax form and arm in this case), Ctrl/⌘-click the thumbnail in the palette to load the transparency mask for the layer as a selection. With this selection active, click the Add Layer Mask icon on the left at the bottom of the palette to make a mask that exactly fits the layer's content. The mask icon in the column to the left of the layer's thumbnail in the Layers

5a

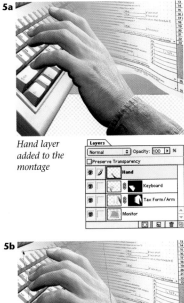

Hand layer added to the montage

5b

Fingers selected, copied to another layer, and rotated slightly

5c

Motion blur applied to the Fingers layer

5d

Layer mask for the Hand layer (left) and Fingers layer in place over masked Hand (right)

5e

Final Layers palette before flattening

palette shows that the mask is active, even though the layer's content, rather than the mask itself, appears in the working window.

Use a gradient tool in Multiply mode to make a gradient from black to white in the mask. Our gradient mask makes the tax form seem as if it's emerging from the monitor. (You could get the same blending effect by making a layer mask that's a simple black-to-white gradient, without making a white shape from the transparency mask. But having the shape there helps you to see how the mask is working.)

4 Making a layer mask with an irregular soft edge. The keyboard photo was the next piece to be added. Again, the element was selected with a path, isolated, color-corrected, and dragged into the composite file as described for the arm and tax form in step 2. Because the keyboard had been photographed in a more "straight-on" view, it had to be rotated and scaled to match its position in the original comprehensive sketch. (Press Ctrl/⌘-T for Free Transform; then drag a handle inward or outward to scale, or move the cursor outside the handles and drag around to rotate. Press the Enter key to accept and finalize the transformation.)

A layer mask was created as in step 3, but this time the transition edge was started with a feathered lasso selection filled with black (Alt/Option-Delete). Then black paint was applied at a low Pressure setting with the airbrush tool with a large soft tip.

5 Creating the illusion of motion. To simulate the motion that can be caught on film with a strobe, you need more than a simple application of Photoshop's Motion Blur filter. The goal is to show both the starting and ending positions, with a blur in between.

The first step in making the fingers of the left hand appear to be typing was to isolate the hand, correct its color, drag it into the composite file, and position it over the keyboard. A slightly feathered lasso was then used to select the four fingers and copy them to a new layer (Ctrl/⌘-J).

With all the layers visible and the Fingers layer active, the Fingers layer was rotated to create a basis for the motion blur. Then Blur, Motion Blur was applied in the direction of the movement between the two positions of the fingers and with a Distance setting of 10 pixels for this 1700-pixel-wide image.

The Opacity of the separate Fingers layer was set at 50%. Then a hand-painted layer mask was added to the original Hand layer to make its fingers partially transparent to add to the illusion of motion.

Saving a flattened copy of the file. When the montage is complete, choose File, Save A Copy; choose a file format, and turn on Flatten Image. This creates a single-layer nontransparent copy of the file. In flattening, Photoshop can retain alpha channels and non-image data such as paths, guides, grids, and color profiles (at your option); all layer masks are applied and discarded, and any remaining transparent areas are filled with white. *Wow!*

Assembling a Scene

Overview *Choose and silhouette the component photos; assemble in one file and match color and tone; create background; add matching shadows; distort and mask shadows to simulate real lighting; adjust color overall; make final adjustments to unify the scene.*

 "Assembly" image

1

The original photos

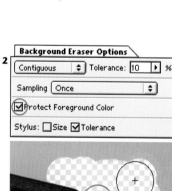

2

Using the background eraser to silhouette the typewriter, with colors sampled from the platen lever to protect it from removal

IF YOU'RE ASSEMBLING OBJECTS IN A STILL-LIFE MONTAGE, your first task is to decide whether you want a stylized illustration — strictly to communicate a concept — or whether you also want to fool the viewer's eye, creating a photorealistic scene.

1 Choosing your objects. If you're not aiming to produce a photorealistic assemblage, you have a lot of freedom in choosing the elements. "Making Montages" on page 158 and "Making Buttons from Photos" on page 320 provide some pointers for assembling conceptually related photos.

But if something more photorealistic is what you're after, you'll need to look for elements with matching lighting, focus, film grain, and shadow color, as well as similar amounts of detail and appropriate perspective. Some of these matching criteria can be adjusted in Photoshop. But all these adjustments take time, so the closer you can come in your choice of photos, the easier the assembly will be.

For the *Global Economy* still-life above we chose four photos: The newspaper-and-eyeglasses photo was important in our choice of other items, since it established the camera angle and included a shadow for the eyeglasses that showed that the lighting was coming from above and to the left. The lighting for the typewriter, globe, and adding machine matched closely enough. The typewriter and adding machine were both angled in a three-quarter view that we could work with and were photographed from above. The intrinsic distortion of the globe's round surface made the camera angle of this straight-on shot less important than the lighting. The lighting and perspective on the passport didn't match the other photos, but since this was a flat element, it would be easy to change by rotating the passport and putting it into perspective.

2 Isolating the objects from their backgrounds. The images that we chose from the Corbis Images Royalty Free volume called *In*

3

The five objects assembled over a gradient background

4

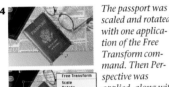

The passport was scaled and rotated with one application of the Free Transform command. Then Perspective was applied, along with final scaling and rotation in another transformation.

5

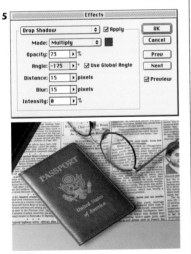

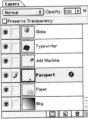

Adding a drop shadow to the passport to match the existing shadow of the eyeglasses

the Office came with alpha channels and clipping paths already prepared for silhouetting the objects. If the image files you want to use are objects on relatively plain backgrounds but aren't equipped with paths or alpha channels, Photoshop 5.5's **background eraser** tool can be very helpful. For instance, to isolate the typewriter (for the purpose of demonstration) we chose the background eraser in the toolbox and pressed the Enter key to open its Options palette. We chose **Contiguous** for the mode setting so that only pixels whose color continued uninterrupted from the pixel under the eraser's hot spot would be erased. That way if we kept the hot spot slightly outside the edge of the typewriter, the contrasting edge of the typewriter would stop the erasure. With the **Once** setting for Sampling, we could click to sample one of the grays in the background, then erase as long as that color continued to do the job, then click again to sample a new shade. We used a low **Tolerance** setting to restrict the erasure to the grays in the background, so we wouldn't be erasing similar colors in the typewriter. We also clicked the check box to turn on **Preserve Foreground Color** so that we could hold down the Alt/Option key to turn the background eraser into an eyedropper that would sample to change the Foreground color, which would then be protected from erasure, even if it fell within the scope of the tool's Tolerance and Contiguous settings. For instance, we used this technique to protect the platen tension lever from being erased.

3 Uniting the elements. When all the elements have been silhouetted, drag-and-drop them into one file. This is the time to scale the elements to approximately their final sizes and to do any major color or tone adjustments and approximate scaling so that all the elements generally match in appearance. (The matching will be fine-tuned at the end of the assembly process, at step 9.)

This is also a good time to add a background: Click the New Layer icon in the middle at the bottom of the Layers palette and drag the new layer down to the bottom of the stack in the palette so you can add a background surface for your items to sit on. We filled the layer with a light-to-dark-gray gradient from corner to corner, using the Linear gradient tool.

4 Adjusting position and perspective. Once all the elements are colored, toned, and scaled to feel at home with each other, you can make any necessary changes in position or perspective. The one item that wasn't in scale and perspective with the rest of the elements in our assemblage was the passport. Also, we needed to rotate it so that the highlight along the left edge was angled to match the lighting of the rest of the objects. Although it would have been nice to accomplish the changes with a single application of the Free Transform command, a two-step transformation is required to get the appropriate foreshortened perspective of a rotated object.

6a *Pasting the drop shadow to linked layers*

First we scaled and rotated the passport (press Ctrl/⌘-T for Free Transform and Shift-drag a corner handle to scale; drag outside the corner handles to rotate). Because of the rotation, the Transform box was now in the wrong position to accomplish the final Perspective and Scale operations, so we pressed Enter to accept the changes and then pressed Ctrl/⌘-T again to get a new "straight-up" Transform box. We then used the Perspective command (right-click [Windows] or Control-click [Mac] inside the Transform box to open the context-sensitive menu so you can choose Perspective; drag on a corner handle to move both that corner and its opposite in or out). Then we opened the context-sensitive menu again and chose Free Transform so we could grab the top center handle and drag downward to foreshorten the passport to its final shape.

Both the Scale and Rotate transformation and the Perspective and Scale transformation involved resampling, so at this point we compared the passport image to the others and decided to sharpen it; we applied Unsharp Mask.

5 Starting with a drop shadow. The next step is to create the shadows that will help all the elements appear to be in the same space. Since the newspaper element had a shadow of the eyeglasses within it, we would use the color of that shadow as we manufactured the others. First we would create a shadow for the passport, as described next, and then copy and paste that shadow to the larger elements as a starting point for the cast shadows.

With the passport layer active, we chose Layer, Effects, Drop Shadow. We clicked the color square in the Effects dialog box to get an eyedropper tool and then sampled the shadow of the eyeglasses. Then we reached outside the Effects dialog and dragged the passport's shadow to match the offset of the eyeglasses' shadow. This automatically changed the Distance and Angle settings inside the Effects dialog box. Then we experimented with the Blur setting until the softness of the shadows also matched.

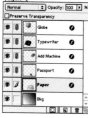

6b

Drop shadows pasted into all object layers

6 Copying and pasting the drop shadow. To make the shadows cast by the typewriter, globe, and adding machine, we started by copying and pasting the passport's shadow. This would automatically give us the right color, angle, and softness to start with. To copy the shadow to all the other objects at once, with the passport layer active we clicked in the Layer's palette's links column (between the eye and the image thumbnail) for each of the other layers except the background. With all these layers linked, we could copy the shadow to all of them at once, using the following method: Right-click (Windows) or Control-click (Mac) on the "f" icon for the layer with the Drop Shadow (in this case the passport layer) to open the context-sensitive menu and choose Copy Effects. Then right/Control-click the "f" again, and this time choose Paste Effects To Linked. All the linked layers will now have the Drop Shadow.

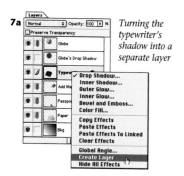

7a *Turning the typewriter's shadow into a separate layer*

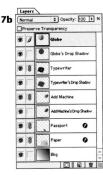

7b

Shadows separated for the typewriter, adding machine, and globe

7c

Skewing the typewriter's shadow

8a

Adding machine shadow and globe shadow cast on the background skewed to match the typewriter's shadow

8

Masking the typewriter's shadow to keep it from overlapping the globe's shadow

7 Skewing the shadows. To be able to turn the drop shadows into cast shadows by skewing them, you'll need to separate the shadows into layers of their own. Since our passport and newspaper were flat items, the Drop Shadow Effect worked fine as it was; we would not need to separate and skew it.

For each of the other elements, we opened the "f" icon's context-sensitive menu and chose Create Layer. Then we started with the typewriter's shadow. Pressing Ctrl/⌘-T and opening the context-sensitive menu allowed us to choose Skew. We wanted to note the amount of skew so we could use it for the adding machine and globe later, so we opened the Info palette (Window, Show Info). As we dragged the top handle to the right to skew the shadow, we watched the angle of horizontal skew (the "H" measurement under the "A" angle measurement in the upper right quadrant of the palette). When we had the skew we liked, the "H" value was –17°. We used the Distort command from the Transform box's context-sensitive menu to fine-tune the alignment of the base of the shadow and the base of the typewriter. Then we applied the same amount of skew to the shadow of the adding machine and used Distort to align it.

8 Visualizing the shadow-and-object interactions. At this point we had to go a step further in visualizing how our elements would actually interact with the light. The globe's shadow would fall on items at three different distances from the globe — the background surface (the farthest away), the adding machine (the middle distance), and the top of the typewriter (right underneath the globe) — and this meant that we needed three copies of the shadow at three different angles.

To make the part of the globe's shadow that fell on the background surface, we dragged the globe's drop shadow layer to the New Layer icon to duplicate it and then dragged the copy down in the Layers palette to a position just above the background. We skewed the shadow to the same –17° horizontal skew angle as we had done for the typewriter and adding machine shadows in step 7. Since the globe is higher above the surface than the typewriter and adding machine are, the angle of the light would be steeper in casting its shadow, and the globe's shadow on the background surface would be shorter. We chose the move tool and dragged the globe's shadow downward a bit, which had the effect of shortening it in the composite.

When soft shadows in Multiply mode overlap in Photoshop, the shadow gets darker in the overlap. But this isn't the way things work in the real world. So some masking is needed to eliminate the overlap. To remove the portion of the typewriter's shadow that overlapped with the globe's shadow on the background surface, we used a layer mask. We knew we wanted to keep the shadow where it fell on the adding machine and the newspaper. So we loaded the transparency masks for these two layers as selections by Ctrl/⌘-clicking on the adding machine in the Layers palette and then Shift-Ctrl/⌘-clicking

9a

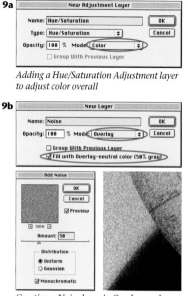

Adding a Hue/Saturation Adjustment layer to adjust color overall

9b

Creating a Noise layer in Overlay mode

9c

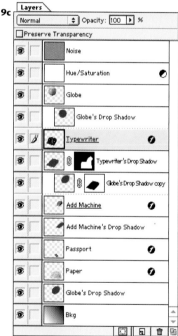

The final Layers palette for the illustration at the top of page ???. "Dark halos" have been added to the typewriter and adding machine, softening their edges and blending them into the atmosphere of the composite image.

on the newspaper to add it to the selection. Then we activated the typewriter's shadow layer and clicked the Add Layer Mask icon on the left at the bottom of the Layers palette.

To make the globe's shadow that falls on the adding machine, we duplicated the globe's background surface shadow layer that we had just made and moved it above the adding machine's layer. Then we used the move tool to drag the shadow up and to the left until it seemed to be in the right position on the adding machine. To eliminate this shadow from the composite everywhere but on the surface of the adding machine, we made a clipping group of the adding machine and this new globe shadow.

To eliminate the darkening where the globe shadow and the typewriter shadow overlapped on the surface of the adding machine, we added a layer mask on the globe shadow's layer: With this shadow layer active, we Ctrl/⌘-clicked on the typewriter shadow layer's thumbnail to load its transparency mask as a selection and then Alt/Option-clicked the Add Layer Mask icon to make a "negative" layer mask that blocked the globe shadow where it overlapped the typewriter shadow. To get the two soft edges to blend, we had to load the typewriter's shadow as a selection again, and this time with the layer mask active on the globe drop shadow above the adding machine, we darkened the mask by filling with black.

For the shadow that fell on the typewriter, we could use the original separated drop shadow layer as it was, simply clipping it inside the typewriter's shape by Alt/Option-clicking on the line between the two layers in the Layers palette.

9 Finishing touches. To enhance the "atmosphere" shared by the assembled objects, we toned down the color and added noise to soften the image overall: First we added an Adjustment layer by Ctrl/⌘-clicking the New Layer icon, choosing Hue/Saturation in the New Adjustment Layer dialog box, and putting the layer in Color mode, so that when we reduced the Saturation in the Hue/Saturation dialog box, the contrast wouldn't be affected.

Above the Adjustment layer we added a New Layer by Alt/Option-clicking the New Layer icon so we could choose the Overlay blending mode in the New Layer dialog box and also fill the layer with Overlay-neutral 50% gray in the same step. We chose Filter, Noise, Add Noise; we turned on the Monochromatic option and experimented with the Amount and Distribution settings until we had the result we wanted.

Our last overall addition was a "dark halo" around the three large objects that would help blend them into the atmosphere created by the noise. We copied and pasted the Drop Shadow from the passport (as we had at step 6), and then worked in the Effects dialog box of the globe, typewriter, and adding machine layers to adjust the Blur.

Now we could fine-tune the separated shadows with the blur tool (the water drop) set to 100% Pressure with a soft brush tip — for instance at the far edge of the globe's shadow on the background.

Alicia Buelow created *Convert* as an illustration for an article in *Internet* magazine about converting traditional published media into electronic media for the Internet. By working with many layers, blending modes, and layer masks, she created a multilevel illustration with much depth.

To create a textured background, Buelow started with a photo she had taken of a painted wall and combined it with overlying layers containing stock photos of a rust texture and peeling paint. Some areas of the peeling paint images were masked out with a layer mask, and the layer was blended in Overlay mode.

To illustrate turning pages, Buelow took three pieces of paper, curled the edges, and laid them on her flatbed scanner. The resulting scan was blended into the background using a layer mask and Hard Light mode, with Opacity reduced to 93%. Likewise, the open book image was created by scanning a book laid open across the scanner and was blended using Luminosity mode.

The jumbled words and letters in the lower left were cut out of a magazine, pasted onto a piece of paper, then scanned and blended into the background using Color Burn mode. Buelow's use of blending modes had the

effect of pulling the overlaid elements toward the warm palette of the background. Though she had a sense of the effect that would be produced by each mode, many of her choices resulted from trial-and-error experimentation, influenced by how the color palette of each layered image blended with that of the others.

The Web page images were "ghosted" with layer masks. Using painted masks for these and other layers made it easy to bring back parts of the images after checking how they looked in the overall composition.

Katrin Eismann's *Nightmare* is a montage of two photos: a winter scene reflected in a puddle, and a fountain at Caesar's Palace in Las Vegas with boutiques behind it. Both were shot with panoramic cameras, which caused the images to curve. Eismann layered the Pegasus on top and the trees underneath. She added a layer mask to the top layer and used the airbrush tool with brush tips of varying sizes to paint the mask so only the horse and some of the clouds and "ghosted" buildings showed through.
▶ *To add a clear layer mask to the active layer, click the mask icon at the bottom of the Layers palette. Then you can paint with black to mask out the parts of the layer you don't want in the image.*

Eismann used Image, Adjust, Replace Color once to change the hue and increase the

saturation of the golden light on the statue and again to reduce saturation on the rest of the animal. ▶ *When you use Replace Color, you can select by color with the eyedropper and then adjust the color of the selected area, all in one interactive step, using the Fuzziness slider to control the way the recolored areas blend with the surroundings. But if you're not happy with the color change and want to undo it, you can't undo just the color because there's no easy way to select exactly that area again. If you need flexibility in case you decide to undo the color change, try this: Instead of Replace Color, use Select, Color Range, save the selection as an alpha channel, and then use Image, Adjust, Hue/Saturation. The trade-off in doing it this way is that you won't be able to adjust Fuzziness and change color at the same time.*

Ups and Downs of Wealth appeared as an opening illustration in *Forbes* magazine for a series on the 400 richest people in America. To create it, **Joyce Hesselberth** started with a teeter-totter concept to convey the idea of people making and losing money but remaining rich. She made economical use of scanned materials to create a strong, hand-crafted collage image, working in grayscale initially and using some elements twice — for example, the two crowns are duplicates, the two textured background areas are from a single scan but with the two sides colored differently, and the figures' clothing employs the same two textures, but differently colored.

The background was created by scanning a piece of paper that she had rubbed with oil pastel to introduce a hand-worked texture.

To create the slightly eerie faces, Hesselberth drew on her collection of black-and-white photos, mostly from the late 1800s. She created composite faces, combining a head and mouth from one person with eyes and nose from another, for example, purposely arranging some of the features slightly out of place. The hint of a smile for the face on the left was created by using the Shear filter to pull up the corners of the mouth a little. To make the faces look more severe, she cut into them a bit as she created the final outlines. ▶ *Since the Shear filter distorts side-to-side, not up-and-down, if you need an up-down distortion, start by rotating the element 90° (Ctrl/⌘-T); then, with a feathered selection, choose Filter, Distort, Shear. Adjust the degree of distortion; click OK. Finally, rotate the element back into its original position.*

Hesselberth created the balance board using a photograph of a wood texture. She scanned the eye-in-a-triangle from a dollar bill, increased contrast with Levels, sharpened it with Unsharp Mask, and added a shadow.

The basic outlines for the crown were created in Adobe Illustrator, then pasted

as paths into Photoshop (Edit, Paste, As Paths). She built a collage of overlapping pieces, using less than 100% Opacity for some layers; the texture for the pieces was made from a close-up black-and-white photo of a face, with a noise pattern added (Filter, Noise, Add Noise). Finally she used the burn tool to darken the edges and the inside of the crown.

The textures for the clothing were derived from hand-woven pieces of fabric that Hesselberth scanned directly on her flatbed scanner. Here, too, she burned the edges of the shapes to add depth.

Once the grayscale collage was assembled in layers, Hesselberth added color. For many of the elements she used Image, Adjust, Hue/Saturation with Colorize turned on. For the balance board she used the pen tool to create selections for the top, end, and side surfaces and filled them with various browns in Multiply mode (Edit, Fill) to add color without hiding the wood grain.

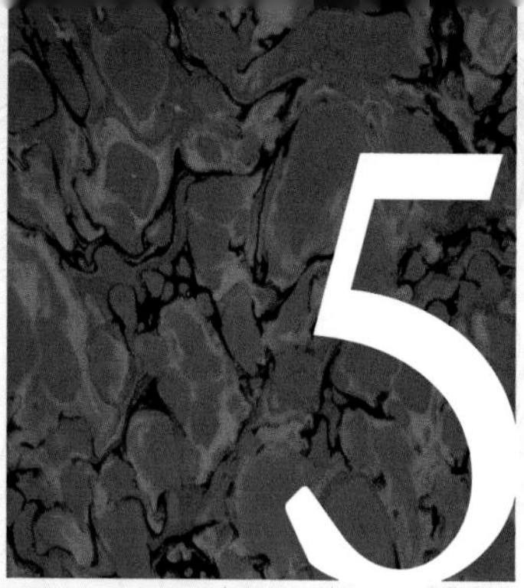

USING FILTERS

IS IT FILTERED YET?

The dialog boxes for many filters include two ways to preview the filter effect before you apply it to an image — the small **preview window** and the **Preview check box**, which makes the effect show up in the main working window. Some filters can take a long time to run. And if you're applying a fairly subtle effect, it may be hard to tell for sure whether it's finished. Check for a flashing line first under the percent figure below the preview window and then under the Preview check box. When the line stops flashing and disappears, it means that the preview or working window now shows the effect of the filter.

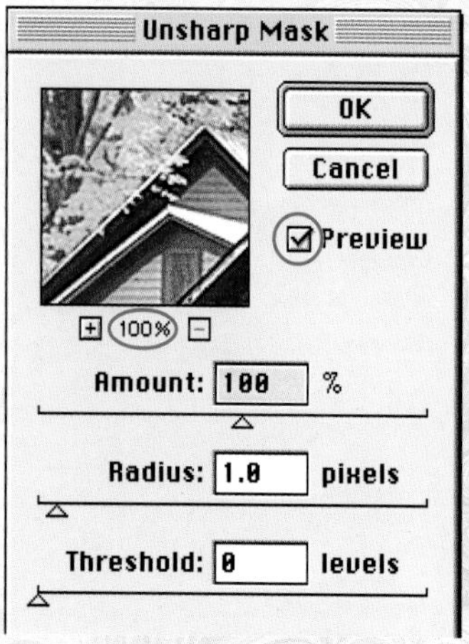

PHOTOSHOP'S FILTERS — SMALL SUBPROGRAMS that are grouped under the Filter menu — can be run on an entire image, a single channel or layer, or a selection. A significant new addition to versions 5 and 5.5 is the 3D Transform filter found in the Render submenu (see page 182), and in version 5.5 the Dither Box is found in the Other menu (see page 192). Also, Lighting Effects and other filters of the Render submenu can add drama to photos. They have great potential for synthesizing entire environments and creating special effects. In addition to these plug-ins and filters designed for special effects (described later in this chapter and in Chapter 8), for artistic effects, and for other special purposes, there are three kinds of filters that can do a lot to improve the quality of scanned photographs, and can even improve illustrations. You'll find these three types of "workhorse" filters in the Sharpen, Blur, and Noise submenus.

SHARPEN

Photoshop provides four sharpening filters. Sharpen and Sharpen More accentuate the color differences between adjacent pixels of different colors. **Sharpen Edges** and **Unsharp Mask** find "edges," areas where a continuous run of pixels of one color comes up against other colors, and then they increase contrast at the edges. Areas that aren't edges, like very slight or gradual color transitions, can be left pretty much unchanged, so they still look smooth, or "soft." The use of sharpening filters comes up again and again throughout the book, but here's a quick list of sharpening tips:

Use only Unsharp Mask. Unlike Sharpen and Sharpen More, which can accentuate blemishes, film grain, and any artifacts you

continued on page 174

FILTER SHORTCUTS

Three keyboard shortcuts can save time once you've applied a filter: **Ctrl/⌘-Shift-F** brings up the **Fade Filter** dialog box so you can adjust the blending mode and Opacity of the filtered image as if it were on a layer above the original unfiltered one. **Ctrl/⌘-F** applies the **last filter** you used, with the same settings. **Ctrl-Alt-F** (Windows) or **⌘-Option-F** (Mac) opens the **dialog box** for the last filter you applied, so you can change the settings before running it again. Ctrl/⌘-F and Ctrl-Alt-F or ⌘-Option-F remain available until you run another filter. But Ctrl/⌘-Shift-F (Fade), like Photoshop's Undo command, is available only immediately after the filter is applied. As soon as you do anything else to the file, the Fade command is grayed out.

Original scan *Sharpen*

Sharpen Edges *Sharpen More*

Unsharp Mask default: 50, 1, 0 *Unsharp Mask: 100, 1, 0*

Unsharp Mask: 100, 3, 2 *Unsharp Mask, 4 times: 25, 3, 2*

Photo delivered at 100 dpi

Resolution increased to 200 dpi *Unsharp Mask applied: 200, 1, 0*

may have created by editing an image, Unsharp Mask accentuates the differences only at "edges," where you want the differences to be distinct. And unlike Sharpen Edges, it gives you precise control. With Unsharp Mask you can set:

- The **Amount** (the strength of the application, or how much the difference at an edge is enhanced by the filter).

- The **Radius** (how many pixels in from the color edge will have their contrast increased). Increase the Radius with increasing resolution, because at higher resolutions the individual pixels are smaller relative to the image components.

- The **Threshold** (how different the colors on the two sides of an edge have to be before the filter will sharpen it). Use higher settings for images that are "grainy" or have subtle color shifts, such as skin tones, so the filter won't sharpen the "noise."

Use it on scanned images. As a rule, run the Unsharp Mask filter to see if it improves a scanned photo by getting rid of blurriness from a poor original or from the scanning process.

Use it on resized or transformed images. Whenever you use Image, Image Size with Resample Image turned on, or when you use the Scale, Rotate, Skew, Distort, Perspective, or Numeric functions from Edit, Transform or Edit, Free Transform, use Unsharp Mask afterwards. Any such change involves *resampling* — that is, creating or recoloring pixels based on calculations — and is bound to "soften" the image (see the flag image at the left).

Use it more than once. Running Unsharp Mask more than once at a lower Amount can sharpen more smoothly than if you run it once at a setting twice as high. (Note that Sharpen More and Sharpen shouldn't be run twice, since they multiply the artifacts they create if you apply them more than once.)

Use it last. Because it can generate artifacts that can be magnified by other image-editing operations, Unsharp Mask should generally be applied after you've finished editing the image.

Original scan

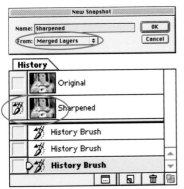

Unsharp mask: 500, 50, 50; oversharpened for a special effect

With the Unsharp Mask filter used in combination with the History function, you can make a Snapshot of the sharpened image and then use it as a source to paint the sharpening exactly where you want it.

EVALUATING SHARPENING

Too much sharpening can give a photo an artificial look, so you don't want to overdo it. But if you're preparing an image for the printed page, keep in mind that sharpening tends to look much "stronger" on-screen or on a laser print than it will when the image is finally printed at much higher resolution on a press.

Use the sharpen tool or History brush for pinpoint precision. For handheld control of the Sharpen filter, you can use the **sharpen** (triangle) tool. If the tool isn't visible in the toolbox, select it from the pop-out palette that also includes the blur (water drop) tool and smudge (finger) tools, or press Shift-R to cycle through these tools. You can control the area and intensity of sharpening by changing the brush size setting in the Brushes palette and the Pressure in the Sharpen Options palette. You can also set the sharpen tool to Use All Layers so that it blurs as if all the visible layers were merged, even though the blur effect is recorded only on the active layer.

Another way to sharpen particular areas of an image is to use Photoshop 5/5.5's **History** function: First sharpen the entire image with the Unsharp Mask filter, using settings that produce the most intense sharpening that you need anywhere in the image; then capture the sharpening as a Snapshot in the History palette by choosing New Snapshot From Merged from the palette's pop-out menu; Undo the overall sharpening effect (Edit, Undo); add a new blank "repairs" layer above the layer you wanted to sharpen (click the New Layer icon at the bottom of the Layers palette), and hand-paint the sharpening precisely where you want it using the History brush and the sharp Snapshot (click in the brush square to the left of the Snapshot's thumbnail in the History palette). If this results in oversharpening some areas, you can undo the effect in those areas by stepping back in the History palette and painting over those spots with the eraser tool set to Airbrush mode.

Using the History method gives you several advantages over using the sharpen tool: First, you can preview the sharpening in the Unsharp Mask filter's dialog box, so you can see the result in advance. This is a distinct advantage over the way the sharpen tool works — when you "paint" it back and forth over the area you want to sharpen, you can't tell that you've reached the optimal sharpening until you see that you've gone too far; then you have to undo the repair and start over, this time stopping one stroke short of the last time. Also, with a repairs layer you can eliminate or reduce the opacity of particular sharpened spots without affecting neighboring areas.

BLUR

Photoshop's blurring filters can be used to soften all or part of an image. **Blur** and **Blur More** (which is three or four times as strong as Blur) smooth an image by reducing the contrast between adjacent pixels. With the **Gaussian Blur** filter, the transition between the contrasting colors occurs at a particular mathematical rate, so that most of the pixels in a black-to-white blur, for example, are in the middle gray range, with fairly few pixels in the very dark or light shades. You can increase the amount of blurring that occurs by raising the Radius value.

Blur the background (right) to reduce the apparent depth of field and to focus attention on the foreground.

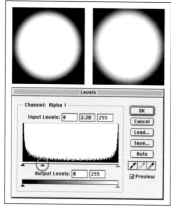

On a Gaussian Blurred mask, move the Input Levels gray slider to enlarge (here) or shrink the mask.

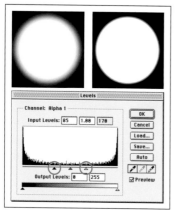

On a Gaussian Blurred mask, move the Input Levels black and white point sliders inward to "harden" the edges.

The Smart Blur filter can be used to make an image (left) "cartoonlike" (right).

Use Gaussian Blur to make the background recede. A common error in Photoshop montage is combining a sharply focused subject with an equally sharply focused image used as background. You can fix the problem by blurring the background slightly to simulate the depth of field a real camera lens might capture. You can also apply this background-blurring technique to a single photo to reduce the perceived depth of field and focus attention on the foreground subject, as described in "Blurring for Attention" on page 130.

Use Gaussian Blur to smooth out flaws in a photo. You may be able to do some photo repair work (such as eliminating water spotting) by using Gaussian Blur on one or all of the color channels.

Use Gaussian Blur to control edge characteristics in alpha channels or layer masks. Once a selection is stored in an alpha channel or layer mask, the Gaussian Blur filter can be run to soften or smooth out the transition between black and white. Then the Image, Adjust, Levels function can be run on the channel to fatten, shrink, or harden the edge of the selection area, as shown at the left.

Photoshop's **Smart Blur** filter, used at high settings, will leave edges sharp but blur the other parts of an image. The result can be a kind of posterization of the non-edge areas — the number of colors is reduced, detail is lost, and the image is presented as blobs of flat colors.

- The higher the **Threshold** setting for Smart Blur, the less "smart" the filter is about recognizing edges — that is, the more different the color and tone of adjacent areas have to be in order for the difference to be recognized as an edge. And since the filter blurs everything that isn't an edge, the higher the Threshold setting, the more blurring occurs.

- At a given Threshold setting, the higher the **Radius,** the farther away from the edge the original color is preserved. A low setting preserves very little, resulting in a lot of blurring. (The exception to this is at the very bottom of the Radius scale, below 0.5 pixels, where the filter seems to be inactive.) A higher Radius setting preserves more of the edges, maintaining more of the image detail. (But once all possible edges are preserved given the Threshold setting, increasing the Radius has no effect.)

- For a particular combination of Radius and Threshold, changing the **Quality** changes the degree of posterization, with Low producing the most colors and High producing the fewest.

- The Edge Only and Edge Overlay **Mode** settings were designed mainly for use in the preview window of the dialog box, to help you see where the filter is identifying edges with your current Radius and Threshold settings.

Use Smart Blur as an interactive posterization tool, with better control of the effect than with Image, Adjust, Posterize.

To turn an image into a drawing, Smart Blur was used in Edge Only mode (left). Then the image was inverted and the file was converted to grayscale.

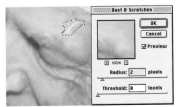

The Dust & Scratches filter (under Noise) can be applied to selected individual blemishes to eliminate the defects.

History

By using the Dust & Scratches filter in combination with the History function, you can pinpoint where you want the repairs — on the image defects — while leaving spots such as the highlights in a subject's eyes untouched.

ADDING DEPTH

Sharpening or blurring can help add depth and form. Sharpen the areas of the image that extend toward the viewer and leave unsharpened (or even blur) the areas that are farther away.

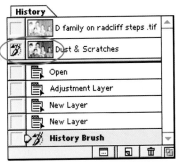

After Francois Guérin painted a still life of fruit in MetaCreations' Painter (left), he used Photoshop's sharpen tool to enhance the three-dimensional look (right).

Experiment with the Threshold and Radius sliders and the Quality setting to get the degree of posterization you want.

Use Smart Blur at "mild" settings for "cosmetic" purposes — to subdue wrinkles in a portrait, for instance, or hide the freckling of a ripe banana.

Use Smart Blur, Gaussian Blur, and Image, Adjust, Levels to produce a drawing from an image: Run the Smart Blur filter in Edge Only mode to generate a white-on-black line drawing. Invert to black-on-white (Ctrl/⌘-I). Then smooth the jaggy lines by running the Gaussian Blur filter at a low Radius setting and using the Input Levels slider (Ctrl/⌘-L) as described on the facing page.

Use the blur tool for precision. This tool (the counterpart of the sharpen tool) gives you pinpoint control of the blur. As with sharpening, you can apply pinpoint blurring with the History brush and a Snapshot instead of the blur tool, using a method like the one described in "Use the sharpen tool or History brush for pinpoint precision" on page 175.

The other three Blur filters fall into the special effects category: **Motion Blur,** which lets you set a direction and an amount for the blur, produces an effect like taking a picture of a moving object. **Radial Blur** provides two options: With **Spin** you can simulate the effect of photographing an object spinning around a center that you specify in a Blur Center box; **Zoom** simulates the effect of zooming the camera toward or away from the center you define.

NOISE

Under Noise in the Filter menu, **Add Noise** can create two kinds of random speckling — Uniform and Gaussian. **Despeckle** and **Median** detect edges and then leave these alone while smoothing out less abrupt changes in color. Median averages the brightness of pixels within an image or selection; you determine the Radius that will be used to select the pixels to be averaged. High Radius settings produce a posterized effect. The **Dust & Scratches** filter looks for "defects" (small areas that are markedly different from their surroundings), and it blurs the surrounding pixels into the defects to fix them without blurring the rest of the image. The Threshold setting determines how different from the surrounding pixels something has to be in order to be detected as a defect. By setting the Threshold high enough, you can maintain the inherent film grain or "noise" of the original scan while you eliminate the higher-contrast defects. The Radius setting determines how far from the edge of the defect the filter goes in its search to get the pixels used in the blur. Dust & Scratches works well if you take advantage of Photoshop 5/5.5's History function, as described in step 3 of "Fixing a Problem Photo" on page 123.

HUE-PROTECTED NOISE

In a color image, Photoshop's Add Noise filter draws from the whole spectrum to change pixel colors; this can produce an artificial "electronic rainbow" look. But you can introduce noise without color change by checking the Monochromatic box in the Add Noise dialog box. Using the Uniform setting keeps most of the noise in the midtones, whereas using Gaussian spreads the noise farther into the highlights and shadows, and produces a more clumped noise pattern.

Original gradient, no noise

Noise, Add Noise, Gaussian, 40

Noise, Add Noise, Gaussian, 40, Monochromatic

Noise, Add Noise, Uniform, 40, Monochromatic

In addition to reorienting pictures of three-dimensional objects, the 3D Transform filter can be useful for applying "labels" to such objects.

Add Noise as the basis for generating a texture. Add Noise used with other filters such as Gaussian Blur, Difference Clouds, and Lighting Effects can generate some interesting textures. Examples appear on pages 191 and 194.

Add Noise to restore film grain. If film grain is eliminated when part of an image is blurred for repair or for a special effect, you can restore the grain by adding noise as described in step 6 of "Blurring for Attention" in Chapter 3. If you've done your blurring on a "repairs" layer (as described in step 3 of "Fixing a Problem Photo" in Chapter 3), you can combine the noise layer and the repairs layer in a clipping group, so that the noise affects only the repairs.

Use Despeckle or Median to reduce scan artifacts. The "ridges" that can appear in desktop-scanned images can be reduced or eliminated by applying the Despeckle or Median filter. (Despeckle is a one-click operation but Median offers more control.) These filters can also help eliminate *moiré,* an interference pattern that happens when the halftone screen in the printed image you're scanning interacts with the scanner's sampling pattern. After these scanner artifacts are reduced, use Unsharp Mask to sharpen the image.

RENDER

The filters of Photoshop's Render menu are some of the most powerful in the program.

The **3D Transform** filter lets you identify a part of an image — such as a picture of a bottle, a globe or a box — to be treated as a three-dimensional object. Once you use the filter's geometry to define the object, you can move and rotate it in perspective as if it were solid. Examples of using 3D Transform can be found in "3D Labeling" on page 182 and on page 194.

The **Clouds** filter creates a cloudlike pattern using the Background and Foreground colors. If you use sky-blue and white, the effect tends to look like high, diffuse clouds. To make bulkier-looking clouds on a darker sky, hold down the Alt/Option key when you select the filter.

Difference Clouds works the same way, except that the cloud effect interacts with the image as if the clouds were being applied in Difference mode. In Difference mode black is the neutral color — that is, black pixels don't cause any change in the target image — so you can use Difference Clouds with the Foreground and Background colors set to black and white to apply a cloudlike pattern of color inversion. Repeated application of Difference Clouds starting with a blank layer in a grayscale image generates a veined effect like marble (see page 191); in a color file you get marble with an "oil slick" rainbow.

The **Lens Flare** filter simulates the photographic effect you get when a bright light shines into the lens of a camera. Immediately

Original photo

A Spotlight with negative Intensity can be used to shade part of an image. This individual light source is set up in the Light Source section at the top of the Lighting Effects dialog box.

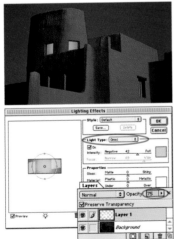

Two windows were selected with the polygon lasso, and copied to a new layer (Ctrl/⌘-J). In the Background layer, negative ambient light was set up in the Properties section of the dialog box. The windows layer was filled with white with Preserve Transparency turned on and an orange Omni light was applied to this layer, as shown here. Opacity was adjusted.

after you apply the Lens Flare, you can use the Filter, Fade command to experiment by adjusting the Opacity.

An essential tool for special effects (see Chapter 8), the **Lighting Effects** filter offers a dialog box that can be used to set up both **ambient** lighting, controlled in the **Properties** section in the lower half of the dialog box, and **individual light sources,** controlled in the **Light Type** section at the top of the box.

Ambient light is diffuse, nondirectional light that's uniform throughout the image, so it casts no shadows, like daylight on an overcast day. And it may have a color, like daylight underwater. The ambient light will affect the density and color of shading that results from any individual light sources that you set up.

There are three varieties of individual light sources: **omnidirectional** lights (sending a glow in all directions, like a light bulb in a table lamp), **spotlights** (directional and focused, to make a pool of light like their counterparts in the real world), and **directional** light sources (too far away to be focused, like bright sunlight or moonlight on the earth), which are ideal for creating textured surfaces and embossed effects.

- **To set the strength of ambient light,** use the Ambience slider in the Properties section of the Lighting Effects dialog box. The more positive the setting, the stronger the ambient light relative to the Directional, Omni, and Spotlight sources you add, and so the less pronounced the shadows produced by these lights. Other settings in the Properties section also affect the overall environment, rather than any individual light source.

- **To color the ambient light,** click on the color box in the Properties section of the dialog box to open the Color Picker.

- **To add a light source,** drag the light bulb icon at the bottom of the palette into the Preview area.

- **To color a light source**, click on the color box under Light Type.

- **To select one of several light sources** so that you can adjust its settings, click on the little circle that represents it in the Preview area, or use the Tab key to cycle through the lights.

- **To move a light source,** drag the central light spot.

- **To control the direction, size, and shape of a Spotlight,** drag the handles on the ellipse. **To control the angle** without changing the shape, Ctrl/⌘-drag a handle. **To change the shape** without affecting the angle, Shift-drag a handle.

- **To duplicate an existing light source,** Alt/Option-drag it.

FIXING OVERBLOWN LIGHTING

If you've set up several light sources in Lighting Effects and your image is now too bright overall, try reducing the global Ambience or Exposure in the Properties section of the box. Or go ahead and run the Lighting Effects filter and then use Filter, Fade after the fact. Either method is easier than adjusting each light source individually.

When you apply a distortion filter, you can often get smoother (though not as crisp) results by running the filter at a low setting several times than at a high setting once, especially if the image includes straight lines. Here we started with a screen dump of a color palette and applied Filter, Distort, Twirl.

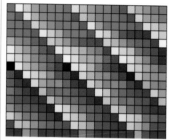

Original palette

Twirl applied 10 times at an Angle setting of 50

Twirl applied once at an Angle setting of 500

- **To turn off a light source temporarily,** so you can see the effect of removing it without actually disrupting its position, click to deselect the On box in the Light Type area of the dialog box.

- **To turn off a light source permanently** (that is, to remove it), drag its circle from the Preview area to the trash can icon.

- **To save a lighting scheme** so you can apply it to other layers or files later, click the Save button. Your new Style will be saved with the Styles supplied with Photoshop, and will be added to the dialog box's pop-out Style menu.

The Lighting Effects filter works well to cast light onto an image as if it were mounted on a wall, as shown on page 181. But here are some other ways you can use it to trick the eye:

- To **unify** several fairly different images in a printed or online publication, apply the same lighting scheme to all of them. You can do this by naming and saving the lighting Style and then loading it to apply to another layer or file.

- To make light appear to come from **inside** something (such as a bulb in a lamp), position an Omni light at the source, as shown in the bottom illustration on page 179.

- To create a **shadowy area** in an image, use a Spotlight set at a negative Intensity with Ambience set to a positive value, as shown on page 179, middle.

- To add a **texture** to the surface of an image, set up a light source and choose a Texture Channel to use as a bump map. A bump map interacts with the light sources for an image or layer, tricking the eye into perceiving bumpiness, or texture. The things that can be used as bump maps for applying Lighting Effects to any layer are the individual color channels (Red, Green, or Blue, for example), any alpha channel in the file, or the transparency mask or layer mask for that layer.

The **Texture Fill** filter gives you a quick way to import grayscale files to use with the Lighting Effects filter. The process is described in "Using Texture Fills with Lighting Effects" on page 195. *wow!*

Combining with Light

Overview *Layer the elements of your montage, adding drop shadows if you like; treat all but the shadow layers with the Lighting Effects filter.*

Wow lighting styles are included on the CD-ROM that comes with this book.

JHD

1

© PHOTOGEAR

Original montage of three images

2

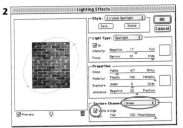

For the bricks layer only, we used a Texture Channel, turning off White Is High to make the white mortar look recessed.

3

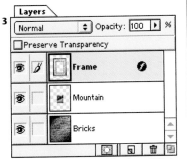

The layered, lit images with a Layer Effects Drop Shadow added to the Frame layer

THE LIGHTING EFFECTS FILTER IS IDEAL for helping the elements of a montage look at home in their surroundings. Here we've combined a drop shadow with the filter's ability to spotlight and to "emboss."

1 Assembling the pieces. Open an RGB file to use as the backdrop for your image. Open each of the other component images, select the part you want to use, drag with the move tool, and drop it into the backdrop file to form a new layer. We used a brick background, a frame, and a landscape photo.

2 Lighting the image. Now choose Filter, Render, Lighting Effects and apply the filter to each layer. Use the same Style setting in each case (we used "2AMSPOT/2 o'clock Spotlight" for the image above). If the image in any layer has an inherent texture, as our brick wall did, use one of the color channels of that layer as a Texture Channel for the filter (we used Green).

3 Adding a shadow. With the Frame layer active we added a drop shadow, positioning it to match the direction of the light source we had created. To add a drop shadow, choose Layer, Effects, Drop Shadow and enter settings for Blur (softness) and Distance and Angle (offset).

Experimenting. Try other settings from the Style list, or create your own and add them to the list by clicking the Save button in the Lighting Effects dialog box. For some kinds of lighting, you may want to separate the drop shadow onto its own layer so you can distort it (as in "Casting a Shadow" in Chapter 8). *Wow*

WOWRGB: Colors for lights are set with the Light Type color square.

WOWSoft: Ambient light (pink here) is set in the Properties section.

WOW3Down: Angles can be set for Spotlights and Directional lights.

3D Labeling

Overview *Open a photo of an object with a generally cylindrical shape; create or import the label to be applied to the object; apply the label with the 3D Transform filter; if appropriate, add the shadow that would be cast by the label.*

 "3DLabel" image

1a

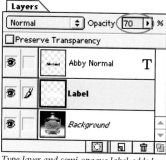

Original image

1b

Type layer and semi-opaque label added

ONE USEFUL APPLICATION for Photoshop 5/5.5's 3D Transform plug-in is to mock up a bottle, jar, or can with a label in place. The label on this jar consists of solid black type on a semi-opaque white base, applied to fit the jar and then enhanced with a subtle shadow.

1 Preparing the label. Starting with a photo of a jar or bottle, build or import label graphics. We started our label by adding a layer (click the New Layer button in the middle at the bottom of the Layers palette) and then using the rectangular marquee to shape a label. We filled it with white by pressing Ctrl/⌘-Delete with white set as the Background color in the toolbox, and then reduced the Opacity of the layer to 70% to make the label slightly transparent.

Next we chose the type tool to open the Type Tool dialog box, and we typed the label text. By choosing Fit In Window we could see the entire block of type as we adjusted its size and spacing. We could also see the type in place in the image, and by moving the cursor into the working window, we could drag to position it. When we had the type set, clicking OK closed the Type Tool box and the type was added as another layer in the stack.

Next, since the 3D Transform dialog box doesn't provide a way to work with linked layers or to save settings and reapply them to another object, we combined the Type layer with the semitransparent white label layer below it so that we would have only one element to fit to the shape of the jar: With the Type layer active, we

1c

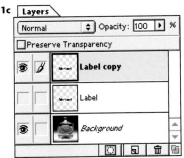

The Type and label layers were merged into one, and this Layer was duplicated for safekeeping before the 3D Transform experimentation began.

2a

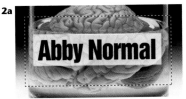

Making a selection of the area of the jar where the label is to be applied

2b

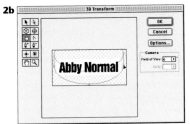

Dragging the cylinder tool to make a primitive as wide as the jar and short enough so the bottom center handle fits inside the window

2c

Using the direct selection tool to grab the center handle

2d

Dragging up to rotate the cylinder primitive to an upright "straight on" position

pressed Ctrl/⌘-E (for Merge Down). The merged layer consisted of fully opaque black type and the 70% opaque white label base.

2 Fitting the label to the jar.

Before you start to work with the 3D Transform filter, it's a good idea to duplicate the label layer so you have a copy for safekeeping. Dragging the layer's thumbnail to the New Layer icon in the Layers palette creates a copy. Then turn off the eye icon for one of the two identical labels and work with the other one.

In working with the 3D Transform filter, the trick is to position the filter's cylinder model to an upright, front, centered view *before* you "attach" the label image, but most would agree that it isn't intuitively obvious how to accomplish this.

Once you get into the 3D Transform dialog box, you won't be able to see the object you're trying to fit the label to. So, as a reference for the width of the object you're applying the label to, before you choose the filter, use the rectangular marquee to make a selection boundary just slightly wider than the object. Then choose Filter, Render, 3D Transform.

In the 3D Transform dialog box click on the cylinder primitive in the toolbox and drag in the preview window to make a cylindrical shape that approximately matches the width of the area where you want to attach it — in this case the jar. But be sure to keep the bottom of the shape in the preview window so you can see the handle in the center of the bottom.

Use the direct selection tool (the hollow arrow) to grab the bottom center handle and drag it up to rotate the cylindrical shape

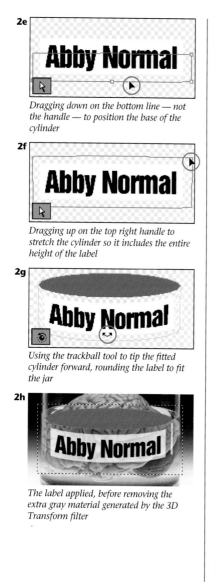

2e

Dragging down on the bottom line — not the handle — to position the base of the cylinder

2f

Dragging up on the top right handle to stretch the cylinder so it includes the entire height of the label

2g

Using the trackball tool to tip the fitted cylinder forward, rounding the label to fit the jar

2h

The label applied, before removing the extra gray material generated by the 3D Transform filter

into a "straight on" view (using this tool won't rotate the label image itself — only the cylinder outline).

Drag on the bottom line — not the handle — to move the straightened primitive so the bottom is below the label image.

Then drag the upper right corner handle up to stretch the primitive up so it encompasses the entire label.

Switch to the trackball tool. As soon as you choose the trackball, the label will automatically "adhere" to the cylinder geometry, and you can use the tool to orient the cylinder and label to the tilt and rotation needed to match your object (the jar). You can also use the pan tool and the Field Of View and Dolly settings to reposition the label, shrink or enlarge it, or change the amount of perspective. Click OK to close the dialog box and render the changes. Then remove the gray disc or any other excess material generated by the filter. You can select this material and press Delete, or use the eraser.

3 Adding the shadow. Because our label was affixed to a transparent jar, we decided to use a Layer Effects Drop Shadow to add the slight darkening that the label would cast onto the brain inside the jar. To add a Drop Shadow, open the Effects dialog box: Position the cursor over the *name* — not the thumbnail — of the transformed label layer, and right-click (Windows) or Control-click (Mac), and drag to open the context-sensitive menu, where you can choose Effects. In the Drop Shadow section of the Effects dialog box, click the color swatch and use the Color Picker's cursor to sample the dark color of a shadow within the image. Adjust the Blur, Angle, Distance, and Opacity to match the lighting in the background image. We used a Blur of 10 for this 1000-pixel-wide image and reduced the Opacity to 50% for a soft shadow. We moved the cursor out of the dialog box and into the image to drag the shadow up to match the lit-from-below ambience of the photo. The resulting Angle setting was –90°, and the Distance was 8 pixels. *wow!*

3

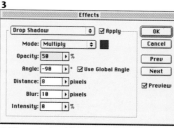

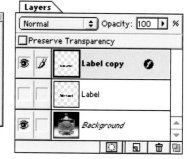

Adding a dark reddish-brown Drop Shadow to complete the labelling illusion

Filter Demos

Overview *For any plug-in filter you want to use, first drag it (separately or in a folder with other filters) to the Plug-ins folder inside the Photoshop folder; start the Photoshop program; open an image; select the area you want to filter (make no selection if you want to filter the entire active layer); choose Filter and select a filter from the pop-out submenus.*

This 800-pixel-wide image is a layered composite of the original image and a copy treated with Photoshop's native Reticulation filter (Filter, Sketch, Reticulation) in the layer above. The filtered layer was in Overlay mode at 50% Opacity. Above that was a Hue/Saturation Adjustment layer with a mask that allowed the Hue change only at the edges of the image.

This is the original image used for the filter demos, before filters were applied. The image is 408 pixels wide, or 1.8 inches wide at 225 dpi.

For filters that create a special effect on a selected area, this version of the graphic (left) was loaded as a selection on a muted background image (right).

FILTER RERUNS

To reapply the last filter effect you used, press Ctrl/⌘-F. To select that filter again but open its dialog box so you can change the settings before you apply the filter, press Ctrl-Alt-F (Windows) or ⌘-Option-F (Mac).

IN ADDITION TO SUPPLYING PLUG-IN FILTERS with Photoshop, Adobe has made available to other software developers the program code they need to write more filters. The following pages provide a catalog of many of the available filters, showing the effects of applying them to two kinds of images — a photo of a hula doll set off from a natural background by a glow, and a "Wow" graphic with a glow behind it. Besides showing you the results of applying the filters themselves, this catalog includes tips for using filters efficiently and creatively.

Some filters are made to work on selections. To show the effect of those plug-ins, we've used a version of the Wow graphic stored in an alpha channel and loaded as a selection in a muted version of a natural background image. Other filters work on an element surrounded by transparency, so we've used only part of the demo image. Where numerical settings are shown in the captions, they are listed in the order they appear in a filter's dialog box, from upper left to lower right. If the default settings were used, no settings are shown. *Wow!*

REPRODUCING FILTER EFFECTS

The size of an image (in pixels) is important for filters and other transformations whose settings are measured in pixels. That's why image widths are given throughout the book. If you see an effect you want to reproduce, here's how to figure out a setting to try:

[Filter setting we used (in pixels) ÷ Width of our filtered image (in pixels)] x Width of your image (in pixels) = Filter setting you should try (in pixels)

(Unlike filters whose settings are measured in pixels, those filters whose settings are in percentages or degrees will produce similar amounts of change whether you apply them to a large or a small image.)

Adobe:
Artistic

Most of the Artistic filters simulate traditional art media. But one, the Plastic Wrap filter, provides highlights and shadows that can add dimensionality and a slick surface texture to type and graphic elements.

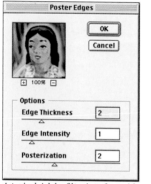

A typical Adobe filter interface with a preview box and sliders for settings

Artistic: Colored Pencil

Artistic: Cutout

Artistic: Dry Brush

Artistic: Film Grain

Artistic: Fresco

Artistic: Neon Glow

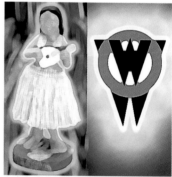

Artistic: Paint Daubs

Artistic: Palette Knife

Artistic: Plastic Wrap

Artistic: Poster Edges

Artistic: Rough Pastels

Artistic: Smudge Stick

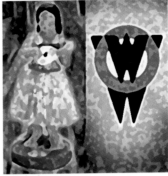

Artistic: Sponge

Artistic: Underpainting

Artistic: Watercolor

NAVIGATING GAUSSIAN BLUR

In the preview window of the Gaussian Blur dialog box (as well as Unsharp Mask and some others), you can scroll by dragging. You can also zoom in by Ctrl/⌘-clicking, zoom out by Alt/ Option-clicking, or move to a particular area of the image by clicking the cursor on the image itself.

Adobe: *Blur*

Two of the Blur filters (Radial Blur and Smart Blur) can each produce two or more very different effects.

TESTING A RADIAL BLUR

Use a Quality setting of Draft (quick but rough) to experiment with the Amount and the blur center; then use Good (or on a very large image, Best) for the final effect.

Blur: Blur

Blur: Blur More

Blur: Gaussian Blur (5)

Blur: Motion Blur (45/30)

Blur: Radial Blur (Spin)

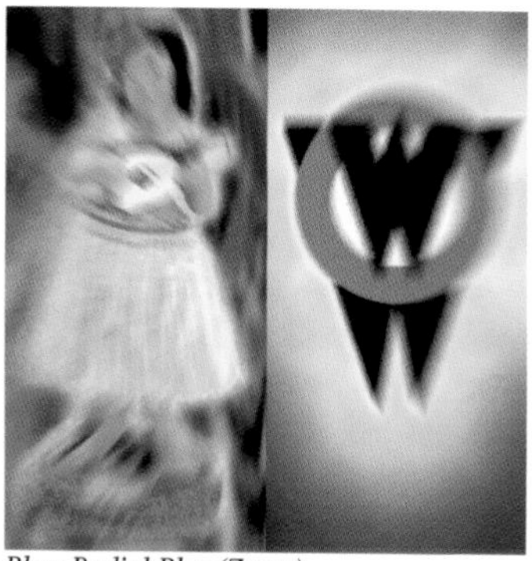

Blur: Radial Blur (Zoom)

Blur: Smart Blur

Blur: Smart Blur (Edges Only)

Adobe: *Brush Strokes*

The Brush Strokes filters simulate different ways of applying paint or ink. Like the Sketch filters, some of the Brush Strokes filters produce results that can be effectively composited with the original image (see "Compositing with Sketch Filters" on page 197).

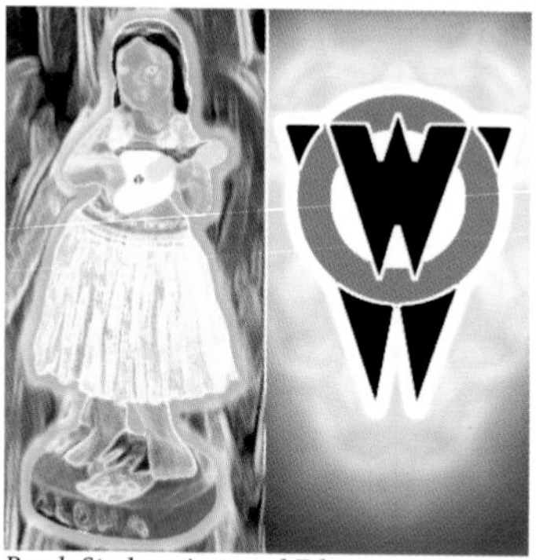

Brush Strokes: Accented Edges

Brush Strokes: Angled Strokes

Brush Strokes: Crosshatch

Brush Strokes: Dark Strokes

Brush Strokes: Ink Outlines

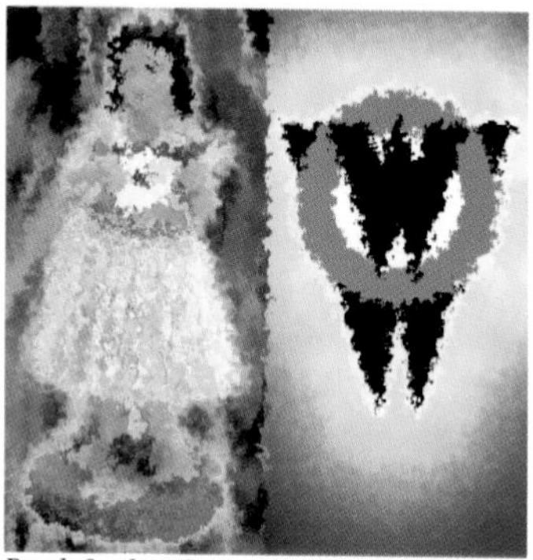

Brush Strokes: Spatter

Brush Strokes: Sprayed Strokes

Brush Strokes: Sumi-e

Adobe: *Distort*

The Distort filters add special effects and textures to an image.

MORE DISPLACEMENT MAPS

The standard Photoshop 5/5.5 installation provides two sets of files to use with Filter, Distort, Displace: in Plug-ins, Displacement Maps and Goodies, Textures. Find more in Textures (Windows) or Textures For Lighting Effects (Mac) on the Photoshop CD-ROM.

Distort: Diffuse Glow

Distort: Displace (Honeycomb)

Distort: Displace (Dispmaps: Random)

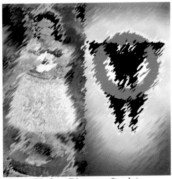

Distort: Displace (Dispmaps: Streaks)

Distort: Glass (Blocks)

Distort: Glass (Custom texture/lightened)

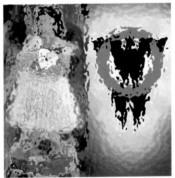

Distort: Ocean Ripple

Distort: Pinch (+100%)

Distort: Pinch (–100%)

Distort: Polar Coordinates (Polar to Rect.)

DISPLACEMENT MODES

Some of the displacement maps that Adobe supplies to be used with the Distort, Displace filter produce quite different effects when applied in Tile mode than when used in Stretch To Fit mode. If you try one of the displacement maps and get an effect that seems uninteresting, try the other mode. (Note that most of the displacement map files are quite small, and Stretch To Fit really distorts them.)

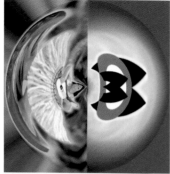

Distort: Polar Coordinates (Rect. to Polar)

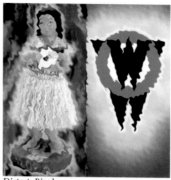

Distort: Ripple

Distort: Shear

Distort: Spherize (+100%)

Distort: Spherize (–100%)

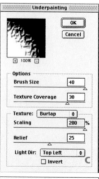

Distort: Twirl

Distort: Wave

Distort: Zigzag (Pond Ripples)

FANCY FRAMING

Some of the filters of the Distort submenu, as well as Spatter and Sprayed Strokes from the Brush Strokes submenu, can be used to create a custom edge treatment for an image. Open an image and open the Layers palette (Window, Show Layers). Turn the *Background* layer into a layer with the capacity for transparency by double-clicking its name in the palette and clicking OK. Then double-click the marquee tool in the toolbox to open the Marquee Options palette. Select the Rectangular or Elliptical Shape, and set a Feather amount. Drag to select the part of the image you want to frame. Then click the Add Layer Mask icon at the bottom of the palette to turn the selection into a layer mask. Adding a white-filled layer below the image layer will give you a better look at the frame edges (**A, B**). For a more unusual effect, experiment on the layer mask with filters that will stylize the edge area of the mask, such as Ocean Ripple or Wave from the Distort submenu, or one of the Brush Strokes or Artistic filters, like Underpainting, as shown here (**C, D**).

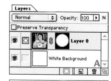

Adobe: *Noise*

One of the Noise filters (Add Noise) "roughens" the color in an image, and the other three (Despeckle, Dust & Scratches, and Median) smooth it.

Noise: Add Noise (Gaussian, 50%, Mono)

Noise: Add Noise (Uniform, 50%)

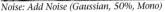

Noise: Despeckle

Noise: Dust & Scratches (4/0)

Noise: Median

CREATING TEXTURES

Try these methods as a start for experimenting to make natural-looking textured surfaces:

Make a stone surface (A) by running the Difference Clouds filter repeatedly on a grayscale file and then colorizing it to make "marble." Then Add Noise at a low setting, Gaussian Blur at a low setting, and run the Lighting Effects filter with a Directional light source, using one of the color channels (Red, Green, or Blue) as the Texture Channel.

Make brushed metal (B) or the start of wood grain by filling a layer with 50% gray and running Add Noise, then using a Motion Blur to create streaks, and finishing with a subtle application of Lighting Effects.

Make rough paper textures for painting (C) by running the Add Noise filter at a low setting, then Blur or Blur More (used here), and then Emboss (from the Stylize submenu). Or try using Facet (from the Pixelate submenu) between the blurring and embossing steps. Use Image, Adjust, Levels to whiten the paper and reduce the contrast.

Adobe: *Other*

The Other submenu houses the eclectic collection of filters shown here. In addition, if you're technically inclined, you can design your own filters with the Other menu's Custom plug-in, as explained in Photoshop's online Help.

Other: DitherBox™ (background only)

Other: High Pass (10)

Other: Maximum (2)

Other: HSL&HSB (HSL-> RGB)

Other: Minimum (2)

Other: Offset

DETERMINING THE DITHER

The DitherBox filter lets you predetermine the pattern used to dither a particular RGB color when you convert from RGB to Web colors. (You can also load other color palettes to use for dithering, but if you're preparing art for the Web, use the Web-Safe Colors. This will ensure that the color won't be further dithered when the image is viewed on a system with an 8-bit monitor.)

To fill an area with a custom dither pattern, first select the area to fill. Then click the RGB color square to open the Color Picker. Now you can specify color in the Color Picker, or use the Color Picker's eyedropper tool to sample from any open image. When you close the Color Picker and click the arrow next to the RGB color square in the DitherBox interface, the filter will automatically generate a Pattern to substitute for the RGB color. If you like, you can edit this pattern by choosing one of the pattern size buttons (2x2, 3x3, and so on) and using the pencil tool to sample from the dialog box's color palette, and then clicking to fill one of the small squares in the preview window.

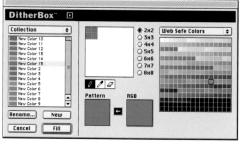

The DitherBox interface, opened by choosing Filter, Other, DitherBox

Adobe:
Pixelate

Most of the Pixelate filters turn an image into patterns of spots of flat color. For all but Facet and Fragment, you can control the size of the spots, producing very different effects depending on the size settings.

Pixelate: Color Halftone (on CMYK)

Pixelate: Crystallize

Pixelate: Facet

Pixelate: Fragment

Pixelate: Mezzotint (Coarse Dots)

Pixelate: Mezzotint (Fine Dots)

Pixelate: Mezzotint (Short Lines)

Pixelate: Mezzotint (Short Strokes)

Pixelate: Mosaic

Pixelate: Pointillize (white Background color)

Pixelate: Pointillize (black Background color)

Adobe: *Render*

The Render filters create "atmosphere" and surface texture. Two of them act independently of the color in the image: Clouds creates a sky, and Texture Fill fills a layer or channel with a pattern. The 3D Transform filter applies the image to a sphere, cube, or cylinder.

Render: 3D Transform

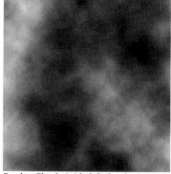

Render: Clouds (with default colors)

RENDERING A STORM

Holding down the Alt/Option key as you choose Filter, Render, Clouds produces a more dramatic cloud pattern with more contrast.

Render: Clouds (with blue Background color)

Render: Difference Clouds

MAKING MARBLE

The Difference Clouds filter can generate a veined, marble look: In the white-filled Background layer of an RGB file, with black and white as the Foreground and Background colors, choose Filter, Render, Difference Clouds. Then press Ctrl/⌘-F repeatedly to build the degree of marbling you want (**A**). Colorize the marble by adding an Adjustment layer (Ctrl/⌘-click the New Layer icon at the bottom of the Layers palette). Choose Color Balance as the Type, and adjust the sliders (**B**). Produce a stucco-like texture (**C**) by treating the uncolored marble (A) with the Lighting Effects filter as follows: In the Channels palette Ctrl/⌘-click on the RGB channel to load its brightness information as a selection, and save the selection as an alpha channel (Select, Save Selection). Apply the filter (Filter, Render, Lighting Effects) using Directional as the Light Type and choosing the alpha channel from the Texture Channel menu, with White Is High turned on.

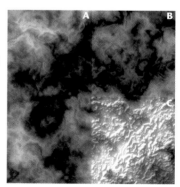

Render: Lens Flare

Render: Lighting Effects (Soft Spotlight)

Render: Lighting Effects (Blue Omni)

Render: Lighting Effects (Directional; Red channel as Texture)

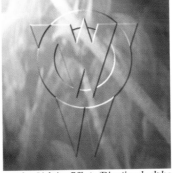

Render: Lighting Effects (Directional; alpha channel as Texture; White Is High on)

Render: Lighting Effects (Directional; alpha channel as Texture; White Is High off)

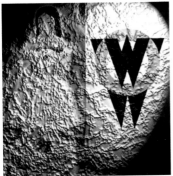

Render: Lighting Effects (Directional; Blistered Paint as Texture)

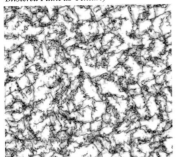

Render: Texture Fill (Blistered Paint)

USING TEXTURE FILLS WITH LIGHTING EFFECTS

The Adobe Photoshop 5/5.5 CD-ROM holds files designed to make seamlessly repeating patterns when used with the Texture Fill filter. Here's how to use one of these textures as a "bump map" for creating surface relief for the Lighting Effects filter's light to act on: Open the Channels palette for the image you want to run Lighting Effects on (Window, Show Channels) and click the New Channel icon at the bottom of the palette to make an alpha channel. With this channel active, choose Filter, Render, Texture Fill. Open the Textures folder (Windows) or Textures For Lighting Effects folder (Mac) and choose a texture. Click the Open button to fill the alpha channel with texture. Then click the RGB channel's name to make it active, and choose Filter, Render, Lighting Effects, picking your texture-filled alpha channel as the Texture Channel in the Lighting Effects dialog box.

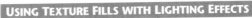

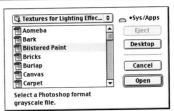

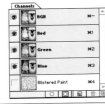

Adobe: *Sharpen*

Although there are four Sharpen filters, the one you'll use most is Unsharp Mask, because it's the only one that lets you control the effect (see "Sharpen" on page 172 for tips on using Unsharp Mask).

Sharpen: Sharpen

Sharpen: Sharpen Edges

Sharpen: Sharpen More

Sharpen: Unsharp Mask (100/1/0)

Sharpen: Unsharp Mask (500/5/0)

Adobe: *Sketch*

The Sketch filters include a number of artistic effects. Some of them imitate drawing methods, while others simulate different dimensional media. The Sketch effects shown here were produced with black as the Foreground color.

Sketch: Bas Relief

Sketch: Chalk & Charcoal

Sketch: Charcoal

Sketch: Chrome

Sketch: Conté Crayon

Sketch: Graphic Pen

Sketch: Halftone Pattern (Dot)

Sketch: Halftone Pattern (Line)

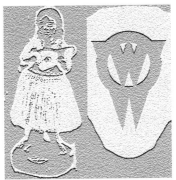

Sketch: Note Paper

Sketch: Photocopy

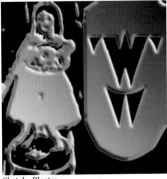

Sketch: Plaster

Sketch: Reticulation

Sketch: Stamp

Sketch: Torn Edges

Sketch: Water Paper

COMPOSITING WITH SKETCH FILTERS

Some of the Sketch filters are ideal for making filtered layers that can then be composited with the original image. Here we've layered an image filtered with Reticulation over the original, reduced its Opacity, and used the Color Dodge blending mode to lighten and brighten the pixels under the white parts of the filtered layer, creating a glowing effect.

Adobe: *Stylize*

The Stylize filters are a diverse collection of edge treatments and other special effects.

NEUTRAL EMBOSSING

To eliminate the color from an image that has been treated with the Emboss filter, keeping only the highlights and shadows, use Image, Adjust, Desaturate.

Stylize: Diffuse

Stylize: Emboss

Stylize: Extrude (Blocks)

Stylize: Extrude (Pyramids)

Stylize: Find Edges

Stylize: Glowing Edges

"SOFTENING" A FILTER

If you run a filter and the result seems too strong, you can choose Filter, Fade Filter and use the Opacity slider in the Fade dialog box to "soften" the effect. With Fade you can also control the blending mode of the filtered image. (Since Fade only works immediately after you apply a filter, the change becomes permanent once you do any other work on the image. For more flexibility later, use this approach instead: Copy your original image to a new layer by dragging its name to the New Layer icon at the bottom of the Layers palette. Apply the filter to this layer and use the layer's Opacity and blending mode controls.)

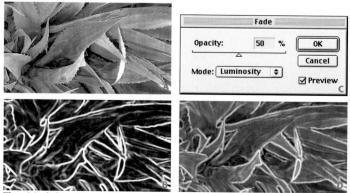

Stylize: Solarize

The original photo (A) was filtered with Stylize, Glowing Edges (B). Then the Filter, Fade command was applied, treating the Glowing Edges version like a top layer, reducing its Opacity and compositing it in Luminosity mode (C), to produce a subtler effect (D).

Stylize: Tiles

Stylize: Wind (Stagger)

Stylize: Trace Contour

Stylize: Wind (Wind)

PHOTOREALISTIC TILES

To get the look of hand-painted tiles, start by running the Stylize, Tiles filter on the image. (Or for a mosaic look with each tile a single color, try the Texture, Stained Glass filter.) Next create an alpha channel (click the New Channel icon at the bottom of the Channels palette), repeat the filter on this channel (Ctrl/⌘-F), and blur slightly (Filter, Blur, Gaussian Blur). Working in the RGB composite channel again (Ctrl/⌘-~ activates the composite), choose Render, Lighting Effects and set up a Directional light source. If the grout in the alpha channel is white, turn off White Is High.

Filtered and blurred alpha channel   *Tiles and Lighting Effects applied*

Adobe: *Texture*

Most of the Texture filters create the illusion that the image has been applied to an uneven surface. But Stained Glass remakes the image into polygons, each filled with a single color.

Texture: Craquelure

Texture: Grain

Texture: Grain (Clumped)

Texture: Grain (Enlarged)

Texture: Grain (Speckle)

Texture: Grain (Stippled)

Texture: Grain (Vertical)

Texture: Mosaic Tiles

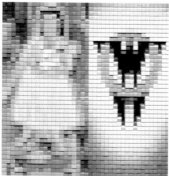

Texture: Patchwork

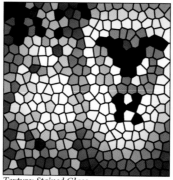

Texture: Stained Glass

Texture: Texturizer (Brick)

Texture: Texturizer (Canvas)

TRYING OUT TEXTURIZER

Choosing Filter, Texture, Texturizer brings up the Texturizer dialog box, which is sort of like a mini version of the Lighting Effects filter. Texturizer doesn't have Lighting Effects' flexibility in setting the type of light source; all its lighting is directional. And it doesn't let you add extra lights or define surface characteristics like shininess. But it's easier to operate, it does let you use images in Photoshop file format as the texture pattern for embossing, and it lets you scale the pattern down to 50% or up to 200% so you can control how many times it repeats. To get a smaller pattern with more repetitions, start with a texture file that's smaller in relation to your background image. To get a rounder edge, apply a slight Gaussian Blur to the texture file before you run the Texturizer filter.

For the image on the left, the Photoshop file used as a texture was scaled to 100%, so it kept its original size relationship to the background image. For the version in the center, it was scaled to 50%. For the image at the right, the texture file was given a slight Gaussian Blur before the filter was applied, which resulted in smoother embossing.

Texture: Texturizer (Load Texture: Weave 7)

Alien Skin:
Eye Candy

Many of the special effects filters that make up the Eye Candy 3.0 set have 10 or more presets (in most cases we've shown only one). All presets can be customized — for color, lighting angle, opacity, relative strength of highlight or shadow, or other qualities. And you can name and save your own settings.

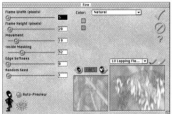

Eye Candy interface

Eye Candy 3.0: Antimatter

Eye Candy 3.0: Carve (Soft light outline)

Eye Candy 3.0: Cutout (Typical)

Eye Candy 3.0: Drop Shadow (Soft)

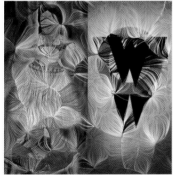

Eye Candy 3.0: Fur (Well defined strands)

Eye Candy 3.0: Glass (Strong distortion)

Eye Candy 3.0: Carve (Chisel)

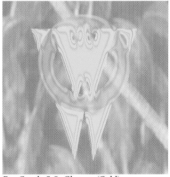

Eye Candy 3.0: Chrome (Gold)

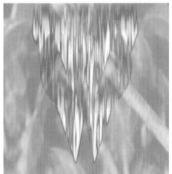

Eye Candy 3.0: Fire (Burning inside)

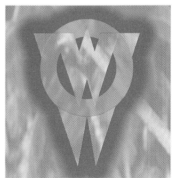

Eye Candy 3.0: Glow (Red glow)

Eye Candy 3.0: HSB Noise (Cells)

Eye Candy 3.0: Inner Bevel (Button)

Eye Candy 3.0: Jiggle (Twisty)

Eye Candy 3.0: Motion Trail (Moving left)

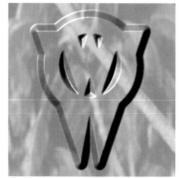
Eye Candy 3.0: Outer Bevel (Dull)

Eye Candy 3.0: Perspective Shadow (Classic)

Eye Candy 3.0: Smoke (Typical)

Eye Candy 3.0: Squint (Beer goggles)

Eye Candy 3.0: Star (Sea urchin)

Eye Candy 3.0: Swirl (Typical)

Eye Candy 3.0: Water Drop (Typical)

Eye Candy 3.0: Weave (Typical)

AlienSkin: *Xenofex*

The Xenofex 1.0 filters create special effects that imitate both natural phenomena and man-made distortion. Each filter has at least 10 presets, and you can make your own changes and then save your settings. For instance, you can control the branching and color of Lightning, or the curvature, static, ghosting, and breakup of the Television effect.

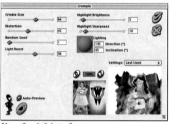

Xenofex 1.0 interface

Xenofex: Baked Earth

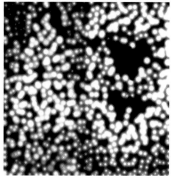

Xenofex: Constellation

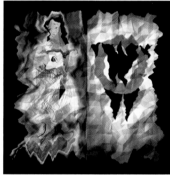

Xenofex: Crumple

Xenofex: Distress

Xenofex: Electrify

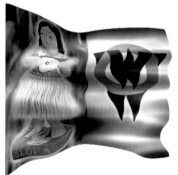

Xenofex: Flag

Xenofex: Lightning (Heat Lightning)

Xenofex: Little Fluffy Clouds

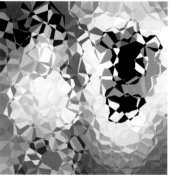

Xenofex: Origami (Shards)

Xenofex: Puzzle (Shiny Cardboard, 5,5,1)

Xenofex: Puzzle (Thick Cardboard, 14,13,3)

Xenofex: Rounded Rectangle (Lead Pipe)

MULTI-LAYER EFFECTS

There's a way to run a filter, such as Lighting Effects, on several layers of a file without flattening the entire file and without affecting all layers. For instance, you might want to filter all the image layers of a poster, but leave the type layers unfiltered. Start by making a merged copy of the layers you want to filter, as follows: Add a new, empty layer at the top of the stack (click the New Layer icon at the bottom of the Layers palette). Turn on the eye icon for this layer and the ones you want to filter. Hold down the Alt/Option key and choose Merge Visible from the Layers palette's pop-out menu.

Xenofex: Shatter (Broken Mirror)

Xenofex: Shower Door (Collage)

Now experiment with filtering the merged copy, making a note of the filter settings when you arrive at the effect you want. If for some reason you later need to work on the individual layers some more, you'll still have them available, separate and unfiltered. After you make the changes you want, you can make a new merged copy and refilter with the settings you noted before.

Xenofex: Stain

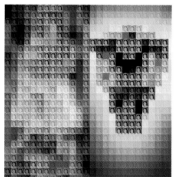

Xenofex: Stamper

Xenofex: Television (70's TV Set)

Xenofex: Television (Scanline Noise)

Andromeda: *Photography*

Andromeda Software's Photography Filters provide special effects similar to those you can achieve with specialized lenses for a 35mm camera. The filters are listed in the Andromeda submenu in the Filter menu.

The cMulti filter interface from the Andromeda Photography filter set

cMulti

Designs

Diffract

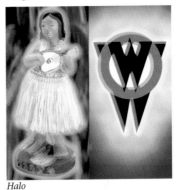
Halo

Prism

Rainbow

Reflection

sMulti

Star

Velocity

Andromeda: *Screens*

Andromeda Software's Screens Filter provides preset Mezzotint treatments for screening images, as well as an interface that lets you choose your own settings and preview several settings at once.

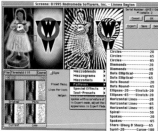

The Andromeda Screens filter's Novice interface

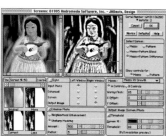

The Andromeda Screens filter's Expert interface, opened by clicking the Expert button while in Novice mode, lets you customize screen settings.

Screens: Patterns (Circles, 65 lpi)

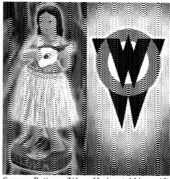

Screens: Patterns (Wavy Horizontal Lines, 45)

Screens: Patterns (Circles) on a Grayscale version of the image

Screens: Mezzoblends (Mezzoblend Lines Wavy Sharp)

Screens: Mezzograms (Mezzogram 65)

Screens: Special Effects (Intaglio, Woodblock)

Screens: Special Effects (Fabric, Well…,Velvet!)

Screens: Mezzotints (Mezzotint 65)

Screens: Mezzotints (Mezzotint 65) on a Grayscale version of the image

Andromeda:
Techtures

Andromeda Software's Techtures filter comes with a library of 900 hand-rendered textures that can be overlaid on, blended with, or embossed into an image. Also included are Environment patterns and Displacement Maps. Examples shown here are blended, except Polished Stone, which is overlaid.

Techtures: Textures (Foliage)

Techtures: Textures (Masonry)

Techtures: Textures (Polished stone)

Techtures: Textures (Tiles)

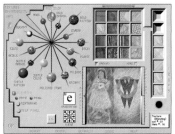
Andromeda Techtures interface

Andromeda:
Measurement

Andromeda Software's Measurement filter lets you draw or import paths to use as measurement devices. Measurements made with these editable paths can be automatically displayed in a number of table and graph formats.

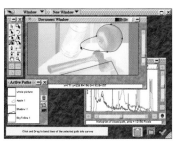
Andromeda Measurement filter interface

Andromeda:
Shadow

Andromeda Software's Shadow filter provides drop and cast shadows with fade and progressively blurred edges. Perspective shadowing is accomplished with a virtual camera, and you can set up as many as four light sources for multiple shadows.

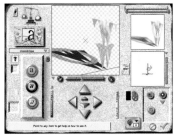
Andromeda Shadow filter interface

Andromeda:
Three-D Luxe

Andromeda Software's Three-D Luxe Filter allows three-dimensional surface mapping in Photoshop. This upgrade to the original Series 2 Three-D filter can combine your image with a number of different 3D shapes and smooth or dimensional surface textures. Over 2000 textures are provided with the filter.

3-D (Cube, Tile, Wrap Corner)

3-D (Cylinder)

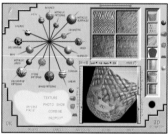

Andromeda Three-D Luxe interface

3-D (Plane)

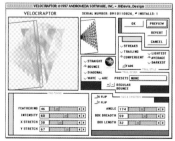

3-D (Sphere, Tile)

Andromeda:
VariFocus

Andromeda Software's VariFocus filter provides variable defocusing to direct attention where you want it. It can simulate short depth of field or create custom expressive effects with the contoured masks that come with the filter or with masks you create yourself.

Andromeda Varifocus filter interface

Andromeda:
Velociraptor

Andromeda's Velociraptor plug-in livens up images by creating customizable motion trails to produce speeding and stutter effects. Among the kinds of trails you can add are arcs, bounces, cascades, loops, spirals, springs, and waves.

Andromeda Velociraptor filter interface

Auto F/X: *Photo/Graphic Edges*

Auto F/X's Photo/Graphic Edges 4.0 filter combines the hundreds of edge effects of previous versions with special effects, including Bevel, Carve, Glow, Burn, and Distort. Effects can be kept live so you can turn them on and off, and can be combined. The package also includes 1000 textures that can be used as backgrounds.

Photo/Graphic Edges Interface

Photo/Graphic Edges

Auto F/X: *Photo/Graphic Patterns*

Auto F/X's Photo/Graphic Patterns makes images look as if they were printed on material surfaces such as marble, wood, or burlap. The filter comes with more than 1000 textures, or you can use your own. The filter adds subtle color, depth, grain, and lighting effects.

Photo/Graphic Patterns Interface

Photo/Graphic Patterns

Auto F/X: *WebVise Totality*

WebVise Totality from Auto F/X is a suite of six Photoshop plug-ins for preparing Web graphics, including GIF and JPEG compression engines, an animator, and an interface for choosing Web-safe colors. WebVise Totality also offers batch processing of files.

WebVise Totality Interface

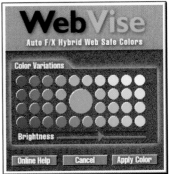

WebVise Totality/Hybrid Web Safe Colors

Extensis: Intellihance Pro 4.0

The Extensis Intellihance Pro plug-in provides a Photoshop Variations-like multiple-preview interface for interactively adjusting tone, correcting color, and sharpening. When incorporated into a Photoshop Action for batch processing, the filter can analyze each image and makes adjustments based on individual needs.

Extensis: PhotoFrame

With Extensis PhotoFrame you can add a wide variety of frames and borders to Photoshop images, combining as many as three frames, adding colors, and rotating to create custom effects. An interactive preview shows you the result of each change as you carry it out. PhotoFrame will import frames in JPEG format.

Extensis: PhotoGraphics

The Extensis PhotoGraphics plug-in provides tools for creating and editing vector shapes that can be stroked and filled, and whose opacity can be individually controlled. The filter also lets you set editable type on a path, even applying more than one text block to a path. It also provides advanced type formatting options, such as coloring single characters.

Extensis Intellihance Pro interface

Extensis PhotoFrame interface

Extensis PhotoGraphics interface

Extensis: Mask Pro 2.0

Mask Pro provides sophisticated tools for silhouetting and creating clipping paths. Mask Pro's EdgeBlender removes background color from partially transparent edge pixels.

Extensis: PhotoFrame (camera_24.frm)

Extensis: PhotoGraphics (Text)

Extensis Mask Pro and EdgeBlender interfaces

Extensis:
PhotoTools 3.0

The PhotoTools 3.0 collection includes special effects, button-building and texture-making tools, and a GIF animator. When PhotoTools is installed in Photoshop's Plug-ins folder, an Extensis menu is added to Photoshop's main menu bar.

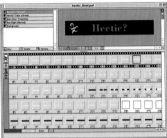

Extensis PhotoTools filter PhotoAnimator interface

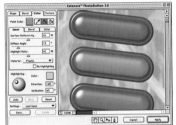

Extensis PhotoTools 3.0 filter PhotoButton interface

Extensis PhotoTools 3.0 filter PhotoTexture interface

Extensis, PhotoBevel: Inner Slope

Extensis, PhotoBevel: Outer Round

Extensis, PhotoCastShadow: Cast Shadow

Extensis, PhotoEmboss: Sample Raise

Extensis, PhotoGroove: Metallic Edge

Extensis, PhotoGroove: Neon Frame

Extensis, PhotoGroove: Transparent Bevel

Extensis, PhotoGlow (Edge, Round)

Flaming Pear: *BladePro*

The BladePro filter lets you combine textures, bevels, and mirrorlike reflections for effects like tarnish, iridescence, and glassiness. The filter comes with 100 presets.

Flaming Pear BladePro interface

Flaming Pear, BladePro

Flaming Pear, BladePro

Flaming Pear: *FeatherGIF*

The Feather GIF plug-in makes cutout GIFs with blurry, transparent edges. Assorted masks and transparency gradients allow Web page backgrounds to show through.

Flaming Pear Feather GIF interface

Flaming Pear: *Solar Cell*

The Solar Cell plug-in lets you design your own fantasy-style suns and solar effects. Or let the filter assign random values to the many control factors.

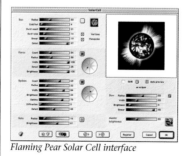

Flaming Pear Solar Cell interface

Flaming Pear: *India Ink*

With the India Ink plug-in you can convert images to etched effects in color or unusual black-and-white halftone screens.

Flaming Pear India Ink interface

Flaming Pear: *Tesselation*

The Tesselation filter lets you control the look of the edges as you create seamlessly repeating tiles. You can build tiled backgrounds in a single step, without having to retouch the edges of the tile.

Flaming Pear Tesselation interface

Human Software: *PhotoSpray*

With the PhotoSpray filter you can spray onto your canvas any of the collections of leaves, flowers, candies, or other images supplied with the plug-in. Or make your own sprays by cloning. You can control color, size, spacing, opacity, shadows, and other characteristics.

Human Software PhotoSpray interface

Human Software: *Squizz!*

Squizz! lets you distort your image by moving the intersections and lines of grids, wrap images onto shapes like cylinders and flags using "envelopes," or distort images by pushing and pulling with brushes of various sizes with unlimited Undo's.

Human Software Squizz! interface

Human Software: *Textissimo*

Textissimo lets you apply any of the more than 400 built-in effects supplied with the filter, including metallic effects, fire, bevel, carving, ice, rock, and drop shadows. You can also customize these effects or create your own.

Human Software Textissimo interface

AltaMira Group: *Genuine Fractals PrintPro*

The Genuine Fractals PrintPro plug-in lets you "res up" images in a way that preserves edge detail and other attributes better than Photoshop's Bicubic resampling.

AltaMira Genuine Fractals PrintPro Interface

MetaCreations: *Kai's Power Tools 3*

The 19 filters in Kai's Power Tools 3, which is part of KPT 5, provide special effects for print and on-screen images. For the "f/x" filters, intensity of the effect and opacity (like that in Photoshop's Fade command) are set on a sliding scale. The interfaces for the KPT filters allow real-time interaction. "Help" buttons provide directions.

KPT Lens f/x interface

KPT Gradient Designer interface

KPT Interform interface

KPT 3.0: KPT 3D Stereo Noise

KPT 3.0: KPT Gaussian f/x

KPT 3.0: KPT Gradient Designer

KPT 3.0: KPT Interform

KPT 3.0: KPT Edge f/x

KPT 3.0: KPT Glass Lens

KPT 3.0: KPT Intensify f/x

KPT 3.0: KPT Noise f/x

KPT 3.0: KPT Page Curl

KPT 3.0: KPT Pixel f/x (Op. 75%, Int. 50%)

KPT 3.0: KPT Planar Tile

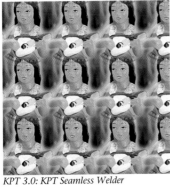

KPT 3.0: KPT Seamless Welder

KPT 3.0: KPT Smudge f/x

KPT 3.0: KPT Spheroid Designer

KPT 3.0: KPT Texture Explorer

KPT 3.0: KPT Twirl

KPT 3.0: KPT Video Feedback

KPT 3.0: KPT Vortex Tiling

MetaCreations: *Kai's Power Tools 5*

The KPT 5 filter set includes the filters of KPT 3 plus several more special effects, listed in a separate submenu of the Filter menu. Each KPT 5 filter has its own full-screen interface.

KPT5: Blurrr/Camera Optics

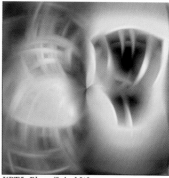

KPT5: Blurrr/Spiral Weave

KPT5: FiberOptix

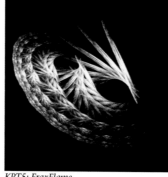

KPT5: FraxFlame

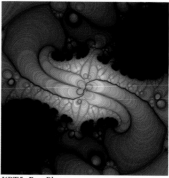

KPT5: FraxPlorer

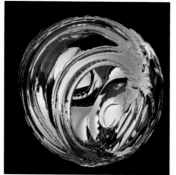

KPT5: Frax 4D

KPT5: Noize (RGB Opacity approx. 50)

KPT5: Orb-It

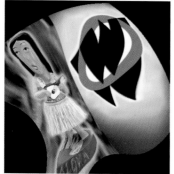

KPT5: Rad Warp

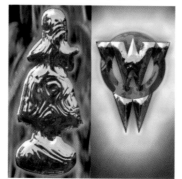

KPT5: ShapeShifter

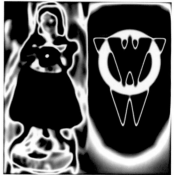

KPT5: Smoothie

RAYflect: *Four Seasons*

The Four Seasons filter lets you generate skyscapes and atmospheric effects, including stormy skies, sunsets, night skies, rainbows, and eclipses. Included is a library of 150 preset skies.

RAYflect Four Seasons interface

RAYflect, Four Seasons

RAYflect: *PhotoTracer*

PhotoTracer provides, inside Photoshop, the functions found in stand-alone programs for creating 3D scenes, including such features as transparency, refraction, bump mapping, and multiple light sources, as well as 230 preformed objects.

RAYflect PhotoTracer interface

RAYflect, PhotoTracer

Right Hemisphere: *Deep Paint*

The Deep Paint plug-in provides "artistic cloning" (applying textured strokes based on the original colors), image spray (using an image as a paint dab), and an airbrush with a true-to-life feel.

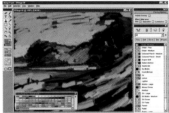

Right Hemisphere Deep Paint interface

Right Hemisphere, Deep Paint

Zaxwerks: *3D Invigorator*

With the 3D Invigorator plug-in you can turn any vector-based art or Type 1 font into a 3D model and then light it, cast reflections on it, and render it. Even after rendering and saving, the original vector artwork can be reshaped.

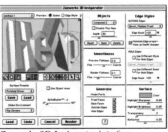

Zaxwerks 3D Invigorator interface

Zaxwerks, 3D Invigorator

Muse No.1 by **Jay Paul Bell** began with a 35mm color photo of a woman wearing a pair of wings from a novelty shop. Bell silhouetted the figure and placed it over a background composed of elements from other original color photographs of pillars, columns, ground surfaces, and landscape textures. To create the impression of an interior space with depth, he used repeating elements that decrease in size and appear to recede into the distance.

To introduce a geometric element, on a separate layer Bell drew lines over the composition, using the pen tool to create

paths. Then, using a brush size and color that worked visually with the composition, he stroked each path with the airbrush tool. ▶ *You can stroke an active path by choosing a painting tool and clicking the Stroke Path icon (second from the left at the bottom of the Paths palette).*

Bell applied the Seamless Welder from the Kai's Power Tools 3 filter set (see page 214) to rectangular, oval, and irregular selections to make some of the line elements repeat. He made a merged copy of the image at this point (Layer, Merge Visible with the Alt/Option key held down) and filtered the copy to produce a neonlike effect on the drawn lines and a

solarized and textured effect on the figure and background (Filter, Stylize, Glowing Edges). A copy of the Seamless Welder/ Geometric Line layer, with the Mode set to Difference and the Opacity set at 100 percent, was placed above the new Glowing Edges layer, which produced a blue cast on the figure. To restore some of the original flesh tones, Bell duplicated the original figure photo and moved it to the top of the stack in the Layers palette. He deleted all but the head, arm, and torso using the eraser tool and put this layer in Difference mode also. The hair area had become flat because of the filtering, so Bell repainted it with the airbrush tool to restore texture.

The Lighting Effects filter played an important part in combining the three black-and-white photos taken by artist **Lisa Cargill** to create *Your Ship Comes In*. The background began with a photo of the desert near Shiprock, New Mexico, taken with a 2¼-inch camera at sunset. The negative was scanned to Kodak Pro Photo CD. The ship is actually an old weather vane photographed with a wide-angle lens to intensify its perceived size and depth. Cargill created both a drop shadow and a cast shadow for the ship. ▶ *To create a cast shadow you can choose Layer, Effects, Drop Shadow, then render the shadow as a layer of its own (Layer, Effects, Create Layer), and reshape it (Edit, Free Transform, using the Alt/Option and Ctrl/⌘ keys to reshape the Transform box to create perspective and distortion.*

Cargill colored all three parts of the image by using the Colorize feature of the Hue/Saturation command, and then used the paintbrush in Color mode to fine-tune the coloring, using a low Opacity setting and a fade from the Foreground color to transparency to build up subtle tints. To add a blue tint to the top of the desert image Cargill created a blue gradient in a separate layer above it and set it to Multiply mode in order to darken the sky without increasing contrast in the highlights. Both the ship and the woman were colorized using Hue/Saturation and brush work with fade and low opacity.

Cargill used layer masks to silhouette the ship and the woman. She created the composition's dramatic, glowing light by working with the Lighting Effects filter on each of the three layers. The woman was already strongly lit, so she used that as a guide for the rest of the lighting. In general, Cargill uses light, warm colors in Lighting Effects for objects she wants to project into the foreground and darker, cooler colors or plain white lights at lower intensity for objects she wants to recede into the background. Cargill also used Lighting Effects to create highlights on the objects, and also to soften certain areas of shadow. One individual layer might have four or five soft Omni lights on it, for example, each with a different color and intensity, all targeted to enhance the effect she wanted in the image. When the lighting of each layer was done, Cargill flattened the image and applied an overall Lighting Effects treatment to the completed piece.

6

PAINTING

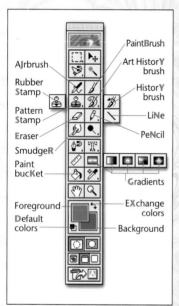

PaintBrush

Airbrush

Art Historƴ brush

Rubber Stamp

Historƴ brush

Pattern Stamp

LiNe

Eraser

PeNcil

SmudgeR

Paint bucKet

Gradients

Foreground

EXchange colors

Default colors

Background

New to Photoshop 5/5.5 are the five separate gradient tools, the History brush, the Art History brush (in version 5.5 only) and the pattern stamp. In addition to these and the other painting tools in the palette, the Fill and Stroke commands from the Edit menu and the Paths palette are part of Photoshop's painting kit.

WITH PHOTOSHOP 5 AND 5.5, THE PROGRAM'S development as a "natural media" painting program has taken several steps forward. Photoshop 5/5.5's History palette and **History brush** allow painters to store and paint from intermediate or alternate versions of their artwork, making it easier to go back and recover work they wish they hadn't painted over, or to sample color from several different stages of an image for painting. Also, the Impressionist capability that used to reside with the rubber stamp tool was moved to the History brush, simplifying the process of reproducing stored images as painted strokes.

With version 5.5 Photoshop took another step beyond version 5's painting capabilities, by extending the default brush tips to include new ones that better imitate bristles, and adding another set of **Natural Media brush tips** as well. (Both the new default brushes and the Natural Media set were developed for Adobe by Jack Davis.) The **Art History brush,** which can use these new brushes to good advantage, was created to automate the process of laying down strokes that follow the color contours of a reference image, thereby applying the paint more like an artist might.

In addition to the History brush and Art History brush, if we define painting tools as those that can apply Foreground color, Background color, Transparency, or pixels cloned from an image, Photoshop's painting tools include the paint bucket, line, eraser, pencil, airbrush, paintbrush, rubber stamp, pattern stamp, smudge, and the five gradient tools. All of these tools (except the gradients and the line, which must be dragged) can be operated either by selecting the tool and then clicking to make a single "footprint" of the brush tip on the canvas, or by holding down the mouse button or stylus and dragging to make a stroke. Most of these tools can also be constrained to a straight line by holding down the Shift key and clicking from point to point or dragging. (The line and gradient tools, which always paint in a straight line, are constrained to 45° and 90° angles when the Shift key is used.)

Each of the painting tools has its own set of controls, found in a Tool Options palette that appears when you double-click the tool's icon in the toolbox or press the Enter/Return key while the tool is active. Tool "footprints" are chosen from the Brushes palette, which by default is nested with the Tool Options palette so you can open it by clicking on the Brushes tab.

continued on page 222

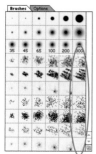

Shown here is Photoshop 5.5's default Brushes palette (top six rows), with the additional Natural Media set loaded below it. The new brushes produce strokes with bristle marks, as shown above.

THE BRUSHES PALETTE
The Brushes palette, which can be opened by choosing Window, Show Brushes or by pressing the default keyboard shortcut F5, makes available all the brushes that come with Photoshop and also lets you define your own, up to 999 x 999 pixels in size.

CYCLING THROUGH BRUSHES

When you're painting, clicking on the Brushes palette to choose a new brush tip can interrupt your work flow. Instead, use the opening bracket key ([ ) to move to the left and up in the palette, and use the closing bracket ( ]) to move down and right. **Shift-[** chooses the first brush in the palette; **Shift-]** chooses the last.

• You can **edit one of Photoshop's standard brushes** by double-clicking it in the palette or by clicking it and choosing Brush Options from the pop-out menu.

• If you want to **add a new brush based on one of Photoshop's round default brushes** but preserve the existing one as well, click the existing brush to choose it and then click in the space at the bottom of the Brushes palette after the last brush, or choose New Brush from the palette's pop-out menu. Then specify characteristics in the New Brush dialog box. (Once you've made a new brush based on one of the round default brushes in this way, if the new one is still round you can use it as a start for others.)

• To **add a custom brush shape,** construct your brush's footprint (see "Brush-Making Tips," below, for ideas) or rasterize a shape made in Adobe Illustrator (File, Place) or choose an area of an existing image. Then surround the new footprint with the rectangular marquee and choose Define Brush from the palette's pop-out menu.

• You can also **delete** brushes from the palette one by one by Ctrl/⌘-clicking on the ones you want to remove.

• You can name and **save** a particular palette of brushes (choose Save Brushes), or **load** a palette you've previously saved instead of the current set of brushes (choose Replace Brushes), or **add** a set of brushes to the current one (choose Append Brushes).

OPTIONS FOR THE BASIC PAINTING TOOLS
Here's a list of the painting characteristics that can be controlled through the **Options** palette for Photoshop's original painting tools. Some of these options also apply to the rubber stamp, pattern stamp, gradient tools, History brush, and Art History brush, but these tools are more like toolkits than single tools, and are covered separately on pages 226 through 231.

Antialiasing: For the paint bucket and line tool. The airbrush, paintbrush, rubber stamp, pattern stamp, and smudge tools are always smooth-edged (antialiased) except in Bitmap or Indexed Color mode; the marks of the pencil tool are never smooth-edged.

Double-clicking one of Photoshop's standard round brushes opens a Brush Options dialog box that lets you change the Diameter, Hardness, and Spacing (how often, as a percentage of the brush's footprint size, a new footprint is laid down). You can also slant and pinch the brush by changing the Angle and Roundness settings or by dragging in the diagram in the lower left corner of the dialog box. All round brushes are antialiased.

For any brush other than a round one, the Brush Options dialog box offers fewer settings. The only things that can be changed are Spacing and antialiasing. In either version of the Brush Options dialog box, if you deselect Spacing using the checkbox, the rate at which brush footprints are laid down is controlled by how fast you drag the cursor.

For the gradient tool, antialiasing depends on the selection into which the gradient is applied. Antialiasing can't be set for the eraser tool. In its Paintbrush and Airbrush modes it's antialiased; in Block and Pencil modes it isn't.

Arrowheads: For the line tool only. You can put a custom arrowhead on the beginning or end of a stroke, or at both ends.

Auto Erase: For the pencil tool. If you start a stroke on an area of the image that is currently the Foreground color, the stroke is made in the Background color. If you start the stroke on a pixel of any other color, the stroke is made in the Foreground color as usual.

Blending Mode: A pop-up list at the upper left of a painting tool's Options palette. It controls the interaction of the paint with the current colors of the pixels in the image. All the modes available in the Layers palette (described in "Blending Modes" on page 82) are also available in Tool Options. In addition, in **Behind** mode, only the transparent areas of a layer will accept color; any already colored pixels in the layer are protected. **Clear** mode is like painting with paint remover. This mode is available for the paint bucket and

BRUSH-MAKING TIPS

Here's a method for making your own brush tips for Photoshop's painting tools:

1 Open a new Photoshop file with the default white *Background*. Choose the airbrush tool and one of the soft round brush tips from Photoshop 5/5.5's default Brushes palette. In the airbrush's Tool Options palette (opened by pressing the Enter/Return key while the airbrush is selected) choose Dissolve mode. Choose a black or a dark gray as the Foreground color. Then click once with the airbrush on the white background. To make more than one brush tip, change brush sizes by choosing other soft round tips in the Brushes palette and click with each one.

2 For each brush you want to make, select one of the brush footprints by surrounding it with the rectangular marquee.

3 Choose Define Brush from the Brushes palette's pop-out menu. The new brush will be added to the current Brushes palette, in the last position.

4 Double-click the new brush in the palette to open the Brushes Options palette. Experiment with a lower Spacing setting and with turning on the Anti-aliased option, and click OK. Try the brush to see if it produces smooth, brushlike strokes. If it doesn't seem smooth enough, you can open the Brushes Options dialog box again and try a lower Spacing setting. Keep in mind, though, that the lower the setting, the slower the brush will operate. This can cause a delay between when you paint the stroke and when it appears on-screen, which can interfere with the "natural media" feel of the painting.

Once you've defined a custom brush or two, be sure to save them in a custom Brushes palette by choosing Save Brushes from the Brushes Palette's pop-out menu. If you simply add them to the default palette, they'll be lost if you forget and choose Reset Brushes from the pop-out menu. (If you want to remove some or all of the default brushes from your custom set, you can Ctrl/⌘-click on them in the Brushes palette.)

1

Clicking with the airbrush in Dissolve mode

2

Selecting a brush footprint

3

| New Brush... |
| Delete Brush |
| Brush Options... |
| **Define Brush** |
| Reset Brushes |
| Load Brushes... |
| Replace Brushes... |
| Save Brushes... |

Defining the brush by choosing from the Brushes palette's pop-out menu

5

Editing the new brush's stroke characteristics: reducing the Spacing and turning on Anti-aliased

Custom arrowheads can be automatically applied to lines drawn with the line tool. Click the Shape button in the Line Tool Options palette and set the Width and Length (as percentages of the line weight) and Concavity. A negative Concavity setting stretches the base of the arrowhead away from the tip, as in the two arrows above on the right. The arrow on the far left was made by clicking with the line tool to place the starting arrowhead and then dragging toward the tip rather than away from it.

Painting with the paintbrush with Wet Edges, using no Fade setting (top), with Fade To Transparent in 25 steps (center), and with Fade To Background in 25 steps (bottom)

Paintbrush Options

| Normal ⬦ | Opacity: 100 ▶ % |

Fade: 0   steps   ☐ Wet Edges

Fade to: Transparent ⬦

Stylus: ☑ Size ☑ Opacity ☐ Color

If you use a graphics tablet and pressure-sensitive stylus, you can imitate the feel of a real brush by turning on both Size and Opacity in the Stylus section of the paintbrush tool's Options palette. Increasing pressure on the stylus will make the strokes bigger and the paint "thicker," as would be the case if you were painting with traditional media.

line tool (the two painting tools that don't have an equivalent in the eraser tool) and for the Fill and Stroke commands from the Edit menu, and only in layers with transparency (in other words, not on the *Background).*

Contiguous: For the paint bucket. With the Contiguous checkbox checked, the paint bucket replaces pixels that are the same color as and continuous with the pixel that the tool's hot spot is clicked on. With Contiguous turned off, all pixels of that color throughout the layer or selection will be replaced with the color applied by the paint bucket.

Erase To History: For the eraser. It restores, stroke by stroke, the History state or Snapshot that you selected (by clicking in the far left column of the History palette.)

Fade: For the airbrush, paintbrush, eraser, and pencil. Strokes fade from the Foreground color to the Background color or to nothing (if the Transparent option is chosen); the Steps setting affects the total distance from the beginning of the stroke (at full-strength Foreground color) to the point where the Background color (or transparency) is full-strength. The eraser tool's fade-out (available in Airbrush, Paintbrush, or Pencil mode, but not in Block mode) is just the opposite — it's always from the Background color (or from transparency for a transparent layer) to the existing image on that layer.

Finger Painting: For the smudge tool only, which normally just smears existing paint, this option instead applies the Foreground color at the start of the smear.

Opacity: For all painting tools except the airbrush and smudge. Opacity of the applied paint can be varied from 1% to 100% by means of the Opacity control, operated by clicking the small Opacity triangle and then dragging the slider. Or press the number keys on the keyboard to change the Opacity setting in 10% increments; the "1" key sets Opacity at 10%, the "2" key at 20%, and so on, with "0" producing 100%. If your fingers are quick, you can be even more precise, typing in two-digit opacities such as 33% or 75%.

Pattern: For the paint bucket and the pattern stamp, which shares a space in the toolbox with the rubber stamp. The paint bucket can fill an area with the currently defined pattern, and the pattern stamp can apply the pattern stroke by stroke. (For more detail see "The Pattern Stamp" on page 227.)

To make a repeating pattern, you can use the rectangular marquee to select an area of an image or an object, and choose Edit, Define Pattern. Now you can fill all or a selected part of an image with your pattern. You can stop there or set the pattern up so the elements in alternate rows are offset, like the prints typically used for wrapping paper or fabric: Fill an image file with your pattern, then select one column of the pattern and use Filter, Other, Offset (with Undefined Areas set to Wrap Around) to shift it vertically by half the height of your original pattern element. Use the rectangular marquee to select this column and the one next to it, and choose Edit, Define Pattern again.

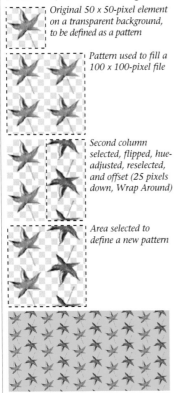

Original 50 x 50-pixel element on a transparent background, to be defined as a pattern

Pattern used to fill a 100 x 100-pixel file

Second column selected, flipped, hue-adjusted, reselected, and offset (25 pixels down, Wrap Around)

Area selected to define a new pattern

Color background filled with the new pattern

Pressure: For the smudge and airbrush tools and the eraser in Airbrush mode, the Pressure setting replaces the Opacity slider. (This slider is different from the stylus pressure that can be set in some tools' Options palettes.) Rather than controlling the opacity of entire strokes, it regulates how much paint the airbrush applies in a given time, or how long a smear is produced by the smudge tool.

Stylus: For all the painting tools except the paint bucket and gradients. You can set the characteristics that will vary when pressure is applied to the stylus of a pressure-sensitive tablet; characteristics that can be varied, depending on the tool, are Size, Opacity, Color, and Pressure.

Use All Layers: For the paint bucket, rubber stamp, or smudge tool. The color (to be filled, cloned, or smeared, respectively) is selected as if all visible layers were merged. When Use All Layers is turned off, only the pixels on the active layer are filled, cloned, or smeared.

Wet Edges: For the paintbrush and the eraser in Paintbrush mode. With Wet Edges turned on, color (in the case of the paintbrush) or transparency (in the case of the eraser) is strongest along the edges of the stroke. For the paintbrush this leaves the center semitransparent as is typical of traditional watercolors.

Weight: For the line tool, set in terms of the number of pixels. Because line weight is set in the Line Tool Options palette, the brush footprint chosen in the Brushes palette has no effect on the line tool.

If you choose View, Show Grid and Snap To Grid, you can make the painting tools follow the grid lines as you paint. But you can give yourself more options in your painting if you make a path first, snapping points and handles to the Grid points to draw symmetrical shapes. Then selecting the path in the Paths palette and choosing a painting tool and pressing the Enter key strokes the path. And you can restroke with different tools, brush sizes, and colors to layer the paint, as we did here.

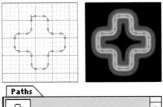

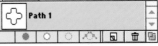

- To fill a selection with the **Foreground** color, press **Alt/Option-Delete**.

- To fill with the **Background** color, press **Ctrl/⌘-Delete**.

- Pressing the **Delete** key by itself fills with **transparency on a transparent layer** or with the **Background color on the** *Background* **layer**.

- To fill with the Foreground or Background color as if **Preserve Transparency** were tuned on, add the Shift key — that is, press **Shift-Alt/Option-Delete** or **Shift-Ctrl/⌘-Delete**.

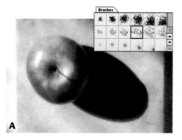

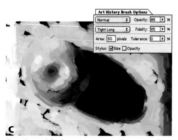

Starting with the same source image and the same brush tip (A), the History brush in Impressionist mode (B) and the Art History brush (C) generate different results. With the Impressionist brush the painter controls exactly where the strokes are laid down; a single stroke can apply more than one color. With the Art History brush each stroke is a single color and the strokes are automatically shaped and placed according to the color in the reference image.

Art History Brush Options

Normal	▲	Opacity:	100	▶	%
Tight Short	▲	Fidelity:	100	▶	%
Area:	50	pixels	Tolerance:	0	▶	%
Stylus: ☑ Size ☐ Opacity

The settings in the Options palette for Photoshop 5.5's Art History Brush include the blending mode, Opacity, painting style (which sets the length and shape of the strokes), Fidelity (which controls how much the color can vary from the actual color of the source), Area (which specifies how big an area will be filled with strokes when you click the tool once), and Tolerance (which lets you protect some areas of your painting from being painted over).

THE HISTORY BRUSH

The History brush can use a previous state or Snapshot of the image, stored in the History palette, as a source of color and detail, applying it stroke-by-stroke to the current image. Its operation in relation to the Snapshots and states of History palette is discussed in "The History Palette" starting on page 20.

As a painting tool rather than an "undo" implement, the History brush is perhaps most effective when it operates in Impressionist mode. With the Impressionist feature turned on in the History brush's Options palette, the History brush can be very helpful in converting a photo to a "hand-painted" work of art. In Impressionist mode the History brush puts down a brushlike smear of color based on the colors in its reference image. If you drag it over several colors in the reference image, the resulting multicolored smear no longer resembles anything that might be produced with a real brush. For this reason, you may want to simplify the coloring of the photo before you use it as a Snapshot for painting. And it will be essential to make your canvas layer temporarily semi-transparent so you can see a copy the original photo through it as you paint. "'Hand-Painting' from History" on page 238 is a step-by-step presentation of using the History brush in Impressionist mode.

THE ART HISTORY BRUSH

New in version 5.5, the Art History brush is an automated painting tool that can lay down several strokes with a single click of the tool. The strokes automatically follow the edges of colored areas of the reference image, which can be either a Snapshot or a state stored in the History palette. (For information on how this palette works, see "The History Palette" starting on page 20.)

Using the Art History brush successfully depends on controlling the tool's automation. As with the History brush in Impressionist mode, it's helpful to be able to see the original image as you paint. Where you click determines which of the color edges in the source will be given the most weight in determining the shape and color of the strokes that are laid down.

Some of the settings in the Art History brush's Options palette are unique to this tool. Besides choosing from a limited set of blending modes and controlling the Opacity, you can set the **paint style** (the relative length of the strokes and how closely they will follow the color boundaries of the original), the **Fidelity** (how much the color can vary from the color in the source image), the **Area** (how big an area will be covered by brushstrokes when you click once with the brush), the **Tolerance** (how different from the source image the current version has to be in order for the Art History brush to be allowed to paint on it), and the Stylus controls.

Details that are lost in the process of painting with the Art History brush can be added later with Photoshop's standard painting tools. "Art History Lessons" starting on page 245 provides step-by-step instructions for taming this tool so the results look "painterly" rather than automated.

THE PATTERN STAMP

Photoshop's pattern stamp lets you apply a pattern, stroke by stroke. A pattern is defined by selecting an area the rectangular marquee and then choosing Edit, Define Pattern. The pattern stamp can paint with the currently defined pattern, either Aligned (painting as if the pattern filled the area behind the image and the pattern stamp was erasing to it) or not (starting a new application of the pattern from the same pattern area each time the mouse button is pressed to start a new stroke).

You can use the pattern stamp tool to make a "brush" to apply multiple copies of an isolated image element, such as the grape shown here.

1 In your image select the element you want to duplicate and copy it to a transparent layer of its own. Apply a drop shadow if it's appropriate for your image by choosing Layer, Effects, Drop Shadow, sampling a shadow color from the image and adjusting the parameters so the direction and intensity of the manufactured shadow also match the image.

2 Use the rectangular marquee to make a selection big enough to include the element and its shadow (be careful not to trim the shadow). Then choose Edit, Define Pattern.

3 In the Brushes palette, double-click one of the brushes in the top row of the default set — a large, round, hard-edged brush. This will open the Brush Options dialog, where you can resize the brush so that it's big enough to completely paint your pattern with one click.

4 Choose the pattern stamp tool in the toolbox (press Shift-S once or twice) and press Enter/Return to open its Options palette. Make sure that Aligned is turned off so you can control exactly where the elements are painted. Then just click, click, click with the brush to position the copies.

1

We wanted to add more red grapes to this tray of grapes and cheese.

2
We used the pen tool to select a single grape, copied it to a layer of its own (Ctrl/⌘-J), added a drop shadow, selected it, and chose Edit, Define Pattern.

3
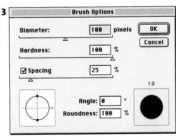
We made a 100-pixel brush, big enough to paint the entire grape-and-shadow image in one click.

4

Using the pattern stamp tool with our new brush tip and with Aligned turned off, we clicked repeatedly to create new piles of grapes.

ORIGINAL PHOTO: © CORBIS IMAGES ROYALTY FREE, BACKGROUNDS FROM NATURE

Starting with the original photo (A), the rubber stamp was used with the Aligned option turned off to replace one of the flowers with greenery (B). Then two more flowers were added, also with Align turned off (C).

With the Linear gradient tool (far left) you apply colors by dragging from where you want the gradient to start to where you want it to end. The other four types — from left to right, Radial, Angle, Reflected, and Diamond — are built by dragging outward from where you want the center to be.

THE RUBBER STAMP

Photoshop's rubber stamp is a cloning tool that makes it possible to apply existing image information in a brush stroke. The tool paints with a portion of a sampled image. The source area is sampled by holding down the Alt/Option key and clicking. Samples can be taken from any open image, from a single layer (if Use All Layers is turned off), or from all layers as if they were merged.

Once the sample has been collected, you drag the tool to apply the clone of the sampled image. If the **Aligned** box is not checked, each time you start a stroke, the clone starts over with a new copy of the sampled point, so you can end up with many copies of the sampled area. If the **Aligned** box is checked, only one version of the clone can be produced, no matter how many stokes are applied; with enough painting, the entire sampled image can be reproduced.

THE GRADIENT TOOLS

Choosing any of Photoshop's gradient tools from the pop-out palette in the toolbox and then double-clicking it opens a dialog box that lets you accomplish some amazing color-transition effects. The gradient tools in Photoshop 5/5.5 are more powerful than the single tool found in previous versions. You have a choice of five gradient tools: Linear, Radial, Angle, Reflected, and Diamond.

In any gradient tool's Options palette, you can choose from the list of Gradient color blends. You can also turn on or off the Transparency, Dither, and Reverse options.

- With **Transparency** turned on, the tool makes use of any transparency information built into a gradient when it was created, so that the gradient may have transparent areas when you apply it. With Transparency turned off, the tool ignores any transparency information, making its transitions from color to color without transparency. If no transparency has been built into the selected gradient, you get the same result whether Transparency is turned on or off. The Transparency checkbox makes it possible to define a single gradient instead of having to define both transparent and solid versions of the same color blend (see the "Transparency Is a Mask" tip at the right).

- Checking the **Dither** box introduces a degree of noise in the color transitions in your

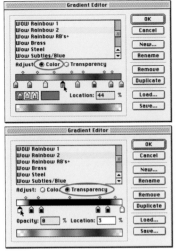

The Gradient Editor set for choosing colors (top) and assigning transparency (bottom). Diamonds indicate the midpoint of a color or transparency transition.

ORIGINAL PHOTO: © CORBIS IMAGES ROYALTY FREE, TREES

A Transparent To Foreground gradient can make an image disappear into the mist. Starting with a dawn image (top), we set white as the Foreground color and applied the gradient, dragging the gradient tool from the middle of the picture upward to a point beyond the top edge.

gradient, to prevent the banding that can occur when gradients are printed.

- The **Reverse** check box lets you apply the colors of the selected gradient in right-to-left order instead of the default left-to-right order shown in the Options palette's preview bar.

Using the Gradient Editor

If you click the Edit button in a gradient tool's Options palette, the Gradient Editor dialog box opens. You can use the Gradient Editor to:

- **Start a new gradient based on an existing one,** by choosing a gradient's name and clicking the Duplicate button. If the Load, Duplicate, and New buttons are dimmed, it's because the gradient list is full (it holds 75 gradients). To make space you can remove one or more gradients by selecting (or Shift-selecting) from the list and clicking the Remove button.

- **Start a brand-new gradient** by clicking the palette's Edit button and clicking New in the Gradient Editor dialog box.

- **Modify an existing gradient** by choosing the gradient's name from the scrolling list. The process of making specific changes is described in "Building a Gradient" below.

Building a Gradient

Each of the little **house-shaped icons** under the gradient bar represents a color specified in the gradient, with the starting color at the left end and the ending color at the right. The **diamonds** above the gradient bar represent the midpoints in the transition between each pair of colors, the point where the color is an equal mix of the two.

- **Change a color** by clicking its icon and then clicking the "F" or "B" icon to set it to the Foreground or Background color. Or click the color swatch to open the Color Picker so you can choose a color. Or click in any open file, or in the Color palette (Window, Show Color) or Swatches palette (Window, Show Swatches) to sample a color.

- **Reposition a color** by dragging it to a new position along the bar or by typing a percentage of the bar length into the Location field.

- **Add a color** by clicking below the gradient bar.

- **Remove a color** by dragging its icon down, away from the bar.

- **Change the rate of color transition** by dragging the midpoint diamond toward one of its two colors.

- **To add transparency** to the gradient, change the Adjust setting in the Gradient Editor dialog box to Transparency. The transparency icons are added, moved, and deleted the same way as the color icons, and the midpoints are set the same way.

- **Change a transparency** by clicking its icon and entering an Opacity setting.

DITHERING

To prevent banding (distinct color steps) in gradients, you can turn on the Dither option in any of the Gradient Options palettes. ☑ Dither

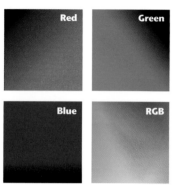

An amorphous multicolor background can be created by applying Black, White Linear gradients (horizontal, vertical, or diagonal) to individual color channels. (The color channels are shown here in color.)

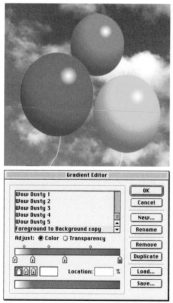

You can offset the "center" of a radial fill by using the Radial gradient tool inside an elliptical selection. For all three balloons white was the starting color; the ending color was a dark pink, red, or yellow; and a bright intermediate version of the color was used in the middle. In each case the Radial gradient tool was dragged from a point off-center within an elliptical selection.

- The Save button lets you name and **save a set of gradients** for loading later.

Applying a Gradient

To fill a layer or a selection with a color gradient, double-click any of the gradient tools in the toolbox to open its Options palette. Choose a Gradient and drag the tool from where you want the first color transition (the one on the left in the palette's preview gradient bar) to begin to where you want the last one to end. For all but the Linear Fill the starting point is the center of the gradient.

You'll find gradients used in artwork throughout the book. Below and on the facing page are a few examples of applying gradients for special effects. Page 231 shows the Photoshop 5.5 default set of gradients, as well as the Wow Gradients supplied on the Wow! CD-ROM that comes with this book. *Wow!*

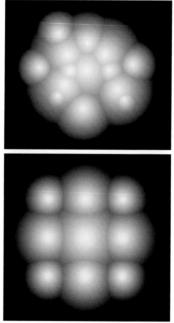

You can get a "molecular" look (top) by setting white and black as the Foreground and Background colors, respectively. First apply a Foreground To Background Radial gradient in Normal mode (set in the Radial Gradient Options palette) to make the central molecule and black background. Then make more of the same kind of gradient around it but with Lighten mode chosen in the Options palette. Starting the Radial gradients on Grid points can create a symmetrically packed appearance (bottom). After all the "atoms" are built, add color with Image, Adjust, Variations.

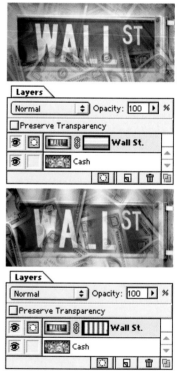

Compositing images using masks filled with two of Photoshop's default gradients applied with the Linear gradient tool: Spectrum (top), which in a mask can only be shades of gray, and Transparent Stripes (bottom, made in Normal mode with black as the Foreground color), which in a mask becomes black-and-white. In each case a Gaussian Blur was applied to the mask to soften the edges of the stripes.

Default Set (v. 5.5)

Foreground To Background

Foreground To Transparent

Black, White

Red, Green

Violet, Orange

Blue, Red, Yellow

Blue, Yellow, Blue

Orange, Yellow, Orange

Violet, Green, Orange

Yellow, Violet, Orange, Blue

Copper

Chrome

Spectrum

Transparent Rainbow

Transparent Stripes

Wow Gradients

Wow Sunset 1

Wow Sunset 2

Wow Sunset 3

Wow Sunset 4

Wow Rainbow 1

Wow Rainbow 2

Wow Rainbow RB's+

Wow Brass

Wow Steel

Wow Subtles/Blue

Wow Subtles/Green

Wow Subtles/Yellow

Wow Subtles/Orange

Wow Subtles/Red

Wow Subtles/Purple

Wow Subtles/Grays

Wow Simple 1

Wow Simple 2

Wow Simple 3

Wow Simple 4

Wow Simple 5

Wow Simple 6

Wow Simple 7

Wow Dusty 1

Wow Dusty 2

Wow Dusty 3

Wow Dusty 4

Wow Dusty 5

Gradients can be used for extreme or subtle effects. Here the Wow Dusty 5 gradient in Overlay mode adds subtle color.

Making an Electronic "Woodcut"

Overview *Trace the contours of a photo; convert that sketch to a pattern; convert a copy of the original photo to a bitmap using the pattern; treat the original photo with the Median filter; layer the bitmap back over the filter-treated photo.*

1a

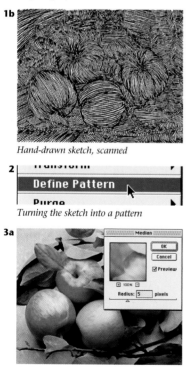

Original photo

1b

Hand-drawn sketch, scanned

2

Turning the sketch into a pattern

3a

Applying the Median filter to the photo

ARTISTS STRIVE TO TAKE ADVANTAGE of the computer's power and automation without losing the hand-crafted look of traditional artists' methods. Here we've achieved a "woodcut" effect by combining the computer's muscle with the subtleties of drawing by hand.

1 Making and aligning the sketch. Open a color photo in Photoshop. Now you'll trace over the photo to make a sketch that follows the shapes of the objects in the image. One way to trace the photo is to add a new transparent layer (click the New Layer icon in the middle at the bottom of the Layers palette) and use a digitizing tablet and the paintbrush tool with the Stylus Size box unchecked to sketch over the image. Another way is to print out a copy of the photo at full size and hand-trace the contours with a marking pen with strokes of uniform width. In either case keep the line width about the same as the white spaces between the strokes, so that if you squint at the page, the drawn areas look 50% gray overall. If you do your artwork by hand (we used a black marker on white tracing paper), scan it into the computer in grayscale mode at 100% size and the same resolution (pixels per inch) as the color photo. (You can find the Resolution of the photo file by choosing Image, Image Size.)

You'll need a fairly full range of gray tones to successfully use the sketch as a pattern in step 3. If the edges of the line work in your sketch file don't have a range of grays, you can experiment with blurring (we used Filter, Blur, Blur More for this 900-pixel-wide scan).

If you're using a scanned sketch, it's time to line it up with the photo. Make the scan file active and use the move tool to drag a copy of the scan into the photo file. Set the opacity of this new layer at about 50% so you can also see the color image. Use the move tool, and if necessary the Free Transform command (Ctrl/⌘-T) to align the sketch with the photo underneath. (To shrink the image without shrinking the window so you can drag with the cursor just outside the

3b

Copy of the photo converted to grayscale

4a

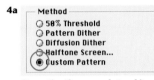

Converting the grayscale to a bitmap

4b

Converted "bitmap" layer

5

Setting the blending mode and Opacity

6a

Soft Light, 100% Opacity over color

6b

Soft Light, 100% Opacity over desaturated

Free Transform box, press Ctrl-minus [Windows] or ⌘-Option-minus [Mac]). Double-click inside the Transform box to accept the change. Set the sketch layer's Opacity back to 100%.

2 Converting the sketch to a pattern. With the sketch layer still active, Select All (Ctrl/⌘-A) and choose Edit, Define Pattern. (Unless you quit the program or use Define Pattern again, Photoshop will hold the pattern in memory until you need it at step 4.)

3 Preparing the color and grayscale images. In the color photo layer run the Median filter (Filter, Noise, Median) to keep the details of the original photo from fighting with the line work. Median averages the brightness of pixels within the Radius you set, generating a new brightness value for each pixel, but it leaves alone those pixels that are greatly different from their neighbors. The overall effect is to blur the fine details of the image while leaving any edges quite distinct (the outlines of the apples, stems, and leaves, for example).

After running the Median filter, duplicate the color photo: Activate the color layer and turn off the eye icon in the sketch layer; choose Image, Duplicate, Merged Layers Only to copy the visible layer to a new file. Convert this file to grayscale (Image, Mode, Grayscale).

4 Converting the grayscale to a "woodcut." With the sketch defined as a pattern (at step 2), convert the copy of the photo to Bitmap mode (Image, Mode, Bitmap), choosing the Custom Pattern option for the Method. (Keep the Output resolution the same as the Input.) Convert the file back to grayscale (Image, Mode, Grayscale).

5 Layering the images. With the converted photo from step 4 active, use the move tool with the Shift key held down to drag-and-drop it back into the color file. Because you made the copy from the color file, it will be exactly the same size as the original, so it will snap into place when dropped. Turn off the eye icon for the original sketch layer so it doesn't contribute to the final image, and turn on the eyes for the newly imported layer and the color layer. Adjust the blending mode and Opacity of the imported layer.

6 Experimenting. We used Screen mode and 75% opacity to get the image at the top of page 232. We also tried applying the custom bitmap layer in Soft Light mode at 100% Opacity. In another experiment, we activated the color layer and added an Adjustment layer (Ctrl/⌘-click the New Layer icon), choosing Hue/Saturation, moving the Saturation slider all the way to the left, and putting the layer in Color mode (for more about desaturating with an Adjustment layer, see page 118). *Wow*

Coloring Line Art

Overview *Scan a pen-and-ink drawing; clean up the line work, increasing contrast and removing extraneous marks; make selections and fill with flat color; airbrush shades and tones; change colors to taste; add highlights.*

TOMMY YUNE

The scanned line art

Adjusting Levels and duplicating the line art to a transparent layer, here viewed alone

TOMMY YUNE'S *JOURNEYGIRL* IMAGE is a tongue-in-cheek spin-off of *The Journeyman Project 3*, a CD-ROM game developed by Presto Studios, for which Yune served as creative director. Though the line work for *JourneyGirl* was inspired by Japanese character design, Yune took a softer, airbrushed approach to color. He started with scanned and fine-tuned line work, built areas of flat color, developed shades and tones, made special modifications to the color, and added highlights. Because of the way he constructed the color work, the line art completely covered its "seams," trapping the color and leaving no gaps.

1 Drawing and scanning. Start by scanning hand-drawn line art in grayscale mode and opening the file in Photoshop. Yune had inked his illustration on LetraMax bright white marker paper, which provided excellent contrast for scanning. He scanned the art at 400 dpi on a flatbed scanner.

2 Cleaning up the line art. Next you'll use Levels — either by choosing Image, Adjust, Levels or by making a Levels Adjustment layer (Ctrl/⌘-click the New Layer icon in the middle at the bottom of the Layers palette, and choose Levels for the Type). In the Levels dialog box, look at the histogram to see what kind of adjustment is needed to get clean, smooth lines with good contrast.

The histogram for Yune's JourneyGirl scan showed two humps (for the black ink and the white paper) with fewer pixels at the intermediate grays — basically, noise from the scanning process. Yune moved the black point and white point Input Levels sliders inward until they were just inside the two humps. He also moved the gamma slider (the gray one) to 1.2 to make the line work appear finer by brightening the image. (Be careful not to brighten your scan too much or the finest lines will begin to disappear.)

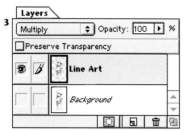

3

Loading the Black channel as a selection, creating a new layer, inverting the selection, and filling with black made a transparent layer with black "line art."

4a **Polygon Lasso Options**

Feather: 0 pixels ☐ Anti-aliased

To select areas for solid color fills, selections were not feathered or antialiased.

4b

Selected areas were filled with flat colors, shown here with the line art layer invisible (top) and visible.

To clean up extraneous marks, make white the Foreground color (you can press "D" for "Default colors" then "X" for "eXchange Foreground and Background colors") and paint over the marks with the paintbrush tool or select them and fill the selection with white (Alt/Option-Delete).

3 Making a line art layer. This step makes a transparent layer with black line art. An important part of this process is to replace the opaque gray antialiasing pixels with semitransparent ones. To create a selection based on the scanned line art, open the Channels palette and Ctrl/⌘-click the Black channel's name to load the channel as a selection. Then invert the selection (Ctrl/⌘-Shift-I) to change the selection from the white areas to the black line work. Going back to the Layers palette,

click the New Layer icon to create another layer. Then fill the selection with black (press "D" for default colors and then Alt/Option-Delete). In the pop-up list of blending modes in the Layers palette, choose Multiply.

4 Making a flat color layer. Convert the file from Grayscale to RGB (Image, Mode, RGB Color); don't merge (or flatten) the file.

So that you'll have a clear view of your cleaned-up line work on its transparent layer, make the *Background* layer active, select all (Ctrl/⌘-A) and fill with white (Alt/Option-Delete if white is still the Foreground color). With the *Background* layer still active, click the New Layer icon to add a layer between the *Background* and the line art layer. Working in this new layer, use the line art layer as a guide as you use the lasso and polygon lasso to select areas to fill with flat color. (Holding down the Alt/Option key while you work with either lasso tool lets you switch back and forth between dragging and clicking to draw the selection boundary.) Fill each selection

5a

Set up with a Tolerance of 0 and no antialiasing, the magic wand tool can be used on the flat color layer to make selections that can then be used to contain airbrushing on a new layer above it.

5b

Layers

Normal	⬦ Opacity: 100 ▸ %

☑ Preserve Transparency

👁   Line Art

👁 🖌 **Colors**

👁   Flats

Shading and toning were done on a copy of the flat-color layer using the HSB setting in the Color palette. The line art and shading and toning layers alone constitute the developing artwork. But retaining the flat color layer provides a way to reselect color areas and to start over if a mistake is made in shading or toning one area.

6

Airbrushing in Color mode changes the color but preserves the shading and toning.

with color as you make it (click the Foreground color square in the toolbox and choose a color or sample from the Color palette, opened by choosing Window, Show Color; then press Alt/Option-Delete to fill). Don't worry about shading at this point — just flat color fills.

5 Shading and toning the color. To make a layer for adding shades and tones, duplicate the flat color layer by dragging its name to the New Layer icon at the bottom of the Layers palette. Select regions of color with the magic wand tool, with Tolerance set to 0, and Anti-aliased and Use All Layers turned off in the Magic Wand Options palette. Shift-click with the wand to add noncontiguous areas to the selection, or in version 5.5 you can uncheck the Contiguous box in the Magic Wand Options palette). Now use the airbrush tool to add shades and tones of color; the active selection boundaries will keep this additional color "inside the lines."

After you've toned a region, the expanded color range will make it hard to select the whole region with the magic wand tool again if you want to add more airbrushing. But you can make the selection by clicking the name of the "flats" layer to activate it and then with the magic wand tool (make sure Use All Layers is *unchecked*) click to select a color area in this layer. Now activate the modulated color layer again and airbrush. To fine-tune the shading and toning, Yune used the dodge and burn tools.

6 Completing the coloring.
Once the primary tonality of the artwork has been established, you can change the color by selecting color regions, again using the magic wand on the flat-color layer, and using the airbrush tool in Color mode (from the list of blending modes in the Airbrush Options palette) to paint over the tonal work. Yune used bright, bold colors, fine-tuning the color with Image, Adjust, Color Balance and with the sponge (saturation) tool.

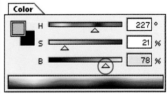

7

After the file was converted to CMYK Color mode, highlights were added in a top layer in Screen mode.

8

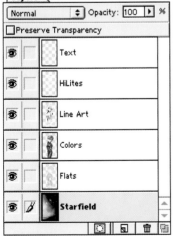

The finished illustration included a starfield background and a top layer with signature and copyright notice.

7 Adding highlights. If your artwork is destined for print, now is the time to convert to CMYK (Image, Mode, CMYK Color), so that what you see on-screen as your highlights develop will be a good predictor of what they'll look like in print (see "Blending and Color Modes" below). Make a new layer at the top of your stack of layers and put it in Screen mode. Use any soft-edged painting tool to add highlights to reflective surfaces such as eyes and metal. If you're working in RGB mode, the color you use on this layer will lighten and tint the artwork beneath. In CMYK mode, the artwork will be lightened, but the tint will be less apparent.

BLENDING AND COLOR MODES

Photoshop's blending modes work differently in RGB Color mode than in CMYK Color mode. That's why you're warned when you choose from the Image, Mode menu.

You can preserve the existing color interactions in a layered RGB file when you convert it to CMYK — by choosing to Merge (or flatten) it before converting. Or you can preserve the layers (Don't Merge) and allow the color blending to change. You can't preserve both the layers and the RGB-specific color interactions.

Choose Merge (or Flatten in version 5.0) to maintain the blending interactions from RGB mode as you convert to CMYK.

Painting with yellow in Screen mode produces a different result in an RGB file (left) than in a CMYK document (right).

8 Adding the background. Yune activated the *Background* layer and dragged-and-dropped a starfield developed for one of the interactive *Journeyman Project* games. He deleted the *Background* and added a layer at the top with his signature and copyright information. 🌊

"TRAPPING" WITH 100K BLACK

If your colored line art is destined for separation and printing, you can ensure that the black linework in your CMYK file doesn't knock out of the other color plates as follows: Make a pure black by clicking the Foreground color square and composing a color with C=0, M=0, Y=0, and K=100. With your linework layer active, press Alt/Option-Shift-Delete to fill the lines with this new black (adding the Shift key to the Alt/Option-Delete shortcut is like temporarily turning on Preserve Transparency for the layer before you fill). Put the layer in Multiply mode. When you flatten the file and then separate it on output, the result will look the same as you would get in a PostScript drawing program or page layout application if you set the black linework to overprint. This makes registration of the color plates more flexible and forgiving.

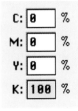

"Hand-Painting" from History

Overview *Define or choose brushes; simplify the color and enhance color contours in the photo that will serve as a resource for painting; make at least one Snapshot to use as a color source for the History brush; establish a semi-transparent contrasting "ground" and a separate painting layer; paint with the History brush; "emboss" the brush strokes; add canvas texture.*

IMAGE "Impressionist History" image

1

Defining brushes made by clicking with the airbrush in Dissolve mode

2a

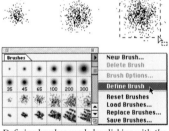

Original photo

NO FILTER OR AUTOMATED PROCESS can provide all the control you might want to include in a painting: the gestural brush strokes, the built-up texture of thickly applied paints, and the texture of the canvas, showing through in areas where paint is thin or absent. MetaCreations' Painter is renowned for its built-in functions that do this kind of imitation of natural media. And Photoshop's Artistic, Brush Strokes, and other filters can automatically generate some pretty amazing painterly effects. Also, the Art History brush, new in Photoshop 5.5, helps to automate the process of converting an image to a painting, by laying down brush strokes that flow and curve to follow the color in the image (see "Art History Lessons" on page 245). But one of the best ways to approximate natural media with Photoshop 5/5.5 is to use the History palette and the History brush in Impressionist mode to lay down paint with "hand-crafted" brush tips. Then use the Emboss and Texturizer filters to add brush stroke and canvas textures.

1 Choosing or making brushes. The natural brushes that come with Photoshop 5.5 are a great starting point for natural media explorations. But if you want to invent brushes of your own, you can use the airbrush in Dissolve mode with black or gray paint to make "footprints" that you can then select with the rectangular marquee and capture as brushes by choosing Define Brush from the Brush palette's pop-out menu. (If you need step-by-step instructions, see "Brush-Making Tips" on page 223.)

2 Preparing the reference image. Open a photo in RGB mode and duplicate it to a second layer (in the Layers palette drag its thumbnail to the New Layer icon in the middle at the bottom of the palette). That way you'll have the original for safekeeping.

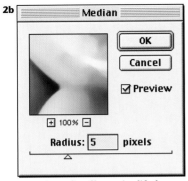

2b

Median

OK
Cancel
☑ Preview

⊞ 100% ⊟

Radius: 5 pixels

Using the Median filter to simplify the coloring of the photo

2c

Using the Posterize filter to define color contours

3a

New Snapshot

Name: Med Version   OK
From: Merged Layers ⧨   Cancel

Making one of the three Snapshots that will be used as sources for painting with the History brush

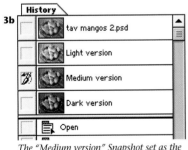

3b

History

tav mangos 2.psd
Light version
Medium version
Dark version
Open

The "Medium version" Snapshot set as the source for the History brush

4a

History Brush Options

Normal ⧨   Opacity: 85 ▶ %

☑ Impressionist

Stylus: ☑ Size ☐ Opacity

Setting up the History brush in Impressionist mode, with Stylus pressure controlling the size of the brush tip

The History brush in Impressionist mode samples color continuously as you paint, from whatever source you choose in the History palette. Because of this continuous sampling, the color variation that occurs in photos of natural subjects, like our basket of fruit, can make an Impressionist stroke look more like a rainbow smear than a stroke of a single color of paint. To retain the edge distinctions of the objects in the photo but reduce the internal color detail so the photo will work better as a source for the Impressionist brush, apply the Median filter to your photo (Filter, Other, Median).

Make any other color adjustments you want. In our image we selected the background and used Image, Adjust, Hue/Saturation to cool its colors so that the contrast made the subject "pop" by contrast.

To further simplify the color and define contours that will be useful in our paint-by-numbers-style painting, choose Image, Adjust, Posterize. We used a setting of 5 Levels in the Posterize dialog box.

3 Setting up the History. Since the History brush relies on the History palette as its source of color, the next step is to make one or more History Snapshots to paint from. We wanted three Snapshots — light, medium, and dark versions.

After we had finished the image preparation in step 2 above, we used Image, Adjust, Levels and moved the gamma (gray) Input Levels slider to the left to lighten the image. Then we Alt/Option-clicked the New Snapshot icon next to the trash icon at the bottom of the History palette to open the New Snapshot dialog box, where we could name the Snapshot "Light version" and choose Merged Layers from the list of sources. Using the Merged Layers option helps to avoid the problems that can arise if you change the layering of your image and then try to use an earlier Snapshot as a source for painting (for a more detailed explanation, see "History Trouble" on page 21).

Pressing Ctrl/⌘-Z undid the lightening of our colored and posterized main image. Then we took another Merged Snapshot of it, naming it "Medium version." Then we adjusted Levels again, this time moving the gamma Input Levels slider to the right, then making a merged Snapshot called "Dark version." Finally we pressed Ctrl/⌘-Z one more time to undo the darkening in the main image.

THE LOWER, THE SMOOTHER

When you define or customize a brush in Photoshop, the lower you make the Spacing setting in the Brush Options dialog box, the smoother the stroke it will produce. That's because the setting is the percentage of the brush's footprint that the brush must move before a new footprint is made. With very low settings, footprints are deposited almost continuously, which results in a very smooth-looking stroke. Unfortunately, this also slows the operation of the brush, so with low settings, painting may feel less fluid as you wait for the on-screen display to catch up with the motion of your brush.

Brush Options

☑ Spacing: 5 %   OK
☐ Anti-aliased   Cancel

Painting on a layer above a black-filled "Ground" layer whose Opacity is reduced to let the "Posterized" layer show through

The "Painting" layer in progress, viewed with the "Ground" and "Posterized" layers (top) and viewed alone

The painting in progress, before applying textures

(At this point we saved the full file under a different name [File, Save As] and deleted the "Original Photo" layer to reduce the size of the working file.)

4 Painting. To give yourself the greatest flexibility for editing the paint strokes you'll apply and for changing the background color later, create a separate "Ground" layer for the painting: Add a layer by clicking the New Layer icon, and fill it with the color you want for your canvas (click the Foreground square in the toolbox and choose a color, then press Alt/Option-Delete to fill the layer with this color). We chose to use black, which would heighten the intensity of our colors. In the Layers palette reduce the "Ground" layer's Opacity to allow for "onion skin" tracing of the posterized image, seen through the background color.

Add another layer to hold the paint, this one completely transparent, by clicking the New Layer icon. With this layer active, you're ready to paint.

To choose the Impressionist setting for painting, double-click the History brush in the toolbox and check the Impressionist box in the History Brush Options palette. Set the Opacity somewhere between 100% (for thick, fully opaque paint) and 75% (for thinner paint that will interact with the colors underneath); 85% is a good starting point. Click next to the "Medium version" Snapshot in the History palette to make it the source of color for the brush.

Looking through the background layer, outline the major features of the painting by tracing the photo with the History brush. Then fill in the shapes, using the color contours of the posterized image to help determine the direction of your strokes.

If you made "Light version" and "Dark version" Snapshots at step 3, you can fine-tune the color of your painting by changing the source for the History brush. You can also add details by switching to a regular paintbrush with a similar or different brush tip (press the "B" key to choose the paintbrush), sampling color from your image by holding down the Alt/Option key to turn the paintbrush into the eyedropper. When you've finished painting, restore the Opacity of the "Ground" layer to 100%.

(At this point we could delete the "Posterized" layer by dragging its thumbnail to the trash icon at the bottom of the Layers palette.)

5 Adding an Impasto texture. To make the paint look more realistic and as if it has been applied thickly, you can "emboss" the brush strokes. The process starts with some fancy footwork back and forth between the Layers palette and Channels palette.

Start by adding a new layer in Overlay mode (Alt/Option-click the New Layer icon so you can choose the mode as you make the layer). With the new layer established, fill it with white (press the "D" key for the default Foreground and Background colors and then Ctrl/⌘-Delete to fill with the white Background color). Turn

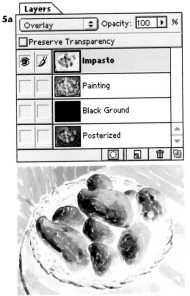

5a

The "Impasto" layer (When the layer is viewed alone, the Overlay mode isn't apparent.)

5b

Applying the Emboss filter to add dimension to the brush strokes

6a

Generating canvas texture with the Texturizer filter

6b

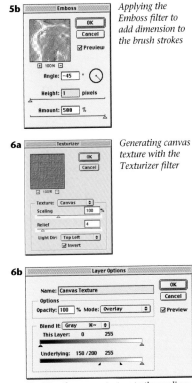

Limiting the canvas texture to the medium-light colors

off the eye icon for this new layer so that only the "Painting" and "Ground" layers contribute to the image.

In the Channels palette Ctrl/⌘-click on the thumbnail for the RGB composite at the top of the palette. This will load the luminance of the image as a selection.

Back in the Layers palette, click in the new white-filled layer's eye column to make it visible again. Then fill the selection with black (with black as the Foreground color in the toolbox, press Alt/Option-Delete) and deselect (Ctrl/⌘-D).

The layer's thumbnail will now look like a "black-and-white negative" of the painting-and-background, but because the layer is in Overlay mode you won't see this. Instead, the layer's effect at this stage will be to exaggerate the color of the image.

Now run the Emboss filter (Filter, Stylize, Emboss), setting the Angle to light the picture from the upper left. We used a Height setting of 1 pixel and an Amount of 500%, to maintain detail in the embossing and at the same time provide strong contrast.

6 Creating canvas texture. To add a canvas texture in areas where the paint is thin, first add another new layer by Alt/Option-clicking the New Layer icon so that you can put the layer in Overlay mode and check the box for Fill With Overlay-Neutral Color (50% Gray). Then run the Texturizer filter (Filter, Texture, Texturizer), choosing Canvas from the Texture list and a matching top left light direction. (Try clicking the Invert box to see if you like this setting better.) When you click OK to close the Texturizer dialog box, you'll see canvas texture over the entire image.

6c

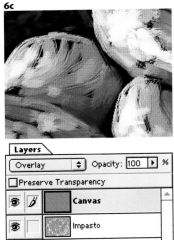

The final Layers palette for the finished painting, shown at the top of page 238

To reinforce the effect of the Impasto, which makes the black and white paint look thickest, you can limit the canvas texture to the light mid-tones, as follows: Double-click the *name* — not the thumbnail — to open the Layer Options dialog box. Move the black slider for Underlying to the right. To split the slider so you can make a gradual rather than abrupt transition between areas that show canvas and those that don't, hold down the Alt/Option key and drag the right half of the slider farther to the right. Adjust the two parts of the slider until you have a canvas effect that you like.

Painting with Light

Overview *Start with a sketch; rough in the color; build volume; add highlights and detail.*

FRANCOIS GUÉRIN

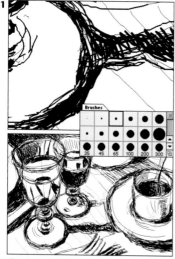

Sketching with the pencil

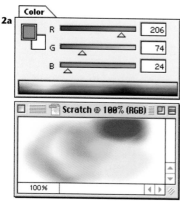

Mixing colors

ACHIEVING ANY PAINTERLY EFFECT with the computer involves some mental translation from traditional tools to electronic ones. Artist/illustrator Francois Guérin, who also works with oils, pastels, gouache, and MetaCreations' Painter, has found several ways to work effectively with Photoshop as a painting program. For *The Meal*, painted from memory, he used primarily the painting tools, the lasso, the Gaussian Blur, and functions from the Image, Adjust submenu. Guérin worked with a Wacom digitizing tablet. He likes the brushlike feel of the stylus but doesn't vary the pressure much.

1 Making a sketch. To start out, click the pencil and begin drawing. Choose pencil tips of different sizes from the Brushes palette. Guérin used a larger tip to darken the shadow areas.

2 Laying down color. You can use the Color palette (Window, Show Color) to mix colors by component percentages. Or make a new small Scratch document (File, New) to mix colors "by hand" that you can then sample with the eyedropper tool. And use the Swatches palette (Window, Show Swatches) to store and recall colors you want to use again. Apply the first strokes of paint with the paintbrush, using brush tips from the top row of the Brushes palette, which provide smooth but hard-edged strokes. Paint in Normal mode so the strokes hide the black-and-white sketch.

3 Building volume. Use your Scratch file to mix the color variations you need to begin painting shapes. At this point, use the paintbrush and airbrush tools, which can have softer edges, to achieve color blending in the painting.

2b

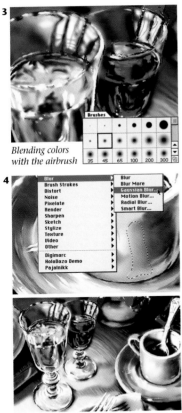

Laying down color with the paintbrush

3

*Blending colors
with the airbrush*

4

4 Indicating textures. Guérin used the smallest pencil point to add "grain" to the wood of the table, which he later smoothed with the smudge (finger) tool. He also used the Blur filters to add a smooth sheen to some of the surfaces in the image. For instance, he used a feathered lasso to select some areas of the cup and saucer, and applied a Gaussian Blur. (With the lasso chosen in the toolbox, press Enter/ Return to open the Lasso Options palette to set the Feather amount.)

5 Putting the colors in context. To modify the colors to be consistent with the light in the scene, you can use a feathered lasso and commands from the Image Adjust submenu as Guérin did, or use Adjustment layers (choose Window, Show Layers and Ctrl/⌘- click the New Layer icon in the middle at the bottom of the palette) for Hue/Saturation, Levels, and Color Balance. You can fine-tune the overall intensity of the adjustment by changing the Opacity of the Adjustment layer. Or, with black and white as the Foreground and Background colors, you can paint the Adjustment layer's built- in mask: Use a feathered lasso and Alt/Option-Delete (to fill with black) or Ctrl/⌘-Delete (to fill with white) or paint with a soft airbrush. Guérin used a highly feathered lasso.

6 Adding modeling and highlights. To mold elements in the painting, you can use traditional painting techniques, such as

applying strokes to follow the form of an object. Guérin shaped the napkin beneath the fork in this way, for example. The blur tool (water drop) can be used to smooth areas such as the reflec- tions on the glass. (If the water drop isn't showing in the tool pal- ette, press Shift-R; you may have to press this key combination more than once to toggle through the tools that share the blur tool's palette position.) The smudge tool (toggle to it by pressing Shift-R) does a good job of adding texture and making color transitions in

*Smoothing color with the Gaussian Blur
filter*

USING A "REPAIRS" LAYER

To smooth the strokes or mix the colors of a painting, try using the blur tool or smudge tool on a new transparent layer above the paint- ing. Add the new, empty layer, choose the blur or smudge tool, and turn on Use All Layers in the tool's Options palette (you can open the palette by pressing the Enter/Return key when the tool is selected). Then apply your smooth- ing or mixing strokes. If you make a mistake, you can erase the offend- ing smudge or blur without damag- ing the painting underneath.

5

Modifying colors

6

Adding texture and highlights

Sketching with the pencil and filling sketched areas with paint

Smoothing color with Gaussian Blur

Differential blurring to create depth

areas where light and shadows meet — in the wood of the table, for instance. It can also be used to pull specular highlights out of white paint, as on the tine of the fork.

Developing electronic painting technique. For a painting of his cactus collection, Guérin again started with an electronic pencil sketch. He poured color into the pencil-drawn shapes with the paint bucket tool and added some detail with the paintbrush. Then he used a feathered lasso and the Gaussian Blur filter to blend the colors. He used the smudge tool to blend the edges where colors met, and added more color with paintbrushes. With the paintbrush and airbrush he built volume in the rounded plants, and he added spines with the paintbrush and pencil. To capture the lighting of the scene, he played with the color balance, brightness, contrast, hue, and saturation of parts of the image, as he had for *The Meal* (see step 5). To create the illusion of depth, he used the Blur filter, applying it three times for the round cactus on the right side of the painting, which was farthest in the background, twice for the closer, spiky one in the upper left corner, and once for a still closer one in the center. *Wow!*

SELECTING BRUSH TIPS

Press the opening or closing bracket key ([or], next to the "P" on the keyboard) to move from tip to tip up or down in the Brushes palette. Using the Shift key along with the bracket selects either the first ([) or the last (]) brush in the palette.

EXTRACTING A PALETTE

To pull a color palette from a painted RGB or CMYK image so you can use it as a resource for a related painting, follow this procedure (don't miss the Revert or History palette step!):

1. First save the painting (File, Save) so you have something to Revert to if you choose that method in step 3 below.

2. Convert the painting to Indexed Color mode (temporarily — you'll be changing it back to full color) by choosing Image, Mode, Indexed Color. In the Indexed Color dialog box, choose Adaptive and 256 or fewer Colors. Click OK.

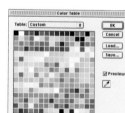

3. Now choose Image, Mode, Color Table. In the Color Table dialog box, click the Save button, give the table a name, and click OK.

4. Convert the painting back to its original color mode: You can choose File, Revert to make this change so you won't lose any of the original color. Or use the History palette to undo the color mode change by dragging the "Indexed Color" step to the trash icon at the bottom of the palette.

5. Now start your new painting (File, New) and choose Window, Show Swatches. Choose Replace Swatches from the Swatches palette's pop-out menu and select the named color table. The Swatches palette will fill with the colors you saved from the first painting.

Art History Lessons

Overview *Prepare the image you want to turn into a painting and take a Snapshot; add a canvas or "Ground" layer and a transparent layer to hold the paint; use Natural Media brush tips with the Art History brush to paint from the Snapshot, adjusting the settings to control stroke size and shape; add details with the paintbrush; add an impasto effect.*

 **IMAGE** "Art History" image

 PHOTO: © JHDDESIGN

1a | **1b**

Original photo, 1000 pixels high | *Saturation boosted overall and in the Red channel*

2

New Snapshot
Name: Color Tweaked   OK
From: Merged Layers ⬥   Cancel

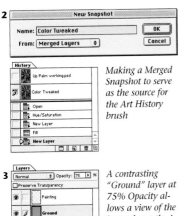

Making a Merged Snapshot to serve as the source for the Art History brush

3

A contrasting "Ground" layer at 75% Opacity allows a view of the image beneath. A separate transparent layer is added for painting.

PHOTOSHOP 5.5'S ART HISTORY BRUSH GENERATES BRUSH STROKES, several with each click of the mouse, that automatically follow the color contours in an image. Although at some settings the result can look like an automated filter application, if you choose your settings carefully and add detailing with other painting tools, you can turn a photo into a very convincing "hand-crafted" painting.

1 Preparing the photo. Choose a photo and adjust its color and tonality to the colors you want to see in the final image. We made overall adjustments to hue and saturation and then made an additional increase in saturation of reds (choose Image, Adjust, Hue/Saturation and work in the default Master image; then change the Edit setting to Reds and make further adjustments).

2 Setting up the History source. Once you have the colors the way you want them, take a Merged Snapshot of the photo by Alt/Option-clicking the New Snapshot icon in the middle at the bottom of the History palette and choosing Merged Layers.

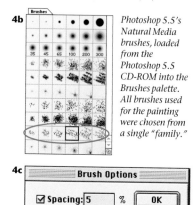

4a

Setting the options for the Art History brush. A large Area and Tight Long strokes are good for "roughing in" the major features.

4b

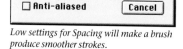

Photoshop 5.5's Natural Media brushes, loaded from the Photoshop 5.5 CD-ROM into the Brushes palette. All brushes used for the painting were chosen from a single "family."

4c

Low settings for Spacing will make a brush produce smoother strokes.

5a

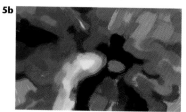

To begin the painting the Area was set to 200, the paint style was set to Tight Long, and a large brush tip was chosen. The first click on the transparent painting layer laid down many "roughing in" strokes. The semitransparent orange "Ground" allowed the image to show through for comparison with the developing painting.

5b

After other large strokes had been laid down, more were added with the same paint style and Area settings but with a medium-size brush tip.

3 Setting up the "canvas." The plan for this painting is to cover the entire "canvas" with color. For maximum control and flexibility, set up a "Ground" layer filled with the color you want for your canvas: Click the New Layer icon in the middle at the bottom of the Layers palette; then click the Foreground color square in the toolbox and choose a color; finally, Alt/Option-Delete to fill the new layer with this color. We chose a contrasting color that would show through gaps in the painting to make the blues and greens of our image jump. Reduce the Opacity of the "Ground" layer somewhat so you can see through to the image below and place your strokes intelligently. Finally, add another new layer above the "Ground" for painting.

4 Choosing brushes. Next set up the Art History brush by choosing it from the toolbox (Shift-Y toggles between the History brush and the Art History brush) and pressing Enter to open its Options palette. We set the options as follows to start the painting:

- The **blending mode** was set to Normal. Later, for detail strokes, it could be changed to Lighten or Darken to add contrast in the highlight and shadow areas.

- The **paint style** (below the mode setting) was set to Tight Long. The paint style controls the length and shape of the strokes (Long, Short, Medium, Curl, or Dab) and how well they follow the color contours in the source image (Tight or Loose). Applied overall, styles other than Tight Long, Tight Medium, and Tight Short produce an effect that looks more like a filter than like hand-painting. We would use Tight Long strokes for roughing in color and switch to Tight Short later to paint details.

- **Opacity** was set to 85%. As brush strokes were layered on, some color would show through from previous strokes.

- **Fidelity** was set quite high — at 85% — so that the color of the strokes laid down with each click of the Art History brush wouldn't vary much from the original colors sampled from the source. Lower this number for more color variation.

- The **Area** was set at 200 pixels for this 1000-pixel-high image. This meant that with each click of the Art History brush, many strokes would be generated, to cover an area approximately equivalent to a circle with a diameter of 200 pixels, though the painted area is not circular. We would use this high Area setting for our "roughing in" strokes and then reduce the setting for finer work later.

- **Tolerance** was left at the default 0 so we could paint anywhere on the current image. Any setting above 0 limits the tool to painting only in areas whose color differs from the source image.

- If you use a digital tablet for painting, you can set the **Stylus** controls so that Size or Opacity will vary with pressure. (Here

5c

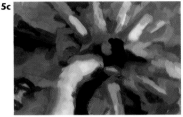

The area was reduced to 100 pixels and a smaller brush tip was chosen.

5d

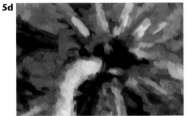

For the finest strokes applied with the Art History brush, the smallest brush tip was used with the Tight Short paint style and Area set to 50.

5e

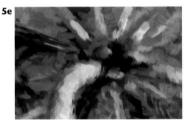

The paintbrush tool was used to add complementary colors and highlights and to put in detail that wasn't possible to add with the automated Art History strokes.

6a

The finished painting layer was duplicated, and the copy was put in Overlay mode and desaturated.

6b

Embossing the desaturated Overlay layer created an impasto effect.

"Size" does not mean the size of the brush tip, but rather the size of the Area, as defined above.)

Next choose a brush tip. We chose from the Natural Media brushes provided on the Photoshop 5.5 CD-ROM. You can load this set of brushes by choosing Load Brushes from the Brushes palette's pop-out menu. (Be sure to use "Load Brushes" rather than "Replace Brushes" so the Brushes palette will also keep the other natural media brushes that are part of the default set.) You can customize a brush by double-clicking its footprint in the Brushes palette and changing its Spacing setting. Lower settings produce bristle-like streaks, while higher settings produce sponge-like dabs.

All the brushes used in this painting were chosen from a single row, so that the painting would appear to have been stroked with a single type of brush, applied with different amounts of paint and pressure.

5 Painting. As you work with the Art History brush, try a quick experiment each time you change the settings: Click once with the brush to see if you like the results. If not, undo (Ctrl/⌘-Z), change the settings, and try again. Once you have settings you like, you can click each time you want to generate strokes. Or hold down the mouse (or stylus) button and watch the strokes pile up until you have the result you want. Or drag the brush to set down several sets of strokes.

In general, paint with Tight strokes to follow the contours of your image. Keep the strokes Long until you need shorter ones for painting detail.

Don't forget to do some hand-detailing with the regular paintbrush, for fine-tuning that can't be effectively generated automatically with the Art History brush. To unify the artwork, use the same kind of natural brushes and Opacity settings as you used for the Art History brush.

6 Adding thickness to the paint. To build up the brush strokes, make a duplicate of your painted layer by dragging its thumbnail in the Layers palette to the New Layer icon. Choose Overlay for the blending mode. Then remove the color from this layer (Image, Adjust, Desaturate). Run the Emboss filter (Filter, Stylize, Emboss) with an Angle setting that lights the image from the top left, varying the Height and Amount settings to get the detail and depth you want. 🎨

ADDING A SIGNATURE

If you have a standard signature that you like to use on your digital paintings, you can keep it on a transparent layer in a Photoshop file of its own. Or keep an object-oriented version in an Adobe Illustrator file. When you finish a painting, just open the signature file and drag-and-drop it into the image.

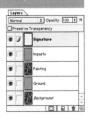

Victor Navone composed *Faerie* in many layers so that he could work on the parts separately and experiment with blending modes. Using a Wacom tablet, Navone chose the paintbrush tool with hard-edged brush tips most of the time. He turned on Stylus Pressure and set the Opacity between 50 and 100 percent. For color blending, he sampled one of the two colors to be

blended, painted lightly over the other, sampled the new hybrid color, painted again, and so on. Keeping a finger on the Alt/Option key made it easy to switch between sampling and painting, which provided the look and feel of brushed color.

Navone used a scanned photo of the legs of an underwater ballerina as a reference, and sketched the rest of the figure. Painting the left arm in sections on two separate layers allowed him to scale and rotate the parts of the limb until he had the position he wanted. He also painted the hair on a separate layer, knowing that it would take several tries to get exactly what he wanted.

The wings were painted in shades of gray, with the veins in a light color. A copy of the wings layer was pasted into an alpha channel, which was chosen as the Texture when the Lighting Effects filter was run on the original wings layer. The wings layer was colored by wildly altering the curves for the individual color channels to produce iridescent colors (Image, Adjust, Curves, as described in "Solarizing" on page 137 in Chapter 3). More color was added by painting on separate layers in Color and Overlay modes. After a test print, the color of the image was lightened overall with a Levels Adjustment layer.

alad and *Entree* are two in a series of images painted by **Kaoru Hollin** to explore the possibility of creating the look of traditional media in Photoshop. Hollin created her palette by selecting colors from the Swatches palette and then adjusting them in the Color Picker. She used black lines in the foreground to provide maximum contrast to intensify the jewel-like quality of the RGB color hues.

To start the background (shown at the right), Hollin used two brush-stroke paintings, one in green tones and the other in blue, originally created in Painter with a Wacom tablet. She combined the two paintings by using a layer mask. Specifically, she opened the blue background, created a new layer in the file, and copied and pasted the green background into it. She then selected a middle portion of the green background layer with the elliptical marquee tool and applied a feather to the selection. She chose Layer, Add Layer Mask, Hide Selection so that part of the green layer was hidden. She used this composite as the background for Salad, then used the Hue/Saturation palette to vary the hue and saturation of the background for each of the other three images.

To create the black line work Hollin used a Wacom graphic pen and tablet to create a hand-drawn effect, using the paintbrush tool and a hard-edged brush tip. Hollin used the graphic tablet for the color work as well, using hard and soft-edged brushes in various sizes.

Layers were essential in the management of the colored areas of the images. Hollin created a new layer for each object in the foreground, and sometimes for each color, so that the final images had as many as 25 layers. She used filters on some of the color layers, including Dry Brush and Blur, to create rougher or smoother textures. For example, to add subtle depth to the background with a dark green color she created a few brush strokes in a new layer, using a soft brush tip with the airbrush in Dissolve mode with a 20-step Fade to Transparent, and then applied the Blur filter. She used the same technique in several other places, including the plate under the salad bowl and the shadow area of the yellow napkin.

Hollin also used the smudge tool to blend colors in some areas. While working, she kept different color areas in separate layers so that she could adjust opacity to get the watercolor look she wanted.

When she was satisfied with the texture and color balance she merged groups of layers to organize the files. Each of the final Photoshop files contains one background layer, one color paint layer, one black brush stroke layer, and one layer with her signature.

These three paintings by **William Low** were created by working back and forth between Photoshop and MetaCreations Painter. He began his *Charles and Ben* painting (shown at the right) with a scanned sketch whose tonality he inverted in Photoshop (Ctrl/⌘-I) to produce white lines on a black ground. This imitated the black gesso ground that Low has used in traditional painting to get the feeling of painting with light as he adds color over the dark background. Each element of the painting—the boy, the bed, the table, and so on— was painted in a separate layer so that Low could more easily edit the composition as it evolved. A layer called "light and shadow," containing only light and dark areas, was used in Overlay mode to exaggerate the effect of the light coming from the window.

For *The Swimmer*, based on a Michaelangelo sculpture, most of the painting was done with round, hard-edged brushes in large sizes, although the water highlights were created by starting with a very soft brush with white at 100 percent Opacity. Low then varied the Opacity setting for the paintbrush by clicking in the Opacity box and then using the arrow keys as he painted. He mixed colors by painting over one color with another color at low opacity, the way a traditional painter builds up a glaze. To use this new color in other areas, he would sample it with the eyedropper and paint at full opacity. For example, to add a blush to the swimmer's cheek, Low applied a red with a brush in Multiply mode at 5 percent Opacity, going over the area until he liked the result. Then he sampled the new cheek color, switched the paintbrush to Normal mode at 100 percent Opacity, and painted the nose.

Wedding was based on a scanned photo. Each element of the image was painted on a separate layer, again using round, hard-edged brushes, and the move tool was used to arrange the composition of the many figures. The texture on the car and on the upper right corner of the background was created by applying a paper texture in Painter, then returning to Photoshop to run the Paint Daubs filter. The rice effect was also created on a layer in Painter.

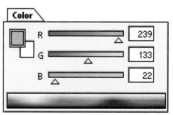

In painting her digital *Self-Portrait*, **Kay Wilson** started with a scan of a loosely rendered self-portrait she had painted in oils. Then, picking various brush tip sizes from the Brushes palette, she began by using a small paintbrush to paint the main lines, and a large paintbrush for the light, medium, and dark areas of color used for modeling the shapes of the face. Medium-sized brush tips added smaller color areas inside the large shapes, building up color on top of the scanned image. All of the painting was done in one layer, with a mouse, and Wilson found the zoom tool helpful for detail work.

Wilson relied on her traditional painting experience to help manage the complex color palette in her self-portrait, exaggerating the colors for the digital version. She modeled the form by using light, medium, and dark values of the same hues, contrasted warm and cool colors, and set off intense colors by surrounding them with grayed ones.

To create the colors she needed, Wilson would often sample from the image with the eyedropper tool, then go to the Color palette (Window, Show Color) and move all three of the RGB sliders a short distance left to darken the color, or right to lighten it. Grayed versions were also created quickly by moving each slider toward the end that's farther away from its current position.

Wilson used the eraser tool (in Paintbrush mode) to modify the edges of color shapes and to develop the background. She had started the background by painting with a neutral color, had covered it with brighter colors, and then erased large areas of the top colors to allow the original color to show through.

▶ *Photoshop 5's Erase To History function, set in the Eraser Options palette, lets you restore the image based on any state in the History palette — either the original or a Snapshot (taken at any time in the development of the painting by choosing New Snapshot from the History palette's pop-out menu). To designate a state as a source for the Erase To History function, click in the column to the left of that state's thumbnail; a History brush icon will appear to show that the state is chosen. Although you can accomplish the same thing by using the History brush tool, using the eraser makes it possible to have two different brush tips at the ready, one chosen for the History brush and the other chosen for the eraser, without having to reset the tip in the Brushes palette. You can move between the two tools quickly by pressing the "E" and "Y" keys.*

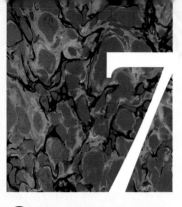

COMBINING
PHOTOSHOP
& POSTSCRIPT

YOU CAN MOVE ARTWORK between Adobe Illustrator 8 and Photoshop 5/5.5 almost seamlessly, and you can import both kinds of files into page layout programs such as Adobe PageMaker, Adobe InDesign, or QuarkXPress. How do you decide when it makes sense to combine Illustrator (or other PostScript object-oriented) artwork with an image created in Photoshop? And when it does, how do you decide whether to import a Photoshop illustration into Illustrator, or an Illustrator drawing into Photoshop, or when to assemble the two in a third program? These pointers can help you make the decision:

- The pen tool in Photoshop can draw smooth Bezier curves, and the other path tools make it easy to modify the curves it draws. The Grid and Guides and the Edit, Transform Path command now allow exact placement, snap-to precision, and easy scaling, skewing, and rotating. But object-oriented drawing programs such as Illustrator, FreeHand, and CorelDraw still excel at all drawing tasks that require layered constructions, automated spacing or copying, transformation from one shape to another through several intermediate steps, or other jobs that are more complicated than *clipping*, or constructing a path for silhouetting part of an image.

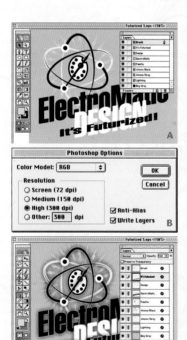

A layered file in Adobe Illustrator 8 (A) can be exported in Photoshop 5 format, with layers preserved, by choosing File, Export, Format, Photoshop 5, and then choosing the desired color model and resolution and enabling the Write Layers option (B). When the file is opened in Photoshop 5 or 5.5, special effects and other treatments can be applied to the individual layers (C). (For more about this process, see "Coloring Clip Art" on page 261.)

- Photoshop's text tool, working with Adobe Type Manager (ATM), can set smooth-looking antialiased type, and the program can add some amazing special effects (see Chapter 2 for more about using type in Photoshop). In versions 5 and 5.5 you can keep type live and editable between working sessions, and the type can be scaled, skewed, rotated, and otherwise distorted without degrading the quality of its edges. Still, for really designing with type or fitting type into a particular shape or along a path, PostScript drawing and page layout programs have much greater capabilities.

- When you want to maintain the PostScript nature of certain elements — for instance, for a brochure cover in which the Photoshop artwork is just one element of an illustration that includes logos, graphics, and typography — incorporate the Photoshop artwork into the PostScript file. That way, you can include the painted or photorealistic Photoshop art and still take advantage of the highest resolution of the output device to produce crisp type and the clean edges of the PostScript elements.

continued on page 254

The Photoshop file was dragged and dropped into Illustrator, where type was set on a path and converted to outlines. Then the sentence was Ctrl/⌘-dragged back into the Photoshop file as a layer of its own so Layer Effects could be added later.

- For a multipage document, or to assemble a number of items with precise alignment, and especially if large amounts of text will be typeset, bring both the Photoshop files and the PostScript artwork into a page layout program. A page layout program also provides a way to assemble Photoshop files of different resolutions.

Although PostScript elements play a role in techniques described elsewhere in the book, this chapter presents some how-to examples of using EPS's produced by PostScript programs to create Photoshop imagery. First, though, here are some tips to help you move artwork from PostScript drawing programs to Photoshop and vice versa.

ILLUSTRATOR TO PHOTOSHOP

Although it's possible to import encapsulated PostScript (EPS) files from other PostScript illustration programs, it's only natural that Adobe Illustrator shows the greatest compatibility with Adobe Photoshop. So the best way to make illustrations available for use in Photoshop may be to save them in (or convert them to) Illustrator EPS format.

- Files from **FreeHand 8** and later versions can be dragged and dropped or copied and pasted directly into Photoshop as pixels or paths. Or they can be exported as Illustrator files or rasterized — converted into pixel-based images — in Photoshop format.

- **CorelDraw** files can be saved in Adobe Illustrator format by using the program's File, Save As, Adobe Illustrator command, or they can be rasterized at the resolution you specify by choosing File, Export, Adobe Photoshop.

  (Translation of a complex file from one PostScript drawing program to another may not be completely accurate. If possible, files translated into Illustrator format should be checked in Illustrator before they are imported into Photoshop. Also, layering will not be retained in an Illustrator EPS file opened or placed in Photoshop.)

Rasterizing Illustrator Artwork into Photoshop

Illustrator 8 files, or selected elements, can be rasterized in any of the following ways:

- **Open** an Illustrator file to rasterize the entire file into Photoshop as a single-layer file at the resolution you choose (File, Open).

- **Place** the file to rasterize all its objects on a single layer of an existing file with the option to align and scale while placing (File, Place).

- **Drag-and-drop** artwork from an open Illustrator file to an open Photoshop file by selecting the Illustrator objects you want to import and dragging from the Illustrator file to the Photoshop file, where they will be rasterized as a new layer. To **center** the

When you paste an Illustrator object from the clipboard into Photoshop, the Paste dialog box lets you choose to rasterize it as pixels or paste it as Bezier paths.

RESOLUTION-INDEPENDENCE

In Photoshop 5 and 5.5, type remains resolution-independent until you render the Type layer or save the file in a format other than Photoshop 5. This means that you can repeatedly edit the type, color it, reshape it (Edit, Transform), and treat it with Layer Effects without deteriorating its edges. To get the same flexibility and control for graphics — such as symbols or logos, you can turn them into a font and then "set" them in Photoshop with one of the type tools.

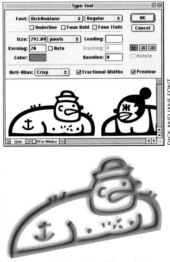

You can get the benefits of Photoshop's type treatment by saving graphics as a font. Programs that can save files as members of a font include CorelDraw (all versions from 3 on); Macromedia Fontographer or FontLab 3.0 for both Mac and Windows; and Softly (shareware) or TypeDesigner for Windows only.

imported art in the Photoshop image, hold down the Shift key while dragging.

- **Export** the file in Photoshop 5 format (in Illustrator: File, Export, Photoshop 5, Write Layers). This will produce a Photoshop file with the objects rasterized on layers, according to the original Illustrator layer structure. Then open the file in Photoshop (File, Open).

- Select a path or paths, **copy** them to the clipboard, and then **paste** them into Photoshop, choosing **Paste As Pixels** in Photoshop's Paste dialog box.

There are several ways to rasterize the individual elements of a file from a "pre-8" version of Illustrator into Photoshop in register but on separate layers, so you can control them as independent elements. For instance, you can define a bounding box for the entire illustration and convert it to crop marks (Object, Cropmarks, Make). With the crop marks at the corners of your artwork, select all objects *except* the ones you want to place together in a layer, and convert them into Illustrator's guide objects (View, Make Guides). Guides aren't imported when a file is opened or placed in Photoshop. By converting back and forth between objects and guides, saving the different versions with different file names, and placing the saved versions into a Photoshop file, you can independently control the elements.

Another approach is to save several copies of the complete Illustrator file and then selectively delete elements from each copy. (This method is described in "Softening the PostScript Line" starting on page 257.) Or, for each element you want to import, turn off printability for the other layers and Save A Copy.

Importing Illustrator Artwork as Paths

Besides *rasterizing* Illustrator files using Export, drag-and-drop, Open, or Place, you can also **transfer Illustrator paths:**

- **Drag and drop** the artwork as paths by holding down the Ctrl/⌘ key as you drag from the open Illustrator file to the open Photoshop file.

- Select the paths you want to transfer, **copy** to the clipboard, and then **paste** them into Photoshop, choosing **Paste As Paths** in Photoshop's Paste dialog box. To center, hold down the Shift key as you paste.

PHOTOSHOP TO ILLUSTRATOR

If you want to import a Photoshop image into Illustrator in order to add type or geometric elements, or to trace parts of it to produce PostScript artwork, there are at least three ways to do it:

- One way is to save the Photoshop file as a **TIFF, GIF, JPEG, PICT, PDF, Photoshop** (turn on visibility for all layers you

GRAPHICS IN PHOTOSHOP

Extensis PhotoGraphics is a plug-in that gives you some of the main object-oriented graphics and type capabilities of PostScript drawing programs such as Adobe Illustrator, Macromedia FreeHand, or CorelDraw. For instance, you can set type on a curve and create paths with Bezier drawing tools right inside Photoshop.

The Extensis PhotoGraphics interface

want to include in the imported image), or **EPS** (include a Preview so you can see it on the screen) and use Illustrator's **Open** or **Place** command to import it onto a printing or nonprinting layer. (If you plan to transform [for example, rotate] the Photoshop art in Illustrator, or if you plan to color-separate and print from Illustrator, use EPS, and *link* the imported image rather than embedding it.)

- If your objective is **to fit type** to a particular part of your Photoshop image, the simplest way may be to open the file in Illustrator, make a path to fit, set type on it, convert the type to outlines, and then drag the converted type back into the Photoshop file.

Or use Photoshop's pen tool to create a path in the shape you want to fit, then export the file (File, Export, Paths To Illustrator), and open it in Illustrator (File, Open). The path will be invisible in Illustrator's Preview mode, being stroked and filled with None. So work in Artwork mode using Illustrator's path type tool to set the type. Then convert the type to outlines (Type, Create Outlines), and then copy and paste, Place, or drag-and-drop the Illustrator art into the Photoshop file. When the Illustrator type on a path is placed back into the Photoshop image, it comes in exactly in register with the original Photoshop path.

WORKING BACK AND FORTH BETWEEN PHOTOSHOP 5.5 AND OTHER PROGRAMS

Photoshop 5.5's new Jump To function allows you to automatically transfer files between Photoshop and other programs, including ImageReady and Illustrator, so that you can work on a file in one program and then another, or simply switch between programs.

- If Adobe Illustrator is already present on the hard disk when you install Photoshop 5.5, Illustrator will automatically be added to the list of programs you can switch to by choosing File, Jump To.

- To add Illustrator to the Jump To list later, or to add another program, make a shortcut (Windows) or an alias (Mac) for the program and drag it into the Jump To Graphics Editor folder inside the Help folder in your Adobe Photoshop 5.5 folder. When you next start Photoshop, the program you added will appear in the File, Jump To submenu (A).

- If you Jump To Illustrator to work on a file and then activate Photoshop again, you'll see a dialog box that notes that the file has been updated outside Photoshop and asks whether you want to keep the updates (B). If you click the Update button, the Illustrator work will appear as a single step in the History palette (C).

- By default, clicking the Jump To button at the bottom of Photoshop 5.5's toolbox (D), or pressing the Jump To keyboard shortcut (Ctrl/⌘-Shift-M), jumps to the ImageReady application. To change the Jump To default to another program, find its shortcut/alias in the Jump To Graphics Editor folder in the Helpers folder and put curly brackets — { and } — around its name (E). When you next start Photoshop, that program will be the Jump To default, and will be launched or activated when you click the button or use the keyboard shortcut.

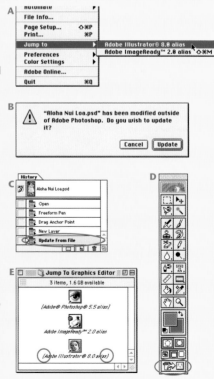

Softening the PostScript Line

Overview *Design graphics and type in Adobe Illustrator 8 using layers; export in Photoshop format; open the artwork in Photoshop; add layer effects; darken edges with the Photocopy filter; adjust color.*

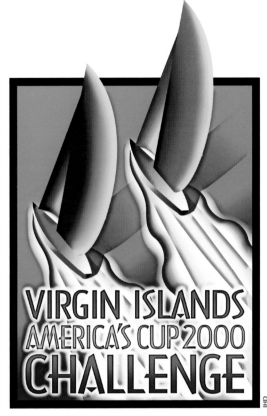

The Illustrator artwork was designed in layers. Since the two sailing boats were identical, we made a copy of the file and deleted one of the boats before saving in Photoshop format.

Saving the Illustrator 8 file in Photoshop 5 format

WORKING WITH BOTH Photoshop and an object-oriented (also called *vector-based*) drawing program gives you access to both kinds of programs' best features. For this poster illustration, shape-blending and typesetting were done in the object-oriented Adobe Illustrator. Then the artwork was opened in the pixel-based environment of Photoshop, where Layer Effects, filters, and soft-edged selections made it easy to produce the kinds of semitransparent effects that are difficult and time-consuming in an object-oriented program — for instance, the interaction between a soft-edged element like a glow or a shadow and a gradient-filled background. Until coloring was needed, we worked in grayscale in order to work out values and contrasts, and to keep the file size and RAM requirements small (a third the size of an RGB file).

1 Preparing the art. Design a layout, draw the objects, and set type in a PostScript drawing program such as Adobe Illustrator, MacMedia FreeHand, or CorelDraw. Start by defining the "canvas" in your object-oriented program by drawing a rectangle and converting it to crop marks. Inside the crop marks in Illustrator we worked in layers and shaped the sailboats with gradient-filled objects, and formed their wakes with object-to-object blends. The type was set and turned into outlines.

Next, with separate layers for all the graphic elements that overlapped each other, we exported the file from Illustrator 8 in Photoshop 5 format, choosing the High Resolution, Anti-Alias, and

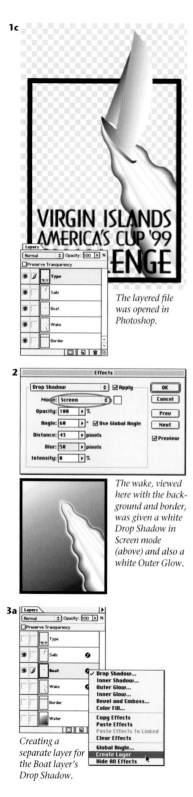

1c

The layered file was opened in Photoshop.

The wake, viewed here with the background and border, was given a white Drop Shadow in Screen mode (above) and also a white Outer Glow.

Creating a separate layer for the Boat layer's Drop Shadow.

Write Layers rendering options in the Photoshop Options dialog box. Next we opened the exported file in Photoshop (File, Open) and opened the Layers palette. (If you don't have version 8 of Illustrator, which can export in Photoshop 5 format, see "Converting a Vector-Based Drawing into Photoshop Layers" on page 260.)

2 Building the background and glow. To make a gradient-filled background, we started by adding a new layer and dragging its name to the bottom of the stack in the Layers palette. Next we dragged with the rectangular marquee to select a rectangle the size of the border element. We double-clicked the Linear gradient tool in the toolbox to open its Options palette, and set up a Foreground To Background gradient with black as the Foreground color and white as the Background color (pressing "D" restores these defaults) and with the Dither option selected to keep the gradient from banding. We dragged from a point beyond the bottom right corner of the selection to a point beyond the top left corner to produce a dark-to-light-gray fill.

To make a glow around one of the sailboat wakes, we used two Layer Effects — Drop Shadow and Outer Glow. We activated the Wake layer and chose Layer, Effects, **Drop Shadow.** In the Effects dialog box we set the Mode to Screen and clicked the color swatch so we could choose white as the color. By using the Drop Shadow effect to create this light glow, we could offset the glow by setting the Angle and Distance, functions that aren't available with the Outer Glow, and we could also extend the glow farther outward than the maximum Blur setting for Outer Glow would allow.

Then we chose **Outer Glow,** clicked the Apply box to turn it on, and set the Blur and Intensity; this added a glow on the right side of the wake and intensified the existing glow that the Drop Shadow effect had produced on the left. The result — a partially transparent glow over a gradient background — would have been very difficult to produce in Illustrator.

3 Shadowing a multilayer element. You can make a shadow for any element on a transparent layer by adding a Drop Shadow Layer Effect. But if you want to make a single combined shadow for elements that occupy more than one layer, you can do it as we did for the shadow of the boat and its sails, by making a shadow for each layer, distorting each one, and then combining them: With the Sails layer active, we added a **Drop Shadow** Layer Effect; we used the default black color and set the Opacity to 100% (using a lower Opacity would have made the area where the two shadows overlapped darker when the two were combined). We turned off the Use Global Angle option, since the Global Angle applies to all angled Effects in the file, and we didn't want these shadows to be off-set in the same direction as the Drop Shadow glow we had applied in step 2. We set the Blur to 0 to keep the shadow edge sharp.

3b

Casting the Sail's shadow with Free Transform's Distort function

3c

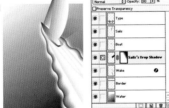

Merging the two drop shadow layers

3d

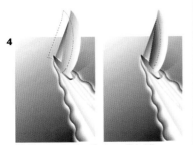

The shadow, with Opacity reduced and a layer mask added

4

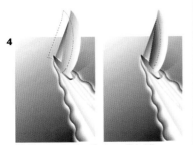

Making a selection that paralleled the curve of the sail, feathering it and trimming it, and then darkening the selected area adds needed volume and dimension.

Next we copied the **Drop Shadow** effect, with exactly the same settings, from the Sails layer to the Boat layer: With the Sails layer active, we right-clicked (Windows)/Control-clicked (Mac) on the layer's "f" icon, and chose Copy Effects from the context-sensitive menu. Then we activated the Boat layer, right-clicked/Control-clicked its *name* (not its thumbnail), and chose Paste Effects.

Before combining the two shadows, we first had to detach them from the Boat and Sails layers, converting them into layers of their own. So for each layer, we opened the context-sensitive "f" menu again and chose Create Layer.

Next we distorted the Boat's Drop Shadow and Sails's Drop Shadow independently before combining them, since this would give us the most flexibility in angling and aligning each one. For each shadow we opened a Transform bounding box around the shadow (Ctrl/⌘-T) and chose the Distort function from the Transform box's context-sensitive menu (right-clicking [Windows]/Control-clicking [Mac] inside the Transform box opens the context-sensitive menu). We reshaped the shadow by dragging on the box's handles, and used the context-sensitive menu again to Skew and Scale the shadow. Double-clicking inside the Transform box completed the transformation.

When we had distorted the two shadows we turned on visibility for the two shadow layers, turned off visibility for all other layers, and chose Merge Visible from the Layers palette's pop-out menu. This produced a single shadow layer. We could now drag this layer down below the Boat in the Layers palette and reduce the Opacity of this combined shadow layer to 30%. A layer mask was added by clicking the Add Layer Mask icon and given a gradient fill to fade the outer reaches of the shadow.

4 Adding dimensionality. Feathered selections can be darkened or lightened to create soft, realistically rounded surfaces like the large sail. Working on the Sails layer we loaded the transparency mask for the sail by Ctrl/⌘-clicking on the layer's name in the Layers palette. We feathered the selection, offset it by dragging, and then trimmed it by using the lasso to deselect everything to the left of the original large sail. (To subtract from a selection, hold down the Alt/Option key while using a selection tool or loading an alpha channel, layer mask, or transparency mask as a selection.) The Image, Adjust, Levels command was used to darken the selected area.

5 Duplicating composite elements. Next we wanted to duplicate the finished boat, its shadow, and its wake and glow. We clicked in the eye icons column in the Layers palette to make all these layers visible and the others (gradient background, border, and type) invisible. We added a new layer, then held down the Alt/Option key while choosing Merge Layers from the Layers palette's pop-out menu (holding down the Alt/Option key while choosing Merge Visible

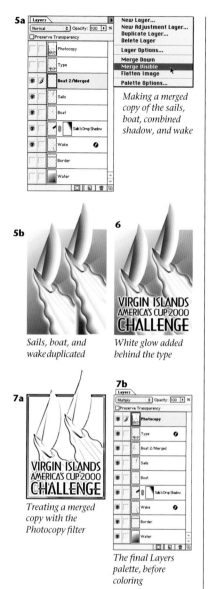

5a

Making a merged copy of the sails, boat, combined shadow, and wake

5b

Sails, boat, and wake duplicated

6

White glow added behind the type

7a

Treating a merged copy with the Photocopy filter

7b

The final Layers palette, before coloring

merges a copy of each of the visible layers into the active layer, at the same time maintaining all but the active layer as separate layers). We dragged with the move tool to offset the new boat layer.

6 Treating the type. The Type layer was made visible and was given an **Outer Glow** Layer Effect like the one added to the Wake layer in step 2.

7 Adding dramatic edges. Photoshop's Photocopy filter can be used to produce soft, thick-and-thin edge treatments in black-and-white. To make a composite layer to filter, we added a new layer at the top and with all layers visible and the top layer active, we held down the Alt/Option key and chose Merge Visible. Then we chose Filter, Sketch, Photocopy and adjusted Detail and Darkness to taste. Putting this layer in Multiply mode overlaid the resulting dark edges onto the layered image below.

Coloring. To get the result shown at the top of page 257, the Grayscale file was converted to RGB (Image, Mode, RGB Color) and color was added to the image: With Preserve Transparency turned on for the Type layer, the individual lines of black type were selected with the rectangular marquee and filled with solid color or gradients. The artwork was colored by applying Image, Adjust, Color Balance to individual layers. For example, for the boat on the right the Shadows and Midtones were pushed toward Red, and the Highlights toward Yellow. *Wow!*

CONVERTING A VECTOR-BASED DRAWING INTO PHOTOSHOP LAYERS

If your object-oriented drawing program (for instance, Adobe Illustrator versions before 8) doesn't let you save layered files in a form that Photoshop can open with the layering scheme intact, here's a way to accomplish the transfer of layers from the drawing program to Photoshop: Include crop marks or a bounding box in the drawing file. Save the finished artwork file several times under different names, so that you end up with one file for every Photoshop layer you want to have. Then reduce the contents of each new file to what you want to see on one Photoshop layer, by deleting everything else. Keep the crop marks or bounding rectangle as part of each file to ensure that all the files have the same overall shape and dimensions. Save the files in Adobe Illustrator EPS format.

Rasterize all the EPS files into Photoshop (File, Open), using the same dimensions and resolution for each file, and then Shift-drag-and-drop each of the elements into a single file to make layers. Because all the files are defined by the same crop marks or bounding box and are exactly the same dimensions, pixel for pixel, Shift-dragging will pin-register all the elements precisely. If you drag-and-drop the elements into the composite file in back-to-front order, you won't even have to rearrange the layers.

Duplicates of the Illustrator 6 file with elements deleted.

Rasterizing the EPS files into Photoshop

Coloring Clip Art

Overview *Divide artwork into the layers you'll need for treating elements with separate Layer Effects; create a white-filled base so you can add color on a separate layer in Multiply mode; apply Layer Effects to add dimensionality.*

 "Color Embossing" image and Action

1a

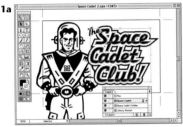

The PostScript artwork, separated into layers in Illustrator

1b

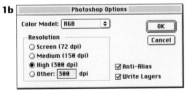

Saving the file in Photoshop 5 format from Illustrator 8

1c

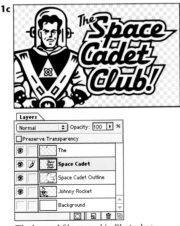

The layered file opened in Photoshop

YOU CAN START WITH YOUR OWN EPS ARTWORK created in a Post-Script drawing program, or take advantage of the thousands of clip art files out there just waiting for the kinds of coloring and special effects that Photoshop 5/5.5 can do so well. We started with a clip art space man, separated the artwork into the appropriate layers in Adobe Illustrator 8, and then moved to Photoshop. The exact step-by-step coloring process will depends greatly on the complexity of your original artwork and how it was created. But the concepts of (1) isolating shapes that can be filled with color on a separate layer in Multiply mode so there are no gaps between the color and the black "linework" and (2) using Layer Effects to add depth and dimension can be useful regardless of the file you start with.

1 Preparing the art. The first step is to organize the artwork in Illustrator and export it as a Photoshop 5 file with layers. We designed a logotype and added it to the Image Club Graphics space man. We used Illustrator's layers to sort the objects that made up the file, using as few layers as we could that would still isolate areas that would need independent color fills or different Layer Effects. We ended up with four layers, three of which contained various parts of the logotype.

Next we exported the file in Photoshop 5 format, setting the Resolution at High and clicking the check boxes to turn on Anti-alias (for smooth edges) and Write Layers (to translate the Illustrator layers directly into Photoshop layers). The resulting Photoshop file kept the same layer names and added a white-filled layer called "Background."

2 Making black-on-transparent artwork. The original Post-Script artwork for the space man had been composed of stacked black and white shapes, a format that often results when ink drawings are scanned and autotraced in a PostScript drawing or tracing

2a

Making only the Johnny Rocket artwork layer visible

2b

Ctrl/⌘-clicking on the composite color channel to load the luminosity of the Johnny Rocket layer as a selection

2c *The inverted luminosity selection filled with black on a new layer to make artwork that could be acted on by Layer Effects later*

3

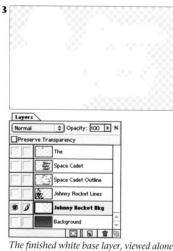

The finished white base layer, viewed alone

4

The Background layer colored with a gradient

program. There was no way to delete the white shapes and still keep the black artwork intact in Illustrator. But in our Photoshop file we needed to have the black artwork on its own transparent layer so we could use its shapes to apply Layer Effects.

To isolate the black "line work," we loaded the luminosity of the Johnny Rocket layer as a selection, as follows: First we clicked to turn off visibility for all layers except Johnny Rocket. Then in the Channels palette we Ctrl/⌘-clicked on the RGB composite channel's name to load its luminosity as a selection. That selected all the white areas in the layer and left the black unselected. We inverted the selection (Ctrl/⌘-Shift-I) so that the black was selected. Now we added a new layer above the Johnny Rocket layer by clicking the New Layer icon at the bottom of the Layers palette. In this new layer, with black as our Foreground color in the toolbox, we pressed Alt/Option-Delete to fill the selection with black.

3 Making a white base layer for the art. Now we had the black linework isolated on its own layer, and the black-and-white art on a layer below. The process of adding color to the artwork (in step 4) depends on using Multiply mode so that solid color will extend all the way to the black "lines," and there won't be a fringe of antialiasing between the color and the black. But in order for Multiply mode to work, there has to be something opaque underneath for the color to affect. The white-filled Background layer would have worked in this example, except that we wanted to use a color gradient for the background. What we needed was a white-filled shape that would underlie the space man and logotype but sit above the Background.

The original Johnny Rocket black-and-white artwork was still in the layer just above the white-filled Background. To turn this layer into a white base for the space man, we activated the layer by clicking its name in the Layers palette and turned on Preserve Transparency at the top of the palette. With white as the Background color in the toolbox we pressed Ctrl/⌘-Delete to fill all the nontransparent areas on the layer with white.

With the developing white base layer still active, we next Ctrl/⌘-clicked on the name of each other layer whose artwork we wanted to include in the white base layer — for instance, the Space Cadet Outline layer. This loaded that layer's transparency mask as a selection, which we could then fill with white in our developing base layer.

4 Coloring the background. With a white base pad in place, you can fill the Background layer. To make a gradient-filled background, we activated the Background layer, chose Foreground and Background colors, and used the Linear gradient tool to fill the layer with a Foreground To Background gradient.

5 Coloring the artwork. Next add a layer for the color. We activated the layer at the top of the Layers palette, added a new layer

5a

Setting up the magic wand for selecting areas to fill with color

5b

The color layer in Multiply mode with all the basic fills in place, viewed alone (top left) and with the other layers

6a

Setting up the magic wand to select filled areas on the color layer

6b

Turning on Preserve Transparency during "fine-tuning," to keep paint from going outside the color-filled shapes

6c

Filling the area behind the type with a gradient

above it by clicking the New Layer icon, and chose Multiply for the new layer's blending mode.

The next step is to select and color each enclosed shape in the artwork. First set up the magic wand, as follows: Double-click the magic wand in the toolbox to open its Options palette, turn on Contiguous and Use All Layers, turn off Anti-aliased, and set the Tolerance at 254.

- The **Contiguous** setting will limit the selection to the single enclosed area clicked with the wand.

- The **Use All Layers** setting will let the wand "see" the artwork in all layers below to make the selection.

- **Turning off Anti-aliased** will make a selection that will fill entirely with opaque color, rather than including some partially transparent pixels at the edges. This will prevent the edge from getting messy if you select and reselect, fill and refill a selection as you experiment with color.

- Setting the **Tolerance at 254** means that all pixels except solid black ones will be included in the selection — in other words, the selection will encroach into the black linework to include all the antialiasing pixels, thus trapping the color-and-line interface.

Click each enclosed transparent area with the magic wand, Shift-clicking if you want to add another area to a selection to be filled with a particular color. Then choose a Foreground color and press Alt/Option-Delete to fill the selection. You can temporarily switch from Multiply to Normal mode and reduce the Opacity of the color layer to see how the edges of the colors overlap the black lines.

6 Refining the color. To fine-tune the color, turn on Preserve Transparency for the color layer to prevent "coloring outside the lines." Use the magic wand again to select the individual color patches if you need a selection to fill, but this time turn off Use All Layers in the wand's Options palette, so that the wand only "looks at" the active layer — the color layer in this case — as it makes selections. Select and paint or refill as you like. We started by adding a yellow-to-green Linear gradient to the outline area around the "Space Cadet Club!" type. We clicked with the airbrush and white paint to make a highlight on the helmet. And we used the dodge and burn tools with a soft brush tip at a low Exposure setting, set to Midtones because of the particular colors we were working on, to lighten and darken various areas to create shading.

7 Adding Layer Effects. When you think the coloring is complete — because of the way you've constructed the color layer, you can always go back and recolor later — you can add dimensionality with Layer Effects. Because we had separated the art and logotype elements into Illustrator layers at the beginning of the project, we

6d Midtones ⬍ Exposure: 50 ▸ %

Fine-tuning the color layer, with dodge-and-burn shading (Note also the airbrushed highlight on the helmet.)

6e

The finished, fine-tuned color layer, viewed alone (top) and with the other layers

7a

Effects		Effects	
Drop Shadow ⬍ ☑Ap		Outer Glow ⬍ ☑Ap	
Mode: Multiply ⬍ ■		Mode: Multiply ⬍ ■	
Opacity: 50 ▸ %		Opacity: 75 ▸ %	
Angle: 50 ▸ ° ☑Use Global		Blur: 18 ▸ pixels	
Distance: 25 ▸ pixels		Intensity: 0 ▸ %	
Blur: 10 ▸ pixels			
Intensity: 0 ▸ %			

Effects		Effects	
Bevel and Emboss ⬍ ☑Ap		Color Fill ⬍ ☑Ap	
Highlight		Mode: Normal ⬍ ■	
Mode: Screen ⬍ □		Opacity: 100 ▸ %	
Opacity: 100 ▸ %			
Shadow			
Mode: Color ⬍ ■			
Opacity: 75 ▸ %			
Style: Inner Bevel ⬍			
Angle: 50 ▸ ☑Use Global			
Depth: 20 ▸ pixels ● Up ○			
Blur: 5 ▸ pixels			

Adding Layer Effects to the logotype to add shadows and dimensionality.

could fine-tune the Layer Effects separately, adding to the back-to-front layered effect we were creating in the artwork.

You can add Layer Effects by activating a layer in the Layers palette and right-clicking (Windows) or Control-clicking (Mac) on its *name* — not its thumbnail — to open the context-sensitive menu that lets you choose Effects. In the Effects dialog box, choose the kind of effect you want from the list in the upper left corner, make sure the Apply check box is selected, and adjust the settings until you get what you want.

The most pronounced Layer Effects in our artwork were added to the main "Space Cadet Club!" logotype. We used a Drop Shadow, offset down and to the left with a large Distance setting. We reduced the Opacity to 50% to soften the lighting. To make a "dark halo" around all sides of the lettering to help add dimension, we used an Outer Glow in Multiply mode, clicking the color square and choosing black, the same color we had used for the Drop Shadow. Because we were working in Photoshop 5.5, we could assign color with the Color Fill Layer Effect, which made it easy to experiment with the main fill color as we adjusted the dimensional effects, all within the Effects dialog box. We used Bevel And Emboss to detail the edge, choosing the Inner Bevel and using yellow for the Highlight and a bright purple for the Shadow color, putting the Shadow in Color mode to override the Color Fill color and to make it look as if another light source was shining from below.

7b

The logotype with Color Fill, Drop Shadow, "dark halo" (provided by an Outer Glow), and lighting from above and below (provided by an Inner Bevel)

7c

Layers

Normal ⬍ Opacity: 100 ▸ %

☐ Preserve Transparency

👁 Color

👁 The 𝑓

👁 🖌 **Space Cadet** 𝑓

👁 Space Cadet Outline 𝑓

👁 Johnny Rocket Lines 𝑓

👁 Johnny Rocket Bkg

👁 Background

The final Layers palette, with Layer Effects applied to the separate elements of the artwork

A shadow and slight embossing were applied to the Johnny Rocket line work layer. The Drop Shadow was used with a lower Distance setting than for the logotype. The Bevel And Emboss Inner Bevel was used with a magenta Highlight in Screen mode and a violet Shadow, also in Screen mode, which again looked like a second light source. Using a lower Blur setting (3 instead of 5) made the bevel look narrower than the bevel on the logotype.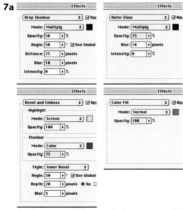

Lance Hidy's 20 x 30-inch five-color *poster for the Gelman Library* of the George Washington University was an exercise in planning and file size economy. He created the components in Photoshop, Adobe Illustrator, and Adobe Streamline, and layered them together in QuarkXPress. Hidy knew he couldn't get the depth of color he wanted for the green-to-aqua sky from process colors alone, so he added a fifth printing ink to his design, Reflex Blue from the Pantone Matching System. ▶ *To add a custom color plate to a Photoshop 5/5.5 file, open the Channels palette and choose New Spot Channel from the palette's pop-out menu. Create your spot-color artwork in this channel, using black where you want to see solid color, white where you want none of the spot color, and shades of gray where you want screens of the color.*

The trees were developed from a scan of a color slide. What seem to be trunks stretching upward in the poster image, in the original photo were actually branches extending outward, since the photo was taken under a tree with the camera pointing straight up. Hidy used Levels to increase the contrast between branches and sky in the 10.5 MB color scan, and then applied Threshold to produce a strictly black-and-white image. The file was converted to Bitmap mode (Image, Mode, Grayscale, and then Image, Mode Bitmap) and saved in EPS format with Transparent Whites selected so the trees could be layered over the background in QuarkXPress. Slightly more than 20 inches wide, the 136 dpi bitmap file was 450K.

The Washington Monument was drawn in Illustrator and filled with a rich gray that included all four process colors (C, M, Y, and K).

Some of the type characters are from Adobe fonts, set in Illustrator and converted to outlines. Others were from printed type, scanned on a desktop flatbed scanner and traced with Adobe Streamline. Characters with counters emerged from the tracing as black-filled type bodies with white-filled counters stacked on top, and each counter-and-body pair had to be converted to a compound object in Illustrator to turn the counter shapes into holes. To color the characters, Hidy selected them all and set

up a pink-to-orange gradient in Illustrator's Paint Style dialog box, which filled each letter with the entire gradient. Then dragging the gradient tool from top to bottom of the whole assemblage spread the gradient over all the characters. Hidy then sampled the gradient to check color composition at three different heights, and used these three colors to make trapping strokes for the type.

A small amount of noise (Filter, Noise, Add Noise) kept the background gradients from banding over the span of the poster's height.

The files were layered into QuarkXPress, where title and text were added in Penumbra, designed by Hidy as an Adobe Multiple Masters font. Rob Anderson at Progress Printing in Lynchburg, Virginia made separated the page into C, M, Y, K and a fifth printing plate. ▶ *When saving Photoshop files with spot color for use in QuarkXPress (or in any other program except Illustrator 7 or later or PageMaker 6.5), first choose Preferences, General and in the Preferences dialog box, turn on the Short PANTONE Names option by clicking the checkbox. Save the file in DCS 2.0 format with spot color channels retained but alpha channels removed.*

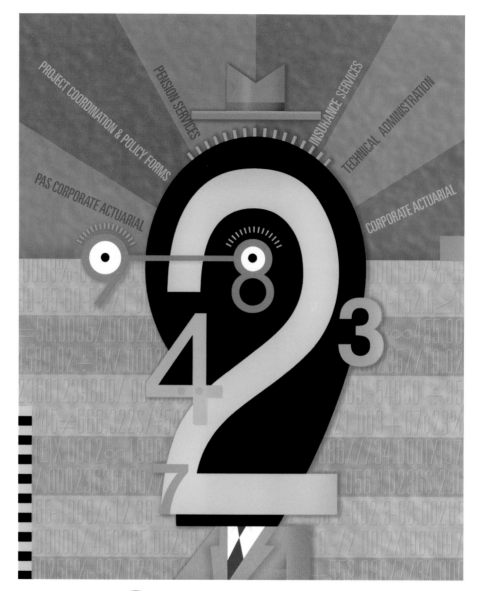

Gordon Studer used a layered Adobe Illustrator file to work out the composition and develop the central figure for *Hire Math: The Actuarial Student Program*, created as cover art for *Topics*, a publication of the pension-planning service TIAA-CREF. The "man" composed of numbers was designed and built in Illustrator (left) and then enhanced in Photoshop, where Studer would have more freedom in working with the elements. ▶ *Adobe Illustrator 8 can export files in Photoshop 5 format, converting the Illustrator layers to Photoshop layers: Choose File, Export, Photoshop 5; then choose the color mode, resolution, and usually antialiasing, and enable Write Layers.*

To help unify (and also soften) the PostScript-drawn elements, Studer scanned a cork texture, then applied Photoshop's Blur and Add Noise filters to create a texture that shows through the geometric stripes and radiating shapes of the background. This mottled texture, as well as a grid of typed numbers and letters in another layer, are used at about 30 percent opacity to add surface interest. In addition, a green drop shadow behind the man helps wed this flat element to the textured background.

© Bert Monroy 1996

To "paint" *Cedar,* **Bert Monroy** began as he often does, referring to a photograph and using Adobe Illustrator's drawing tools to construct the building and its details. Still in Illustrator he assigned color fills to the elements he had built, saved them, and then imported them into Photoshop, where he added highlights, shadows, and textures. ▶ *In Illustrator 8 you can save layered files in Photoshop 5 format, checking the Write Layers box to translate Illustrator layers into Photoshop layers.*

Monroy painted the tree on its own layer in Photoshop, using a large, round brush for the trunk and decreasing brush sizes for the branches. He added Noise and then applied the Craquelure filter (from Filter, Texture) to make the bark texture.

To paint the leaves on the tree and shrubs, Monroy created a set of custom brushes. For the tree's leaves, about a dozen different shapes were drawn in Illustrator and imported into Photoshop, where each was selected and made into a

brush by choosing Define Brush from the Brushes palette. Copies of the leaf shapes were also skewed, rotated, and distorted to make more brushes, thus creating enough variety to fill the tree with individual-looking leaves. Using the paintbrush tool and various shades of green, Monroy added the leaves by clicking the paintbrush all over the branches, starting with the dark, shadowed ones in the back. He added dappled light to the forward leaves, trunk, and branches with the dodge and burn tools.

The tree's late afternoon shadow was added by duplicating the tree layer and filling the copy with black. ▶ *Pressing Shift-Alt/Option-Delete fills nontransparent areas of the active layer with the Foreground color. (Using the Shift Key preserves transparency.)*

The shadow layer was scaled, skewed, faded, and blurred using methods like those described in "Casting a Shadow" in Chapter 8, except that the blurring of the shadow was done with Motion Blur.

GRAPHICS SPECIAL EFFECTS

Combined special effects, like these found in the Effects layers of the **Wow Layer Effects** files on the CD-ROM that comes with this book, can be copied and pasted into your own documents. Choose the Wow Layer Effects document that corresponds most closely to the size of your type or graphic — 200, 100, or 50 pixels high. Then right-click/Control-click on the "f" icon on the Effects layer you want to copy and choose Copy Effects from the context-sensitive pop-out menu. Next, in the Layers palette of the document where you want to apply those effects, right-click/Control-click on the name of your target layer and choose Paste Effects. Note that the effects will look somewhat different if your graphic or background is different in color or tone than those shown here.

MOST OF THE SPECIAL EFFECTS in this chapter are designed to simulate what happens when light and materials interact — from a simple drop shadow to the complex reflections and refraction of chrome, brushed metal, or crystal. The next 10 pages present an overview of using Photoshop's layers, Layer Effects, layer masks, Adjustment layers, alpha channels, and filters to start a wide range of dramatic dimensional treatments. Then pages 278 and 279 describe how Photoshop can help with full-fledged 3D work.

The step-by-step special effects techniques later in the chapter give you all the details you need for creating objects and textures where none existed before. And you can find many photorealistic and superrealistic special effects, with more variations, on the Wow CD-ROM. Some are saved in the three **Wow Layer Effects** files as Effects that you can copy and paste to your own files. Others are recorded as Actions, so you can load them into Photoshop's Actions palette and apply them "automatically." You can also copy and paste Effects from the files in the Wow Layered Images folder of tutorial files.

PHOTOSHOP'S "SPECIAL EFFECTS TOOLS"

With Layer Effects, Photoshop 5/5.5 has made a significant addition to what was already an impressive set of tools for turning flat graphics into lighted, solid-looking, even glowing objects. Here's a very brief introduction to the easy-to-use new tools and a quick review of some old ones, which still have important talents to contribute, especially for more sophisticated dimensionality and lighting:

- The **Layer Effects,** new with Photoshop 5, provide a way to automate the process of adding dimension and pseudo-lighting to an isolated image element. It's now easy to "custom-fit" basic shadows, glows, and embossing to follow the edge of the graphic, type, or other element on a transparent layer. With a little creative massaging, these simple Layer Effects can produce fairly complex and dynamic graphic effects such as the Wow Layer Effects shown at the left or just for subtle shading techniques (as in step 12 of "Exercising Layers" in Chapter 2, for example).

- The **Lighting Effects filter** is still invaluable for creating believable dimensional effects. Supplied with the right raw materials in the form of RGB images to be carved, stamped, or otherwise dimensioned, and grayscale channels to shape the

continued on page 270

This dimensional treatment of type was produced with a combination of a "hands-on" Lighting Effects method (like the one shown in 5f on page 277) and quick-and-easy Layer Effects. First, for a sharp edge and dramatic spotlighting, the embossed effect was created with the Lighting Effects filter and an alpha channel. Then the embossed type element was selected and copied to a new layer (Ctrl/⌘-J) and a drop shadow was added with Layer Effects, as described in "Using Layer Effects," starting on page 250.

This debossed effect was produced like the embossing above, except that "White Is High" was unchecked in the Lighting Effects filter's dialog box and Layer Effects Inner Shadow was applied instead of the Drop Shadow. The shadow inside the recessed type adds to the depth and realism of the effect.

dimensioning, Lighting Effects can produce a wide variety of effects. The number, colors, and Styles of lights you set up and the overall Properties settings can make the difference between subtle and startling results.

- For special purposes, other filters — like **Emboss** or **Texturizer** — can also do the dimensioning. And filters like **Glass, Chrome,** and **Plastic Wrap** can play an important role in modelling the play of light on dull, shiny, transparent, translucent, or reflective surfaces.

- **Alpha channels** (and even color channels) store grayscale images that can be loaded as *bump maps* to create tactile effects like embossed textures. Or they can be duplicated and applied as layer masks to help trim the dimensional effects created with the Lighting Effects filter.

- **Levels, Curves, Color Balance,** and **Hue/Saturation** can be varied, either directly or through Adjustment layers, to provide subtle changes in color or brightness.

CHOOSING THE RIGHT METHOD

Most of the special effects techniques in this chapter showcase some variation of adding thickness to a shape. By adding dimension you can either raise the shape from the surface, which we can call ***embossing,*** or the opposite — sink it into a surface, called ***debossing.***

The addition of Layer Effects to Photoshop 5/5.5 made it much easier to create these special effects. In many cases it makes sense to use this new easy method and simply apply Layer Effects to the contents of a layer. But in other cases, it pays to use a more "hands-on" method, adding dimension by creating modified versions of an original grayscale graphic and using these versions with Lighting Effects or other filters for more specialized or sophisticated effects.

Before we get into the basic "how-to's" of the easy method in "Using Layer Effects" on page 272 and of the hands-on method in "Digital Embossing 'By Hand'" starting on page 275, here are some pointers for choosing when to simply use Layer Effects and when to invest the time and thought in a more complicated method:

- For **halos** and **glows,** using Layer Effects — with some custom tweaking — is definitely the best method, as described in "Adding a Multicolor Glow" on page 283. You can achieve spectacular results using the simple Layer Effects approach. Any other method requires more work, takes up more memory, and is less flexible if you decide to make changes.

- A **drop shadow** or a **cast shadow** can always be started as a Layer Effects Drop Shadow or Inner Shadow. Once Photoshop has built the shadow, you can keep it as a simple drop shadow that makes your image element look like it's floating slightly above the background surface, or you can turn the Effects into

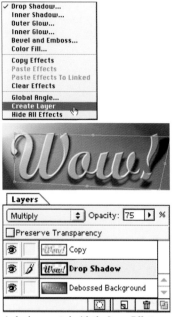

A shadow created with the Layer Effects Drop Shadow can be separated from its graphic element and rendered as a layer of its own (A). Then it can be distorted with the Free Transform command to produce a cast shadow (B). The Layers palette for the final effect shows the distorted shadow layer after it has been separated from the copy of the embossed graphic (top layer). You'll find the "how-to" details of this shadow technique in steps 3 through 5 of "Casting a Shadow," which starts on page 280.

separate layers and distort the drop shadow to convey something about the quality or the angle of the surface behind your shadowed object, as shown at the left. You can also take it one step further and turn it into a cast shadow that makes it look like your layer's content is standing up on the surface instead of floating in front of it, as in "Casting a Shadow" on page 280. Or it can add to the illusion that your object is embossed, as in "Chiseled in Stone" on page 291, or debossed, as in "Carving" on page 288.

- An **embossed** or **debossed dimensional effect** can be achieved either by applying Layer Effects or by using channels and the Lighting Effects filter to achieve more dramatic lighting. **Layer Effects** are quick, flexible (you can reopen the Layer Effects dialog box and edit them later), memory-efficient (they're stored as instructions rather than pixels, so they don't take much memory), and easy to copy and paste from one layer to another. They also take advantage of the shape information that's already built into a layer's transparency mask or layer mask, so no additional graphic is required.

  But the pseudo-lighting that's applied in Layer Effects is *directional* — that is, the light comes from a distance and from a particular angle, like bright sunlight. With the **Lighting Effects filter** and alpha channels, you invest more time and memory, but you have the additional pizzazz of omnidirectional lights (like the light from a glowing lamp) and spotlights (directional but focused lights) for creating pools of light. You can use several light sources, combining their effects (with Layer Effects, the maximum number of lights you can imitate is two — one color for the embossing highlight and one for the shadow). Finally, with the Lighting Effects filter you have some control over ambient lighting and the material characteristics of the surfaces in your image — shiny or matte, dull or reflective.

- When you want to **add dimensionality other than at the edges** of an element in a layer (such as imitating a rough surface texture on a graphic or an entire image), you'll need to use either an alpha channel and the **Lighting Effects filter** or the **Emboss filter**. The Emboss filter is limited — it uses only a single directional light — but it's quick and easy, and for certain texture effects it works very well when you put the embossed layer into Overlay mode, as described in "'Hand-Painting' from History" and "Art History Lessons" in Chapter 6.

- The **reflected and refracted highlights** that cause chrome, brushed metal, liquids, crystal, and glass to sparkle and shine can be manufactured by setting up multiple spotlights in the **Lighting Effects** dialog box as in "Forging Steel" on page 302, or with a combination of a photo, Lighting Effects, and a

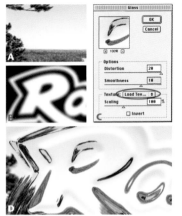

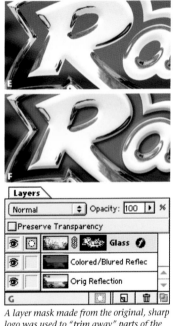

Starting with a duplicate of a background image (A) that would make a good reflection for a chrome effect, we used a separate grayscale file with a blurred version of a black-and-white logo (B) as the texture for applying the Glass filter (C) to create a rounded and raised shiny chrome effect (D).

A layer mask made from the original, sharp logo was used to "trim away" parts of the "Glass" version of the logo, allowing a darkened and blurred version of the original image to show through from the layer below (E). Finally a Layer Effects Drop Shadow was added to the Glass layer (F), making the dimensional effect more realistic. The mask provided the edge needed to create the shadow effect, as shown in the Layers palette for the finished image (G). This method is described in detail in "Chrome Plating" on page 298.

special-effects filter — **Glass, Plastic Wrap,** or **Chrome** — as in "Chrome Plating" on page 298.

With all these possibilities, here are some things to consider when choosing a method for implementing a special effect:

- **Is the illusion convincing?** Sometimes a well-placed Lighting Effects spotlight can do a lot to make a special effect look more realistic and dramatic. In other cases, adding Layer Effects can heighten a dimensional effect that you've already created with a more complicated hands-on method, such as the Lighting Effects filter or the Glass filter, as shown at the left.

- **Does it give you the control you need?** If you want a flat top surface on your dimensioned graphic, with a sharp edge where the bevel starts, the hands-on Lighting Effects/alpha channel method is the only way to get it.

  Also, some methods that lighten or darken an edge using only layers and blending modes don't let you change the color balance of a highlight or shadow individually. This is the case with the Emboss filter, for instance. But with alpha channels, layer masks, or Adjustment layers you can target the fine-tuning of color and tonality. Even with Layer Effects, you can control the color balance of highlights and shadows independently. And if you split the individual Effects off into separately rendered layers, you can then recolor or otherwise modify each effect.

- **Is it flexible?** With Layer Effects you can edit and re-edit to your heart's content — you can change all the parameters that Photoshop uses to create each effect, time and time again, without spoiling the edge. If instead you use alpha channels and the Lighting Effects filter, you may want to create your embossed or debossed element on a copy of the background image in a separate transparent layer and use a layer mask to trim it out of its surroundings so that the original background shows behind it. By using a separate layer instead of applying the effects directly to the image, you'll be able to apply Adjustment layers or make clipping groups so you can affect the dimensioned element alone, leaving the background unchanged.

USING LAYER EFFECTS

Photoshop 5 provides five kinds of dimensional effects (and version 5.5 adds a sixth) that can be chosen from the Layer, Effects submenu or from the Effects list in the context-sensitive menu that appears if you right-click/Control-click on the name of a layer in the Layers palette. The six categories of Effects are:

- **Drop Shadow,** which not only drops a shadow of the element onto the surface behind, but also provides a good starting point for cast shadows.

Layers

Normal ▼ | Opacity: 100 ▶ %

☐ Preserve Transparency

👁 ✎ ▨ **Rock'et**

👁 ▨ *Background*

As a starting point for the samples shown at the right, a Background image was opened and a selection in the shape of the "Rock'et" logo was made with the horizontal type mask tool. A new layer with only the logo on it was created with the Layer, New, Layer Via Copy command (Ctrl/⌘-J). Isolated on its own layer, the logo was lightened slightly with the Levels command, and then the Layer Effects shown at the right were applied.

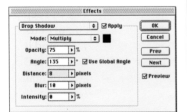

Effects

Drop Shadow ▼ | ☑ Apply | **OK**

Mode: Multiply ▼ ■ | **Cancel**

Opacity: 75 ▶ % | **Prev**

Angle: 135 ▶ ° ☑ Use Global Angle | **Next**

Distance: 8 ▶ pixels | ☑ **Preview**

Blur: 18 ▶ pixels

Intensity: 8 ▶ %

Choosing Layer, Effects, Drop Shadow opens the Effects dialog box to the Drop Shadow effect. If Apply is chosen, a drop shadow will be created. By increasing the Distance setting from its default 0 and changing the Angle, you can move the shadow. Or you can move the shadow by hand, dragging on the image while the Effects dialog box is open to the Drop Shadow. If you select Use Global Angle, all the Effects that you apply in that file are created as if the lighting was coming from the same direction, and changing the Angle for any single effect changes all of them.

- **Inner Shadow,** which casts a shadow inward on the element, as if the element were sunk into the surrounding image.
- **Outer Glow,** which creates the effect of a glow shining out from behind the element, visible only beyond its edges.
- **Inner Glow,** which creates a glow that extends inward from the **Edge** of the element, or outward from its **Center.**
- **Bevel and Emboss,** which provides settings for Emboss, Inner Bevel, Outer Bevel, and Pillow Emboss. **Emboss** highlights some of the edges, and shades the opposite ones to give the element a bevel that makes it look raised (if Up is chosen) or sunken (if you choose Down); this effect builds a bevel whose width is half inside the original edge and half outside. **Inner Bevel** creates the entire bevel inside the original edge, and **Outer Bevel** creates it entirely outward from the edge. **Pillow Emboss** creates a "reverse bevel" that gives the element a sort of "quilted" look, creating the impression that the surface of the element is level with the rest of the image, and only the outline of the element is indented, or "stitched down."
- **Color Fill,** found only in version 5.5, which colors the entire element, taking into account the blending Mode and Opacity that you choose for this effect.

Some of the attributes you can set for the Layer Effects are the

Drop Shadow

Inner Shadow

Outer Glow

Inner Glow with the Edge option chosen

Inner Glow with the Center option chosen

Emboss

Inner Bevel

Outer Bevel

Pillow Emboss

Color Fill in Multiply mode (v. 5.5 only)

Color Fill, Photoshop 5.5's new Layer Effect, lets you chose a color, Opacity, and blending Mode to apply to the area defined by the layer mask or transparency mask of the active layer. Here are a few of the things you can do with Color Fill:

• Darken a recessed element, as if it were in a shadow created by carving it into the surface.

• Create a series of matching buttons or a set of button states (idle and rollover, for instance) by copying a layer with a button graphic that has been treated with several Layer Effects and changing only the Color Fill of each one.

• Store color information that you have to apply often — the corporate color for a logo, for instance — so you can copy and paste this Color Fill wherever you need it.

A GLOWING EXAMPLE

Spending a little time experimenting with Layer Effects settings can greatly expand their potential. For instance, simply by changing the Mode of the Drop Shadow to Screen, we could use it here for the outermost (red) glow. You'll find step-by-step instructions for this three-color glow effect in "Adding a Multicolor Glow" on page 283.

Intensity of the highlight or shadow, the **Angle** of the light (this controls where the highlighted and shadowed edges are and where a drop shadow falls), the **Color** cast of the light or shadow, the amount of **Blur** (this establishes the softness of shadows and the roundness of bevels), the blending **Mode** with which the effect is applied to the layer, and the **Opacity.**

All of the techniques in this chapter involve using Layer Effects, and examples of the default settings for the Effects are shown on page 273. All of the Effects can be **applied singly or in combination.** If you go beyond the defaults, modifying the settings and combining effects in ways you might not think of at first, you'll find that you can dramatically extend the special-effects possibilities of Layer Effects.

Once you have the effects you want, you can split them off into layers of their own as in the example shown on page 271 by choosing Layer, Effects, Create Layer or by right-clicking/Control-clicking on the "f" icon for that layer in the Layers palette and choosing Create Layer from the context-sensitive menu. Splitting them off allows you to modify the Effects in ways that aren't available through the Effects dialog box. But separating the Effects into layers of their own also puts an end to their flexibility: They are now pixels rather than Effects instructions, so you can't go back into the Effects dialog box and change them further.

PRESERVING LAYER EFFECTS

If you apply a Layer Effect to a layer and then reduce the pixel dimensions of the image (as you might to repurpose artwork for the Web, for instance), the effect won't shrink along with it. That is, the offset Distance of a shadow or the Blur for a glow won't change automatically, and so the shadow will be offset too far or the glow will be disproportionately large in the reduced image. Here are three ways to ensure that the effect stays in proportion. The one you choose will depend on how far along you are in your image development.

• If you're sure your image is completed, before you resize, flatten the image.

• If you think you may need to make changes, before you resize, choose Layer, Effects, Create Layer to rasterize the effect. When you resize, the effect will shrink along with the image, but you'll still be able to control it separately from the artwork it was added to.

• Or after you reduce the size of the image, double-click the "f" icon on the layer and reset the parameters in the Effects dialog box.

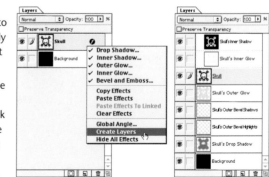

One way to produce the original white-on-black graphic to be used for embossing is to build it in Adobe Illustrator, copy it, and paste it into a Photoshop alpha channel. Another way is to make it directly in Photoshop.

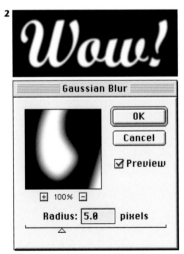

Blurring a copy of the graphic produces "gray matter" at the edges, which will give a smoother emboss or deboss.

DIGITAL EMBOSSING "BY HAND"

Here's a "primer" that provides the foundation for the sophisticated dimensional effects you can apply "by hand" — with Lighting Effects and other filters, rather than with the quick-and-easy Layer Effects method. The Lighting Effects, Displace, and Glass filters add dimensionality by using the light and dark information in a Photoshop file (typically a Grayscale file), an alpha channel, or even a color channel to change the shape or shading of your image. If you understand the fundamentals of how this works as presented in this section, it will be easier to carry out the hands-on techniques in the rest of the chapter, where instructions are provided at the click-and-drag level of detail.

1 Starting with a graphic. Photoshop's Lighting Effects filter can use the grayscale information of a black-and-white graphic as the basis for creating dimensionality in an RGB file. So a good first step in creating a dimensional effect is to store a black-and-white graphic in an alpha channel, as we do in most techniques in this chapter. By default the white in the channel will raise the surface when the channel is used with Lighting Effects' default settings, and black will leave the surface flat. If the graphic is only black and white, with no more gray than you find in an antialiased edge, sharp vertical sides are created at the edge of the graphic.

2 Generating "gray matter." For a smooth, realistic, embossed or debossed appearance, you need a range of gray tones, to make a gradual transition between the raised or sunken graphic and the surrounding surface. So the next step in creating a dimensional effect is often to store a blurred copy of the graphic in a second alpha channel. Blurring a black-and-white graphic spreads gray tones both inward and outward from where the black and white meet, making a soft "shoulder" at the edge instead of a "cliff." By using the Gaussian Blur filter, you can control the character of the edge: The larger the Radius setting for the Gaussian Blur, the more the edge softens up, and the more gradual the transition will be between the low and high surfaces of the emboss. (The "hand-made" blur that you create by

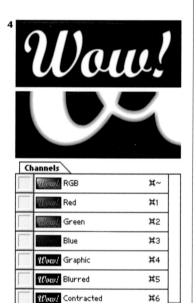

3

The third of the "basic" embossing channels is a "thin" version of the original, to be used for "trimming" the top edge of a copy of the blurred graphic.

4

A copy of the blurred alpha channel (#5) can be trimmed with the original (#4) and thin (#6) alpha channels, making a specialized channel (#7), shown above.

MATCHING BLUR AND TRIM

When you use a "thin" version of a graphic to trim a blurred version, the setting you choose for Select, Modify, Contract is related to the Radius setting you used for the Gaussian Blur. Using the same or a slightly smaller setting for Contract often does a good job of creating a sharp edge.

Gaussian-blurring the alpha channel is the counterpart of the Blur setting for Emboss in Layer Effects.)

3 Making "cookie cutters." Once you have a grayscale channel with the original graphic and another with a blurred ("gray matter") copy of it, you may need another one for additional control: a slimmed-down (less bold) version of the original. Then both the original and this thin version can be used to create sharper top and bottom edges for the embossing graphic, while keeping some rounding and "slope" in the shoulder itself. This thin graphic can be produced by creating a new black-filled alpha channel, loading the original graphic as a selection in it, shrinking the selection a little (Select, Modify, Contract), and filling the selection with white.

4 Shaping the gray matter with the original graphic and the thin graphic. With the three alpha channels described in steps 1 through 3 you can create specialized alpha channels for producing a variety of dimensional effects. For instance, loading the thin version as a selection in a copy of the blurred channel and filling the selection with white removes the blurring that had encroached into the graphic. The sides and outside edges of the graphic are still gray. So when the graphic is used for embossing, the sides will still rise gradually from a softly curved bottom edge, but the top surface will be flat and its edges will be sharp. (This result is similar to the Outer Bevel of Layer Effects, but the trimmed alpha channel gives you more control of the sharpness and position of the top edge of the bevel.)

On the other hand, if you load the original (fatter) graphic as a selection in a copy of the blurred channel, then reverse the selection to select the black background instead of the white graphic, and fill this new selection with black, you effectively trim away the blurring that had extended into the background. So when you emboss, the top edge will be rounded, but the edge where the graphic meets the surrounding surface will be sharp. (The result is like the Inner Bevel of Layer Effects.)

5 Embossing and debossing with Lighting Effects. One of the many amazing things the Lighting Effects filter can do is to emboss or deboss a surface image using an alpha channel as the Texture Channel. The White Is High option raises the surface where the graphic is light. In contrast, turning off White Is High raises the surface where the graphic is dark.

Enhancing embossed images. Adjusting the Gloss and Material settings to simulate a shiny or matte surface, which can be done in the Lighting Effects dialog box, helps make dimensional images look more realistic. Adding cast or drop shadows with Layer Effects also adds to the photorealism, as shown in the examples on pages 270 and 271.

5a

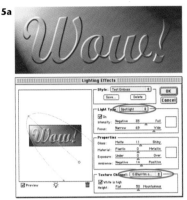

The Lighting Effects filter can be applied to an RGB image, with an alpha channel used as the Texture Channel. The spotlights available with Lighting Effects can make the effect more dynamic or dramatic than the directional lighting available with Layer Effects.

ACTION The "Embossing Sampler" Action on the Wow! CD-ROM starts with an RGB file and a graphic in the first alpha channel and generates five of the additional kinds of alpha channels shown in the illustrations for step 5 on pages 277 and 278. It then brings up the Lighting Effects dialog box so you can choose one of these alpha channels as the Texture Channel for experimenting with embossing or debossing effects.

CHOOSING A SURFACE

When you choose an RGB "surface" to emboss, look for an image with colors in the middle of the tonal range, so that the highlights and shadows produced in the embossing process will show up well.

5b

The alpha channel that holds the original graphic (#4) was used as the Texture Channel when the Lighting Effects filter was applied to a gold-colored surface for embossing (center) and debossing (right). It produced the look of a thin cut-out laid on top of a background.

5c

When the blurred alpha channel (#5) was used as the Texture Channel for the Lighting Effects filter, both the inner (top surface) and outer (bottom) edges of the "W" were rounded. The result produced with this channel is similar to the Emboss effect in Layer Effects Bevel And Emboss.

5d

The surface of the embossed/debossed "W" was flattened by "trimming" a duplicate of the blurred channel (#5) with the "thin" channel (#6) and using the result as the Texture Channel. The result produced with this channel is similar to the Outer Bevel effect in Layer Effects Bevel And Emboss.

5e

The outer edge of the "W" was sharpened by trimming a copy of the blurred channel (#5) with a reversed selection made from the "original" (#4); the result was used as the Texture Channel. The result produced with this channel is similar to the Inner Bevel effect in Layer Effects Bevel And Emboss.

5f

To make a beveled edge like the one used to emboss the "Wow!" graphic at the left, both the inner and outer edges of the blurred "W" channel (#5) were trimmed, as described for the two versions above, and the result was used as the Texture Channel. This hard-edged precision cannot be achieved with Layer Effects Bevel And Emboss.

5g

To make a Texture Channel for "pillow" embossing, the "original" channel (#4) was loaded as a selection in a duplicate of the blurred channel, the tonality of the selected area was inverted (Ctrl/⌘-I), and the result was used as the Texture Channel. The result produced with this channel is similar to the Pillow Emboss effect in Layer Effects Bevel And Emboss.

5h

The best way we've found to create a raised or sunken chiseled look with a sharp central ridge is to load the "original" channel (#4) as a selection in a new black-filled alpha channel and run the KPT Gradient Designer from MetaCreations' Kai's Power Tools 3 (also included with KPT 5). Then use this alpha channel as the Texture Channel for the Lighting Effects filter. Though it means buying a set of plug-ins, it's worth the expense if you want to get results like these. (You'll find step-by-step directions and filter settings in "Chiseled in Stone," starting on page 291.) This effect can't be achieved with Layer Effects alone.

PHOTOSHOP AND THE THIRD DIMENSION

There are times when you need to go beyond embossing and debossing to create an image with a true 3D look. A **Levels** Adjustment layer with a customized mask can create shadows and highlights that add depth to a scene, as shown at the left. In addition, three of Photoshop's Edit, Transform functions (**Skew, Perspective,** and **Distort**) allow you to select part or all of an image and telescope or "bend" it to exaggerate perspective; the **Spherize** filter can also create depth illusions. And the **3D Transform** filter lets you select an element of your image and treat it like a 3D object, changing the perspective as you turn it with the filter's trackball tool (using the 3D Transform filter is explained step-by-step in "3D Transformation" on page 170). Filters supplied by other developers can also add dimensionality, such as the KPT Glass Lens (from MetaCreations' Kai's Power Tools 3) and Andromeda's Three-D Luxe. These and other plug-ins are described in "Filter Demos" in Chapter 5.

Stand-alone 3D programs create solid objects by *modelling*. Two of the simplest ways to model are to *extrude* or *revolve* two-dimensional vector-based artwork into a 3D shape. They also allow you to *stage* an entire scene by arranging the models you make, and then quickly change the viewpoint or lighting to produce a new perspective. All 3D programs can also *render,* producing a photo-like view of the scene that assigns surface characteristics to the models and includes the interaction of light and shadows with these textures.

Two plug-ins for Photoshop — Rayflect's PhotoTracer and Zaxwerks' 3D Invigorator — provide many of the functions of

TYPE DESIGN: JOHN ODAM DESIGN ASSOCIATES / ILLUSTRATION: JHD

Photoshop techniques can be useful in creating the illusion of 3D space, as in the illustration for this book cover. For instance, the Edit, Free Transform, Perspective command could be used to turn a layer containing a flat assemblage of flags into a "floor." A pseudo-reflection of the flags was applied to the globe by copying part of the original flags image into a layer of its own, running the Spherize filter on that layer (Filter, Distort, Spherize), and reducing the layer's Opacity. A drop shadow could be added to the globe (Layer, Effects, Drop Shadow) and then rendered into a separate layer (Layer, Effects, Create Layer), and scaled and skewed into a cast shadow (Edit, Free Transform). A Levels Adjustment layer was added above the floor layer, with a mask that limited its darkening effect to the back left corner.

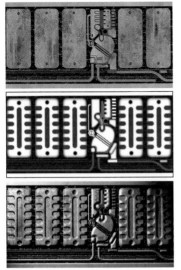

To quickly test this alpha channel (center) as a bump map before committing to a time-consuming 3D rendering process, Frank Vitale and E. J. Dixon of Presto Studios ran Photoshop's Lighting Effects filter on the painted RGB image shown at the top, using the alpha channel as the Texture Channel to produce the illustration at the bottom.

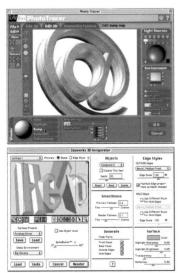

Rayflect's PhotoTracer (top) and Zaxwerks' 3D Invigorator, described on page 217, are Photoshop plug-ins that provide many of the modelling and rendering functions of stand-alone 3D programs.

simple stand-alone 3D programs. With these additions, you can create and render without leaving Photoshop.

There are two ways that Photoshop can work with the artwork from 3D programs or plug-in filters. It can serve as the recipient of an object or scene modeled and rendered in three dimensions, so you can then retouch or enhance it. Or it can serve as a generator for images to be used as surface maps to add color, texture, and detail to a model in a stand-alone 3D program.

Photoshop to 3D

All 3D programs accept color files that can be applied to 3D models as flat surface textures (called *texture maps*) or for tactile effects (called *bump maps*). Photoshop's Lighting Effects filter can be useful to quickly test out *bump maps* to be used in 3D images, as in the example at the left. Some programs (such as MetaCreations' Bryce 3D) can also generate 3D models from grayscale images, translating the shades of gray as different distances above or below a surface, to create mountains, canyons, or other 3D models.

3D to Photoshop

Programs like Adobe Dimensions are designed to make relatively simple 3D models from type or from artwork drawn in PostScript programs such as Adobe Illustrator, Macromedia FreeHand, or CorelDraw. They can extrude or revolve models around the height, width, or depth axes and they can create perspective views, but they can't provide the complex texture, lighting, and shadowing effects of more powerful 3D programs. Effects such as highlights, shadows, and embossed textures can be added by hand to Dimensions artwork with Photoshop's filtering and layering techniques.

Even if you use a more sophisticated 3D program or plug-in with advanced modelling and rendering functions, starting and ending with Photoshop can still save you time. Setting up your models, lighting, and camera angles in a 3D program is time-consuming, and rendering can take a long time. So if you find that you want to change the color or brightness of a 3D image once it's rendered, it may make sense to adjust Color Balance or Hue/Saturation for all or part of the image in Photoshop instead of going back to the 3D program to change the lighting and rerender the scene. Also, some kinds of shadows and other details look more convincing if applied "by hand" with Photoshop's airbrush or other techniques than by a 3D program's rendering algorithms.

In addition to full-color rendered images, most 3D programs can produce a mask that accompanies the file, appearing as an alpha channel when the file is opened in Photoshop. This channel can then be used in any of the ways Photoshop masks are applied — for instance, to isolate parts of an image so the color can be changed, to apply a blur or another filter selectively, or to composite the image into a new background.

Casting a Shadow

Overview *Set type; add a background and put it into perspective; add a drop shadow to the type; separate, distort and progressively blur the shadow; color and bevel the type.*

"Cast Shadow"
image and Action

Original photo

Applying Perspective to the image after scaling it to a fraction of its original height

Making a temporary mask for adjusting Levels

Setting the type

ONE WAY TO HELP TYPE OR A GRAPHIC look at home in its environment is to make it cast a shadow onto the background. We started by setting type in Photoshop, added a drop shadow with an Effects layer, and then turned it into a cast shadow that falls onto our flag, breaking the shadow out onto a layer of its own. We then added dimension and lighting to the type layer with a customized beveled edge and a glow applied as Layer Effects, which we could keep live in case we wanted to change them later.

1 Preparing the background. Choose a background image and alter it if necessary. We started with a 1000-pixel-wide flag image and distorted it using the Perspective command: We pressed Ctrl/⌘-T for Free Transform, right-clicked/Control-clicked to get a context-sensitive menu, and chose Perspective. To distort the image, we dragged one lower handle of the transform box outward and then one upper handle inward.

We lightened the stars and stripes at the top of the flag with a Levels change through a temporary gradient mask: To do this, press "Q" to activate Quick Mask mode, then choose the Linear gradient tool from the toolbox's gradient tool pop-out palette, then press "D" for default colors. Drag the gradient tool from the bottom of the image to the top, then turn this gradient Quick Mask into a selection by pressing "Q" again. Now we could apply Image, Adjust, Levels, moving the black slider on the Output Levels bar to lighten the top of the image and reduce its contrast.

2 Setting the type. To open the Type Tool dialog box, choose the type tool in the toolbox (pressing "T" selects the tool) and click on your canvas. Choose the font, style, size, leading, alignment, and other characteristics. Click the color swatch in the dialog box to open the Color Picker so you can choose a color; we chose a green.

Then type in the wording you want. If you want to move the type around, you don't have to close the Type Tool dialog box to do it. Just move the cursor onto the canvas and drag. When you click OK to close the dialog box, the type tool will automatically generate its own transparent layer. (Choosing View, Show Layers

2b

The type in place in a layer above the flag

3a

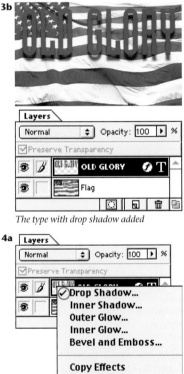

Adding a Drop Shadow Effects layer

3b

The type with drop shadow added

4a

Choosing Layer, Effects, Create Layer to make a separate layer of the drop shadow

opens the Layers palette so you can see this, and so you can use the palette for steps 3 through 7.)

3 Adding the shadow. To cast the shadow, we first added a drop shadow to the "OLD GLORY" layer using the Drop Shadow layer effect, as follows:

Right-click/Control-click on the *name* of the new type layer in the Layers palette (be sure to click the name, not the icon, because each component has its own context-sensitive menu); choose Effects from the context-sensitive menu that appears; and choose Drop Shadow from the list at the top of the Effects dialog box.

Working directly in your image, drag the shadow far enough so it's no longer covered up by the type and you can see what happens as you change the Blur setting. At this point all you need is enough of a blur to slightly soften the sharp edge.

After blurring the shadow, we set the color for the drop shadow, as follows: We clicked the color swatch next to the Multiply mode setting to open the Color Picker and then clicked to pick up color from an existing shadow on one of the white stripes of the flag.

4 Casting the shadow. The next step is to separate the shadow to its own layer so you can distort it without distorting the type. Right-click/Control-click the *"f"* symbol in the type layer and choose Create Layer from the context-sensitive menu.

5 Distorting the shadow. With the new Drop Shadow layer active, we used the Edit, Free Transform command like this: We pressed Ctrl/⌘-T to bring up the Free Transform frame. To flip and stretch the shadow, we dragged the frame's top center handle down past the bottom edge. Then we right-clicked/Control-clicked inside the Transform box to bring up the context-sensitive menu, where we chose Perspective. Dragging outward on a bottom corner handle

---

INTERACTIVE FLIPPING

It's easy to have fingertip control of what happens when you flip an element — a shadow layer, for instance. You can flip the element in place or flip it so it's above, beside, or below where it started, stretching or shrinking it in the process.

After you press Ctrl/⌘-T to bring up the Free Transform frame, put the cursor on a center handle on the top, bottom, or side of the frame.

• To flip the element around an edge or corner, drag the handle all the way across the frame and beyond the opposite edge or corner, as shown.

• Hold down the Ctrl/⌘ key to be able to skew as you flip.

• To flip the element around its center so it ends up in its original position but facing the other direction, Alt/Option-drag the handle past the center mark.

• To be able to skew the element as you flip it around its center, hold down the Ctrl/⌘ key as you Alt/Option-drag.

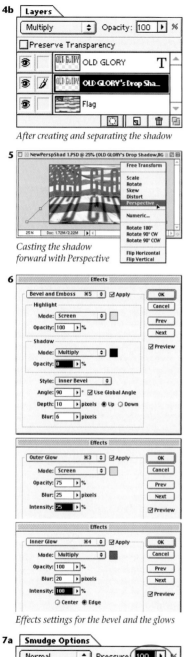

4b

After creating and separating the shadow

5

Casting the shadow forward with Perspective

6

Effects settings for the bevel and the glows

7a

The shadow was retouched with the smudge tool with a soft brush tip, and faded with a layer mask.

and then inward on a top corner handle created the perspective effect. Before pressing the Enter key to finalize the transformation, we dragged inside the box to move the shadow into place so we could check its alignment with the type.

6 Adding a bevel and glows. Now that the shadow effect has been separated from the type layer, you can add other effects to the type layer and keep these new effects "live." (If you had added them before step 3, they would have been broken into separate layers, along with the drop shadow, when you chose Create Layer.)

We chose Layer, Effects, Bevel And Emboss to open the Effects dialog box and set the bevel highlight and shadow. We made sure the Apply box was checked, then chose Inner Bevel (to construct the bevel inward from the existing edge of the type), 90° (to light the type from above), 10 pixels for the depth, Up (to make the faces of the type characters rise above the surface rather than sink into it), and a 6-pixel blur for a slight rounding of the edge. We left the blending modes at the default Screen (for the highlight) and Multiply (for the shadow). We specified a light blue for the Highlight by clicking the color square next to the mode setting and choosing a color. We set the Opacity of the Shadow to 0%; this effectively turned off the bevel's shadow and added to the illusion that we were looking down on the type rather than viewing it straight on.

To make the type glow around its edges, we then chose Outer Glow from the list at the top of the Effects box, clicked the Apply box, left the default Screen setting for the mode, picked a color, and experimented with the Blur (softness of the glow), Intensity (extent of the glow), and Opacity until the glow looked right.

To darken the type at its edges, we chose Inner Glow from the list, clicked the Apply box, picked a color, switched the mode to Multiply, and experimented with Blur, Intensity, and Opacity.

7 Blending the shadow into its surroundings. To make the dimensional type even more at home in its surroundings, we used the smudge tool (press Shift-R once or twice to toggle to it, then press Enter to open its Options palette). To limit its effects to the shadow layer, we turned off Use All Layers. We set the Pressure to 100%, chose a soft brush tip from the Brushes palette (Window, Show Brushes), and used the smudge to distort the edges of the shadow to match the folds in the flag.

7b

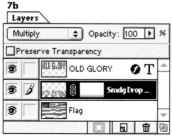

A layer mask fades the shadow.

Finally we added a layer mask (click the mask icon at the bottom of the Layers palette); chose white for the Foreground color and gray (about 50% black) for the Background color, and Shift-dragged with the Linear gradient tool (press "G") to "fade" the forward edge of the shadow.

Adding a Multicolor Glow

Overview *Prepare a background; add a graphic element in a transparent layer; use Layer Effects — Drop Shadow, Outer Glow, Inner Glow, and Bevel And Emboss — to create a multicolor glow.*

 "Glow" image and Actions

Original image

Treating the background image with a Hue/Saturation Adjustment layer: Increasing the Saturation to boost color intensity and decreasing Lightness to darken the image

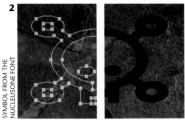

The graphic was pasted as paths from Illustrator (left), turned into a selection, and filled with black in a new layer (right).

CREATING A GLOW that goes from hot white to fiery red turns out to be easy once you start thinking of some of the Layer Effects options in new ways. Because the Effects are so simple to edit and re-edit, this method gives you tremendous control and flexibility.

1 Preparing the background. Choose an image for your background and make any necessary changes to prepare it to "host" your glowing object. We added an Adjustment layer (Ctrl/⌘-click the New Layer icon at the bottom of the Layers palette) with Hue/Saturation as the Type. We increased the Saturation since a bright, glowing light would be shining on the surface, and reduced the Lightness to create a darkened environment for good contrast.

2 Adding the graphic. Now add a layer with the element that you want to set aglow. For instance, you can drag-and-drop an element from another Photoshop file. Or do as we did: In Adobe Illustrator we converted a character from a symbol font (NucleusOne) into paths (Type, Create Outlines), stretched it a bit horizontally, then copied it to the clipboard (Ctrl/⌘-C). In Photoshop we pasted the clipboard contents (Ctrl/⌘-V), choosing Paste As Paths in the Paste dialog box. Then we turned the path into a selection (click the marching ants circle icon at the bottom of the Paths palette, near the center). We clicked the New Layer icon in the center at the bottom of the Layers palette and filled the selection with black (press "D" for the default Foreground and Background colors and then Alt/Option-Delete to fill with the Foreground color). Deselect (Ctrl/⌘-D).

3 Making the outer glow. With the new layer active, move the cursor over its *name* (not its thumbnail) in the Layers palette. Right-click (Windows) or Control-click (Mac) to open a context-sensitive menu where you can choose Effects to open the Effects dialog box so the glowing colors can be added. Although we tend to think of a Drop Shadow as being a darkening effect, you can begin to explore other possibilities simply by changing the color and blending mode. Change the Mode to Screen and click the color swatch so you can change the color to red.

3a

Opening the Effects dialog box by choosing from the context-sensitive menu

3b

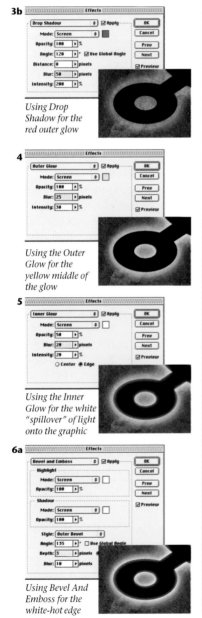

Using Drop Shadow for the red outer glow

4

Using the Outer Glow for the yellow middle of the glow

5

Using the Inner Glow for the white "spillover" of light onto the graphic

6a

Using Bevel And Emboss for the white-hot edge

Set the Opacity, Blur, and Intensity fairly high for this outermost glow. We used settings of 100% for Opacity, 50 pixels (the maximum setting) for Blur, and 200% for Intensity. Leave the Distance setting at 0; this way, no matter what the Angle setting is, the glow will be centered behind the graphic, spreading out equally in all directions.

4 Making the middle glow. For the yellow glow, choose Outer Glow from the list in the upper left corner of the Effects dialog box and make sure the Apply box is checked. (For any Effect, until the Apply box is checked, all the choices will be dimmed and you won't be able to add the Effect.) You can use the standard yellow glow in Screen mode at 100% Opacity. The Blur and Intensity should be set lower than for the red glow. We used 25 for the Blur and 30 for the Intensity.

5 Creating a "spill" of light. You can use the Inner Glow to create the light that spills over the edges and around to the front of the graphic. Use white for the color — the same color that will be used in step 6 for the innermost, hottest glow just outside the edge. Use smaller Blur and Intensity settings than for either of the other glows. We used 20 for both the Blur and the Intensity and reduced the Opacity to 50% for a subtle effect.

6 Making the hottest glow. For the final edge treatment, choose Bevel And Emboss from the list of Effects. Choose Outer Bevel for the Style in the bottom section of the box. To make a soft glow rather than a sharp bevel, use a low setting for Depth; we used 3. We set the Blur at 10 to produce a fairly intense glow just at the edge. For both the Highlight and the Shadow, choose Screen for the Mode and white for the color. The result will be a glow that spreads out on both sides of the Angle you designate. In some areas the glow will be very narrow, so the overall glow effect won't be uniform. But the variation actually makes the effect more dynamic.

7 Experimenting. To try other colors, duplicate the Effects layer by dragging its name to the New Layer icon. Then turn off the eye icon for the one of the copies and in the other copy double-click the "f" icon to open the Effects box so you can try different colors and settings.

6b

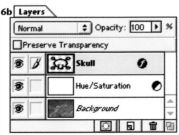

The final Layers palette for the image shown at the top of page 283

7

A variation made by changing colors and boosting Intensity of the outer and middle glows

Lighting a Fire

Overview *With graphics stored in an alpha channel, duplicate the channel; run a series of filters to create gray "flames"; convert to Indexed Color and apply the Black Body color table; convert to RGB; make a layer from the original "Graphic" channel; apply glows.*

"Fire" image file and Action

Original "Graphic" alpha channel in a 1000-pixel-wide Grayscale file. A duplicate alpha channel was created for filtering.

2a

The image is rotated 90° clockwise and the Wind filter is applied several times to the duplicate alpha channel.

2b

The results of applying the Wind filter and rotating the image back to its original orientation

A CONVINCING FLAME EFFECT can be helpful in making the point that something is not just hot — but *hot!* To create flames that rise from the name of this golden chili pepper, we started with a display font called Whimsy Baroque and elaborated on "Sal's Flaming Text Effect" developed by Sal Giliberto. After developing the flames in a grayscale file, we used Photoshop's Black Body color table to really light them up. We recorded an Action as we developed the flame treatment, so it can be quickly and easily applied to other type and graphics.

1 Starting with type. Open a new Grayscale file (File, New) to contain the type or graphics that you want to set afire. We used a 1000-pixel-wide file. In the Channels palette, add an alpha channel by clicking the New Channel icon next to the trash icon at the bottom of the palette. With this new channel (#2) active, import or create white type or graphics. (Step 1 of "Carving" on page 288 and step 2 of "Adding a Multicolor Glow" on page 283 provide pointers for adding type or graphics to an alpha channel.)

2 Starting the flames. Retaining the original "Graphic" channel #2 so you can use it later, duplicate it by dragging its name to the New Channel icon. The new alpha channel will be visible and active.

The first step in generating the gray matter that will become the flames is to apply the Wind filter. This filter creates a horizontal distortion, but you want the flames to rise. So start the process by choosing Image, Rotate Canvas, 90° CW to turn the graphic on its side. Then choose Filter, Distort, Wind. Choose Blast for the Method, and From The Right for the Direction, and click OK to run the filter.

For our 1000-pixel-wide file, we ran the filter a total of three times. (If you're starting with a higher-resolution file, you'll probably want to run the filter a few more times, and in later steps you'll also want to proportionally increase any filter settings that are expressed in pixels.)

3 Generating grayscale information. The Wind filter that you just applied has made white streaks on the black background. To broaden the range of gray tones that you'll be translating to color later, use the Gaussian Blur filter (Filter, Blur, Gaussian Blur). We used a Radius setting of 3 to blur the pixelated lines but still retain the general shapes produced by the Wind filter.

3

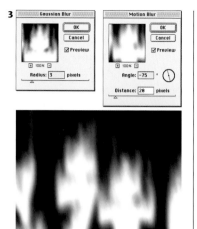

Generating gray tones with a Gaussian Blur and adding a "breeze" with Motion Blur

4a

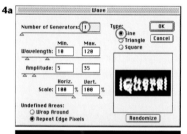

Applying the Wave filter

4b

Adding edge detail with the Ocean Ripple filter

4 Blowing on the flames. To make the flames more dynamic, you can introduce a slight breeze and wavering fluctuations. For the breeze we used the Motion Blur filter (Filter, Blur, Motion Blur), dragging the Angle dial to set the direction at just off vertical, and setting the distance at 20.

The Wave filter can supply most of the wavering: Choose Filter, Distort, Wave. We changed the Number Of Generations to 1 but otherwise used the default Sine settings. Experiment with the settings until you get a result you like in the Wave dialog's preview box, then click OK.

Even without changing the settings between runs, the result of running the Wave filter is slightly different each time since the effect is random within the Max and Min settings established in the dialog box. So if you want to try a few variations to see if you get a result you like even better, you can do it this way: After you've achieved a result you like pretty well and clicked OK to close the dialog, duplicate the file (Image, Duplicate) so that you have an untouched copy if your experiments don't work out. Go back to the original file and press Ctrl/⌘-Z to undo the Wave filter. Then press Ctrl/⌘-F to rerun the filter. Compare the result with the untouched copy, and keep the one you like — or continue to undo and rerun until you're satisfied.

To add detail at the edges of the flames, you can use the Ocean Ripple filter (Filter, Distort, Ocean Ripple). We used the maximum setting for Ripple Size (wave length) and a low Ripple Magnitude (wave height).

5 Adding color. To translate the grays to fire colors, you'll need to put the flaming graphic into a layer: With the finished alpha channel active, select all (Ctrl/⌘-A) and copy (Ctrl/⌘-C). Press Ctrl/⌘-1 to make the main Black channel (#1) active, and paste (Ctrl/⌘-V) to create a new layer. Then press Ctrl/⌘-E to merge it with the original *Background* layer, flattening the file.

Now start the coloring process by converting the file to Indexed Color — not RGB (Image, Mode, Indexed Color). You won't see any

4c

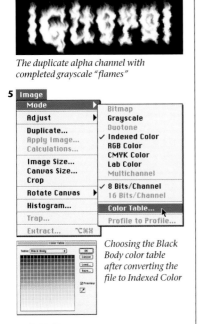

The duplicate alpha channel with completed grayscale "flames"

5

Choosing the Black Body color table after converting the file to Indexed Color

6

The result of converting from Indexed Color to RGB Color and adding a layer with black type

7a

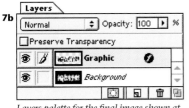

Heating up the edges of the black type with Layer Effects — Inner Glow (shown) and Outer Glow

7b

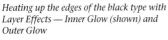

Layers palette for the final image shown at the top of page 285

color change with the mode conversion, but now you can "remap" the Grayscale indexed palette to the fire colors by choosing Image, Mode, Color Table and choosing Black Body. The whites remain white, light grays become yellow, and middle grays become red.

6 Topping with black type. In order to add another layer to put your original black type or graphic in front of the flames, you'll need to convert the file to RGB, since Indexed Color files can't include more than one layer. Choose Image, Mode, RGB Color.

Now add a new layer by clicking the New Layer icon in the middle at the bottom of the Layers palette. To load the original "Graphic" channel (it's now channel #4 of the color file) as a selection, Ctrl/⌘-click its name in the Channels palette; this loads the channel but does not activate it. Fill the selection with black (press the "D" key to set the default colors, then Alt/Option-Delete to fill).

7 Heating the type. To slightly wrap the fire around the edges of the type, you can use two Layer Effects — the Inner Glow and Outer Glow. Choose Layer, Effects, Inner Glow and adjust the settings in the Effects dialog box. We increased the Blur to 10 pixels and the Intensity to 50. Next choose Outer Glow from the list at the top of the box, and adjust the settings. We used the same settings as for Inner Glow. Click OK to close the Effects box. *Wow*

VARIATIONS ON A THEME

The flame treatment in "Lighting a Fire" can be reproduced on any grayscale file with type or another element in the first alpha channel (#2), named "Graphic." With such a file ready and waiting, load the **Wow Actions** by choosing Load Actions from the Actions palette's pop-out menu and choosing Wow Actions from the Wow CD-ROM. In the Actions palette, pop open the Wow Actions folder by clicking the arrow in front of its name. Click on the "8-Fire" name and click the Play (arrow) button at the bottom of the palette.

If you start with a file that's very much bigger than 1000 pixels wide and find that the effect isn't dramatic enough, you can make changes to the Action before you start over and run it again: Add more repetitions of the Wind filter by dragging one of the Wind steps to the New Action button next to the trash icon at the bottom of the Actions palette. To change settings for any of the filters, click in the dialog toggle box to the left of that step in the Actions palette to make the Action stop at that point and let you change the values for that filter.

The Wow Fire Action was applied to a grayscale file with the TV graphic stored in an alpha channel. After the Action was run, the color was changed by applying a Hue/Saturation Adjustment layer.

Carving

Overview *In an Adjustment layer above the background, use Layer Effects to create the edges and shadows for the carving and to darken the "recessed" area; offset the recessed area to increase the dimensional effect.*

"Carving" image and Action

1

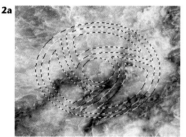

The original Background image and the white-on-black graphic stored in channel #4

2a

Channel #4 loaded as a selection

2b

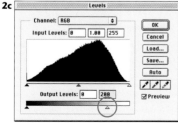

Adding a Levels Adjustment layer

2c

Darkening the "recessed" areas

SOMETIMES ALL YOU NEED to create the illusion of the third dimension is an edge, defined by subtle highlights and shadows that add thickness to a two-dimensional graphic to make it look carved or cut out. The technique that produced the carving above uses an Adjustment layer with Layer Effects applied. This method is not capable of creating results as sophisticated as the Lighting Effects filter. But the effect is convincing. And because the dimensionality is created on an Adjustment layer, you can change materials instantly, just by dragging and dropping a new background image.

1 Setting up the file. The starting point is a background image suitable for carving, with a white-on-black graphic stored in an alpha channel; the white areas should be the areas you want to recess, or carve. To put a graphic into an alpha channel you can open the RGB image you want to "carve," open the Channels palette, create an alpha channel by clicking the New Channel icon to the left of the trash icon at the bottom of the palette, and place the graphic into it (File, Place). If necessary, center and scale the graphic before pressing the Enter/Return key to finalize the placement.

2 Adding an Adjustment layer. To make an Adjustment layer that includes a mask in the shape of your graphic, start by loading the alpha channel as a selection (Ctrl/⌘-click on the channel's name in the Channels palette, or press Ctrl-Alt-4 [Windows] or ⌘-Option-4 [Mac]).

Then Ctrl/⌘-click the New Layer icon, in the middle at the bottom of the Layers palette, to add an Adjustment layer. Choose Levels as the Type and click OK.

In the Levels dialog box, move the white Output Levels slider inward to darken the background image in the selected areas of the

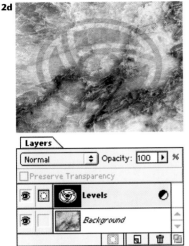

2d

The result of adding the Levels Adjustment layer

3

Using the Inner Shadow Layer Effect to cast a shadow into the recessed area

4

Creating the bevel highlight and shadow with the Outer Bevel Effect

graphic without increasing contrast as would happen if you darkened them using the Input sliders.

3 Casting a shadow into the recessed interior. In general, when you add multiple Layer Effects it's easier to see how the overall treatment is developing if you start with the most significant of the Effects you will apply and then add the subtler ones. The settings you use will depend on the effect you want and the texture you're carving.

To create the shadow for the carving, choose Layer, Effects, Inner Shadow and choose the settings you like for Opacity, and Blur. Use the default black color or click on the color swatch to open the Color Picker, and use its cursor to sample a dark color from the background. Instead of entering values for Angle and Distance, you can use the cursor directly in the image to move the shadow interactively, and the Distance and Angle settings will reflect what you've done. If you leave the default Use Global Angle turned on, the same Angle will be used for any other Effects you add. Don't close the Effects dialog box yet.

4 Creating the beveled edge. Once you've created the shadow, you can choose Bevel And Emboss from the list in the upper left corner of the Effects box. Click the Apply checkbox and enter settings to create the effect you want. We chose Outer Bevel for the Style, which would build the bevel outward from the white area of the mask. We increased the Intensity to 100% for both Highlight and Shadow. We also changed the Blending modes: For the Highlight, the Color Dodge mode would exaggerate the specular highlight on the beveled edge by increasing the saturation of the colors. For the Shadow, the Soft Light mode would maintain detail and colors on the shaded areas of the bevel. For a sharp bevel we used a high Depth setting and a low Blur.

5 Enhancing the shadow. You can use the Inner Glow, as we did, to create a dark "halo" that will help define the edge of the carved area. We used a black shadow in Color Burn mode to maintain the colors in the darkened areas, lowered the Opacity, and increased the Blur setting. Since we wanted the shadow at the edges, we left the default Edge choice.

Next we used the Drop Shadow for an even more subtle (and somewhat counter-intuitive) addition to the shading. Adding a drop shadow to the white area of the mask actually "threw" the effect onto the bevel edges and the top (uncarved) surfaces. We put the Drop Shadow in Overlay mode to increase the contrast and saturation. Using a large Blur setting made the effect subtle and spread it from bevels onto the top surfaces. Since we wanted the effect to spread evenly from the edges, we left the Distance setting at 0.

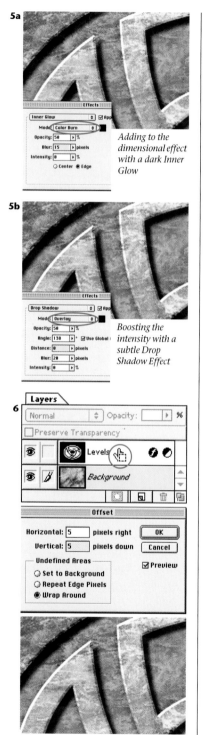

5a

Adding to the dimensional effect with a dark Inner Glow

5b

Boosting the intensity with a subtle Drop Shadow Effect

6

Offsetting the recessed surface. Note the shift in position of the orange vein in the marble.

6 Offsetting the recessed surface. To add to the illusion of depth, we shifted the image slightly in the recessed areas. To do this, click on the background layer to activate it and then load the Adjustment layer's mask as a selection by Ctrl/⌘-clicking on the name of the Adjustment layer's name in the Layers palette; this will select the recessed areas of the carving. Choose Filter, Other, Offset and enter values that will offset the texture just enough so it doesn't align with the texture in the raised areas.

7 Experimenting. Once you've developed your carving effect, it's easy to apply it to different backgrounds. Simply dragging-and-dropping other textures below the Adjustment layer and turning on or off the appropriate eye icons will apply the Adjustment layer's Effects to the new images. Then you can run the Offset filter as in step 6.

8 Using two textures. To use two different textures, one for the face of the carving and the other for the recessed areas, drag-and-drop the texture for the recessed area into the file above the background. Then make a layer mask that allows the texture to show only the interior areas, as follows: Ctrl/⌘-click the Adjustment layer's thumbnail to load it as a selection again. Then click the new texture's thumbnail to make it the active layer. Click the Add Layer Mask icon, on the left at the bottom of the palette. ✐

7

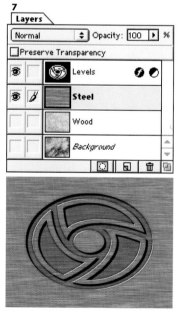

Changing the texture

8

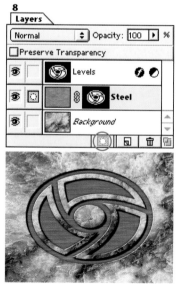

Using a second texture for the recessed areas

Chiseled in Stone

Overview *Import type or graphics into an alpha channel in a background texture file; run the KPT Gradient Designer filter on a new, black-filled alpha channel; use the gradient-filled channel and the Lighting Effects filter to "emboss" the background; apply Layer Effects to add shadows and enhance highlights.*

IMAGE "Chiseled" image

1a

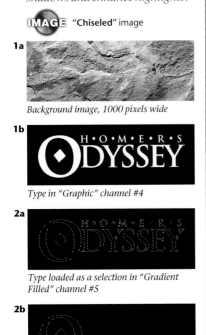

Background image, 1000 pixels wide

1b

Type in "Graphic" channel #4

2a

Type loaded as a selection in "Gradient Filled" channel #5

2b

Part of the selection removed, leaving only the single large letter

2c

Setting up a gradient with the KPT Gradient Designer

A KEY CHARACTERISTIC OF CHISELED TYPE is the sharp "V"-shaped cross-section of the carved strokes of the letters. Whether you raise the lettering or cut it in, the key to creating chiseled type in Photoshop is the KPT Gradient Designer filter, which is part of Kai's Power Tools (any version from 3.0.1 on; see page 214). **Note:** The KPT Gradient Designer plug-in is *not* included on the CD-ROM that comes with this book. If you want to use it, you'll have to buy the Kai's Power Tools filter set from MetaCreations (see the Appendix).

Using the KPT Gradient Designer filter in Circular Shapeburst mode with a black-to-white gradation gives you the grayscale material that the Lighting Effects filter can work with to create the smooth, raised center ridges and sharp corners characteristic of raised chiseled lettering, or the sharp-sided channels of recessed carving. As an artifact, the filter even produces the gouge marks of the chisel. To give the chiseled lettering the same "weathered" look as the background, you can use the grayscale information from one of the background's color channels to modify the filtered type before you apply Lighting Effects.

1 Assembling the raw materials. Start with an RGB image of the surface you want to carve, and type or graphics stored in an alpha channel (#4). (If you need instructions for getting type or graphics into an alpha channel, see step 1 of "Carving" on page 288.)

2 Making a channel for chiseling. Next you'll use channel #4 to help generate the chiseling channel (#5). To make the new channel, Alt/Option-click the New Channel icon next to the trash icon at the bottom of the palette; Alt/Option-clicking opens the New Channel dialog box so you can name the channel as you add it. Then load channel #4 as a selection by Ctrl/⌘-clicking on its thumbnail in the Channels palette.

If your type varies in size as ours did, you'll need to apply the KPT Gradient Designer separately to the different sizes. To deselect the smaller type, leaving only the "O" selected, we used the polygon lasso: We subtracted the other letters from the selection by holding down the Alt/Option key as we clicked from point to point to surround them.

With the KPT Gradient Designer installed, choose Filter, KPT 3.0, KPT Gradient Designer, and choose Circular Shapeburst from the Mode pop-up menu. Position the cursor at the left end of the

2d

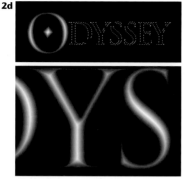

The gradient was applied first to the "O" and then to the other letters

3a

The Green channel

3b

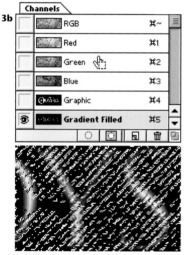

Loading the Green channel as a selection in channel #5

3c

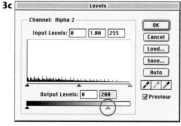

Darkening the selected areas with Levels

gradient band (below the curved bracket that extends across the middle of the Gradient Designer interface) and press and hold the mouse button. The cursor will turn into an eyedropper; a spectrum gradient band will appear, and above it a black-to-white gradient; drag the eyedropper over to the white end of this gradient and release the mouse button. Then repeat this color-sampling procedure, but this time drag the eyedropper from the white to the black end of the gradient band. When you finish, the interface should look pretty much like the one in figure 2c, with a shapeburst in the center box that's white in the middle and black at the edges. (If it's black in the middle instead, pop out the menu from the gradient icon and switch from Sawtooth B–>A to Sawtooth A–>B, or vice versa, so your Gradient Designer setup matches figure 2c.) Click OK. If you have different-size letters as we did, repeat the process of loading channel #4 as a selection in channel #5, deleting parts of the selection and running the KPT Gradient Designer on the remaining letters (you can rerun the filter by pressing Ctrl/⌘-F). We ran the Gradient Designer once more — on "DYSSEY," since all these letters are the same weight.

We decided to use a different treatment on "H•O•M•E•R•S," as described in step 5.

3 Adding texture to the letters. Now you can add texture to the dimensionality created by the Gradient Designer, to make the letters look like they were chiseled from the same substance as the original background. The texture can be found in one of the color channels (Red, Green, or Blue). You can press Ctrl/⌘ and the channel number (1, 2, or 3) to look at each channel in turn, to see which shows the best contrast in the texture detail. When you've chosen one, in the Channels palette click on the thumbnail of the channel that contains the gradient-filled type (channel #5) in order to make it the active channel. Then Ctrl/⌘-click the thumbnail of the color channel you've chosen to load that channel as a selection. We used the Green channel because it best showed the surface texture of the stone.

With the selection active, choose Image, Adjust, Levels and move the Output Levels white point slider inward to slightly darken the gray tones in the selected areas of the gradient-filled type. This slight texturing of the light-to-dark gradient will allow the embossing effect that follows in step 4 to generate surface detail that matches the background photo.

4 Chiseling the surface. In the Layers palette, duplicate the *Background* layer by dragging its name to the New Layer icon in the middle at the bottom of the palette. Then, with this new layer active, choose Filter, Render, Lighting Effects. In the Lighting Effects dialog box make sure White Is High is turned on and choose the gradient-filled alpha channel (#5) as the Texture Channel.

The other settings you use will vary, depending on the pixel dimensions of your file, the darkness of your background, and the

3d

Channel #5 with texture applied

4a

A duplicate layer made for chiseling

4b

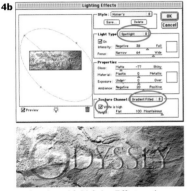

Embossing with Lighting Effects, using a Spotlight and Texture Channel

5a

Copying letters to a new layer so that Layer Effects could be applied

5b

Adding Layer Effects: The Drop Shadow color was sampled from the image. The Outer Glow added a dark halo for contrast. And the Inner Bevel was set to create a diffuse brightening effect.

amount of contrast you want between the background and the chiseled letters. Using a Spotlight for the Light Type will add drama; it will also provide a visual clue about whether the chiseled graphic is raised or recessed. For a less dramatic emboss, try a Directional light, but keep in mind that it won't be as easy for the viewer to tell whether the carved type or graphic is projecting from the surface or receding. The Properties settings and the Height setting for the Texture Channel affect the shadow density and contrast of the chiseled ridge.

5 Enhancing the shading. In order to use Layer Effects to create a shadow and other effects that will add to the illusion of raised lettering, you'll need to isolate a copy of the chiseled type on a layer of its own, separate from the lighted background that now holds it. To do that, load channel #4 as a selection (we then subtracted the "H•O•M•E•R•S" from the selection) and copy the selected type to make a new layer (Ctrl/⌘-J).

In the Layers palette, position the cursor over the *name* — not the thumbnail — of the new layer, and hold down the right mouse button (Windows) or Control key (Mac) as you drag to open the context-sensitive menu and select Effects. In the Effects dialog box, you'll be applying the Drop Shadow, Outer Glow, and Bevel And Emboss Inner Bevel.

Use the **Drop Shadow** to make the shadow cast by the raised letters onto the background. Click the color swatch and sample a dark color from the image. We sampled the deep shadow that appears in the background just above the "Y." The shadows in the background image are quite sharp. A Blur setting of only 5 pixels made a matching sharp-edged shadow for this 1000-pixel-wide image. With the Effects dialog box still open, move the cursor onto the image itself and drag to offset the shadow.

Use the **Outer Glow** to add contrast at the edge of the letters. Again, sample a dark color from the image, and set the mode to Multiply. We found that a Blur setting of 15 pixels created the darkness we wanted.

Use the **Inner Bevel** to enhance the brightness and contrast on the highlighted bevel edges. Reducing the Shadow's Opacity to 0 will mean that the Shadow component of the Bevel has no effect. For the Highlight, set the Blur high so that no edge will be created — just an overall brightening of light areas; we used the maximum setting of 50 pixels. We used Overlay for the Mode and chose a light color. The effect was to lighten the highlighted bevels without adding another color and without lightening the dark areas of the texture.

6 Making type stand out. We made the small "H•O•M•E•R•S" lettering black, and then set it off by adding a white outline and by brightening the area immediately around each character. To "set" the type, we added a new layer, loaded the original graphic (channel #4) as a selection, subtracted all the large lettering from the selection, and filled the remaining selection with black, then deselected.

5c

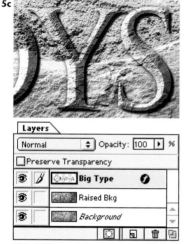

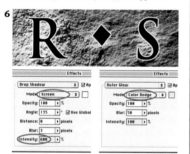

Chiseled type with Layer Effects applied

6

The small type, outlined with a high-intensity white Drop Shadow in Screen mode and spotlighted with the Outer Glow in Color Dodge mode

7

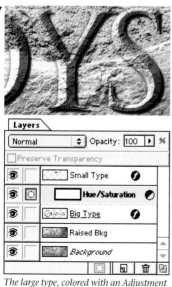

The large type, colored with an Adjustment layer in a clipping group

We opened the Effects dialog box and used the Drop Shadow to create a white outline: We set the Mode to Screen and clicked the color swatch and chose white. To get a sharp, strong outline we used a very slight Blur (3 pixels), and boosted the Intensity to 600%.

Next we used the Outer Glow to "shine" the rock face behind the letters: We used a 50-pixel Blur for a diffuse glow, and set the Mode to Color Dodge to saturate the colors of the rock in the glowing area around each letter.

7 Coloring the chiseled letters. You can leave the color of the chiseled type as it is, or change it to make it more distinct from the background, as we did. We used an Adjustment layer clipped to the Big Type layer so that only the large chiseled type would be affected: We clicked on the Big Type layer to activate it and added an Adjustment layer (Ctrl/⌘-click the New Layer icon at the bottom of the Layers palette). We chose Hue/Saturation as the Type, and clicked in the checkbox for Group With Previous Layer to make the clipping group. In the Hue/Saturation dialog box we moved the Saturation slider to the left and also changed the Hue. 〰

CHISELING IN

To make chiseled type look carved in instead of raised, turn off White Is High when you run the Lighting Effects filter at step 4 of "Chiseled in Stone." By experience we expect light to shine from the top down, whether it's sunlight outdoors or a ceiling light indoors. So position the light source to shine from somewhere above the image. We tend to view images and pages from the upper left, so positioning your light source there helps make the chiseling look recessed. Make sure the lighting you establish is dramatic, so the viewer will have no doubt where the light source is. Instead of the shadows and glows added at step 5 of "Chiseled in Stone," use Layer Effects that will enhance the "carved in" look: You can use Drop Shadow to better define the edges of the highlighted sides of the bevels; use black or a dark color sampled from the image, use a fairly small Blur setting and a relatively low Opacity, and drag the shadow just a little bit down and to the right (assuming that your light source is above and to the left). You can also use an Inner Bevel with both Highlight and Shadow in Overlay mode, using white for the Highlight color and black for the Shadow. This will add contrast without overwhelming the details of the texture. Using large Depth and Blur settings spreads the lighting across the bevel.

A Drop Shadow with a narrow offset helps define the edges of the letters. A diffuse Inner Bevel in Overlay mode increases contrast between carved faces.

Crystal Clear

Overview *Use the Glass filter and a custom-made displacement map to raise graphics from a background image; overlay an "environment" image to create reflections for the water or crystal shapes; use a clipping group to trim the shapes and apply Layer Effects to enhance refraction and reflection.*

 "**Crystal**" image and Actions

The original background (top left), the "environment" reflection photo, and the white-on-black graphic

2a

The blurred copy of the graphics channel

2b

Duplicating the blurred channel to create a separate grayscale Photoshop file to use with the Glass filter

JHD / ORIGINAL PHOTOS: © CORBIS IMAGES ROYALTY FREE, EXECUTIVE TEXTURES

SEVERAL OF PHOTOSHOP'S FILTERS use the lights and darks of a *displacement map* file to distort an image. If you use a recognizable shape as a displacement map, you can get some very interesting results, such as the look of water or crystal.

Besides the subtle highlights and shadows it uses to simulate the reflections and refractions of glass, Photoshop's Glass filter works like its cousin the Displace filter, by moving the pixels of the layer it's applied to. The distance each pixel moves depends on the luminance (or brightness) of the corresponding pixel in the displacement map. Any image in Photoshop format except a bitmap can serve as a displacement map. White pixels move their corresponding pixels in the filtered image the maximum positive (up or right) distance, black pixels produce the maximum negative (down or left) displacement, and 50% brightness produces no displacement at all. Here we used the Glass filter twice — once to distort the background to create the watery type and graphics, and again to add a distorted reflection of the environment. Several Layer Effects enhanced the lighting, adding to the realism of light interacting with the shapes.

1 Setting up the file. Choose an RGB background file and an RGB "environment" file to be reflected in the crystal or water you will create. It works well to choose a background image with detail that will show a distortion. And choose an environment photo with areas of contrasting light and dark. We chose a stone background and a dramatic abstract photo for the reflections.

Start working in the background image (you'll add the environment image at step 5). Open the Channels palette (Window, Show Channels) and create an alpha channel in the background file by clicking the New Channel icon, next to the trash icon at the bottom of the Channels palette. Create a white-on-black graphic in the

3

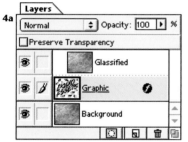

Before (top left) and after applying the Glass filter

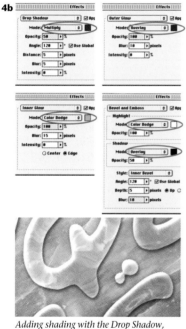

4a

Using a copy of the original graphic to "clip" the "glassified" refraction layer and apply Layer Effects

4b

Adding shading with the Drop Shadow, Outer Glow, and Bevel And Emboss, and internal reflections with Inner Glow.

channel or import an EPS from Adobe Illustrator or another Post-Script program using the File, Place command or copy-and-paste. If the background or alpha channel extends beyond the edges of the "frame" of your image, crop the file now to get rid of any unseen "big data" sticking out beyond the edges: Select all (Ctrl/⌘-A) and choose Image, Crop.

2 Making the displacement map. The next step is to create the Photoshop file that will be used as the displacement map with the Glass filter to raise the type and graphics out of the background image. Duplicate the graphics channel (#4) by dragging its icon to the New Channel icon to make channel #5. With the original graphic preserved in channel #4, you can blur channel #5 to create gray information that will round the edges of the type and graphics when the Glass filter is applied in step 3: With channel #5 active, choose Filter, Blur, Gaussian Blur. For our 1000-pixel-wide image, we used a setting of 7 pixels.

Next, since the Glass filter needs a separate file in Photoshop format to use as its displacement map, duplicate the blurred channel as a file by choosing Duplicate Channel from the Channels palette's pop-out menu. Choose *New* for the Destination Document in the Duplicate Channel dialog box. This will produce a new Grayscale file; save it in Photoshop format (File, Save As).

3 Creating refraction. Working in your main image file, duplicate the background image by dragging its name to the New Layer icon in the middle at the bottom of the Layers palette. Run the Glass filter on this layer, using the displacement map file you made in step 2: Choose Filter, Distort, Glass; choose Load Texture from the pop-out Texture list, and load the displacement map. The Distortion setting determines the degree of refraction — lower settings produce an effect that's more like water, higher settings a result that looks like crystal, which is denser than water and bends the light more. Adjust the Smoothness to taste, and don't change the Scaling.

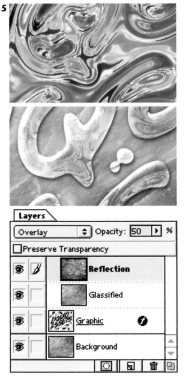

Adding the reflections layer to the clipping group

There are many ways to create a faded edge treatment like the edge on "Liquid Assets" at the top of page 295. One way is to add a layer with a soft-edged white frame, as follows: Add a new transparent layer above the image. Use the rectangular marquee to select the area that you want to keep. Feather the selection to round the corners and soften the edge (Select, Feather). Then invert the selection (Ctrl/⌘-Shift-I) and fill with white.

4 Trimming the edges and adding highlights and shadows. Now you'll add a copy of the original graphic as a layer between the original background and the "glassified" layer so you can use it to "clip" the glassified layer: Click the background layer's name in the Layers palette to activate it, and then click the New Layer icon. To add the original graphics to this layer, in the Channels palette Ctrl/⌘-click on the unblurred graphic channel (#4 here) to load it as a selection. Then fill the selection with black on your new transparent layer (pressing "D" restores the default black Foreground color and then pressing Alt/Option-Delete fills the selection with black). Deselect (Ctrl/⌘-D).

In the Layers palette, clicking on the border between the new layer and the glassified layer above it turns the two layers into a clipping group. First, it hides the glassification effect everywhere outside the graphic. And second, if you now use Layer Effects on the graphics layer to add shadows and highlights, they will also apply to the glassified layer.

We used a drop shadow to add depth to the raised water graphics (Layer, Effects, Drop Shadow), using the default Multiply mode and clicking the color swatch and sampling a shadow color from the background image.

To imitate the light reflected up from the background through the water, we used the Inner Glow effect (choose Inner Glow from the pop-out list in the Effects dialog box), this time sampling a color from the background and then using the Color Picker to choose a brighter and more saturated version of the hue; we used Color Dodge for the Mode setting.

We experimented with other Layer Effects, using a dark Outer Glow in Overlay mode, and an Inner Bevel (from Bevel And Emboss) with white Highlight in Color Dodge mode and black Shadow in Overlay mode. The combination of Layer Effects created a luminous effect and at the same time created strong directional lighting. We turned on Use Global Angle for the Drop Shadow and Inner Bevel (the only Effects we used that had an Angle setting), so the highlight and shadow directions would be coordinated for these two effects.

5 Creating reflections. With the glassified layer active, use the move tool to drag-and-drop your reflection image into the developing file. Again, as you did in step 1, select all and crop, so the Glass filter will work predictably. Run the Glass filter (as at step 3) on this new dragged-and-dropped reflections layer with the Distortion setting at least twice as high as you used in step 3. (We used 5 at step 3 and 20 here for the reflection.)

To complete the water or crystal effect, include the reflection layer in the existing clipping group by Alt/Option-clicking on the border between it and the glassified layer in the Layers palette. Change its blending mode to Overlay, and adjust its Opacity until you get the result you like best.

Chrome Plating

Overview *In an "environment" photo with a graphic in an alpha channel, use the Glass filter and a blurred displacement map to "emboss" the graphic on the photo; add shadows and highlights with Layer Effects; use a Plastic-Wrapped version of the graphic to add specular highlights; add hand-painted glints.*

ACTION IMAGE "Chrome" image and Action

1

A white-on-black graphic is stored in the first alpha channel of an RGB image that will serve as the reflection in the chrome.

2a

The Plastic Wrap filter is applied to an inverted (black-on-white) copy of the alpha channel.

2b

The artifacts at the edges of the "wrapped" graphic are cleaned up by loading the original graphic as a selection, contracting and inverting the selection, and filling with black.

2c

The completed "wrapped" channel

POLISHED CHROME IS UNIQUELY SHINY and reflective. One way to create chrome in Photoshop is by using the Glass and Plastic Wrap filters to produce the characteristic mirrored and curved surfaces. Then a gleam can be added to the edges by using Layer Effects to lighten the highlights, darken the shadows, and imitate colored lighting. Finally, hand-painted glints complete the illusion.

1 Setting up the file. Start with a photo that will provide the image material to be reflected in the chrome, and a white-on-black graphic stored in an alpha channel (#4). (If you need more information on getting a graphic into an alpha channel, see step 1 of "Forging Steel" on page 302.)

You might also want to add another photo as a contrasting background behind the chrome element you're about to generate, but in this case we would produce a polished but not mirrorlike background directly from the reflection image (in step 9), so we didn't need an additional photo.

At this point, to ensure that the Glass filter will perform as expected in step 4, get rid of any "big data" (parts of layers that extend beyond the edges of the image; see the "Bye-Bye Big Data" tip on page 296): Select all (Ctrl/⌘-A) and crop (Image, Crop).

2 Generating specular highlights. Next you'll use a duplicate of the alpha channel graphic to generate some surface highlights for the chrome. Duplicate the graphic channel (#4) by dragging it to the New Channel icon next to the trash icon at the bottom of the Channels palette. Then invert the tonality of the new (#5) channel (Ctrl/⌘-I) so you have a black-on-white image.

We could have used the Lighting Effects filter to produce the highlights we needed (this technique is described in step 3 of "Forging Steel" on page 303), but

OFFSETTING THE HIGHLIGHT

The highlight produced by the Plastic Wrap filter is always right in the middle of the area being filtered. If you want to move the highlight off dead center, increase the canvas size (Image, Canvas Size, adding new canvas disproportionately.

3a

Blurring a copy of the original graphic generates a range of grays at the edges.

3b

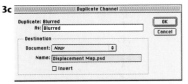

Duplicating the blurred alpha channel as a separate Photoshop file to use as the displacement map for the Glass filter.

3c

The "As" entry in the Duplicate Channel dialog box is the name of the layer that will be created. The "Document" entry is the name of the new file.

3d

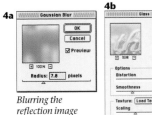

The displacement map file has to be saved before it can be used.

4a **4b**

Blurring the reflection image eliminates detail that would distract the eye, but keeps the "environmental" content needed to simulate chrome.

In general, the higher the Distortion setting in the Glass filter's dialog box, the shinier the surface appears to be.

4c

The relief and reflectivity created by the applying the Glass filter

the Plastic Wrap filter alone did a good job in this case, creating the "organic"-looking highlights we wanted for the curved surfaces. With the new channel (#5) active, apply the filter by choosing Filter, Artistic, Plastic Wrap.

Now trim off the background and the edge artifacts that Plastic Wrap can produce, as follows: With the wrapped channel active, load the original graphic channel as a selection by Ctrl/⌘-clicking on its name in the Channels palette. Shrink the selection (Select, Modify, Contract, 1 pixel). Then invert the selection (Shift-Ctrl/⌘-I) and fill with black (with an alpha channel active, pressing "D" makes *black* the Background color; then pressing the Delete key fills the selection with black). This specular-highlights channel can sit until you need it at step 7.

3 Making a displacement map. To make the grayscale displacement map image that the Glass filter needs for "embossing" the graphic out of the background image, you'll start with another copy of the original graphic: Duplicate the graphic channel by dragging it to the New Channel icon (to make channel #6). To get the gray information needed for a rounded edge, choose Filter, Blur, Gaussian Blur; we used a Radius setting of 7 for this 1000-pixel-wide image. Like Photoshop's Displace filter, the Glass filter requires the displacement map to be a file in Photoshop format. So the next step is to duplicate the blurred channel as a file: Choose Duplicate Channel from the Channels palette's pop-out menu and choose *New* for the Destination Document. Save the new file to disk (File, Save As).

4 Embossing the graphic. In your developing chrome file, work in the Layers palette to duplicate the reflection photo for safekeeping by dragging its layer's name to the New Layer icon, in the middle at the bottom of the palette. Then blur the top copy of the two (our "Bkg Blurred" layer) so its details won't distract the eye when it becomes the reflection in the chrome (Filter, Blur, Gaussian Blur).

Next, duplicate the blurred background layer and use the Glass filter to raise the graphic from the surface of this new layer (ours is called "Glassified"): Choose Filter, Distort, Glass and choose Load Texture from the pop-out Texture menu, choosing the displacement map file you saved in step 3. Experiment with the Distortion and Smoothness settings, but don't change the Scaling.

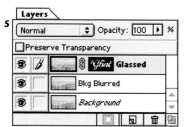

5

A layer mask is added to the "glassified" layer to define an edge to which Layer Effects can be applied.

6a

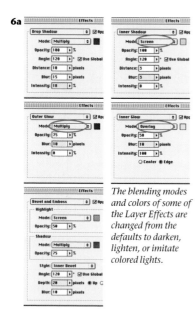

The blending modes and colors of some of the Layer Effects are changed from the defaults to darken, lighten, or imitate colored lights.

6b

The result of applying the Layer Effects

5 Trimming the outer edge. Now you can remove the background of the raised graphic, leaving a clean, sharp edge. If you do this by means of the layer mask, you'll still have the rounded outer edge available if you want to experiment with it later, expanding or softening the edge. To make the layer mask, make sure the newly "glassified" layer is active and load the original graphic as a selection by Ctrl/⌘-clicking on it (#4) in the Channels palette. Back in the Layers palette, click the Add Layer Mask icon.

6 "Popping" the chrome graphic. Now you can use Layer Effects to make the chrome graphic stand out from its background and to add some of the specular highlights that will make it shiny. To accentuate the depth, use a Drop Shadow and dark Outer Glow: right-click (Windows) or Control-click (Mac) on the *name* (not the thumbnail) of the glassified layer to open a context-sensitive menu and choose Effects. You'll use the Drop Shadow to create an offset shadow, and the Outer Glow to produce a narrower dark "halo" around the entire chrome graphic. In the **Drop Shadow** section of the Effects dialog box, click the color swatch and sample a dark color from the image. Adjust the Blur, Distance, Angle, and Intensity settings to make a fairly soft shadow. Then choose **Outer Glow** from the pop-out list of effects. Change the Mode to Multiply, and use the same shadow color or choose another one from the image.

To further accentuate the edges, choose **Bevel And Emboss** from the pop-out list in the Effects dialog box and choose **Inner Bevel** for the Style. Again sample colors from the image, using the default Screen and Multiply modes to create highlights and shadows. Adjust the Depth and Blur settings to create the kind of bevel you want for the edge. We used settings of 20 for Depth and 10 for Blur to create distinct but rounded edges.

7a

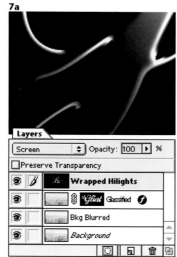

The "wrapped" layer (shown by itself here) is added in Screen mode.

7b

In Screen mode the light areas of the Wrapped Hilights layer brighten the image in the layers underneath. The dark areas of the layer have no effect in this mode.

8a

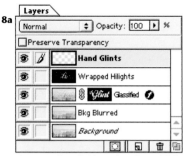

A separate layer in Normal mode provided a place for adding white glints that wouldn't be trimmed by the mask in the Glassified layer and that could easily be erased or changed if necessary.

8b

Before (left) and after adding hot spots at some of the corners of the chrome element

9a

A Hue/Saturation Adjustment layer was used to color and darken the background.

You can add subtle color highlights with the Inner Shadow and Inner Glow effects, experimenting with the Mode and color of each to imitate colored light sources.

5 Adding the gleam. Now it's time to use the Plastic-Wrapped alpha channel (#5) to generate the gleaming edge of the top surface of the chrome. Click the wrapped channel's name in the Channels palette to activate the channel (#6). Then select all (Ctrl/⌘-A) and copy (Ctrl/⌘-C). In the Layers palette, activate the top (glassified) layer, and then paste (Ctrl/⌘-V) to add a new layer containing the wrapped graphic. Set this layer's blending mode to Screen so the light parts of the image will lighten the image below. Use Levels (Ctrl/⌘-L) to adjust the intensity of the highlighting.

8 Putting on the glints. To add to the believability of the chrome treatment, you can add the small specular "hot spots" characteristic of a really shiny surface: Add an empty layer at the top of the stack by clicking the New Layer icon. Click with a small soft-tipped airbrush with white paint to apply a few sparkles at the edges of the graphic.

9 "Painting" the surface underneath. To colorize and darken the blurred background as we did, as if it were a painted and polished but not mirror-shiny surface, you can activate that layer by clicking on its name in the Layers palette and then add an Adjustment layer above it by Ctrl/⌘-clicking the New Layer icon. Choose Hue/Saturation for the Type, click the Colorize checkbox to turn on this feature, and adjust the color until it looks the way you want it. We reduced the Saturation and Lightness and shifted the Hue.

To finish the chrome shown at the top of page 298, we used another Hue/Saturation adjustment layer, this one with a layer mask that would allow us to "groove" the surface to make a panel. We used the rectangular marquee to select the shape we wanted for the contrasting panel, then Ctrl/⌘-clicked the New Layer icon to make the Adjustment layer, and adjusted the color. This time it wasn't necessary to turn on the Colorize box; we merely adjusted the Hue.

A **Bevel And Emboss Layer Effect** was also added to this second Hue/Saturation layer, and **Pillow Emboss** was chosen for the Style.

9b

Another Hue/Saturation Adjustment layer with a built-in mask is used to change the color across the middle of the background image and to add "pillow" embossing.

Forging Steel

Overview *Make two alpha channels, one with a white-on-black graphic and one with a blurred and trimmed version; "emboss" a 3D version of the graphic on a white background with the Lighting Effects filter; add more highlights with the Plastic Wrap filter; color with Adjustment layers; trim the "metal" with a clipping group; add a brushed texture and a dark "halo."*

ACTION **IMAGE** "Brushed Steel" image and Actions

1

Original graphic in channel #4 of a 1000-pixel-wide file

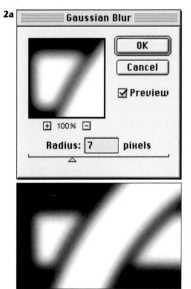

2a Gaussian Blur

Blurring a duplicate graphic in channel #5

STEEL CAN HAVE A HIGHLY POLISHED, mirrorlike surface, or it can be dull, burnished, or brushed. Starting with a white *Background* layer and a white-on-black graphic in an alpha channel, you can use Photoshop to manufacture the steel. Then heat it to the point where it shows a rainbow sheen, brush the surface, and cut out a 3D version of the graphic, with perfectly beveled polished edges.

Step 3 of this technique uses the Lighting Effects filter, rather than Layer Effects, to make the bevel. We chose to do it this way because Lighting Effects — with its multiple colored lights, spot-lighting, and material settings — provides better control of the glint and shine on the beveled edges of the graphic. And the bevel itself, made from a specially prepared alpha channel, can be sharper-edged than bevels produced with Layer Effects.

1 Setting up the file. Start a new RGB file (File, New) with a white-filled *Background*. Open the Channels palette (Window, Show Channels) and add an alpha channel by clicking the New Channel icon next to the trash can icon at the bottom of the palette. You can either create a graphic in this channel by making a selection and filling with white, or import one as we did. Our logo was created in black in Adobe Illustrator, placed in the Photoshop file with the alpha channel (#4) active (File, Place), stretched to fit the file, turned into a selection by double-clicking inside the placement box, and filled with white.

(The pixel settings used for commands that come later in this technique were chosen based on our 1000-pixel-wide file size, on the relative width of the graphic shapes that made up our logo, and on how wide we wanted the bevels to be. If your file is a different size, or if the thicknesses of your graphic elements or the desired bevel are very different from ours, you'll need to adjust accordingly for any command that requires a setting in pixels.)

2 Making the alpha channel to use with Lighting Effects. In addition to the original graphic in channel #4, you'll need a

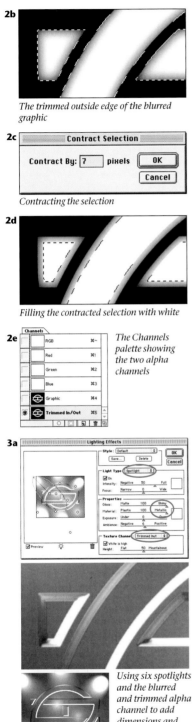

2b

The trimmed outside edge of the blurred graphic

2c

Contracting the selection

2d

Filling the contracted selection with white

2e *The Channels palette showing the two alpha channels*

3a

Using six spotlights and the blurred and trimmed alpha channel to add dimensions and specular highlights on the embossed layer

modified version of the graphic to produce the bevel when you apply the Lighting Effects filter in step 3. The channel will need to be white where you want it to create the top surface of the metal logo, black outside the logo shape, and shades of gray where you want to create the bevel. The edge between the bevel and the top surface should be sharp, so you'll want a sharp transition between the gray ramp that defines the bevel and the white area that forms the top surface. You can produce this alpha channel from a copy of the original graphic as follows: In the Channels palette, duplicate channel #4 by dragging its name to the New Channel icon next to the trash icon at the bottom of the palette. If you have a selection active, deselect (Ctrl/⌘-D). To create the "gray matter" for the bevel, blur the graphic by choosing Filter, Blur, Gaussian Blur; we used a Radius of 7 pixels.

Next trim the outside and inside edges: For the outside trim, load the original graphic as a selection by Ctrl/⌘-clicking Channel #4's name in the Channels palette; then invert the selection (Ctrl/⌘-Shift-I) and fill with black (if black is the Foreground color, you can press Alt/Option-Delete; to make black the Foreground color, press "D" for the default colors).

For the inside edge, load the original graphic as a selection (either re-invert the selection you just filled with black by pressing Ctrl/⌘-Shift-I, or Ctrl/⌘-click channel #4's name again). Then make the selection smaller by choosing Select, Modify, Contract. For the Contract By setting, use the same number of pixels you used for the blur, or a few pixels less for a narrower bevel. Fill the selection with white and deselect (Ctrl/⌘-D).

Finally, soften the edges of the alpha channel slightly to cut down on the artifacts that the Lighting Effects filter can sometimes produce: With channel #5 active and nothing selected, choose Filter, Blur, Gaussian Blur and set the Radius at 0.5 pixels.

3 Creating the 3D effect. Next you'll use the Lighting Effects filter to create a 3D beveled metal version of the graphic. In the Layers palette click on the name of the *Background* layer. Choose Filter, Render, Lighting Effects. Choose channel #5 from the Texture Channel pop-out list, and set up several spotlights to create the multiple specular highlighting associated with shiny metal; you can duplicate a light by Alt/Option-dragging its icon. You can get radically different results in the "personality" of the metal, depending on how you design the play of lights on the embossed object. In the Properties area of the dialog box, move the Gloss setting all the way to Shiny and the Material setting to Metallic. When the preview shows a result you like, click OK to accept it.

At this point we converted our *Background* layer to a layer with the option for transparency just by double-clicking its name in the Layers palette to open the Layer Options dialog box. We also renamed it, typing in the new name (we called ours "Embossed"), and clicked OK.

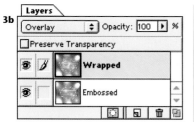

A duplicate layer for adding color and more highlights

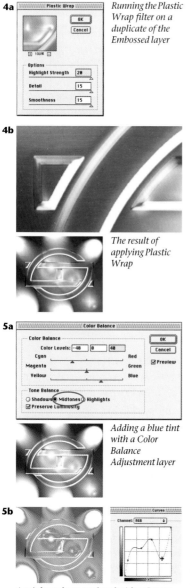

Running the Plastic Wrap filter on a duplicate of the Embossed layer

The result of applying Plastic Wrap

Adding a blue tint with a Color Balance Adjustment layer

A rainbow sheen produced with a Curves Adjustment layer

4 Adding more highlights. To make a layer whose highlights and color you can further adjust, Alt/Option-drag the Embossed layer's name to the New Layer icon in the middle at the bottom of the Layers palette. Running the Plastic Wrap filter (Filter, Artistic, Plastic Wrap) will make highlights and shadows that conform to the curves of the graphic. From the Layers palette's pop-out list of blending modes, choose Overlay. This mode will blend the new highlights and shadows, but not the midtones, with the layer below.

5 Coloring the steel. With the new layer active, Ctrl/⌘-click the New Layer icon to make an Adjustment layer that will store information for coloring the steel. In the New Adjustment Layer dialog box choose Color Balance for the type. In the Color Balance dialog box adjust the color sliders for the Midtones; we made adjustments that would give our steel a blue tone.

To get the multicolored sheen of heated or oiled steel, add another Adjustment layer, this time choosing Curves as the Type. In the Curves dialog box use the curve tool to place points that make a "roller coaster" curve and thus dramatically alternating colors.

6 Trimming away the excess. An easy way to get a clean edge for cutting the three-dimensional graphic from its background is to use a clipping group: Make a new layer, load the original graphic as a selection by pressing Ctrl-Alt-4 (Windows) or ⌘-Option-4 (Mac), and fill with the Foreground color (Alt/Option-Delete). Deselect (Ctrl/⌘-D). Drag the layer's name to the bottom of the list in the Layers palette. To make the nontransparent part of this layer (the graphic) serve as a mask for all the layers above, hold down the Alt/Option key and click on the border between the new layer's name and the one above it; continue Alt/Option-clicking up the Layers palette until all the layers are clipped by the graphic layer at the bottom. Because a single graphic makes the antialiased edge for all the layers above it, there is no "edge interference" from overlaid antialiased cut-outs created by deleting the background area or using layer masks. We also added another layer and filled it with white (Ctrl/⌘-Delete) so we could see the edges clearly.

6a

After trimming away the background area with a clipping group

7 Brushing the steel. To create the surface texture for the steel, start by adding another new layer, this one filled with gray: With the Curves Adjustment layer active, Alt/Option-click the New Layer icon. Name the new layer and put it in Overlay mode. Click in the check box for Fill With Overlay-Neutral Color (50% Gray). You can also check the Group With Previous

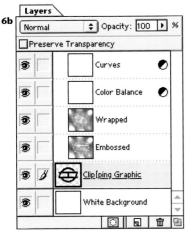

6b

The Layers after trimming the 3D logo with a clipping group and adding a white-filled layer as a background

7a

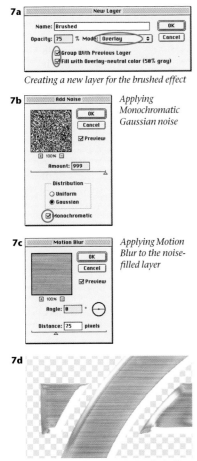

Creating a new layer for the brushed effect

7b

Applying Monochromatic Gaussian noise

7c

Applying Motion Blur to the noise-filled layer

7d

A layer mask eliminates the brushed effect from the bevel (viewed with the white background layer's eye icon turned off).

Layer box to include it within the clipping group. Finally, click OK. With the new layer active, choose Filter, Noise, Add Noise and add Monochromatic Gaussian noise at the highest setting. Then choose Filter, Blur, Motion Blur and set up a horizontal blur.

UNIFORM MOTION BLURS

The Motion Blur filter, applied to a noise-filled layer, can be useful for making textures like brushed metal. But the blur isn't complete at the edges. To make the blur uniform, use the rectangular marquee to select the uniform center of the layer, press Ctrl/⌘-T (for Free Transform) and Alt/Option-drag a middle handle to stretch the uniform part to the edge of the layer. (The Alt/Option key scales the selected area from the center outward.) Double-click in the selected area to complete the transformation.

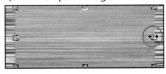

The developing file should now show a "brushed" surface over the entire logo. To remove the texture from the bevel, you can use a layer mask: In the Channels palette Ctrl/⌘-click on channel 4's name to load the original graphic as a selection; then choose Select, Modify, Contract and enter the same setting you used for the bevel size at step 2. With the brushed layer active, click the Add Layer Mask icon, on the left at the bottom of the palette. A "constricted graphic" layer mask will be created, allowing the brushed texture to show on the flat surface of the 3D logo but eliminating it from the beveled edge.

8a

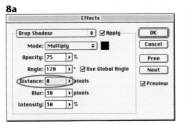

A Drop Shadow Effect with Blur set to 30 and Distance to 0 provides a dark "halo."

8b

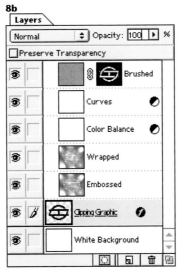

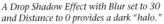

The layers palette for the finished 3D graphic, with Opacity for the Curves layer reduced to diminish the rainbow effect

8 Adding finishing touches. To add a shadow, or dark "halo," to set off the graphic, we used a Layer Effects Drop Shadow on the clipping layer (Layer, Effects, Drop Shadow). To subdue the rainbow sheen, we experimented with lowering the Opacity of the Curves and Color Balance Adjustment layers. A multi-pointed star created in Adobe Illustrator was dragged and dropped into the file to finish the logo shown at the top of page 302.

To make the *Crystal Hands Ad* for Kenwood's CyberTitler, **Jack Davis** began with two photos, one of the device alone and one with hands in typing position on the keyboard. He used the second photo as a reference for the size and orientation of the crystal hands, and the first as a background in Strata StudioPro, to help create realistic reflections and refractions in the crystal. The hands themselves were made from a purchased articulated model.

In StudioPro, the hands were arranged to match the photo and then fused so they would look solid when rendered with raytracing. Davis rendered the hands twice, once in front of the CyberTitler photo, and once with no background photo. He needed the second rendering to create an alpha channel that could be used to select the hands from the first rendering, so they could be layered above a silhouetted version of the original high-resolution photo, since the

rendering process had degraded the background photo used in StudioPro.

Davis made a drop shadow for the hands and then used the smudge tool to bend the shadow as it fell over the various edges of the keyboard. He also used Levels to exaggerate the highlights and shadows on the CyberTitler and enhanced the front edge of the keyboard with purple to match the lighting on the hands and in the background image.

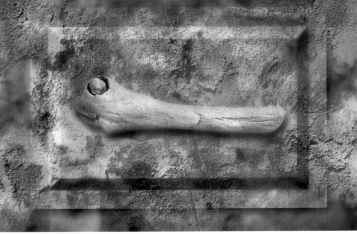

For his series *Kane, Kani, Ki,* **Russell Sparkman** created the textured backgrounds from two scanned photos layered together using the Layers palette's Opacity slider and the Layer Options dialog box.

After the combined texture was completed, the two layers were merged into one. This texture layer was then duplicated. An object — metal, crab shell, or driftwood — was dragged from another file into the texture file to create a third layer. A drop shadow was created under the object (see "Casting a Shadow" on page 280), and then the object, shadow, and top texture layer were merged, reducing the file to two layers again.

Sparkman created a new layer, specifying Overlay mode and Fill With Overlay-Neutral Color (50% Gray) in the New Layer dialog box. ▶ *To open the New Layer dialog box when you add a layer so you can set the blending mode and Opacity and name the layer, Alt/Option-click the New Layer icon in the middle at the bottom of the Layers palette.*

A bevel highlight and shadow were created on this layer, and the neutral layer was then merged with the object-shadow-texture layer.

Sparkman applied a Gaussian Blur to the underlying layer and darkened it using Image, Adjust, Levels. Then he used a combination of feathered selections and layer masks to delete parts of the upper layer to transparency, to partially reveal the underlying blurred and darkened original texture layer.

All layers were then merged and a duplicate of this layer was made. A Gaussian Blur was applied to the top layer and then it was darkened with the Output slider of the Levels dialog box. Then, using Layer Options in the top layer, Sparkman held down the Alt/Option key and dragged the left-hand portion of the "This Layers" white point slider over to a setting between 20 and 25. This began to reveal the brighter, sharper underlying layer through the darker, blurred upper layer.

Using heavily feathered selections, he made small "amoeba-like" selections of the upper layer and deleted these areas to transparency, revealing more of the underlying layer. After many areas had been selected and deleted, the end result was an effect of mottled light, with areas of sharpness and softness.

PHOTOSHOP AND THE WEB

The layered Photoshop file for the Electro-Matic Design logo is provided on the Wow CD-ROM. The logo was created in Illustrator, then finalized in Photoshop 5.5. The lightning elements were designed to be animated, with the artwork for the frames created in different Photoshop layers. In ImageReady the layers could be turned on and off to produce the animation frames. For efficiency in downloading, the file was divided into "slices" — only the parts that change as the lightning flashes are downloaded for the animation.

To save the "hot spots" for an image map graphic, create them as separate layers. You can assign the links in ImageReady by activating each layer in turn, and choosing Layer Options from the Layers palette's pop-out menu, or double-click the layer's name, just as in Photoshop. In the Layer Options dialog box, turn on the Use Layers As Image Maps option and assign the URL.

IF YOU'RE PREPARING WEB GRAPHICS in Photoshop, it really makes sense to upgrade to version 5.5 and give your Web graphics workflow the one-two punch provided by the new Photoshop and ImageReady combination. Version 2.0 of ImageReady comes on the Photoshop 5.5 Application CD-ROM, so adding it to your Web-graphics production kit is just a matter of upgrading from Photoshop 5 to 5.5. The techniques presented in this chapter were designed to take full advantage of the features in version 5.5 and ImageReady, though you'll find some workarounds to use with Photoshop 5 alone.

ESTABLISHING AN EFFICIENT WEB WORKFLOW

There's a great deal of overlap between the Web-related features in Photoshop 5.5 and ImageReady 2. This means that if you have both programs, there are many ways to proceed, moving back and forth between programs as you develop Web graphics. In general, though, it's often more efficient to create the graphics and images in Photoshop, and then move to ImageReady for final animation, coding, and export. Here are some suggestions:

- Photoshop is better equipped for creating and editing images than ImageReady is. So if you're developing simple **static images** to be posted on the Web, it makes sense to use Photoshop to create them and then use its File, **Save For Web** command to *optimize* them, which means to balance image quality with file size. In the Save For Web interface you can even preview how the file will look when viewed within a Web browser.

  With its ability to use an alpha channel for transparency, the File, Export, **GIF89a Export** command still has one trick that can't be done with Save For Web. You'll find an example of this workflow, which is the same in version 5 and 5.5, in "Silhouettes, Soft Shadows, and Transparency" on page 336.

- An *image map* is a single image on a Web page that contains multiple "hot spots," or areas that link to other files. If you're creating an **image map,** you can prepare the image file and separate the hot spots as layers in Photoshop or ImageReady. But assigning each layer to a link has to be done in ImageReady.

- Since several small image files download faster than a single large image, one way to reduce download time is to *slice* the

continued on page 311

Photoshop 5.5's Save For Web Interface

Photoshop 5.5's Save For Web interface is designed to help you balance image quality and file size. In its four-up mode (shown here) it shows your original image, the format and compression you're currently considering, and two other compression options. The display for each preview includes a listing of file sizes and typical download times. The toolbox in the Save For Web interface includes a hand tool for moving the preview to different areas of the image, a zoom tool for changing preview magnification, an eyedropper for sampling color, and a square that shows the current Foreground color.

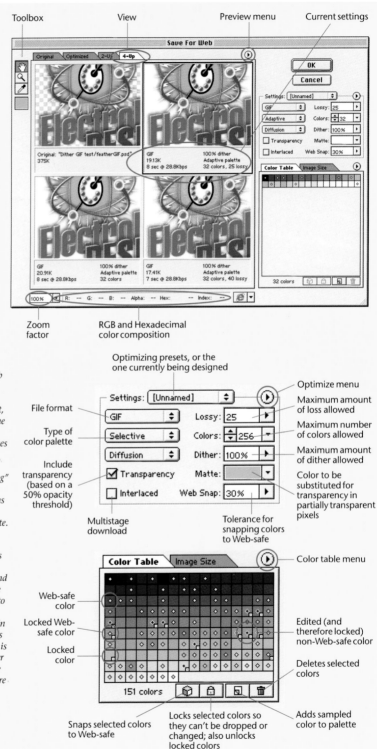

Toolbox · View · Preview menu · Current settings

Zoom factor

RGB and Hexadecimal color composition

The Optimize section of the Save For Web interface (shown at the right) lets you choose a preset compression scheme or design your own, including the file format, the type of color palette to be used, and the kind and extent of dithering that will be produced by Photoshop. Dithering increases the apparent number of colors in a GIF file's palette, but it makes the image less "compressible" (see "Run-Length Encoding" on page 315). The Web Snap setting determines how close a Web-safe color has to be to the original color before it will automatically snap to the Web-safe palette.

Optimizing presets, or the one currently being designed

Optimize menu

File format

Type of color palette

Include transparency (based on a 50% opacity threshold)

Multistage download

Maximum amount of loss allowed

Maximum number of colors allowed

Maximum amount of dither allowed

Color to be substituted for transparency in partially transparent pixels

Tolerance for snapping colors to Web-safe

The Color Table found in Photoshop 5.5's Save For Web interface and in Image-Ready's Optimize palette lets you select and sort colors and lock them so they won't be changed in the process of reducing colors to decrease file size. Small white diamonds indicate Web-safe colors; a small square in the lower right corner shows that a color is locked; a thick outline means that a color is currently selected. A black dot in the center indicates that the color has been edited by hand and is not Web-safe; edited colors are automatically locked.

Web-safe color

Locked Web-safe color

Locked color

Color table menu

Edited (and therefore locked) non-Web-safe color

Deletes selected colors

Adds sampled color to palette

Snaps selected colors to Web-safe

Locks selected colors so they can't be dropped or changed; also unlocks locked colors

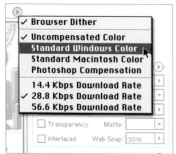

The Preview menu that pops out from Photoshop's Save For Web interface lets you see how your artwork will look on a Web browser and various kinds of monitors. You can also change the download rate used to compute the download time shown in the preview window, although the default 28.8 Kbps is typical for most Web visitors.

The Optimize To File Size dialog box opens from the pop-out Optimize menu in the Optimize section of Photoshop 5.5's Save For Web interface. Here you can enter a file size as a target for the Save For Web operations. If you choose the Current Settings option, Photoshop will use the file format, type of palette, and dither currently in the Settings section of the Save For Web interface as a starting point for reducing the file size to hit the target. On the other hand, if you choose the Auto Select option, Photoshop will analyze the colors in the image and choose a GIF or JPEG profile. ImageReady's Optimize palette offers the same option.

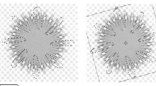

To animate the lightning in the ElectroMatic Design logo, the yellow highlight elements were rotated, with three different positions stored on different layers in Photoshop.

image file, dividing it into sections that will be reassembled seamlessly when downloaded. Prepare the image file in Photoshop and then move it to ImageReady and **optimize** it with the **Optimize palette.** Then **slice** it, defining the areas for the separate links with the **slice** and **slice select** tools. Finally, ImageReady can save the optimized graphic and the HTML code for the image with the **Save Optimized** command. "Plastic Pushbuttons" on page 330 makes use of this workflow.

- If you're developing an **animation,** in most cases it makes sense to create all the graphics that will be used for the frames as individual layers in Photoshop. Then move the file to ImageReady. Choose the optimization settings for the graphics so there will be no surprises later, and then use ImageReady's **Animation palette** to assemble and pace the animation. Finally save the animation as an animated GIF file with the Save Optimized command. This workflow is used for "'Onion-Skinning' a GIF Animation" on page 325. When you build an animation using this workflow, you can preview it at every stage of development — in Photoshop by scrolling the Layers palette (as described in "Previewing Animation in Photoshop" on page 327), in ImageReady's Animation palette (as in step 8 on page 329), and by loading the working file into your Web browser, which can be launched from ImageReady's View menu.

- If you're developing button graphics that include alternate versions for animated **rollovers** (using JavaScript) to show the buttons in resting (normal) and rollover (when the cursor passes over) or mouse-down (pressed) states, you can develop all the graphics you need in Photoshop. Then assign the rest, rollover, and mouse-down states in ImageReady's **Rollover palette.** Save the automatically generated HTML and the button graphics with the Save Optimized command, and then preview the rollover states in your browser. "Making Buttons from Photos" on page 320 and "Plastic Pushbuttons" on page 330 follow this workflow.

For very simple buttons, it may be better to do all the work in ImageReady, which has a few button-making tools that Photoshop lacks. Page 319 shows an example of buttons made entirely in ImageReady.

PLANNING ART FOR THE WEB

No matter what Photoshop/ImageReady workflow you use, planning is essential for designing Web graphics. Although many of the same basic rules of design and composition apply whether you're designing for the screen or for print, in some ways creating images for the Web or for multimedia is fundamentally different from creating images for the printed page:

- Almost everyone understands the **"information architecture"** of a printed book or magazine. But getting around on a

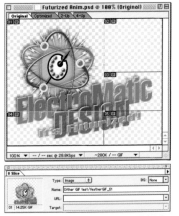

The ElectroMatic Design logo was divided into five named slices in ImageReady, to make downloading more efficient. Slicing allows one part of an image (slice #01) to be saved as an animated GIF and downloaded as an animation, while the other slices are saved as static GIFs. Also, slices can be constructed to get the most from compression. For instance, the "empty" slice in the upper right corner downloads very quickly.

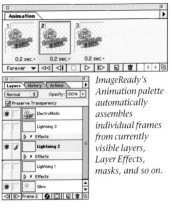

ImageReady's Animation palette automatically assembles individual frames from currently visible layers, Layer Effects, masks, and so on.

When slicing and animation are complete, choosing File, Save Optimized creates an HTML document along with the associated sliced images.

Web site or in a multimedia program is still a less familiar and less intuitive process for most people. As a result, one of the goals of most on-screen presentations is to make it clear how a user can get to the information stored at the site or on the disc. Easy-to-interpret buttons and other navigational "controls" become essential. In this chapter "Making Buttons from Photos," and "Plastic Pushbuttons" provide methods for button design and manufacture.

- The typical **layout and design grid** for on-screen images is horizontal, to match the aspect ratio of the monitor, rather than vertical, to fit a typical printed page.

- The **resolution** of on-screen images is a lot lower than that used for print. That means precautions should be taken to ensure smooth edges on type and graphics. This low resolution is also one of the reasons that type on-screen has to be bigger than type in print in order to be readable. When creating low-resolution display type and graphics, you can get more flexibility in the design process and therefore better-looking results if you design them at twice or four times the size you need and then scale them down with Image, Image Size.

- **Color reduction, image compression,** and **file format** become all-important, in the attempt to deliver good-looking Web graphics that can be downloaded quickly. Most computers sold in the last few years and used to explore the Web have 16-bit or 24-bit color capabilities, so, depending on your target audience, limiting yourself to the 216-color Web-safe palette may not be mandatory. However, you may often need to design or "massage" graphics to look good when displayed with the limited color depth of 8-bit color systems and thus within the Web-safe palette. To keep image files small, which may be a more important goal than strictly adhering to the Web-safe palette, you may need to restrict color depth even more, as described in "Preparing Web Art in Photoshop" on page 313.

  GIF and **JPEG** are the standard formats used for compressing graphics files for the Web, with the **PNG** format showing great promise but still limited browser compatibility. "Choosing a Format" on page 314 discusses the advantages of each of the formats that Photoshop and ImageReady provide for Web graphics. And all of the techniques presented in this chapter deal with color reduction, image compression, and file format.

- Making artwork for the Web opens up the opportunity to use motion. **Animation** is discussed in "'Onion-Skinning' a GIF Animation" on page 325. In addition, the two button-making techniques described in "Making Buttons from Photos" and "Plastic Pushbuttons" include designing alternate states for buttons and "animating" them as JavaScript rollover states.

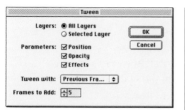

ImageReady's Tween command (from the Animation palette's pop-out menu) builds frames automatically. You can choose the start and end frames and the number of frames to be added, as well as which characteristics and layers to modify and which to leave "as is."

When you open an ImageReady-generated HTML file for an animation in your browser for testing, the browser uses the HTML and the associated files in the Images folder to show the animation.

A WEB-DESIGN RESOURCE

Before you put Photoshop or ImageReady to work in building a Web site, it's important to base the information architecture of site and page design on solid communication concepts and well-implemented design principles. A book that we find particularly useful for designing for the Web is *The Web Design Wow! Book* (Davis and Merritt, Peachpit Press), winner of the Computer Press Association's Best Advanced How-To Book award.

PREPARING WEB ART IN PHOTOSHOP

Almost any effect you can create in Photoshop can be adapted for use on Web sites. Special-effects treatments for text and graphics like those in Chapter 8 make excellent styling for the buttons that activate Web links. Photo treatments like those in Chapter 3 and montages like those in Chapter 4, adapted to meet the special challenges of downloading from the Web, can be ideal for background illustrations or for image maps.

When you prepare artwork to be included in Web pages, you're aiming for good image quality and fast downloading. You want the image to be attractive and the colors to be as accurate as possible (the latter is especially important in fine art or in online catalog images, for instance, or in displaying a corporate logo). Unfortunately, image quality and speed tend to work against each other, exerting exactly opposite pressures on the development of artwork. The more detail and color subtlety in an image, the bigger the compressed file tends to be, and thus the slower to download.

Keeping Files Small

Here are some general tips for reducing the bulk of the images you prepare for the Web:

- **Reduce the dimensions.** Make the image as small as you can and still get the impression you want.

- **Avoid horizontal or diagonal gradients.** Because of *run-length encoding* methods used to compress images in the GIF format, vertical gradients compress smaller than horizontal or diagonal ones. ("Run-Length Encoding" on page 315 explains how this works.)

- If you use Indexed color, **avoid or limit dithering**. *Dithering* is the interspersing of dots of two different colors to create the illusion of a third color; Photoshop provides it as an option when you convert from RGB to Indexed color, either with the Image, Mode, Indexed Color command or with File, Save For Web. Because it interferes with run-length encoding, dithering increases the size of a compressed file. Sometimes, though, color rendition is so much better with dithering that the extra file size is worth it, especially since dithering now involves a variable setting rather than an all-or-nothing decision. (See the "Dither, Dither" tip on page 314.)

- When you convert from RGB to Indexed color, choosing one of the adaptive palettes (Adaptive, Perceptual, or Selective) lets you **try out palettes with less color depth,** such as 16 or 32 colors. See "'Shaping' Adaptive Palettes" on page 36 in Chapter 1 for advice on customizing adaptive palettes.

- **Use tiled backgrounds.** For an individual Web-page (or frame) background, instead of making an image file the size of

In run-length encoding, which is the type of compression scheme used in the GIF file format, color data is compressed by reading across the image, one row of pixels at a time, and storing information about color *changes* rather than storing the color of each individual pixel. The fewer color changes there are in each row of pixels — or the more *horizontal color redundancy* there is—the more the file can be compressed. So, for example, a vertical color gradient — one that changes color from top to bottom — contains only one color per row and can be compressed quite small. But a horizontal or diagonal gradient — changing color from side to side or corner to corner — involves many color changes per row and therefore can't be compressed as much. Solid colors also compress better than dithered colors, since a color change has to be recorded with each color change in the "dotted" mix.

Both of these files are 256 pixels wide, with 256 colors and no dither. The diagonal gradient on the left compresses to 20K, while the horizontal gradient compresses to 10K.

the page, make a small repeating *tile* that a Web browser can use to fill the background (see "Tiling Backgrounds" on page 315).

Choosing a Format

Among the file formats Photoshop can save or export are three that are compatible with the Web. If you're using Photoshop 5.5, the Save For Web dialog box can help a great deal in choosing a format. Even so, knowing the strengths and weaknesses of the different formats will help in planning your artwork.

- **JPEG** (for *Joint Photographic Experts Group*) excels at compressing **photographs**. It allows 24-bit color, so that people whose computer systems can display this color (or 16-bit) will see the file at its best (or close to it). (Those with 8-bit systems will see a browser-dithered version.) But JPEG doesn't allow you to make part of the image transparent to let the background of the Web page show through. At best, the transparency can be faked as described in "'Transparent' JPEGs on page 340. Also, if applied with too high a degree of compression, JPEG can cause serious image degradation, especially around edges.

- **GIF** (for *graphics interchange file*) is great for **flat-color artwork**, but poor for photos because it supports only 256 colors or less, and its compression method is optimized for areas of flat color. It does allow limited, hard-edged transparency, however. So you can have graphics that are silhouetted against the Web page background.

- **PNG** (pronounced "ping") is the relatively new *Portable Network Graphics* format that allows either 8-bit or full 24-bit color and

In Web graphics there are two sources of *dithering,* or simulating a color with patterns of dots of other colors. Photoshop and ImageReady introduce *application dither* to simulate additional colors that occur in the original artwork but not in the limited palette you've chosen for the Web graphic. Without application dithering, you tend to get sharp color breaks and banding rather than smooth color transitions. Photoshop's Save For Web dialog box includes a pop-out list of dithering types (No Dither, Diffusion, Pattern, and Noise) and a Dither slider for controlling how much dither can be introduced. The Save For Web previews let you see the dithering that results from the current setting. The same options are found in ImageReady's Optimize palette.

Browser dither is the pixel pattern that a browser introduces when the image as you've optimized it includes colors not used by an 8-bit system. You can preview simulated browser dither in Photoshop by choosing Browser Dither from the Preview menu that pops out from the preview panel in the Save For Web dialog box. In ImageReady you can preview it by choosing View, Preview, Browser Dither.

The **DitherBox filter** — found in the Other submenu of the Filter menu in both Photoshop 5.5 and ImageReady — lets you define your own custom pixel patterns for the solid RGB colors you want to simulate using Web-safe colors. The DitherBox filter is described on page 192.

To get a textured background for a Web page and still reduce the time needed for downloading, you can use a background tile — a small, repeating element for filling an individual Web page (or frame), starting at the top left corner and proceeding across and down. The smaller the tile, the less time it will take to download. If you make Web background tiles in Photoshop, be sure to try them out with the common browsers at typical download speeds.

The same randomized pattern that was used to make the seamlessly tiled Web-page background was incorporated into this graphic that included soft shadows. Then it was saved as a JPEG. (For more details, see pages 340 and 341.)

In preparing an image for export in GIF format, one way to reduce file size is to stylize the image with posterization (Image, Adjust, Posterize). Both of the GIFs for this 250 x 380-pixel image use 32 colors. Here the posterized image (on the right) uses no dither; its size is 24K. The image on the left uses 100% dithering to maintain image quality. It's quite a bit bigger than the posterized version (40K) because the dithering interferes with the run-length encoding used for GIF compression. Finding the balance between size and quality is the key.

precise control of transparency (through the use of alpha channels, which can be full 8-bit grayscale masks). PNG can usually produce a smaller file than GIF. It also takes into consideration the different gamma characteristics (brightness) of the monitors used on Mac, Windows, and Unix platforms, so that images created on one system are less likely to look too light or too dark when viewed on another platform.

The PNG formats available in Photoshop and ImageReady (8-bit and 24-bit) promise big improvements in graphics-handling for the Web. But not many of the currently used browser versions support them. For general distribution, Photoshop's GIF and JPEG formats are still the best bets for now.

With all three formats — JPEG, GIF, and PNG — you have the option of displaying a blurry or chunky version of the image first, which then builds to a complete detailed version. This is done through *interlacing* or *progressive display*.

If you create Web graphics, the Save For Web command alone makes the upgrade from version 5 to 5.5 worth the price. In Photoshop 5, without version 5.5's Save For Web preview interface, the choice of a format (GIF or JPEG) and within that format a degree of compression is a trial-and-error process. One method of comparing and contrasting possible compression schemes and formats is to take a representative Web-destined image and save it in several versions of both GIF and JPEG. Then reopen the compressed files and compare the appearance and size of the different results, and choose the best compromise.

Analyzing Your Artwork

When deciding whether to use GIF or JPEG and figuring out how to set up the graphic to begin with, you'll need to answer a series of questions about the artwork. The first is "What kind of artwork are you starting with?" Your approach will be different depending on whether you're working with

- A full-color image like a photo or artwork with color gradients, where it's important to preserve the full color range,

- Monochromatic artwork,

- Flat-color artwork originally created for print,

- Or flat-color artwork that you're creating from scratch specifically for the Web

Starting with a Full-Color Image

If you want to preserve the quality of a full-color photo or illustration destined for the Web, your options will differ, depending on whether your image is partly transparent — a vignette, for example, with soft edges that let the Web page background show through — and whether it's a shape other than rectangular.

The only way to make a "pseudo" soft-edged transparent mask for exporting a GIF file in Photoshop or ImageReady is to convert the file from RGB using Photoshop's Image, Mode, Indexed Color command and then export it using File, Export, GIF89a Export. The GIF89a Export dialog box allows you to choose an alpha channel as a transparency mask source.

An alpha channel used as a transparency mask for a GIF (as shown at the top of this column) must be a black-and-white-only bitmap. If you use a grayscale image in the alpha channel (A), the GIF89a Export will automatically convert it to a bitmap using a "threshold" edge method (B). You can get a much better transparency mask by using dithering, as described in steps 3 and 4 of "Silhouettes, Shadows, and Transparency" on page 336.

Flaming Pear's FeatherGIF filter (see page 212) automates the process of producing a GIF with a soft-edged vignette using a dithered bitmap mask. Instead of producing a grayscale transparency map in an alpha channel, then producing a Bitmap file from this channel, and finally importing the Bitmap image back into an alpha channel in the image file, you can simply run the filter.

If your image is rectangular and it doesn't have any areas that need to be transparent, use JPEG. In the Save For Web dialog box, try several Quality settings (or let Photoshop choose them for you automatically), comparing the resulting files for image quality and loading time. Often Low quality works for photos, while Medium may be needed for color gradients. Photoshop 5/5.5's JPEG option lets you set quality on a sliding scale. You can also choose Optimized to avoid the blurred edges and "chunked" color that JPEG can sometimes produce. Or choose Progressive for a display that appears quickly (though pixelated) and then builds sharp detail.

If your image has a shape other than rectangular, especially if it has a soft, feathered edge, JPEG is still an option if your Web-page background consists of a solid color or a seamless, randomized texture that doesn't require precise alignment (see pages 340 and 341 for an example). In that case, transparency can be faked by incorporating the background color or tile pattern into the image.

If you don't know what the Web-page background will be, or if it consists of a complex image, or if your silhouetted or soft-edged image will need to appear on more than one background, you'll probably want to use the **GIF89a format,** realizing that you'll have to compromise color depth in order to get transparency. You can use the GIF conversion process described in "Adapting Existing Flat-Color Artwork," below. "Silhouettes, Shadows, and Transparency" on page 336 also tells how to prepare such a graphic element for silhouetting.

Grayscale or Other Monochromatic Art
Often you can get decent-looking monochromatic artwork with many fewer than the 256 shades that a full Indexed Color Adaptive palette would provide. Follow the directions below for flat-color art, but try setting the number of colors as low as 16 colors when you convert to an adaptive palette, and then go higher if needed.

Adapting Existing Flat-Color Artwork
GIF is the best format for flat-color artwork. Starting in RGB mode, choose Save For Web and try different options. You can force the colors closer to a Web-safe palette by (1) choosing Selective from the pop-out list of color palette types in the Settings section of the Save For Web interface, (2) setting a fairly high Web Snap tolerance percentage in the lower right corner of the Settings section, and (3) forcing individual colors outside the Web Snap tolerance into compliance with the Web-safe palette by clicking the Web Snap cube icon, on the left at the bottom of the Save For Web Color Table.

If you need transparency so the background of the Web page can show through your artwork, In Photoshop 5.5 you can turn

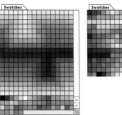

*Photoshop 5/5.5's **Web Spectrum.aco** and **Web Hues.aco** Swatches files provide two arrangements of Web-safe colors to choose from when creating Web graphics from scratch.*

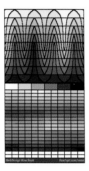

*The **Wow Web Color Pal.gif** file on the Wow CD-ROM provides two "spectrum" layouts of Web-safe colors. It also isolates the four pure grays that exist in the Web-safe palette and provides extra "wells" where you can put colors that are important for a particular job.*

on the Transparency option in the Settings section of the Save For Web interface. The Transparency option, which also works the same way in ImageReady's Optimize palette, uses the transparency mask information in the currently visible layers of the image file to create the 1-bit mask. The Matte color (also in Save For Web's Settings section) determines what color will be used to replace the transparency in the semi-transparent pixels at the edges.

If you want to create transparency based on a mask stored in an alpha channel, or if you're working in Photoshop 5.0, create the transparency with the File, Export, GIF89a Export command rather than Save For Web or Image-Ready's Optimize. "Silhouettes, Soft Shadows, and Transparency" on page 336 provides an example of transparency based on a mask. The "GIF Transparency in v. 5" tip at the right tells how to handle transparency in this version of the program.

Type or Flat-Color Artwork Built for the Web

If you're building artwork by importing shapes from Illustrator and filling them with color, or by making selections and filling them, or by drawing directly in Photoshop, it's easy to ensure

that all your colors are Web-safe. Create your artwork with colors chosen from a browser-safe Swatches palette such as Web Safe Colors (v.5) or Web Hues.aco or Web Spectrum.aco (v.5.5) provided on the Adobe Photoshop 5 or 5.5 Application CD-ROM. Or open the **Wow Web Color Pal.gif** file provided on the CD-ROM that comes with this book and use it to sample colors, as described next. This file presents the Web colors in an easy-to-use arrangement. That way, no matter what method you use for saving and compressing your files, the important flat areas of the artwork won't be forced to dither on 8-bit systems.

Start out working in RGB Color mode with your Web Swatches palette or Wow Web Color Pal file open. **If your graphics will appear on a single-color background,** start with a layer filled with your background color. Choose the colors for your graphics by sampling from the Swatches palette or Color Pal file with the eyedropper tool — you can toggle to the eyedropper from any painting tool simply by moving the tool over the Swatches palette.

When your artwork is complete, choose File, Save For Web (or if you're working in ImageReady, use the Optimize palette). Choose

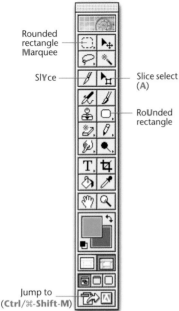

Rounded rectangle **Marquee**

SlYce

Slice select (A)

RoUnded rectangle

Jump to (**Ctrl/⌘-Shift-M**)

Unique to ImageReady's otherwise Photoshop-like toolbox are the slicing tools, the rounded rectangle marquee, and the object-oriented geometric drawing tools, which also include a rounded rectangle.

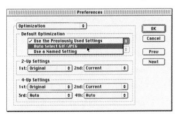

If you choose File, Preferences, Optimization in ImageReady, you can choose to have the program automatically choose its best compromise between file size and image quality, including whether to use GIF or JPEG. You can override the automatic choice at any time by making entries in the Optimize palette.

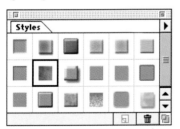

Preset Layer Effects combinations can be applied to the graphics on a transparent layer in ImageReady by choosing from the Styles palette, shown here, or by applying as in Photoshop 5/5.5.

GIF for the file format and Selective for the palette type. In the Lossy section of the interface try a setting between 20 and 40. Experiment with the setting to see how changes affect the quality of the artwork and the file size or download time.

USING IMAGEREADY

Much of ImageReady's graphics-creation interface works the same way as Photoshop. The tool palette looks much the same, with the addition of object-oriented drawing tools and tools for making and editing the *slices* that divide a large cumbersome image into a number of smaller files that can be downloaded simultaneously, and thus much more quickly. The ImageReady toolbox is missing the magnetic lasso, background eraser, History brush, and pen tools, and the painting tools are limited compared to those of Photoshop. Its selecting and image editing commands are also limited.

Where ImageReady really shines, though, is in slicing, in generating the JavaScript for rollover states in the Rollover palette, and in turning layered Photoshop files into animations with the Animation palette. Once you've made your choices for compression and color of a typical image slice or animation frame in ImageReady's Optimize palette, the Save Optimized command can apply the same size and color criteria to all slices, states, and frames in your project.

Like Photoshop 5.5, ImageReady lets you preview what a Web browser will do to your color on an 8-bit system as you make optimizing decisions (View, Preview, Browser Dither). To launch a specific browser so you can check a final animation or the rollover states of buttons, choose File, Preview In, and choose from the list of available browsers.

ImageReady's Modus Operandi

Two of ImageReady's important palettes — the Animation palette and the Rollover palette — share a common way of working. Once you get the hang of it, developing animations and rollover states from imported layered Photoshop files is easy. Briefly, the routine is "duplicate and change, duplicate and change," and so on.

In the Animation and Rollover palettes, the next graphic (the next frame in an animation or the next state for a button) is created by duplicating the palette's current frame or state and then changing the image file to the way you want it to look for the new frame or state. For instance, if you've created a layered Photoshop file with all the elements you need for your animation or button states, you can duplicate the current frame or state and then make changes in ImageReady's Layers palette by turning on or off the visibility or changing the settings for any of the layers, masks, or effects.

ImageReady Does It Better . . .

Although a typical Web-graphics workflow is to develop the graphics in Photoshop 5.5 and then move to ImageReady for slicing,

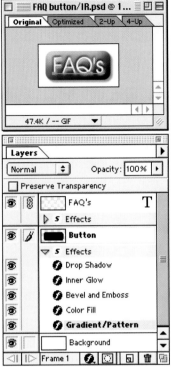

A simple button can be created by setting type on one layer and applying Layer Effects, and drawing a button shape with the rounded rectangle tool on another layer and applying different Layer Effects. The button color can be set with the Color Fill Layer Effect, which is also found in Photoshop 5.5 (but not in version 5). Unique to ImageReady is the Gradient/Pattern Layer Effect, which was used to emphasize the upper-left lighting of this button. The Layer Effects for each layer are stored as an "s" list that can be toggled open to show the individual Effects. Any Layer Effect can be changed by double-clicking its "f" icon to open its palette and changing the entries. Clicking to turn off the eye icon for an Effect hides that Effect.

For the file whose Layers palette is shown above, simply by turning on and off particular Effects as the different button states are selected in the Rollover palette, you can create the graphics for the states.

optimizing, animating or creating rollovers, and finally for exporting the image files and HTML code, there are some things in the "graphics-creation" category that ImageReady can do but Photoshop can't. This may make it worthwhile to "jump to" ImageReady while you're developing a file in Photoshop.

- ImageReady's toolbox includes a rounded rectangle tool that Photoshop doesn't have. If you start a simple round-cornered button in ImageReady, you might even want to stay there and complete the buttons, as we did for the example shown on this page.

- ImageReady's Layer Effects include all the ones found in Photoshop *plus* the Gradient/Pattern effect. Like the other Layer Effects, this one makes it easy to make changes without permanently changing the art-work on the layer, or to change the shape of the art-work on the layer and have the Effects automatically adjust themselves to the change in shape. When a file with the Gradient/Pattern effect is imported into Photoshop, the Effect won't show up, but you'll see it when you take the file back into ImageReady.

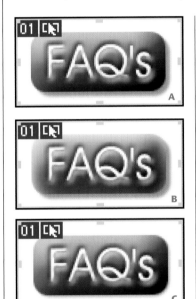

To create these button states, a gold Outer Glow for the Button layer was turned on to create the Over (rollover) state (B) in the Rollover palette. For the Normal (rest) state (A) and the Down (mouse-down, or pressed) state (C), the glow was turned off. In addition, for the Down state the move tool and arrow keys were used to move the button 2 pixels down and right, and the Drop Shadow was moved 1 pixel up and to the left by changing the Distance setting in the Drop Shadow palette.

You can choose from ImageReady's View menu to launch a Web browser to test rollover states, animations, and so on.

- ImageReady has a Styles palette, where it can store sets of Layer Effects, with thumbnails that let you choose them visually. The program comes with a number of preset Styles, and you can add your own by choosing New Style from the Styles palette's pop-out menu. In Photoshop the process of storing Layer Effects is a bit more complex. You can save a file in which you've applied them, and then copy (Layer, Effects, Copy Effects) and paste (Layer Effects, Paste Effects) them into another transparent layer.

Making Buttons from Photos

Overview *To unify a set of buttons, crop and silhouette each subject; add a border, background, color treatment, glows, and a drop shadow; in ImageReady, produce and save the normal, rollover, and mouse-down states.*

AS PEOPLE MANEUVER THROUGH CYBERSPACE, as long as they can distinguish the buttons that make things happen from the informational elements around them, buttons for World Wide Web sites and other interactive projects can be created from a wide range of imagery. When you plan to craft buttons from photos or full-color illustrations, sometimes the biggest design challenge is turning a diverse collection of images into a unified set. Here we've unified three photos by applying a consistent series of graphic treatments: cropping, silhouetting, adding a border, desaturating, applying a consistent background, adding a glow, colorizing, and adding a shadow. Then we added an edge glow and modified the shadow to make rollover and mouse-down states for the buttons.

1 Preparing the photos. To begin the process, open all the images in Photoshop that you want to use for making buttons. For each image, choose File, Save A Copy so you'll have the original, untouched version if you need to start over. You can develop each button in its own file as described here, or bring them together into a single large master file, as in "Plastic Pushbuttons" on page 330.

Most scanned photos consist of a single opaque background layer, but you'll need transparency for later steps in the process. Open the Layers palette. If any of your photos consists of *Background* only (the italic type in the Layers palette indicates that this layer can't include transparency), give that layer the capability for transparency by double-clicking its name to open the Make Layer dialog box. Simply opening the dialog box, accepting a new name, and clicking OK changes the *Background* to a layer that allows you to erase to transparency. (We renamed the layer "Photo.")

For a cohesive design, a set of buttons will work best if their images are roughly the same size and orientation. So that you can see their relative sizes, display all the files at the same magnification (50%, for instance). Press Ctrl/⌘-A (for Select, All) and then Ctrl/⌘-T (for Edit, Free Transform); Shift-drag on a corner handle of the Transform box to resize proportionally, and drag around outside the box to rotate. After pressing the Enter/Return key to accept the transformation, sharpen the image (Filter, Sharpen, Unsharp Mask).

2 Cropping. Now you'll make a marquee for cropping all the buttons to be the same size and shape. Select the marquee tool in the toolbox and press Enter/Return to open its Options palette. Set the

The three original photos

2   3a

Each of the photos was cropped close.   *Removing the background from each photo left only the subject.*

3b

Similarly cropped and without their backgrounds, the three photos looked more alike. They could be scaled to final size at this point.

4   5

Adding a border defined the shape of each button.   *Removing all color prepared each element to receive a unifying color scheme.*

6a

Setting up the gradient

6b **7a**

A gradient was added by dragging diagonally with the Linear gradient tool.

A Layer Effects Outer Glow added to the Photo layer helps the image pop.

7b

With border, glow, and background gradient in place, the layered button file looks like this.

7c

The matching backgrounds and glows make the buttons look more like a cohesive set.

8a

Adding an Adjustment layer for Color Balance

Style to Fixed Size, enter Height and Width values, set Feather to 0, and set Shape to Rectangular. Click the marquee tool to produce the marching ants, and drag the marquee into place to frame each subject the way you want it for the button. While the marquee is still active, complete the cropping by choosing Image, Crop to eliminate pixels outside the marquee.

3 Silhouetting and scaling. Now display your buttons at 200% so you can see the detail in the edges of the subjects. Isolate the elements you want by precisely selecting their silhouettes and eliminating dissimilar backgrounds. You can use the Extract command or magic eraser if a subject's edge is well-defined (if you need help in choosing and using a selection method, read "Making Selections" and the following sections, starting on page 60).

Because Layer Effects will be used in developing glows and drop shadows for these buttons, go ahead and open the Transform box again (Ctrl/⌘-T) and Shift-drag a corner handle of the Transform box to size the photo down so that at 100% magnification it appears at the size you want it to be in the final buttons. Scaling the button element earlier in the process would have eliminated detail that would be helpful for selecting the subjects for silhouetting. Waiting until later in the process to scale the button elements would require editing the Layer Effects to reduce them to fit the resized elements. Editing Layer Effects is not difficult to do — you simply double-click the "f" icon and enter new parameters for the Effects. But since these button elements are photos, not hard-edged graphics, reducing them now will work fine. Complete each photo's transformation by pressing the Enter/Return key, and run the Unsharp Mask filter.

4 Creating a border. To outline the button, first add a layer for the border by Alt/Option-clicking the New Layer icon at the bottom of the Layers palette and naming the layer "Border." By putting the border on a separate layer, you'll be able to add a glow to the silhouetted photo with Layer Effects (in step 7) without making the border glow also. To add the border, press "D" (for "Default colors") to ensure that the Foreground color is set to black, then select all (Ctrl/⌘-A), and choose Edit, Stroke, Inside. For our oversized 70-pixel-high buttons (approximately 1-inch-square on-screen) we used a 1-pixel stroke Width.

5 Removing color. Even if you want to make the buttons more colorful in the long run (as we do later, in step 8), removing the color from them now can be useful as a first step toward a consistent color scheme: Activate the Photo layer and choose Image, Adjust, Desaturate.

6 Adding a background treatment. Using the same background for each button is another unifying technique. Create and name a new layer (we called ours "Gradient," since that would be its content), and make it the backmost layer by dragging its name to be

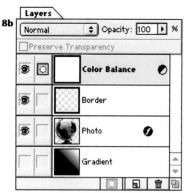

The Adjustment layer in place

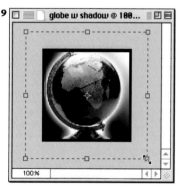

Adding canvas to make room for the drop shadow

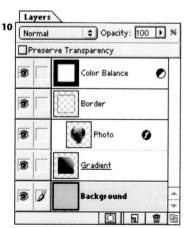

A background was added, the Color Balance Adjustment layer was masked so it didn't affect the background, and the Photo and Gradient layers were made into a clipping group to keep the Photo layer's glow from spilling onto the background and onto the drop shadow that would be added to the Gradient layer.

lowest in the Layers palette. Then fill the layer; we used the Linear gradient tool. To add a diagonal black-to-white gradient, choose the Linear gradient tool; press Enter/Return to open its Options palette; choose Foreground To Background from the Gradient pop-out list; and drag from the corner where you want the background to be black to the diagonally opposite corner, where you want the background to be white. We dragged from lower left to upper right.

7 Adding a glow. To add a glow to the button element, activate the Photo layer and choose Layer, Effects, Outer Glow. Set the color to white and the Opacity to 100% and experiment with the Blur and Intensity until you have a glow you like; the Blur controls the extent of the glow and the Intensity controls its brightness and contrast.

8 Applying a color scheme. Now add back some color to the highlights, midtones, and shadows of the button. In your button file, add an Adjustment layer at the top of the stack by activating the Border layer and then Ctrl/⌘-clicking the New Layer icon. In the New Adjustment Layer dialog box, choose Color Balance. In the Color Balance dialog move any or all of the three sliders until the developing button is the color you want.

9 Making room for a drop shadow. To make your button stand out from the information elements on a Web page, you can pop it into the third dimension with drop shadows. But first you'll need to add some space to each button file to make room for the shadow. Open your working window beyond the canvas size (you can do this by shrinking the image without shrinking the window, by pressing Ctrl-hyphen [Windows] or ⌘-Option-hyphen [Mac]). Choose the crop tool (pressing "C" chooses it) and drag across the entire image to select all of it. Then expand the crop box beyond the existing canvas by holding down the Alt/Option key and dragging outward on a corner handle (the Alt/Option key expands the crop box from the center). Press the Enter/Return key to accept the enlarged canvas.

10 Housekeeping. To make the buttons look and feel interactive, you can create alternate states, or appearances. The *normal* state is the way the button looks when it's sitting idle. The *rollover* state is the how it looks when the cursor passes over it. The *mouse-down* state is the way it looks when it's clicked. For these buttons we used a drop shadow and a glow just inside the edge to develop the three states. (The normal and mouse-down states are shown at the top of page 320, and the rollover state is shown in figure 11, on page 323.)

Before adding the shadow and glow, you'll need to do a few things to tidy up the file. First create a new layer below the button for the shadow to fall on: Click the New Layer icon and drag the new layer's thumbnail to the bottom of the stack in the Layers palette. Fill this layer with your Web page's background color. One way to do this is to open your master Web-page background file

11

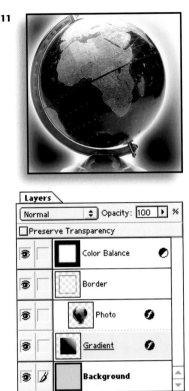

Drop Shadow and Inner Glow added to the Gradient layer to make the rollover state of the button

11

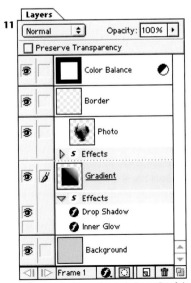

Setting up the Normal state in ImageReady's Layers palette, with the Inner Glow turned off

and use the eyedropper to sample a representative color. This will make it the Foreground color, and pressing Alt/Option-Delete will fill the new layer with the color.

Once you've added the background, you may notice a few things that need fixing. First, the glow on the cropped, silhouetted photo may now be bleeding out beyond the edges of the gradient-filled square because of the canvas that was added. And second, the Color Balance Adjustment layer affects not only the button elements but the Background layer also, changing its color.

To address the Color Balance situation first, add a mask to the Adjustment layer by Ctrl/⌘-clicking the Gradient layer's name in the Layers palette to load its transparency mask as a selection. Activate the Color Balance layer, invert the selection (Ctrl/⌘-Shift-I), and fill with black. The Color Balance layer will no longer affect the Background layer.

To trim the glow so it doesn't spread out beyond the edges of the button, use the Gradient layer to mask, or *clip,* the Photo layer: Alt/Option-click on the line between the Gradient and Photo layers in the Layers palette. The line will become dotted, the Photo layer's thumbnail will be moved over to show that it's clipped, and the Gradient layer's name will be underlined to show that it's the clipping layer. Anything in the Photo layer that's beyond the Gradient layer's transparency mask will be hidden.

11 Adding the shadow and glow. Now you can add the drop shadow by activating the Gradient layer and choosing Layer, Effects, Drop Shadow. Leave the default Multiply mode setting and adjust the other settings to taste. The shadow should be angled down and to one side.

Next choose Inner Glow from the pop-out list in the upper left corner of the Effects box. Choose the Edge option, leave the mode at Screen, and adjust the other settings to taste — the effect we were looking for was just a brightening inside the edge of the button.

12 Making the three states. Now you can take each button file, which contains the normal, rollover, and mouse-down versions of the button, into ImageReady (see the "Photoshop to ImageReady" tip on page 324). There you'll optimize the color (using the method described in step 5 of "'Onion-Skinning a GIF Animation" on page 328), generate the three states of the button, and crop.

In ImageReady's Layers palette, click the small triangle next to the "s" icon that designates Layer Effects for the Gradient layer. This will show a list of all the Effects applied to that layer. Open the Rollover palette (Window, Show Rollover).

First you'll define the **normal** state for the button. When the Normal state is active in the Rollover window, as it is now, whatever is visible in the working window will be included in the Normal button state. Since the button was designed to have a normal

12b

The three states, shown in the Rollover palette. Each has its own layer contents and Effects.

13

Using the slice select tool to eliminate extra background at the edges

14a

Saving the HTML, images, and cropping (slice) specifications

14b

The HTML and image files

---

state with a drop shadow but no glow, we clicked the eye icon next to the listing for the Inner Glow to turn it off.

To make the **rollover** state, click the New Rollover State icon (next to the trash icon at the bottom of the Rollover palette). This will duplicate the Normal state, and the copy will be called "Over." With the Over state active (outlined with a black border in the Roll-over palette), make changes to the Layers palette so the rollover state is visible. In this case, we clicked in the eye column for the Inner Glow to turn it back on.

To make the **mouse-down** state, with the Over state active in the Rollover window, click the New Rollover State button. This will duplicate the Over state, and the copy will be called "Down." With the Down state active, make changes in the Layers palette so the mouse-down state is visible. In this case, the mouse-down state has the shadow directly under the button so it looks like the button has been pressed closer to the surface. We achieved this by clicking on the "f" icon for the Drop Shadow, which opened the Drop Shadow palette, and then changing the Distance setting in this palette to 0.

13 Trimming the button. To trim away any unnecessary background around the button and thus cut down on both the file size and the amount of screen real estate occupied by the button, you can "slice," or crop it. All three states for this button and for the others in the set need to be cropped to the same size and shape so they will be easier to align in your Web editor.

Start the slicing process by clicking on the Normal state in the Rollover window so it shows in the working window. Choose the slice select tool (pressing the "A" key chooses it) and drag the handles inward to crop the image, being careful not to trim off the edges of the shadow. In our photo buttons, the shadow is offset to the left and down in the Normal state and doesn't show at the top or on the right. To be sure that we didn't trim too close on the top or right side, we next clicked the Down state in the Rollover window and dragged the top and right side handles of the slice box outward so the crop would be big enough to include the entire shadow.

14 Saving and testing the file. Now you'll save an HTML file and the associated images for the button states. Choose File, Save As Optimized. In the Save Optimized dialog box, type in a name for the button and *turn on all three checkboxes:* Save HTML File, Save Images, and Save Selected Slices Only. ImageReady will save the HTML file and a folder with all three of your button states, trimmed according to the slice you made.

To preview the button's states, open the HTML file in your browser and test it by moving your cursor over the button to see the rollover state and then clicking to see the mouse-down state. When all the buttons in the set are complete, bring their files into your Web editor to lay out and link the buttons to your site. *Wow*

"Onion-Skinning" a GIF Animation

Overview *Prepare artwork as a series of sequential layers in a Photoshop file; make changes to the artwork to create individual animation frames, temporarily reducing Opacity settings to see several layers at once; create the animation in ImageReady.*

"AstroPup" file and GIF animation

GRAPHICS: HAVANA STREET, IN THE MOOD

1a

The original EPS clip art

1b

Heads cropped and resized

2

Line work thickened and Web color applied

3a

Aligning the second head. A 50% Opacity setting reveals the layer below (left). Restoring Opacity to 100% shows the finished artwork.

THERE ARE CERTAINLY MORE SOPHISTICATED WAYS of doing animation for the Web (vector-based Flash animation, for example). But creating frames in layers using the Photoshop equivalent of the old animator's onion-skinning process and turning the layers into an animated GIF in ImageReady can produce a simple animation that can be viewed by any browser that supports graphics. Once the frames are painted in Photoshop, the production process is fairly automatic. Here we started with clip art and produced an eight-frame "cartoon" of an astro pup counting rockets.

1 Preparing the graphics.

You'll build each frame of your animation in a Photoshop layer. We started with a series of clip art images, opening each of the dogs as an RGB file in Photoshop and selecting and filling with white everything but the head, except in the file with the space suit. We started working at approximately 200% of what we thought would be our final pixel dimensions.

2 Coloring the artwork. So

that all the line work from the different source files would match, the black-and-white artwork was slightly blurred and

2X OR 4X

When you're designing for on-screen display, it's a good idea to start out with artwork that's two or four times the pixel dimensions you think you want for the screen. This gives you several advantages: You can see more detail, so it's easier to make selections and fine adjustments; you can make a 1-pixel stroke and it will look like a smooth hairline when you reduce it; you have enough pixels so you can make the on-screen display bigger than you originally planned if you change your mind; and if you ever need to use the images in a coordinated print piece, they'll reproduce better.

then treated with Image, Adjust, Brightness/Contrast, using the method described in "Cleaning Up Masks" on page 78. Color was added to the artwork with the paintbrush with hard-edged brush tips (from the top row of the default Brushes palette), and with Multiply mode chosen in the Paint Brush Options palette so that painting onto the black lines wouldn't change their color. About a

3b

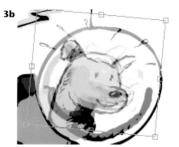

Aligning the last of the heads, with all but the bottom layer at 50% Opacity

3c

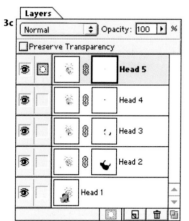

Heads aligned and masked

3d

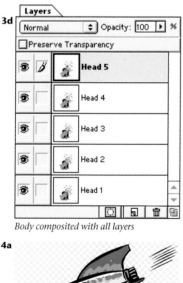

Body composited with all layers

4a

Rocket clip art with Web colors added

dozen Web-safe colors were used (see "Getting Colors Organized" at the right).

3 Using the "onion-skinning" process. Our aim was to animate a sequence of the astro pup watching rockets fly over, so we first had to get all the parts into one file at roughly the right size. We selected and dragged-and-dropped each head into the main astro pup background file to become a layer of its own, arranging the layers in the appropriate order for the animation.

Visibility was turned off (by clicking the eye icons in the Layers palette) for all but the bottom layer and the next layer up. The second layer's Opacity setting was reduced to 50% so we could see through to the full dog underneath. The head on the second layer was selected and moved by pressing Ctrl/⌘-T for Free Transform and dragging inside the Transform box; it was scaled by dragging the handles inward or outward, and rotated by dragging around the outside of the box, until it aligned with the dog on the bottom layer. Being able to see through the layer was essential in aligning the frames.

We made a layer mask by clicking the Add Layer Mask icon (on the left at the bottom of the Layers palette) and painting with black paint to make a smooth transition from the new head to the dog body. Then we turned on visibility for the next layer up, reduced its Opacity to 50%, aligned its head with the body on the bottom layer, and added another layer mask. This process was repeated for the other two heads, and a copy of the tail was also positioned on each layer.

Once all the heads and tails had been moved into position, we added a body to the head and tail on the second layer by selecting the body on the bottom layer and duplicating it to a new layer (Ctrl/⌘-J), which appeared in the Layers palette between the bottom layer and the Head 2 layer. This new layer was duplicated (by dragging its thumbnail to the New Layer icon at the bottom of the palette), and the copy was dragged between Head 2 and Head 3 in the palette. The duplication and moving process was repeated until each Head layer had a body layer underneath it.

We clicked the Head 2 layer to activate it, and then pressed Ctrl/⌘-E to merge Head 2 with the body copy below it. The merging process was repeated for each of the other Head layers, until all heads had bodies.

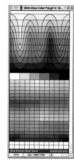

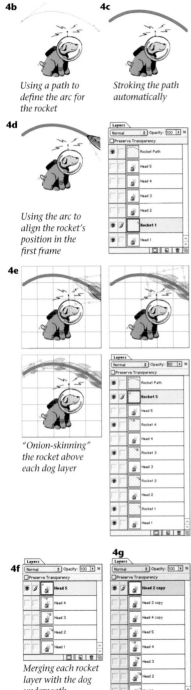

4b

4c

Using a path to define the arc for the rocket

Stroking the path automatically

4d

Using the arc to align the rocket's position in the first frame

4e

"Onion-skinning" the rocket above each dog layer

4f

Merging each rocket layer with the dog underneath

4g

Adding rocketless dog layers to return the head to its starting position

4 Using a guide for motion. If your animation involves an object moving through the frame, sometimes it's helpful to have a guide — an arc for a bouncing ball or for a rocket flying overhead, for instance. To make such a guide for our rocket, we activated the top layer of our file, clicked the New Layer icon to add a layer on top of that, and used the pen tool to form an arc. To make the arc easier to see, you can stroke the path with paint as we did by choosing a color from the Swatches palette, clicking the path name in the Paths palette to activate it, choosing the paintbrush tool, and clicking the Stroke Path icon (second from the left at the bottom of the palette). (The paint stroke layer won't be part of the animation — it's just a temporary guide.)

Another aid in aligning moving elements is Photoshop's Grid. We turned on the Grid (View, Show Grid) to help gauge the horizontal distance to move the rocket in each frame.

We opened a clip art file of a rocket and colored it as we had the dogs. Then we clicked on the name of the bottom layer of the dog file in the Layers palette to activate it, and dragged the rocket into the file. We used Layer, Free Transform, dragging around the outside of the box to rotate the rocket so its nose lined up with the green arc and pressing the Enter key. We duplicated the rocket layer, moved the copy up the Layers stack above the next dog, changed its Opacity to 50% so we could see through it to the rocket below, and used Free Transform to move it, rotate it, and scale it.

We continued making copies of the rocket, moving up the stack of layers to the top. Then we merged each rocket layer with the dog layer below it, using the same process as in step 3 (Ctrl/⌘-E). To return the dog's head to its starting position (in case we decided to loop the animation), we added duplicate dog layers. Finally, we deleted the layer with the green arc by dragging its thumbnail to the palette's trash can icon. We turned off the Grid (View, Hide Grid) and saved the file in Photoshop format (File, Save As).

Once you have a layered Photoshop file, you can animate it in ImageReady as described in steps 5 through 9. Or if you're working

---

PREVIEWING ANIMATION IN PHOTOSHOP

You can use the Layers palette to preview an animation whose cels have been created as a stack of Photoshop layers before taking the file into ImageReady or another animation program for final preparation. Set the Layers palette's thumbnails to the largest size (choose Palette Options from the palette's pop-out menu). Shorten the palette until only one layer's thumbnail shows, and move the scroll box up or down the scroll bar, or press and hold the palette's up or down scrolling arrow, to run the movie as a kind of digital flipbook. If your first frame is in the bottom layer of your file and your last frame is in the top layer, scrolling with the up arrow will run the animation forward; using the bottom arrow will run it backwards.

5a

As you change parameters in ImageReady's Optimize palette, the GIF image in the 2-Up working window shows the size of the file and a typical download time.

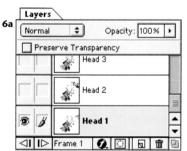

5b

When we specified 32 Colors, Image-Ready's Color Table displayed them. Since we had chosen to use the Web palette for optimizing, all 32 colors were Web-safe, as indicated by the white diamonds in the Color Table display.

6a

In the ImageReady Layers palette, the image that was to become Frame 1 of the animation was activated and made visible.

6b

After Frame 1 was established, clicking the Duplicate Current Frame button copied Frame 1 to a new frame in ImageReady's Animation window.

in Photoshop 5 and don't have ImageReady, you can animate with GIFBuilder (freeware for Mac) or GIF Construction Set (shareware for Windows). **Note:** GIFBuilder and GIF Construction Set can be found on the Web; neither is provided on the Wow! CD-ROM.

5 Optimizing in ImageReady. Open your layered file in Image-Ready by clicking the Jump To button in Photoshop 5.5's toolbox or by choosing File, Open in ImageReady. It's a good idea to choose the type of optimization and compression of your file before you assemble the animation. That way, as you preview the animation you can see if problems arise in specific frames.

Start by picking the layer that has the most color complexity — the most colors and the most broken-up distribution of color patches. That way you'll know that the compression choices you make for this image will also work for all the other layers. In the Layers palette, Alt/Option-click in the eye column for this layer to turn on its visibility and turn off visibility for the other layers; also click its name to make it the active layer.

In the working window, click the 2-Up or 4-Up tab so you'll be able to see your original and also the current optimized version as you change the color and compression parameters. Then open the Optimize palette (Window, Show Optimize), choose **GIF** (the only format that supports ImageReady animation), and set the **Matte** color if necessary. There was no **Transparency** in the Astro pup file, so the Matte color was irrelevant. **Interlaced** was turned off, since it's inappropriate for animation.

Then adjust the other parameters to reduce the number of colors and increase the GIF compression. As you tweak the settings, check the readouts for file size (K) and download time (for a 28.8 baud transfer, a realistic rate for most Web users) in the GIF side of the 2-Up working window.

For the **palette,** we chose Web. In creating the Astro Pup file we had initially chosen flat colors from a Web-safe palette, so we knew there would be no surprises when we chose to use the Web palette in ImageReady. The trick was to find out how few of the 216 colors we could use and still maintain the quality we wanted. We had used only a dozen basic colors for the original illustration, so we "guesstimated" that a **Colors** setting of 32 would provide enough colors for both the original hues and the antialiasing. Choosing the Web option had ensured that the 32 colors would be Web-safe, so there was no need for **Dither** and no need to use **Web Snap** to bring the colors into the Web palette.

We increased the **Lossy** setting until we started to notice unacceptable degradation of the image. Often this point will be somewhere between 10% and 50%. Sometimes the savings in file size is considerable, and sometimes negligible, depending on the complexity of the image.

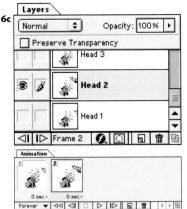

6c

With Frame 2 active in ImageReady's Animation palette, a new layer was activated in the Layers palette, which updated Frame 2 in the Animation palette.

6d

Each new frame was added by duplicating the current frame as shown here. Then ImageReady's Layers palette was updated to create the image for the new frame.

7

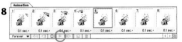

Using the pop-out menu to set the delay time for each frame and to set the animation for continuous looping

8

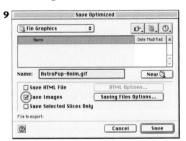

Clicking the Play button in the Animation palette runs the animation at full size in the working window.

9

Turning on ImageReady's Save Images function to save all the frames as a single GIF file

Once your image is optimized, turn off Auto Regenerate in the Optimize palette's pop-out menu so that the process of creating the animation won't be slowed by ImageReady displaying each frame in its optimized condition. (If you want to double-check the individual frames, you can turn Auto Regenerate back on after you finish animating, at step 8.)

6 Assembling the animation. In the Layers palette Alt/Option-click in the eye column for the layer you want to use for the first frame of your animation and click its name to make it the active layer. Open the Animation palette (Window, Show Animation). You'll find your currently active layer automatically designated as Frame 1.

Start Frame 2 by clicking the Duplicate Current Frame button, next to the trash icon at the bottom of the Animation palette. This puts a copy of Frame 1 — the current frame at the time you clicked the button — in Frame 2. Go back to the Layers palette and activate the layer you want to use for Frame 2, making sure it's the only layer that's visible. This will automatically update Frame 2 in the Animation palette.

To make each of the remaining frames of the animation, repeat the process of duplicating the current frame (now Frame 2) to create the next frame (Frame 3 in this case) and setting the Layers palette to update the new frame.

7 Adjusting the timing and looping. By putting the cursor over the time delay number at the bottom of each frame and dragging upward, you can choose a frame delay time. By choosing the minimum delay (0.1 second) you can ensure that your animation won't flash by too fast on systems with high-speed connections. The 0.2-second setting (5 frames per second) is the slowest rate that still produces fairly smooth animation. Use the pop-out list in the bottom left corner of the Animation palette to set the number of times the animation will play — Forever, Once, or a custom Other setting.

8 Previewing the animation. To see the animation running, turn the Auto Regenerate feature back on in the Optimize palette, click on the Optimized tab in the main working window so that it shows only one image at a time, and click the Play button (the triangle immediately to the right of the square Stop button) at the bottom of the Animation palette. If you see something that needs changing, go back to the appropriate palette or window and make the necessary change. The animation will be updated to reflect the change.

9 Saving the file. When the animation is complete, choose File, Save Optimized As. In the Save Optimized dialog box, click the checkbox to turn on Save Images. This will save all the images of the animation as a single GIF file. *new!*

Plastic Pushbuttons

Overview *Add Layer Effects to the graphics and icons for a panel of buttons, changing the effects to produce three button states; in ImageReady optimize the color and file size; slice the file into separate buttons; assign button states to produce an HTML file and images.*

ACTION IMAGE "**Plastic**" image files, HTML, and Action

1

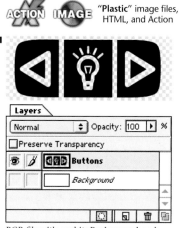

RGB file with a white Background *and button shapes with cut-out icons*

TO MAKE A PANEL OF TRANSLUCENT BUTTONS, Photoshop 5/5.5's Layer Effects can be used to give a clear, beveled appearance to a graphic on a transparent layer to create the button faces. Then you can color the button icons, creating variations to use as rollover and mouse-down states. When you've completed the Photoshop file with all three states, you can open the file in ImageReady for optimizing, slicing, defining the rollover states, and saving the HTML file and sliced images.

There are five main parts to the button-making process described in the next six pages: Designing the button graphics (steps 1 through 6), producing and saving alternate states for the buttons (steps 7 through 10), optimizing color and file size (step 11), slicing the buttons apart (step 12), and assigning and saving the button states (step 13).

Note: The buttons shown above were designed to be used on a white Web page background. If you want to use similar buttons on a colored background, you'll need to experiment with the Layer Effects, especially those in Screen and Multiply modes, to get the result you want. For instance, a color glow Layer Effect in Screen mode doesn't color the white background — that is, it disappears where it overlays the white gap between buttons. In contrast, on a dark color, the glow *does* show up against the background, so the glow from one button can "bump into" or overlap the glow from the one beside it, unless you reduce the Distance setting for the glow, or increase the space between buttons. Also, a shadow in Multiply mode will have no effect on a black background, so if your background is black, you can't count on the shadow to differentiate the "rest" state from the rollover or mouse-down condition.

1 Setting up the buttons file. Start with the graphic you want to use for your set of buttons — in our case, button shapes with cut-out graphics — on a transparent layer above a *Background* filled with white. One way to get to this point is by opening a new Photoshop file (File, New) with the default white *Background* and then dragging and dropping your button panel graphics from Adobe Illustrator. At this starting stage of your Photoshop file, your set of buttons should be twice (or more) as big as you will want them to be when you finish. By working at this larger size, you'll be

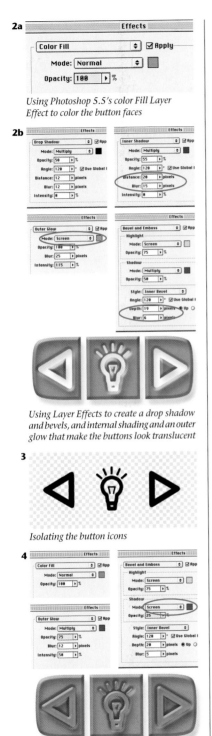

2a

Using Photoshop 5.5's color Fill Layer Effect to color the button faces

2b

Using Layer Effects to create a drop shadow and bevels, and internal shading and an outer glow that make the buttons look translucent

3

Isolating the button icons

4

Applying Layer Effects to the icons layer to create the "rest state for the buttons

able to create more detailed and subtle effects than if you start with your file at the final on-screen size.

If you're working in Photoshop 5.5, you don't need to worry about the color of the graphics at this point. Adding the color with Layer Effects in step 2 will give you more flexibility and efficiency in coloring the various button states. But if you're working in version 5, which lacks the Color Fill Layer Effect, fill the graphics with color. Pick a Web-safe color to reduce dithering when the graphics are viewed on an 8-bit (256-color) monitor. If you're working in version 5.5, you can limit your color choices to Web-safe colors by clicking the Foreground color square in the toolbox to open the Color Picker and then clicking the Only Web Colors checkbox.

2 Turning the buttons to plastic. Now you'll apply Layer Effects to the buttons layer. Right-click/Control-click on the buttons layer's *name* (not its thumbnail) and choose Effects. If you're working in Photoshop 5.5, start by choosing **Color Fill** from the pop-out list in the upper left corner of the Effects dialog box. Click the color swatch and choose a bright Web-safe color and leave the Mode set at Normal. Once you get the other Layer Effects set up, you can return to Color Fill and experiment if you like.

Choose **Drop Shadow** from the pop-out list of Effects and set the Blur, Distance, and Opacity to produce a soft, offset shadow.

To add some variability to the color of the button face, choose **Inner Shadow** from the Effects list, click the color swatch, and choose a darker shade of the button color. Use relatively large Blur and Distance settings. The large Blur will produce fairly amorphous shadows, and the large Distance setting will offset them. The result will be a variegated light-and-dark shadowy effect.

Add dimension to the buttons by choosing **Bevel And Emboss** from the Effects list and choosing **Inner Bevel** for the Style. To make a sharply beveled edge, set the Depth to a fairly high value (20 is the maximum; we used 19) and the Blur to a relatively small number (we used 6). For the Shadow color use a darker shade of the button color. For the Highlight color choose a lighter shade of the color you plan to use for the graphics inside the buttons (we used a light blue).

What really makes the buttons at the top of page 330 look translucent is the way light seems to shine through the plastic to brighten and color the shadowed area underneath. To achieve this effect, choose **Outer Glow** from the Effects list and pick a lighter version of your button color. Leaving the Mode setting at Screen, set the Opacity at 100%, increase the Intensity, and use a large enough Blur setting so the glow lightens part, but not all, of the offset drop shadow.

3 Isolating the button graphics. The next step is to separate out the icon graphics so you can make variations for the three

5

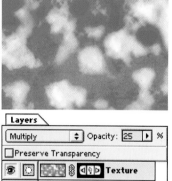

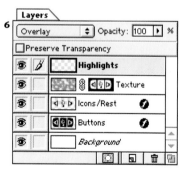

Adding a tortoise-shell texture to the button faces

6

Airbrushing specular highlights on a separate layer

button states. First add a transparent layer above the buttons layer by clicking the New Layer icon, in the middle at the bottom of the Layers palette. Then load the outline of the button graphics by Ctrl/⌘-clicking on the buttons layer to load its transparency mask as a selection. Inverting the selection (Shift-Ctrl/⌘-I) will deselect the button faces and instead select the button icons and the space outside the buttons. To limit the selection to the icons, hold down the Alt/Option key and use the lasso tool to surround (and thus subtract) the unwanted parts of the selection.

4 Coloring the button icons. With the selectin active, the next step is to add Layer Effects to the layer with the isolated icons, to define the "rest" state for the buttons. Once this is done, duplicating the layer twice and changing the Layer Effects for each of the two copies will define the rollover and mouse-down states. If you're working in version 5.5, you can take advantage of Color Fill again, as explained next. But if you're working in Photoshop 5, at this point you'll need to choose a new Web-safe Foreground color that contrasts with your button faces and press Alt/Option-Delete to fill the icons with color.

You can get a head start on the Effects for the icons layer by copying the Effects from the buttons layer: Right-click/Control-click the "f" icon on the buttons layer and choose Copy Effects from the context-sensitive menu that pops out. Then right-click/Control-click on the *name* (not the thumbnail) of the icons layer and choose Paste Effects from the context-sensitive menu. If you're using Photoshop 5.5, change the color by choosing **Color Fill** in the Effects dialog box, clicking the color swatch, and choosing a new color.

For the **Drop Shadow** and **Inner Shadow** effects, leave the settings as they are. But make changes to the Outer Glow and Bevel And Emboss: For the **Outer Glow** choose a darker shade of the button color (not the icon color) and reduce the Opacity and Intensity. For the **Inner Bevel** set both Highlight and Shadow modes to Screen so the icons seem to be internally lit, and increase the Depth setting to help make the icons look raised above the button surfaces.

5 Adding a tortoise-shell texture. To add interest to the plastic material of the button faces, we added a layer above the icons layer by clicking the New Layer icon. To add a tortise-shell effect as we did, choose colors by clicking the Foreground and Background squares in the toolbox. Then run the Clouds filter (Filter, Render, Clouds) and adjust the color and contrast to create a mottled texture (Image, Adjust, Hue/Saturation and then Image, Adjust, Levels). Choose Multiply for the layer's blending mode so that the dark areas of the texture will darken the plastic underneath. To apply the texture to the button faces alone and prevent it from affecting the icons or the drop shadows and glows, make a layer mask that limits the texture to the buttons themselves: Ctrl/⌘-click the name of the

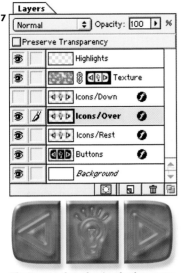

The Layers palette showing the three states of the panel of buttons, with the rollover state visible

8a

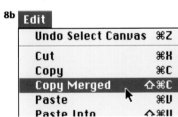

Making a merged duplicate file of the rest state of the buttons

8b

Edit

Undo Select Canvas	⌘Z
Cut	⌘H
Copy	⌘C
Copy Merged	⇧⌘C
Paste	⌘U
Paste Into	⇧⌘U

Making a merged copy of the rollover state of the buttons

8c

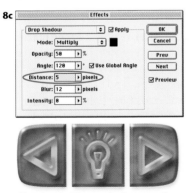

Changing the Distance for the mouse-down state's drop shadow more nearly centers the shadows under the buttons.

buttons layer to load the button graphics as a selection. Then with the Texture layer active, click the Add Layer Mask icon, on the left at the bottom of the Layers palette.

6 Adding specular highlights. Hand-painted specular highlights can turn the plastic from dull to shiny instantly. So that it's easier to fix any painting mistakes, add another transparent layer to paint on. Then choose the airbrush, a small soft brush tip, and white paint (pressing "D" restores the default colors, and pressing "X" exchanges them, making white the Foreground color). Click with the airbrush to add highlights.

7 Making the other button states. The rollover state for these buttons can be created by changing the color of the icons. First duplicate the icons layer by dragging it to the New Layer icon. Then duplicate it again. Give each new layer a name that indicates the button state it represents (to rename a layer, double-click its name in the Layers palette and enter the name change); we used "Icons/ Over" and "Icons/Down."

For the rollover and mouse-down icons layers, experiment with changes to the color fills and glows (click the "f" icon to open the Effects dialog box). For the Icons/Down layer we changed the Color Fill to green and changed the Outer Glow to a lighter green in Hard Light mode. For the mouse-down icons layer, we changed the Color Fill to gold and changed the Outer Glow to red in Color mode.

8 Creating the final buttons file. At this point it's a good idea to save your fully layered file with Layer Effects "live" (File, Save) in case you decide to make changes later. Though most of this next step could be done in ImageReady, for the sake of simplifying the rest of the project, you can also make a duplicate file with finished merged button panels in all three states. This also helps in visualizing how the buttons will operate.

Start by turning on visibility for all the layers you need to make the buttons in the rest state. (For our file this would be the Highlights, Texture, Icons/Rest, Buttons, and *Background* layers.) Choose Image, Duplicate and click the Merged Layers Only checkbox, so that the new file will have a single layer that is a composite of all the visible layers in the source file.

To add a layer with the buttons in the rollover state, first turn on visibility for the appropriate layers in the fully layered source file. (For our file this meant turning on visibility for the Icons/Over layer in addition to those already on.) Then make a merged copy and paste it into the duplicate file as follows: Select all (Ctrl/⌘-A), and copy by choosing Edit, Copy Merged or pressing Shift-Ctrl/⌘-C. In the duplicate file you just started, paste the merged copy into the file (Ctrl/⌘-V) to make a separate layer.

To add a layer with the buttons in the mouse-down state, go back to the fully layered source file again and turn on the appropriate

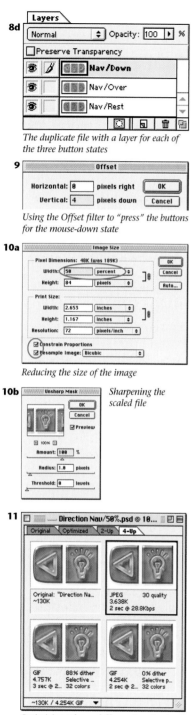

8d

The duplicate file with a layer for each of the three button states

9

Using the Offset filter to "press" the buttons for the mouse-down state

10a

Reducing the size of the image

10b

Sharpening the scaled file

11

Optimizing color and file compression in ImageReady

layers. (We now turned on visiblility for the Icons/Down layer also.) This time, though, before you make a merged copy, change the position of the drop shadows to make it look like the shadow is moving as its button is pressed down, as follows: Click the "f" icon on the buttons layer and reduce the offset of the Drop Shadow by changing the Distance setting. We changed the setting from the original 12 pixels used in step 2 to 6 pixels. The result was to pull the button shadows closer underneath the buttons. Now make another merged copy and paste it into the simplified file. (After you've made this layer for the mouse-down state, you may want to go back into the Effects dialog for the buttons layer in the fully layered file and reset the Distance to its original setting. That way it will be set up in its "finished" state if you need to use the file again later.)

9 Making the buttons move. For one last touch of realism, you can make the pressed buttons actually move down by doing some final tweaking to the simplified file. In this file all the effects and textures have been "flattened," or combined, in a single layer for each state. Activate the layer for the mouse-down state. Choose Filter, Other, Offset; use 0 for the Horizontal setting, and for the Vertical entry use a value that's smaller than the difference between the original Distance setting for the buttons layer's Drop Shadow used in step 2 (in this case 12 pixels) and the changed Distance setting used in step 8 (in this case 6 pixels); we used 4 pixels.

10 Reducing the size of the graphics. With the graphics completed, it's time to size them down to their final on-screen dimensions. To save a version of the file at full size, choose File, Save A Copy. Then reduce the size of the active file by choosing Image, Image Size. Make sure the Constrain Properties and Resample Image (Bicubic) boxes are checked. Then choose Percent for the units of the Width setting and type in "50." The other dimensions will change automatically; click OK to complete the resizing. Run the Unsharp Mask filter on each layer (Filter, Sharpen, Unsharp Mask) to fix any softening caused by resampling in the scaling process.

Now you'll move to ImageReady to optimize file size and color, slice the buttons panel into individual buttons, animate the rollover states, and save the HTML code and the images. Keep Photoshop open and jump to ImageReady by clicking the Jump To button at the bottom of Photoshop's toolbox. (If you're working in Photoshop 5 and you don't have ImageReady, you can save the buttons, and then use a Web editor to assign the button states.)

11 Optimizing in ImageReady. After opening the file in ImageReady, click the 4-Up tab in the main window, open the Optimize palette (Window, Show Optimize), make sure that Auto Regenerate is turned on in the Optimize palette's pop-out menu so the previews will be updated, and experiment with GIF and JPEG settings. (Step 5 of "'Onion-Skinning' a GIF Animation" on page 328 tells more

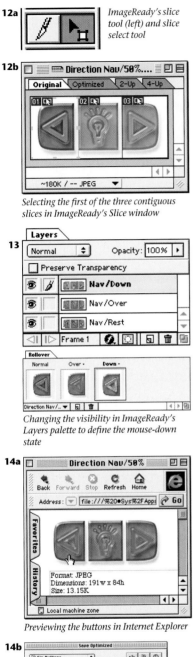

12a

ImageReady's slice tool (left) and slice select tool

12b

□ ≣ ▭ Direction Nav/50%.... ≣ ⊟ ⊞

Original \ Optimized \ 2-Up \ 4-Up

01 ◀ 02 💡 03 ▶

~180K / -- JPEG ▼

Selecting the first of the three contiguous slices in ImageReady's Slice window

13

Layers

Normal ⬦ | Opacity: 100% ▶

☐ Preserve Transparency

👁 ✎ | 🔲🔲🔲 **Nav/Down**

👁 | 🔲🔲🔲 Nav/Over

👁 | 🔲🔲🔲 Nav/Rest

◁ ▷ Frame 1 🎯 ☐ 📄 🗑 📄

Rollover

Normal | Over · | Down ·

◀ | ◀ | ◀

Direction Nav/... ▼ 📄 🗑 | ◀ ▶ 📄

Changing the visibility in ImageReady's Layers palette to define the mouse-down state

14a

□ ▭ Direction Nav/50% ⊟ ⊞

Back Forward Stop Refresh Home 🅔

Address: ▼ | file:///%20●Sys%2F Apps ⟳ Go

Favorites History

Format: JPEG
Dimensions: 191 w x 84 h
Size: 13.15K

☐ Local machine zone

Previewing the buttons in Internet Explorer

14b

Save Optimized

Fin Buttons ⬦ | ⬆ 📄 ⏱

Name | Date Modified

Name: LeftBut.html | New 📄

☑ Save HTML File | HTML Options...
☑ Save Images | Saving Files Options...
☑ Save Selected Slices Only

Saving HTML and images

about choosing settings in the Optimize palette). Because of all the shading in this image, JPEG at a low setting did a better job of compressing the file without degrading the color than GIF did with a reduction to 32 colors.

12 Slicing the buttons apart. Open ImageReady's Slice window (Window, Show Slice) and click the Original tab in the main window to display the panel of buttons. Choose the slice tool and turn on Snap To Slices in the Slice menu. Then drag the slice tool across the leftmost button to create the first slice. We dragged all the way to the left edge of the middle button to select enough of the white background so that the glowing edge of the middle button's mouse-down state wouldn't have room to show. Similarly, create a slice for the middle button, and another for the rightmost button.

> **PREVENTING OVERLAP**
>
> With Snap To Slices turned on in ImageReady's View menu, dragging a side handle snaps the slice edge to the one next to it, so that slices won't overlap. Another way to ensure that slices won't overlap is to turn on the rulers (View, Show Rulers) and drag guides from the left ruler to provide snapping lines for the slices.

13 Assigning states. When all the slices are set, click the first button slice with the slice select tool to make it active. Open the Rollover palette (Window, Show Rollover) and you'll find the first button in its rest, or Normal, state waiting for you. Duplicate this button by clicking on the New Rollover State icon next to the trash icon at the bottom of the window; the duplicate becomes the Over state. Then click in the visibility column of ImageReady's Layers palette to make visible the rollover state layer of your buttons file. This will change the Over image in the Rollover window. Duplicate the Over state by clicking the New Rollover State icon, and change the visibility in the Layers palette so the mouse-down buttons layer is visible as the Down state in the Rollover window.

14 Previewing and saving. When you finish this process, you can preview the operation of the buttons in your browser from within ImageReady: Choose File, Preview In, and choose the browser. You can move the cursor and press the mouse button to check the rollover and mouse-down states, although the entire panel of buttons will act like one big button. If the states look the way you want them to, export the buttons slice-by-slice: Click the first slice with the slice select tool, and choose File, Save Optimized As. In the Save Optimized dialog box, enter a name for this button (we called ours "LeftBut") and turn on all three saving options: Save HTML File, Save Images, and Save Selected Slices Only.

Select each of the other slices and save them in the same way. Then work in your Web editor to combine all the elements and set the final links. *Wow!*

Silhouettes, Soft Shadows, and Transparency

Overview *Create a soft-edged graphic above a Background layer; crate a transparency map in an alpha channel; convert the transparency map to 1-bit; convert the file to Indexed color; export as a GIF, using the 1-bit mask.*

ACTION **IMAGE** "Transparency" image and Action

1

Layers
Normal ‡ Opacity: 100 ▶ %
☐ Preserve Transparency
👁 ✏ [Graphic] **Graphic**
[ ] *Background*

Setting up the file, with the graphic on a transparent layer above the Background

2a

Effects
Drop Shadow ‡ ☑ Apply	OK
Mode: Multiply ‡ ■	Cancel
Opacity: 75 ▶ %	Prev
Angle: 43 ▶ ° ☑ Use Global Angle	Next
Distance: 5 ▶ pixels	☑ Preview
Blur: 5 ▶ pixels	
Intensity: 0 ▶ %	

Adding a Drop Shadow that will become the cast shadow

SILHOUETTING A DESIGN ELEMENT for a Web page, even if you need to add a soft shadow or a vignette, isn't especially hard to do when the Web page's background is a single color, and you know the color in advance. You can build the background into the graphic, or in Photoshop 5.5 you can choose your Web page background color as the Matte color in the Save For Web dialog box.

But the process of creating soft-edged transparency gets more complicated when the background is a pattern or texture rather than a flat color, or when the element you're designing must be used on several backgrounds of different colors — in other words when a vignette or the illusion of an element standing there in thin air casting a shadow has to work in all background situations. Until the PNG Web graphics format, with its ability to include a grayscale mask for partial transparency, becomes universally accepted, we're limited in Photoshop 5, 5.5, and ImageReady to defining 1-bit masks — with each pixel either fully ON or fully OFF. Here's a technique for creating a 1-bit mask that uses a diffusion dither to simulate partial transparency and soft edges. It works whether you're using version 5 or 5.5.

1 Preparing the element. Start with an RGB file with your graphic element in a transparent layer above the *Background.* The file should be at the final size and resolution you want to use on the Web. We use a "running star."

2 Adding a cast shadow. Add a drop shadow to the graphic (Layer, Effects, Drop Shadow), experimenting to get the Opacity (shadow density) and Blur (softness) that you want. (Make a note of the Blur setting; you may need it again at step 5.) Since you will be distorting the shadow to turn in into a cast shadow, the Distance setting (offset) isn't so important — the shadow just has to be offset enough so you can get a good look at the density and softness as you experiment.

To be able to distort the shadow so it looks like it's falling behind the graphic, it needs to be separated from the graphic layer. Right-click/Control-click the "f" icon to open the context-sensitive Layer Effects menu and choose Create Layer.

At this point you can further adjust the shadow density. Simply reduce the layer's Opacity setting. We changed the Opacity to 75%.

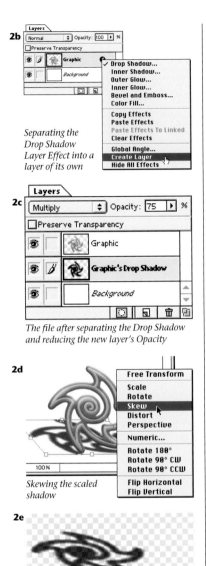

2b

Separating the Drop Shadow Layer Effect into a layer of its own

2c

The file after separating the Drop Shadow and reducing the new layer's Opacity

2d

Skewing the scaled shadow

2e

The finished shadow, viewed alone

3a

Loading the luminosity of the shadow layer by making it the only visible layer and then Ctrl/⌘-clicking the RGB channel in the Channels palette

Next, press Ctrl/⌘-T (for Edit, Free Transform). Grab the top center handle of the Transform box and drag down to scale the shadow. We made our shadow about half as high as the graphic. Then right-click/Control-click inside the Transform box to open the context-sensitive menu and choose Skew. Now dragging on the top center handle will skew the shadow. Experiment with scaling and skewing until the shadow looks right to you. Drag inside the transform box to move the shadow, aligning its base with the base of the graphic. Press Enter to complete the transformation.

3 Building a "transparency map."

Making a mask that exactly fits the shadow starts with loading a selection that not only includes its shape information but also includes the partial transparency of the shadow itself. Loading the shadow layer's transparency mask would give us the shape information, differentiating between pixels that are fully transparent and those that aren't. But it wouldn't take into account the partial transparency throughout the shadow. The way to include the transparency is as follows: First make only the shadow layer visible (Alt/Option-click in its eye column in the Layers palette) and also make it the active layer (click on its thumbnail in the Layers palette). Now when you open the Channels palette, you can load the layer's luminosity (or gray values) as a selection by Ctrl/⌘-clicking on the RGB channel in the palette. (If

no pixels of more than 50% luminosity are present, you won't see any marching ants. But don't worry, the selection will still be active.) To turn this selection into an alpha channel, click the Save Selection As Channel icon (second from the left at the bottom of the Channels palette).

To add the silhouette of the graphic to the alpha channel

3b

The "transparency map" selection saved as an alpha channel

3c

The shadow stored in an alpha channel as the first step in building a transparency map

3d

Adding a mask for the graphic to the developing transparency map in the alpha channel

3e

Inverting the tonality of the transparency map in the alpha channel

4a

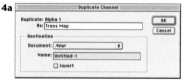

Duplicating the transparency map alpha channel as a separate file

you just created, go back to the Layers palette and Ctrl/⌘-click the thumbnail of the graphic layer to load its transparency mask as a selection. In the Channels palette, click on the new alpha channel's thumbnail to activate the channel, and then fill the selection with black.

As it is now, with the graphic and shadow dark, loading the alpha channel would select *everything but* the graphic and its shadow, so the channel's tonality needs to be inverted. Press Ctrl/⌘-I to invert black and white. You now have an 8-bit grayscale mask, or transparency map, for the graphic and its shadow. The next step will be to convert it to the kind of 1-bit mask that can be used with a GIF image.

4 Making the 1-bit mask. To make a 1-bit mask from the 8-bit alpha channel transparency map, start by duplicating the alpha channel: Choose Duplicate Channels from the Channels palette's pop-out menu and choose *New* for the Document setting in the Duplicate Channel dialog box. Then convert this new Grayscale file to Bitmap mode (Image, Mode, Bitmap) using Diffusion Dither and keeping the Output resolution the same as the Input. The Diffusion Dither will convert the grays in the file to a pleasing pattern of black-and-white pixels.

Select all (Ctrl/⌘-A) and copy the dithered image to the clipboard (Ctrl/⌘-C). In your original file, open the Channels palette and create a new alpha channel (click the New Channel icon, next to the trash icon at the bottom of the palette). Then, with this new channel active, paste the dithered image from the clipboard into the channel (Ctrl/⌘-V) and deselect (Ctrl/⌘-D).

The new alpha channel now contains a dithered mask that will allow some of the pixels of the soft shadow to show (in the white areas of the mask) and will hide others (in the black areas of the

4b

Converting the transparency map file to Bitmap mode

mask). When the masked image appears over a background, the background's color will show through in the masked spots. At the antialiased edge of the original graphic, some of the pixels will also be allowed to show and some will be masked.

5 Making a temporary background. Now you can temporarily supply a background for your graphic and shadow. The background will contribute to the color at the antialiased edge of the graphic and to the color of the soft shadow.

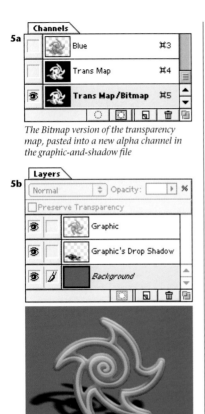

5a

The Bitmap version of the transparency map, pasted into a new alpha channel in the graphic-and-shadow file

5b

Alternative #1: adding a color sampled from the Web-page's background texture to the file

5c

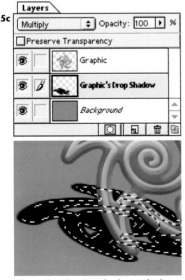

Alternative #2: using a background color from the graphic and "solidifying" the shadow to pure black

Alternative #1: If you know the approximate color of the textured background that your graphic and shadow will appear on, or if it will appear on a known solid color, activate the *Background* layer in your graphic-and-shadow file by clicking on its thumbnail in the Layers palette, and fill the layer with this color. (One way to do this it to click with the eyedropper tool to sample color from the Web-page background image file and make it the Background color; then press Alt/Option-Delete.)

Alternative #2: If you don't know the background color, or if your file has to appear against several background colors, your strategy will be different. In this case your best bet is to fill in the semitransparent edges of the graphic with the color of the graphic itself, and to make the shadow completely black. Here's how you can do it: Use the method in the previous paragraph to color the *Background* layer, except sample the color of the graphic itself to set the Background color. Activate the shadow layer by clicking on its name, and make the shadow opaque, as follows. Start by setting the Opacity for its layer at 100%. Then load the layer's transparency mask as a selection (Ctrl/⌘-click its name in the Layers palette). Fill the selection with black (press "D" for default colors and press Shift-Alt/Option-Delete to fill only the nontransparent pixels. Then fill in the soft edge of the shadow with black by stroking the selection (choose Edit, Stroke and enter a Stroke Width setting that's the same as the Blur you used for the Drop Shadow at step 2. The result will be a fairly ugly shadow layer, but it will prevent the background color from showing through and so it will provide the pure black pixels needed in step 7 when you apply the transparency map you've stored in the alpha channel.

6 Converting to Indexed color. Photoshop 5.5's File, Save For Web File command offers many options for optimizing color and file size when you save an image as a GIF. But it doesn't offer the opportunity to use an alpha channel as a transparency map.

Using the File, Export, GIF89a Export command instead *does* allow you to use the alpha channel, as long as the file is already converted to an indexed palette. Therefore, the next step is to convert to Indexed Color: Choose Image, Mode, Indexed Color; set the number of Colors and choose a type of Palette. We chose a 32-color Selective palette, which is an adaptive palette that aims to preserve the coloring of your

Converting the file to Indexed color mode using a 32-color Selective palette and Diffusion Dither

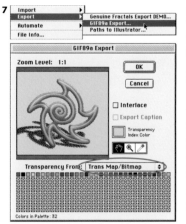

Exporting the shadowed graphic using the bitmap transparency map channel

The exported GIF file as it appears when opened in Photoshop

Against a textured green Web-page background, the GIF file (made using Alternative #1 at step 5) blends seamlessly.

Against a multicolor Web-page background, the GIF file (made using Alternative #1 at step 5) shows occasional specks of green at the edges of the shadow and graphic. Using Alternative #2 would eliminate the green.

image but leans toward colors from the Web palette if they are close. All adaptive palettes let you reduce the number the colors more than nonadaptive palettes, while still keeping the image looking good on most monitors.

7 Exporting the file. Once the file is in Indexed Color mode, choose File, Export, GIF89a Export. In the "Transparency From" pop-out list in the GIF89a Export dialog box, choose the alpha channel with the transparency map, and click OK. The result will be a GIF file with a transparent background and a "see-through" shadow that will let the background show through.

"TRANSPARENT" JPEGS

The JPEG format, which often produces the best-looking reproduction of silhouetted or vignetted photos and soft-edged graphics, doesn't really allow transparency. But if your Web-page background will be a solid color or a randomized texture so there's no alignment problem, transparency can be faked successfully. The technique depends on using a small pattern tile for the Web page background, saved at exactly the same JPEG settings you use for the image file.

Start with two files: First, the image element on a transparent layer above the *Background* layer. This should be cropped tightly (A). Second, a seamlessly repeating tile used to make the Web-page background pattern. This second file should be in its original uncompressed form (that is, not yet JPEGged) (B).

The graphic, isolated on a transparent layer

The seamless textured background tile, created with an embossed random pattern that doesn't require alignment to look good

In the tile file select all (Ctrl/⌘-A) and choose Edit, Define Pattern. Then in the image element file activate the *Background* layer and choose Edit, Fill, Pattern (C). Next choose File, Save For Web. Use JPEG as the type, and optimize the image by experimenting with different compression settings. When you've chosen the one you like, note the Quality and Blur settings, because you'll need them when you save the tile for the Web page background, next. Click OK to save the file.

The Background layer filled with the pattern and ready to be JPEG-compressed

With the tile file open, use the Save For Web interface again, and specify the same settings you used for the graphics file so that the graphic will blend seamlessly with the tiled background (D).

The JPEG in place on the Web page background with other similar graphics (see the finished Web-page graphics on page 341).

The Inn
about the inn
location & sights
reservations

The Islands
the virgin islands
st. thomas
charlotte amalie

The Contest
why a contest
what's the prize
how do i enter

A list of addresses and phone numbers of the publishers of these recently published collections on CD-ROM appears on page

A list of addresses and phone numbers of the publishers of these recently published collections on CD-ROM appears on page

A list of addresses and phone numbers of the publishers of these recently published collections on CD-ROM appears on page

Jack Davis "painted" the logo for the *Danish Chalet Inn* in Adobe Illustrator using a pressure-sensitive stylus. He saved the layered artwork in Photoshop format so he could open it in Photoshop and add Layer Effects. He used soft drop shadows on the type and pillow embossing on the oval that surrounded the painting. He saved the design at high resolution (top) for use on a custom-printed T-shirt, and reduced the file size of a copy for use on the Web.

For the background of the Web site (www.wininn.com) he used a seamlessly repeating, fine-grained randomized texture tile, starting with Noise and following a method like the rough paper texture (**C** on page 191).He turned the texture into a seamlessly wrapping pattern

so the individual tiles wouldn't be perceived in the Web-page background.
▶ *To make a randomized pattern or texture repeat seamlessly, apply the Offset filter (Filter, Other, Offset), entering Horizontal and Vertical settings that will move the edges of the image into the center — in other words, the settings should be about half the width and height of the tile. Choose Wrap Around for the Undefined Areas (so pixels that are pushed off the right and bottom edges will reappear at the left and top to fill the empty space created there). To eliminate the seams, double-click the rubber stamp tool in the toolbox to open its Options palette. For a random grain, click in the check box to turn off Aligned. Choose a soft brush tip from the brushes palette, about twice the size of the "grain" of your texture.*

Hold down the Alt/Option key and click the tool on a part of the image away from any seam to pick up cloning texture. Rubber stamp over the seam, using short strokes. Stay away from the edge of the image so you don't create another seam. You can see if you've accidentally made a new seam by using the Offset filter again.

The small tile, which was saved as a JPEG to match the graphics placed over the background, would download quickly to fill the frame. Davis also used the same tiled background in constructing each of the four main Web graphics, using the method described in "'Transparent' JPEGs" on page 340.

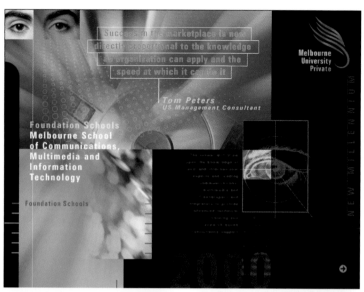

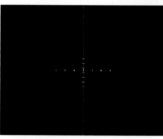

Wayne Rankin found Photoshop's layers and masks especially helpful in creating an *interactive CD-ROM for Melbourne University Private*. He could assemble the image material in separate layers and then use masks to control how much of each element showed in the final composition of each screen.

To unify the project, Rankin repeated a number of symbols and other graphic elements from screen to screen. For example, a faint grid of receding white circles appears on most screens to create a feeling of depth. The circles were drawn in Illustrator and imported as a layer in Photoshop. The concept of "vision" and a focus on innovation, with the client taking a position as "The University for the New Millennium," gave rise to a photo of two eyes in the upper left corner of most screens, with one eye that remains constant, while the other changes through the application of color overlays. In a rectangular area in the lower left corner of most screens Rankin used luminous color with radiating streaks to convey a sense of innovation. This graphic was created using painting and blurring techniques in Photoshop.

Rankin chose solid black as the screen background because it makes the colors project, looks good on larger monitors, and helps to de-emphasize the rectangular look of the screens, as the combinations of bright graphics define their own overall shapes and patterns.

Rankin developed other graphic devices to communicate the strengths of the University. For example, to convey the idea of a modern institution that retains the underlying strength of experience, he combined old and new images, such as recent photography and scans of old etchings. Rankin used circles and squares as geometric elements for containing and setting off images and areas of type. This adds a rhythm and cohesiveness to the composition of each screen and also works to convey a sense of the University's careful planning and systems.

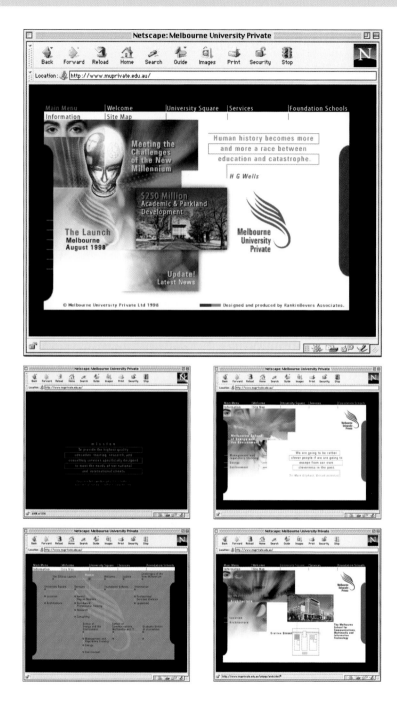

Wayne Rankin designed a *Web site for Melbourne University Private*, drawing on the designs already created for the CD-ROM. In this case however, the client wanted a white background. Despite the change, Rankin maintained a similar look and feel so that the Web site is clearly related to the visual style established for the CD-ROM, using black border areas as one of the ways of tying the disc and Web site together.

Like the CD-ROM graphics, the Web art makes use of repeating elements that vary in color. Graphics for the Web artwork tend to be simpler than those used on the CD-ROM. The files are smaller, for quick downloading, and the sound and video elements created for the CD-ROM were eliminated so the Web site would load and function more quickly.

The navigational system for the site is understated, with "buttons" that are small blocks of plain type. The initial splash screen lists the browser requirements for getting the most out of the site, and a site map uses a simple, easy-to-remember layout to show how information is organized.

Appendix A: Images

Most of the publishers listed on the next three pages supply photo collections that cover a wide variety of subject matter. The image sizes given are for open RGB files (or CMYK where noted). Before you use any digital stock photo, be sure to read the license agreement that applies to it, and confirm all rights with the image publisher.

Artbeats Software
TIFF; to 25 MB; 40–80 images per disc, $139–$199 per disc; 541-863-4429, 800-444-9392; **www.artbeats.com**

Artville
JPEG; approx. 29 MB; 50–100 images per disc, $60–$290 per disc; 608-240-2140, 800-631-7808; **www.artville.com**

Aztech New Media
TIFF; to 11 MB; 4500 images, $50; 416-449-4787, 888-820-8324; **www.aztech.com**

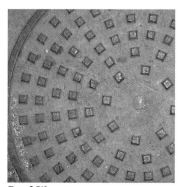

BeachWare
TIFF; to 17 MB; 100 images per disc, $25 per disc; 760-735-8945; **www.beachware.com**

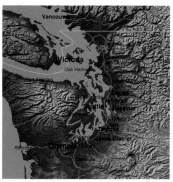

Cartesia MapArt
Layered Photoshop and GIF; to 26 MB; 50–2500 images per disc, $99–$499 per disc; 609-397-1611, 800-334-4291; **www.map-art.com**

Classic PIO Partners
TIFF; to 28 MB; 40–80 images per disc, $50–$150 per disc; 626-564-8106, 800-370-2746; **www.classicpartners.com**

Comstock Klips
JPEG; to 28 MB; 104 images per disc, $79–$499 per disc; 212-353-8600, 800-225-2727; **www.comstock.com**

Corbis Images
TIFF; to 28 MB; 100 images per disc, $199–$349 per disc; 760-634-6500, 800-260-0444; **www.corbisimages.com**

Corel
Kodak Photo CD; to 18 MB; 100 images per disc, $20 per disc; 613-728-3733, 800-772-6735; www.corel.com

Creativ Collection Verlag
EPS with clipping paths; to 6 MB; 90–350 images per disc, $139–$149 per disc; 941-739-2554, 888-244-8822; atlantech@centralstock.com

Definitive Stock
JPEG; to 45 MB; 54–100 images per disc, $40–$299 per disc; 206-340-0069, 800-234-2627; www.definitivestock.com

Digital Vision
CMYK; JPEG; to 37 MB; 50–100 images per disc, $150–$300 per disc; 309-688-8800, 800-255-8800; www.dgusa.com; www.digitalvision.ltd.uk

Digital Wisdom
TIFF and JPEG; 78–267 images per disc, $49–$496 per disc; 804-758-06740, 800-800-8560; www.digiwis.com

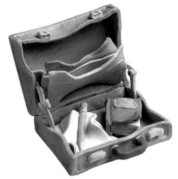

Dynamic Graphics Artworks
EPS with clipping paths; to 7 MB; 50–100 images per disc, $150–$300 per disc; 309-688-8800, 800-255-8800; www.dgusa.com

EyeWire Images
JPEG; to 42 MB; 40–100 images per disc, $230–$300 per disc; 403-294-3195, 800-661-9410; www.eyewire.com

Harpy Digital
Kodak Photo CD; to 18 MB; 40–100 images per disc, $25-30; 310-397-7636; www.harpydigital.com

Image Farm
JPEG; to 50 MB; 50–130 images per disc, $99–$129; 416-504-4161, 800-438-3276; www.imagefarm.com

Image Ideas
*JPEG; to 33 MB; 60–100 images per disc,
$149–$249; 905-709-1600,
888-238-1600; www.image-ideas.com*

Imagedrome
*TIFF; to 28 MB; 100 images per disc, $100
per disc; 415-841-9384;
www.imagedrome.com*

Imagin
*JPEG; to 30 MB; 60 images per disc, $179–
$199; 941-761-3339, 888-244-8822;
atlantech@centralstock.com*

PhotoDisc
*JPEG; to 29 MB; 100–336 images per disc,
$150–$290; 206-441-9355,
800-979-4413; www.photodisc.com*

PhotoSphere
*Kodak Photo CD; 80–100 images per disc,
$195–$250; 604-876-3206, 800-665-1496;
www.photosphere.com*

PhotoSpin
*TIFF; to 20 MB; 50–100 images per disc,
$60-$90; 310-265-1313, 888-246-1313;
www.photospin.com*

RubberBall
*Some CMYK; JPEG; to 45 MB; 100 images
per disc, $250–$300; 801-224-6886,
888-224-3472; www.rubberball.com*

Transmission Digital
*Grayscale and CMYK; TIFF; to 37 MB;
38–43 images per disc, $130–$150;
212-244-2661, 800-585-2248;
www.transmissiondigital.com*

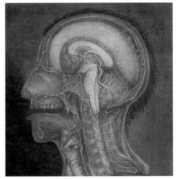

Visual Language
*JPEG; to 37 MB; 24–200+ images per disc,
$75–$150; 626-431-2778, 888-702-8777;
www.visuallanguage.com*

Appendix B
Artists &
Photographers

Darryl Baird 151
dbaird@flint.umich.edu

Jim Belderes 103

Jay Paul Bell 218
107 Mattek Avenue
DeKalb, IL 60115
jbell11750@aol.com

Alicia Buelow 99, 169
336 Arkansas Street
San Francisco, CA 94107
415-522-5902
abuelow@sirius.com

Lisa Cargill 219
4206 N. Ashland, 1A
Chicago, IL 60613
888-975-1729
lisacargill@worldnet.alt.net

Jack Cliggett 157

E. J. Dixon 279
818-769-7910
ej@hotmail.com

Katrin Eismann 170
Katrin@photoshopdiva.com
www.photoshopdiva.com

Louis Fishauf 59
Reactor Art + Design Ltd.
51 Camden Street
Toronto, Ontario, Canada M5V1V2
416-703-1913, ext. 241

Francois Guérin 177, 242, 244
33 Rue Alexandre Dumas
Paris 75011, France
43-73-36-62
74067.1513@compuserve.com

Eric Hanauer 150
ehanauer@earthlink.net
home.earthlink.net/~ehanauer

Joyce Hesselberth 171
410-235-7803
joyce@spurdesign.com

Lance Hidy 167
2 Summer Street
Merrimack, MA 01860
lance@lancehidy.com

Kaoru Hollin 249
khollin@earthlink.net

William Low 250
william@williamlow.com

Bert Monroy 269
11 Latham Lane
Berkeley, CA 94708
510-524-9412
bmonroy@crl.com

Victor Navone 248, 279
vnavone@bigplanet.com

Donal Philby 128

Wayne Rankin 57, 342, 343
502 Albert Street East
Melbourne, Victoria 3002
Australia
613-9662-1233
wayne@rba.com.au

Roy Robinson 134

Phil Saunders 98
Presto Studios, Inc.
5414 Oberlin Drive, Suite 200
San Diego, CA 92121
619-622-0500
phil@presto.com

Russell Sparkman 307
2-100 Issha
Meito-ku, Nagoya
Japan 465
052-703-6305
vfe04663@niftyserve.or.jp

Gordon Studer 58, 266
1576 62nd Street
Emeryville, CA 94608
510-655-4256
gstuder@dnai.com

Frank Vitale 279
1833 11th Street, #2
Santa Monica, CA 90404
vitalef@earthlink.net

Kay Wilson 251
330 Verdant Lane
Canfield, OH 44406
330-533-3851
karson@cboss.com
www.geocities.com/~Kay Wilson

Tommy Yune 90, 234
Ursus Studios
P.O. Box 4858
Cerritos, CA 90703-4858
tommyyune@aol.com

Appendix C
Resources

Suppliers of software and other products mentioned in The Photoshop 5/5.5 Wow! Book

Adobe Systems, Inc.
345 Park Avenue
San Jose, CA 95110
408-536-6000
www.adobe.com

Alien Skin Software
2522 Clark Avenue
Raleigh, NC 27607
919-832-4124
www.alienskin.com

AltaMira Group
www.altamira-group.com

Andromeda Software Inc.
699 Hampshire Road, Suite 109
Thousand Oaks, CA 91361
805-379-4109
www.andromeda.com

Artbeats Software, Inc.
Box 709
Myrtle Creek, OR 97457
541-863-4429
www.artbeats.com

Artville
2310 Darwin Road
Madison, WI 53704
608-240-2140
www.artville.com

Auto FX Software
31 Inverness Center Parkway, Suite 270
Birmingham, AL 35242
205-980-0056
www.autofx.com

Aztech New Media Corp.
1 Scarsdale Road
Don Mills, Ontario M3B 2R2
Canada
416-449-4787
www.aztech.com

BeachWare, Inc.
9419 Mount Israel Road
Escondido, CA 92029
760-735-8945
www.beachware.com

Cartesia Software
80 Lambert Lane, Suite 100
Lambertville, NJ 08530
609-397-1611
www.map-art.com

Classic PIO Partners
87 East Green Street, Suite 809
Pasadena, CA 91105
626-564-8106
www.classicpartners.com

Comstock Stock Photography
30 Irving Place
New York, NY 10003
212-353-8600
www.comstock.com

Corbis Images
750 Second Street
Encinitas, CA 90064
760-634-6500
www.corbisimages.com

Corel Corporation
1600 Carling Avenue
Ottawa, Ontario K1Z 8R7
Canada
613-728-8200
613-761-9176 fax
www.corel.com

Creativ Collection
Atlantech, Inc.
6695 Cortez Road
Bradenton, FL 34210
941-761-3339
www.creativcollection.com

Definitive Stock
One Union Square
600 University Street, Suite 1701
Seattle, WA 98101
206-340-0069
www.definitivestock.com

Digital Vision
230 Fifth Avenue, Suite 512
New York, NY 10001
309-688-8800
www.digitalvision.ltd.uk

Digital Wisdom
P.O. Box 2070
300 Jeanette Drive
Tappahannock, VA 22560
www.digiwis.com

Dynamic Graphics, Inc.
6000 N. Forest Park Drive
Peoria, IL 61614
309-688-8800
www.dgusa.com

Extensis Corporation
1800 SW First Avenue, Suite 500
Portland, OR 97201
503-274-2020
www.extensis.com

Flaming Pear
612-253-8400
www.flamingpear.com

HumanSoftwareCo, Inc.
19925 StevensCreek Blvd
Cupertino CA 95014
408-399-0057
www.humansoftware.com

EyeWire, Inc.
1525 Greenview Drive
Grand Prairie, TX 75050
403-294-3195
www.eyewire.com

Harpy Digital
P.O. Box 66023
Los Angeles, CA 90006
310-397-7636
www.harpydigital.com

Image Farm, Inc.
398 Adelaide Street, West, Suite 1004
Toronto, Ontario M5V 1S7
Canada
www.corel.com

Image Ideas
105 West Beaver Creek Road, Suite 5
Richmond Hill, Ontario L4B 1C6
Canada
905-709-1600
www.image-ideas.com

Imagin
Atlantech, Inc.
6695 Cortez Road
Bradenton, FL 34210
941-761-3339
atlantech@centralstock.com

Intense Software Incorporated
www.intensesoftware.com

Macromedia, Inc.
600 Townsend Street
San Francisco, CA 94103
415-252-2000
www.macromedia.com

MetaCreations
6303 Carpinteria Avenue
Carpinteria, CA 93013
805-566-6200
805-566-6385
www.metacreations.com

Peachpit Press
1249 Eighth Street
Berkeley, CA 94710
510-524-2178
www.peachpit.com

PhotoDisc
206-441-9355
www.photodisc.com

PhotoSphere
604-876-3206
www.photosphere.com

PhotoSpin
29916 South Hawthorne Boulevard
Rolling Hills Estates, CA 90274
310-265-1313
www.photospin.com

Quark, Inc.
1800 Grant Street
Denver, CO 80203
307-772-7100
www.quark.com

RAYflect
www.rayflect.com

RightHemisphere
www.righthemisphere.com

RubberBall Productions
102 South Mountain Way Drive
Orem, UT 84058
801-224-6886
www.rubberball.com

Symantec Corporation
10201 Torre Avenue
Cupertino, CA 95014
408-253-9600
www.symantec.com

Transmission Digital Publishing
Earl Ripling
242 West 30th Street
New York, NY 10001
212-244-2661
www.transmissiondigital.com

Visual Language
626-431-2778
www.visuallanguage.com

Zaxwerks
626-309-9102
www.zaxwerks.com

Index